Waiting for Godot in Sarajevo

RADICAL
TRADITIONS

THEOLOGY IN A POSTCRITICAL KEY

Series Editors: Stanley M. Hauerwas, Duke University, and Peter Ochs, University of Virginia

BOOKS IN THE SERIES:

Waiting for Godot in Sarajevo: Theological Reflections on Nihilism, Tragedy, and Apocalypse, *David Toole*

Wilderness Wanderings: Probing Twentieth-Century Theology and Philosophy, *Stanley M. Hauerwas*

Revelation Restored: Divine Writ and Critical Responses, *David Weiss Halivni*

FORTHCOMING:

Reasoning After Revelation: Dialogues in Postmodern Jewish Philosophy, *Steven Kepnes, Peter Ochs, and Robert Gibbs*

After the Spirit: The Story of the Holy Spirit Eclipsed by Nature, Grace, and Law, *Eugene F. Rogers, Jr.*

Ascending Numbers: Augustine's *De Musica* and the Western Tradition, *Catherine Pickstock*

Radical Traditions cuts new lines of inquiry across a confused array of debates concerning the place of theology in modernity and, more generally, the status and role of scriptural faith in contemporary life. Charged with a rejuvenated confidence, spawned in part by the rediscovery of reason as inescapably tradition constituted, a new generation of theologians and religious scholars is returning to scriptural traditions with the hope of retrieving resources long ignored, depreciated, and in many cases ideologically suppressed by modern habits of thought. *Radical Traditions* assembles a promising matrix of strategies, disciplines, and lines of thought that invites Jewish, Christian, and Islamic theologians back to the word, recovering and articulating modes of scriptural reasoning as that which always underlies modernist reasoning and therefore has the capacity—and authority—to correct it.

Far from despairing over modernity's failings, postcritical theologies rediscover resources for renewal and self-correction within the disciplines of academic study themselves. Postcritical theologies open up the possibility of participating once again in the living relationship that binds together God, text, and community of interpretation. *Radical Traditions* thus advocates a "return to the text," which means a commitment to displaying the richness and wisdom of traditions that are at once text based, hermeneutical, and oriented to communal practice.

Books in this series offer the opportunity to speak openly with practitioners of other faiths or even with those who profess no (or limited) faith, both academics and nonacademics, about the ways religious traditions address pivotal issues of the day. Unfettered by foundationalist preoccupations, these books represent a call for new paradigms of reason—a thinking and rationality that is more responsive than originative. By embracing a postcritical posture, they are able to speak unapologetically out of scriptural traditions manifest in the practices of believing communities (Jewish, Christian, and others); articulate those practices through disciplines of philosophic, textual, and cultural criticism; and engage intellectual, social, and political practices that for too long have been insulated from theological evaluation. *Radical Traditions* is radical not only in its confidence in nonapologetic theological speech but also in how the practice of such speech challenges the current social and political arrangements of modernity.

Waiting for Godot in Sarajevo

Theological Reflections on Nihilism, Tragedy, and Apocalypse

David Toole

Westview Press
A Member of Perseus Books, L.L.C.

Radical Traditions: Theology in a Postcritical Key

Published in 1998 in the United States of America by Westview Press, 5500 Central Avenue, Boulder, Colorado 80301-2877, and in the United Kingdom by Westview Press, 12 Hid's Copse Road, Cumnor Hill, Oxford OX2 9JJ

Library of Congress Cataloging-in-Publication Data
Toole, David, 1962–
Waiting for Godot in Sarajevo : theological reflections on nihilism, tragedy, and apocalypse / David Toole.
p. cm. — (Radical traditions)
Includes bibliographical references and index.
ISBN 0-8133-3503-5
1. Nihilism—Religious aspects—Christianity. 2. Tragic, The—Religious aspects—Christianity. 3. Christianity and politics.
I. Title. II. Series.
B828.3.T66 1998
909.82—dc21 98-11336
CIP

The paper used in this publication meets the requirements of the American National Standard for Permanence of Paper for Printed Library Materials Z39.48-1984.

10 9 8 7 6 5 4 3 2 1

To my mother and father
Joan Trimble Toole
and
Kenneth Ross Toole
(1920–1981)

Contents

Preface xiii
Acknowledgments xix

1 **Waiting for Godot in Sarajevo** 1
Susan Sontag, Sarajevo, and Suffering, 1
MacIntyre's Diagnosis of the Current Disaster, 4
The Encyclopaedic Enterprise, 6
MacIntyre's Response to Nietzsche, 8
The University and the Moral Life, 11
Antigone and MacIntyre Against the Imperium, 13
Waiting for Godot in Sarajevo, 15
Nihilism, Tragedy, Apocalypse, 19

2 **From Out of the Abyss: Nihilism According to Nietzsche and His Critics** 23
The Pre-Homeric Abyss and the Question of Suffering, 24
The World as It Is and the Birth of Nihilism, 27
Of Slaves and Nobles, 29
The World as It Ought to Be, 32
The World as It Ought to Be Does Not Exist, 33
Final Forms of Nihilism, 35
Ethical Nihilism, Absolute Historicism, and Ontological Violence, 38
Heidegger on "Classical Nihilism," 42
Nihilism as Insurrection: Heidegger's Critique of Nietzsche, 44
Nihilism Before Nietzsche, 47
Nihilism and the Politics of Description, 50

3 Between Nihilism and Apocalypse: The Tragic Theology of John Milbank 53

Milbank's Postmodern Augustinianism, 55
Revisiting MacIntyre: From Dialectics to Rhetoric, 58
Metanarrative Realism, 61
Linguistic Idealism, 63
The Analogical Code, 66
Augustine and Heidegger on Being, 69
Dismantling MacIntyre's Castle, 70
Charity and Forgiveness, 73
The Logos Crucified, 75
Misreading Deleuze, 77
Baroque Risks of Harmony and the Moment of Undecidability, 80
Adjusting Milbank's Christology, 84

4 Toward a Metaphysics of Tragedy: Justifying the World as Art 89

Aesthetic Justification and Musical Dissonance, 89
Vultures Are No Reproach to the World, 93
Dionysus, Apollo, and the Birth of Tragedy, 96
Euripides' *Bacchae,* 99
Visions of Dionysian Apocalypse, 103
The Dionysian Subversion of the Polis, 108
Tragic Drama and the Artistic Taming of the Horrible, 110
Tragedy According to Aristotle and Schopenhauer, 112
Toward a Tragic Culture, 115
The Story of Mann Gulch: Courage Struggling for Oxygen, 117
From Catastrophe to Tragedy: Wonder-Altered Grief, 121
From Scientific Instinct to Tragic Insight, 123
Pausing to Take Pictures of the World as Art, 126

5 From a Metaphysics to a Politics of Tragedy: Michel Foucault and the Lyricism of Protest 129

Toward a Metaphysics *and* a Politics of Tragedy, 131
Waiting for Godot in Paris, 134
Madness and Civilization, 137
Madness and Tragedy in the Classical Age, 140
Madness as the Truth of Confinement, 142
The Lyricism of Protest, 144

From the Necessity of Metaphysics to
the Real Work of Writing History, 147
A Pure Gaze That Would Be Pure Language, 150
The Confinement of Language, 152
The Madman and the Poet, 154
Enslaved Sovereignty and the Homeland of History, 157
Murdering History, 160

**6 On the Borders of Heaven and Earth:
The Tragic Politics of Michel Foucault** 167

The Material Reality of Discourse and Effective History, 168
The Panopticon, Disciplinary Power,
and the Carceral City, 171
The Soul Is the Prison of the Body, 176
Below the Thresholds of Visibility, 179
Discursive Resistance, Heterotopia,
and Subjugated Knowledges, 182
Physically Committed Resistance, 186
A Technology of the Self, 188
An Aesthetics of Existence, 191
Returning to the Theater in Sarajevo, 193
A Politics of Dying, 197
A Difficult Hope and the Politics of Lamentation, 201

**7 Worthy Are the Slaughtered:
Toward a Metaphysics of Apocalypse
and an Apocalyptic Politics** 205

Toward an Apocalyptic Style, 206
Politics as the Art of the Impossible, 210
From the Politics of Effectiveness to
the Politics of the Cross, 212
The Metaphysics of Apocalypse, 216
The Powers, 218
The Power of the Air, 220
The Concreteness of the Cross, the Church,
and the War in Heaven, 222

**8 Revolutionary Subordination:
The Apocalyptic Politics of Jesus and the Church** 227

The Messianic Pattern of New Testament Narrative, 228
The Tactical Calculus of Jesus' Provocative Acts, 230
Infrapolitics and the Hidden Transcript, 232
Parables as Tactics of Resistance, 235

Itinerancy and the Articulation of a Poetic Geography, 241
Of Demons and Lepers, 243
The Weapon of Table Fellowship, 246
Jesus in Jerusalem: Symbolic Acts of Defiance, 248
Revolutionary Subordination, 252
Resisting Auschwitz, 257
Immeasurable Victory, 262

Epilogue: Returning to Sarajevo 267

Notes 273
Index 317

Preface

It is a common thought among historians that the twentieth century did not begin in 1900, or even in 1901, with the turning of the calendar. Rather, the century began on June 28, 1914, on Franz Josef Street in Sarajevo, when Gavrilo Princip shot and killed Archduke Franz Ferdinand, heir to the Hapsburg throne. This event, of course, led Austria-Hungary to declare war on Serbia, and before long the whole of Europe found itself embroiled in a war that would last for four long years and claim the lives of almost an entire generation. Here, say historians, in the trenches of World War I, the twentieth century began—and what a beginning it was for the century that would produce Hitler and Stalin, Auschwitz and the Gulag, Hiroshima, Korea, Vietnam, Cambodia, Nicaragua, Guatemala, El Salvador, Afghanistan, Rwanda, Chechnya, and, of course, Bosnia.[1]

In the spring of 1992, through some strange twist in history, the century that began in Sarajevo returned there, bringing with it the cumulative horror of a century's worth of war and genocide. The century that began with the assassination of the Archduke had circled around and come home to roost, with the result that between 1992 and 1996, Sarajevo was all but destroyed. It may well be that historians of the future, as they sort through the past, will declare that the twentieth century ended where it began, in the streets of Sarajevo, on April 6, 1992, the day the siege of the city began.

But even if historians let the century live on for another few years, Sarajevo cannot help but symbolize for us the borders of a century that we can remember only with the astonishment that accompanies grief. And, of course, if the twentieth century has come to an end in the rubble of Sarajevo, then we need to wonder what the future might hold. For Sarajevo was famous not only as the place where the Archduke met his end but also as the city that embodied in a concrete way all the hopes of the Enlightenment: a city where Jews and Muslims and Christians (both Catholic and Orthodox) lived together in peace, overcoming (but not abandoning) their religious differences. More than any other city in Europe—or for that matter, in the world—Sarajevo, because of its unique history, had become a city of hope. It had become, as Dzevad Karahasan says, the new Jerusalem.[2] But that city now lies in ruins. And what does that suggest about Enlightenment dreams? What does the fate of Sarajevo—as the city that has come to symbolize both the atrocities and the hopes of our century—say about the future?

In the pages that follow, I reflect upon these questions, and others that follow in their wake, taking my lead from Susan Sontag, who traveled to Sarajevo in the summer of 1993 to stage a performance of Samuel Beckett's *Waiting for Godot*. Although Sarajevo itself begins to bring into focus the sweeping events of our century, it is in fact only in conjunction with *Waiting for Godot* that the full focal power of Sarajevo becomes evident—a focal power that draws us both into the presence of suffering and into questions about what suffering might mean, if indeed it means anything at all. These questions concerning the meaning of suffering, which are metaphysical in nature, stand at the center of this book, but they do not stand alone. For Sontag's performance of *Godot* in Sarajevo raises another question, as well—a question concerning the character of a politics adequate to the task of living the good life in the face of suffering.

After taking one lead from Sontag, I take another from Nietzsche. It is Nietzsche who allows me to place these questions about the metaphysics and politics of suffering within the tripartite frame of my title—nihilism, tragedy, apocalypse; and it is Nietzsche who gives initial shape to my reflections on both nihilism and tragedy.[3] Roughly halfway through the book, however, I leave Nietzsche behind and turn to the work of Michel Foucault. I turn to Foucault because, although Nietzsche—in response to the meaninglessness of nihilism—offers us the meaningfulness of tragedy, he does so in mostly metaphysical terms. Foucault, on the other hand, with his account of power and resistance, turns Nietzsche's metaphysics of tragedy into a politics and thus gives us one answer to our question about how to live the good life in the face of suffering. Taken together, Nietzsche and Foucault are only part of the story, however, for there remains another answer to the same question. Hence my account of Nietzsche and Foucault on the metaphysics and politics of tragedy gives way to an account of John Howard Yoder and the New Testament on the metaphysics and politics of apocalypse.[4]

At this point I could, no doubt, begin to explain myself further by offering a formal, chapter-by-chapter, introduction to my argument. However, for reasons I will explain later, I have chosen not to do so. And so I ask of the reader a certain measure of patience as he or she takes up this book and tries to discern where things are headed. For the impatient reader, I perhaps should note that the first chapter, although not a formal introduction and although short on details, does introduce the overall design of my narrative. There are two matters, however, that do not find sufficient explanation there, and so it is to these matters that I devote the remainder of these prefatory comments. The matters in question bear the names of "theology" and "method."

In the first chapter, the title of this work gains sufficient explanation, with the exception of one term: "theological." Why "theological reflections"? Part of the answer is obvious, since the explicit concern of three of the eight chapters is Christian theology. But discounting the first chapter (which is mostly introductory), what about the other four—two each on Nietzsche and Foucault? In what sense are my reflections on Nietzsche and Foucault theological? The complete answer to this question will have to wait until all is said and done, which is to say that in the end the theological character of my reflections should be clear. Still, I can perhaps at least gesture here toward an answer to this question by invoking Nietzsche's famous words, "We are not rid of God because we still have faith in grammar";[5] or as Foucault puts it, "God is perhaps not so much a region beyond knowledge as something prior to the sentences we speak."[6] Neither Foucault nor Nietzsche utter these words in order to characterize their own view. Foucault is speaking about the understanding of language at the end of the eighteenth century; and Nietzsche is in fact criticizing those who suppose that the very existence of human reason indicates the presence of divinity. Nonetheless, the notion that the existence of grammar somehow leads to the existence of God, that language itself compels us to think about divinity, is an idea that lurks throughout the works of both Nietzsche and Foucault. In the final analysis, it seems to me the question is not how one can read Nietzsche and Foucault theologically, but rather how one can *not* read them this way, given their own understanding both of the mysterious character of language and of those equally mysterious beings whose existence is defined most centrally by the capacity to speak and write.

I should note, too, that in the case of Foucault my reflections are theological for another reason—or perhaps for the same reason in another form, since it is not only Foucault's account of language that requires theological reflection but also his account of power and resistance. What is it, Foucault asks, that "enables people there, on the spot, to resist the Gulag, what makes it intolerable for them, and what can give the people of the anti-Gulag the courage to stand up and die in order to be able to utter a word or a poem"?[7] Foucault never answers this question exactly. But, as we will see, all his works gather around it; and it is an inherently theological question. It is a question that leads us in the same direction as the analysis of language, that leads us beyond ourselves toward the mystery that exists not only prior to the sentences we speak but also prior to all our acts of resistance.

So much for the theological character of my reflections; now let me say a few words about method.

To put it bluntly, if a bit too simply, this work has no method. In the pages that follow, I attempt simply a close and imaginative reading of dozens upon dozens of texts that have aligned themselves with one another mostly by chance. In many ways, the meeting of Michel Foucault and John Howard Yoder in this text, which is the meeting that inspired me originally to begin this project, is as unlikely as the meeting of these two men in real life. If Foucault and Yoder meet here, it is not because a method of investigation, a way of proceeding, either required or allowed them to do so. Rather, Foucault and Yoder meet here because they met in my life a few years ago when, quite by chance, I encountered both of them in different courses in the same semester as a first-year Ph.D. student at Duke University. Had I not read them side by side, I might not have thought to engage them with each other.

And even reading them at the same time was not enough of an impetus to begin thinking about how they might illuminate one another. That impetus came not from the chance meeting of texts but from the more complex texture of my life as a non-Christian who studied among Christians and who married a Catholic, and who then found himself raising Catholic children—and who, all the while, continued to read Foucault and Yoder.

To articulate the method of this work would be to articulate, on the one hand, the narrative of my own life, and on the other, the forces of chance (or providence) that allowed not only for the meeting of Foucault and Yoder but also for that of Nietzsche and Norman Maclean, Yoder and Ian MacMillan, and for the meeting between all of these folks and Samuel Beckett. Indeed, the story of how I came across the essay by Susan Sontag that inspired my title is another example of chance or providence at work.

A friend mentioned the essay to me in passing. Months later I ran into the essay accidentally, remembered my friend's words, and read it. A year later I wrote a few words about it. Almost a year after that it became the gathering force of all my efforts. And then, still months after that, I reread James Miller's book on Foucault and discovered (or remembered) that one of his chapters is titled "Waiting for Godot" because Foucault himself established a crucial link between his work and Beckett's play. I could continue to tell stories like this, stories about the way texts have met one another and about the way those texts have resonated with my life experience. But I think I have said enough to illustrate the point that the work has no method. I doubt that it is possible to give an account of the events that have made this work what it is. In any case, I know I am not up to the task.

Faced with this inability to speak of method, I can, nonetheless, say a few words about the character of this work, both as a whole and in the details of its close readings. Taken as a whole, this work is, I think, what Foucault called an "experience-book":

> The books I write constitute an experience for me that I'd like to be as rich as possible. An experience is something you come out of changed. If I had to write a book to communicate what I have already thought, I'd never have the courage to begin it. I write precisely because I don't know what to think about a subject that attracts my interest. In so doing, the book transforms me, changes what I think.[8]

Foucault goes on to say that an "experience is, of course, something one has alone; but it cannot have its full impact unless the individual manages to escape from pure subjectivity in such a way that others can—I won't say re-experience it—but at least cross paths with it or retrace it."[9]

Like Foucault's books, this work "functions as an experience"[10] because the writing of it constituted an experience that transformed me (for instance, somewhere in the midst of writing it, I converted to Catholicism). The test of this work, however, is whether it functions as an experience for the reader as well. For only if I can share this experience, only if the reader can cross paths with what I have experienced while writing this work, will it have its full impact. And it is for this reason that I have not offered the reader a traditional, formal introduction. For to tell you how things come out before you have even begun would be already to distance your experience from mine—since I did not know, as I worked through these reflections, how things would come out. It is also for this reason that the subtitle calls attention to the *reflective* character of this work.

Lest all this talk of "experience" mislead, it is important to note that what is at stake is finally the truth. Hence, Foucault notes that in order for a book to function as an experience, "it is necessary that what it asserts is somehow 'true.' "[11] But to paraphrase Foucault, the truth of such an experience does not lie in a series of arguments but in the experience "the book permits us to have."[12] This last point allows me to say one final thing about the character of this work as a whole.

The reader will discover that from the beginning my narrative unfolds at two radically different levels, or perhaps I should say in two distinct genres, and that at times I switch from one to the other rather suddenly without stopping to explain. Many of the pages that follow are filled with academic commentary, with the sometimes painstaking exposition of difficult philosophical and theological texts. On the other hand, a significant number of the following pages are devoted to the much different enterprise of interpreting works of literature. At times one might wonder what purpose these flights into literature serve. Or perhaps the converse will be true, and one might see clearly how my recourse to literature functions to advance the narrative but wonder about the role, for instance, of my extended commentary on Foucault. My hope is that both the academic commentary and the flights into literature work together to create the richest experience possible—an experience that was not only mine in the writing but that will also be the reader's in the reading. Of course, I could have advanced the argument without recourse to literature; or I could have left the academic commentary behind and sought simply to create a literary experience. But to follow either of these paths would have been to leave behind the truth.

I said above that in spite of my inability to articulate the method of this work, I could say a few things not only about the character of the work as a whole but also about the details of its close readings. I can, in other words, say a few words about how I read the texts that have, quite by chance, aligned themselves with one another in this work.

First of all, it was in fact wrong for me to say that I am involved in the writing of academic commentary. For I have simply learned too much from Foucault to think that the writing of commentary is desirable, since it pretends to be nothing more than a restating of what has already been said, even if in fact, as Foucault notes, to state "what has been said, one has to restate what has never been said."[13] I have chosen not to pursue this inherently problematic task; thus my close readings should not be taken as commentaries. Rather, let me say of my reading of Nietzsche, Foucault, Milbank, and the rest what Foucault said of his reading of Nietzsche:

> I am tired of people studying [Nietzsche] only to produce the same kind of commentaries that are written on Hegel or Mallarmé. For myself, I prefer to utilise the writers I like. The only valid tribute to thought such as Nietzsche's is precisely to use it, to deform it, to make it groan and protest. And if the commentators then say that I am being faithful or unfaithful to Nietzsche, that is of absolutely no interest. . . .
>
> I can't help but dream about a kind of criticism that would not try to judge, but to bring an oeuvre, a book, a sentence, an idea to life; it would light fires, watch the grass grow, listen to the wind, and catch the sea-foam in the breeze and scatter it. It would multiply, not judgments, but signs of existence; it would summon them, drag them from their sleep. Perhaps it would invent them sometimes—all the better. All the better. Criticism that hands down sentences sends me to sleep; I'd like criticism of scintillating leaps of the imagination. It would not be sovereign or dressed in red. It would bear the lightning of possible storms.[14]

It is in the spirit of these words and amidst such inventions and scintillating leaps of the imagination that I offer the reader the following experience.

David Toole

Acknowledgments

My debts are many. I would like to thank *Soundings: An Interdisciplinary Journal* for permission to reprint here in Chapters 6 and 8 an altered version of an essay published originally as "Witnesses and Voyeurs: The Perils of Remembrance in *Orbit of Darkness* and *Schindler's List*," vol. 77 (1994): 271–293. And I would like to thank, as well, Copper Canyon Press (P.O. Box 271, Port Townsend, WA 98368) for permission to reprint Hayden Carruth's poem "On Being Asked to Write a Poem Against the Vietnam War," from *Collected Shorter Poems*, © 1992 by Hayden Carruth.

Albert Borgmann, Phil Fandozzi, and the rest of the members of the Philosophy and Liberal Studies programs at the University of Montana, Missoula, made it possible for me to teach two courses in which I first explored many of the ideas that I present here. Ron Perrin introduced me both to Susan Sontag's essay on Sarajevo and, long before that, to the philosophical life. Stanley Hauerwas molded my philosophical interests into theological reflection, and he also read the manuscript all along the way. Rom Coles introduced me in a studied way to the works of both Nietzsche and Foucault. Mary McClintock Fulkerson, Tom Langford, and Ken Surin read the manuscript in its entirety and provided me with helpful criticisms. Both Dale Martin and Peter Ochs not only read the manuscript but saved me, in different ways, from major blunders in the final chapters. Any blunders that remain are, of course, my own.

The list could go on. But let me add just one more set of names: Nancy, Gabe, and Ben. Ben just turned three, and he knows nothing of an existence that does not include Daddy's book. Gabe is now six and perhaps has vague memories of a time before Daddy's book but mostly just wants to know when Daddy's book will be finished. Nancy remembers a time before the book and longs to recover something of our pre-book life.

No doubt, it is not a good thing that the writing of a book can so dominate the life of a family. And it is a miraculous thing that that family made it possible for me to write this book. To these three people I owe everything that counts.

D. T.

I

Waiting for Godot in Sarajevo

Susan Sontag, Sarajevo, and Suffering

In the summer of 1993, Susan Sontag traveled to the besieged and battered city of Sarajevo to stage a production of Beckett's play *Waiting for Godot*. The idea to stage not only a play but *this* play came about in the midst of a conversation during Sontag's visit to the city a few months earlier. As she reports,

> Realizing suddenly that I was talking to a producer as well as a director, I asked Pasovic if he would be interested in my coming back in a few months to direct a play.
>
> "Of course," he said.
>
> Before I could add, "Then let me think for a while about what I might want to do," he went on, "What play will you do?" And bravado, following the impulsiveness of my proposal, suggested to me in an instant what I might not have seen had I taken longer to reflect: there was one obvious play for me to direct. Beckett's play, written over forty years ago, seems written for, and about, Sarajevo.[1]

As it turned out, the prospect of staging a play in a city that had become at once a battlefield and something of a concentration camp presented unique difficulties. For example, although both good actors and a cultivated audience remained in the city, as did two of Sarajevo's five theaters, the journey to and from the theater for both the actors and the spectators was a matter of risking the sniper bullets and the mortar shells that were all too common. And the theaters themselves were without power (and hence lighting); they were also death traps by design, were they to take a hit from a shell when full of people. Furthermore, when the actors did arrive for rehearsal after what for some had been a two-hour walk, they were tired and weak. As Sontag notes, the "actors were visibly underweight and tired easily. . . . Whenever I halted the run-through for a few minutes to change a movement or a line reading, all the actors . . . would instantly lie down on the stage." This fatigue, coupled with the distraction and fear caused by exploding shells, also made it more difficult for the actors to memorize their lines.

Given these often life-threatening obstacles, it may seem odd—indeed, perhaps it *should* seem odd—that Sontag spent more than a month in Sarajevo putting together a performance of *Waiting for Godot.* Why did she risk not only her own life but the lives of actors and spectators alike to, of all things, stage a play in a war zone?

If, by itself, the act does not seem odd, then certainly Sontag's explanation of her motivation does. She did it, she says, "because it gave me a practical reason to return to Sarajevo. . . . I had spent two weeks there in April. . . . But I couldn't again be just a witness: that is, meet and visit, tremble with fear, feel brave, feel depressed, have heart-breaking conversations, grow ever more indignant, lose weight. If I went back, it would be to pitch in and do something." Fair enough. But in a world where to "do something" involves UN sanctions and soldiers, airdrops, air raids, negotiations between heads of state, and acts of Congress, by what account can the staging of a play in a war zone be considered *practical*?

Sontag reports that her efforts did in fact meet criticism, in part because of the choice of the "pessimistic" *Godot,* but also because, as one journalist asked, "Isn't putting on a play [in Sarajevo] like fiddling while Rome burns?" Does not such an action founder precisely on its impractical nature, not to mention its insensitivity to the horrors of genocide?

In spite of the risks and the criticism,

> *Waiting for Godot* opened, with twelve candles on the stage, on August 17. There were two performances that day, one at 2:00 PM and the other at 4:00 PM. In Sarajevo there are only matinees; hardly anybody goes out after dark. Many people were turned away. . . . I think it was at the end of [the third] performance—on Wednesday, August 18 at 2:00 PM—during the long tragic silence of the Vladimirs and the Estragons which follows the messenger's announcement that Mr. Godot isn't coming today, but will surely come tomorrow, that my eyes began to sting with tears. Velibor was crying too. No one in the audience made a sound. The only sounds were coming from outside the theater: a UN APC thundering down the street and the crack of sniper fire.[2]

Sontag's account of her journey to Sarajevo seems the perfect place to bring into focus, here at the beginning, the questions and concerns that fill the following pages—questions and concerns that gather around the legacy of the Enlightenment. To begin in Sarajevo, amidst the ravages of war and the unspeakable horrors of yet another twentieth-century genocide, is to begin smack in the middle of the suffering that belies the optimism of Enlightenment dreams.

What better place to go to refute the Enlightenment dream of a universal humanity endowed with a single reason, embodying a single morality, than the Balkans and a war where Christians and Muslims are killing one another. It's the crusades all over again, except the knights now drive tanks and any thought of actually finding the grail has long since been given up and replaced with the more pragmatic goal of securing national boundaries. That human beings might rise above such "religious" differences and reach a higher order of reason, whereby differences could be adjudicated without the violence of the crusades, was an understandable dream. But it was, as even Kant understood (and this is the Kant that we forget to teach to undergraduates, Kant the philosopher of history), only a dream—although in Kant's day it was at least a dream with some merit.[3] In our day it is a dream that simply has not withstood the test of time. Too many corpses lie strewn across the terrain of the last three centuries, although the number of corpses in which our own century stands buried is more than enough to make the point.

And what exactly is the point? Simply this: that we live now not in a world fueled by Enlightenment dreams of unity and peace and progress (although the rhetoric of the global village persists) but in a fractured, fragmented world of endless and often escalating conflicts. Nietzsche had a name for this world, and we should listen to him because in this at least he has proved to be so right:

> What I relate is the history of the next two centuries. I describe what is coming, what can no longer come differently: *the advent of nihilism*. This history can be related even now; for necessity itself is at work here. This future speaks even now in a hundred signs, this destiny announces itself everywhere; for the music of the future all ears are cocked even now. For some time now, our whole European culture has been moving as toward a catastrophe, with a tortured tension that is growing from decade to decade: restlessly, violently, headlong, like a river that wants to reach the end.[4]

Nietzsche wrote these words in 1887 or 1888. We should wonder what the next century holds, given that we now know with great precision the extent of the catastrophe so far, and we have lived only through the first of Nietzsche's *two* centuries. In any event, it seems assured that whatever the next century holds will emerge as the further unfolding of nihilism—a slippery term that I will discuss at some length later, but for now need denote nothing more than a world at war with itself.

Given *this* world and *this* century, with its attendant corpses, Sarajevo seems a likely place to begin. To begin in Sarajevo is to keep both myself and the reader awake to the suffering that lies at the heart of the world. As Jan Kott has it, the "road from exile out of paradise to the new paradise, which has been promised, is littered with corpses." Tragic drama, Kott goes on to say, "is the spectacular exhibition of those corpses."[5] Although theology and philosophy cannot, like tragic drama, offer a spectacular display of the dead, these disciplines should nonetheless never lose sight of the fact that the world is littered with corpses. I begin in Sarajevo, in part, in order to make a preemptive strike against the abstraction that will necessarily enter this text as it leaves images of Sarajevo behind and begins to focus instead on the words that fill texts. The problem that confronts any writing, but particularly that kind of writing that postures itself as academic, is how not to lose the stuff of the world amidst all the words. How do you keep words tethered to the world in which the corpses live, while at the same time allowing yourself, as you must, to become absorbed in texts?

By staging *Godot* in Sarajevo and then writing an account of that event, Sontag has given me at least an initial tether between text and world. When she says that Beckett's *Godot* was written for and about Sarajevo what she means, it seems to me, is that the circumstances in Sarajevo in July of 1993 were such that to stage a performance of *Godot* then and there allowed for a remarkable convergence of text and world. To begin by waiting for Godot in Sarajevo, then, is to begin both with a reminder of the suffering that holds a central place in our world and with a reminder of the relationship between this suffering and any attempt to think seriously about this world. Indeed, perhaps I should say with T. W. Adorno that it is nothing other than the suffering at the heart of the world that compels us to think at all.[6]

Note, however, that to begin by waiting for Godot in Sarajevo does not serve simply as a reminder about suffering but serves also to pose a set of questions about the practical, political character of certain responses to suffering. What are we to make of Sontag's claim that the staging of *Godot* in Sarajevo was a practical response to a genocidal war? It is that question that stands at the center of this book. In order to both develop that question and begin to answer it, let me leave behind for the moment both Sarajevo and Godot and turn instead to the philosophical project that Alasdair MacIntyre launched in 1981 with the publication of *After Virtue*.[7]

MacIntyre's Diagnosis of the Current Disaster

After Virtue begins with the "disquieting suggestion" that contemporary moral debate has reached an impasse because we no longer have a coherent account of the moral life. What we have instead are linguistic and theoretical fragments from what were once coherent accounts of the moral life embodied in the equally coherent lives of real communities. The fragmentary character of our moral language is the result of a fall, which, as MacIntyre elaborates the story in later works, is a fall both from the picture of the moral life we find in Aquinas's *Summa Theologica* and from the embodiment of the moral life in communities such as Benedictine monasteries and, for a brief moment in the thirteenth century, the University of Paris.[8]

As MacIntyre narrates the story, what Aquinas accomplished in the *Summa*—with his dialectical synthesis not only of the Augustinian and Aristotelian traditions but also of Arab commentaries upon the latter, the works of the Jewish philosopher Maimonides, Sacred Scripture, and the Platonic, Neoplatonic, and early patristic traditions—was to initiate and partially institutionalize a novel method of enquiry. Had this method of enquiry been adopted (instead of marginalized and partially rejected) by thirteenth- and fourteenth-century institutions such as the university and the church, the history of the West would have been quite different. Indeed, although MacIntyre does not say so explicitly, he implies that had the method of the *Summa* been fully institutionalized, the scientific revolution and theological reformation that dominated the fifteenth through the seventeenth centuries might not have occurred, which is also to say that the Enlightenment might have been avoided.[9]

Of course, all this is hindsight, and speculative hindsight at that, but it is also the driving assumption behind MacIntyre's entire project. And it is this assumption of a fall, together with a critique of the Enlightenment, that stands as the foundation of MacIntyre's conclusions about contemporary moral debates—conclusions that MacIntyre summarizes in the context of a discussion of what he terms "modern radicalism":

> The modern radical is as confident in the moral expression of his stances and consequently in the assertive uses of the rhetoric of morality as any conservative has ever been. Whatever else he denounces in our culture he is certain that it still possesses the moral resources which he requires in order to denounce it. Everything else may be, in his eyes, in disorder; but the language of morality is in order, just as it is. That he too may be being betrayed by the very language he uses is not a thought available to him. It is the aim of this book to make that thought available to radicals, liberals and conservatives alike. I cannot however make it palatable; for if it is true, we are all already in a state so disastrous that there are no large remedies for it.[10]

MacIntyre wants to suggest, then, not only that when we use moral language to speak of contemporary conflicts like abortion or war, we do not know what we are talking about, but also that we are in "a state so disastrous" that it is not immediately apparent we can even know that our moral language and our moral lives are in such a mess. The possibility that we live in the midst of this kind of disaster brings MacIntyre to the "drastic conclusion" that "nothing less than the rejection of a large part of . . . the *ethos* of the distinctively modern and modernizing world . . . will provide us with a rationally and morally defensible standpoint from which to judge and act."[11]

When MacIntyre arrives at this conclusion, we are still in the preface; as the book concludes, he has not changed his mind. In the closing paragraphs he asserts that all political traditions within our culture have exhausted themselves and that all that is left for us to do is wait "for another—doubtless very different—St. Benedict."[12] In other words, all that's left for us now is to do what certain "men and women of good will" did as the Roman Empire lost its foothold on the world and began to slip into the Dark Ages. They "turned aside from the task of shoring up the Roman *imperium* and ceased to identify the continuation of civility and moral community with the maintenance of that *imperium.* What they set themselves to achieve instead . . . was the construction of new forms of community within which the moral life could be sustained so that both morality and civility might survive the coming age of barbarism and darkness."[13] According to MacIntyre our task is like theirs: "What matters at this stage is the construction of local forms of community within which civility and the intellectual and moral life can be sustained through the new dark ages which are already upon us."[14]

The Encyclopaedic Enterprise

The new dark ages that are already upon us are, of course, the latter days of Enlightenment liberalism, the central tenants of which MacIntyre captures so nicely with his discussion of the Ninth Edition of the *Encyclopaedia Britannica* in *Three Rival Versions of Moral Enquiry,* the second sequel to *After Virtue*. MacIntyre notes that the editor of the Ninth Edition of the *Encyclopaedia Britannica* "made it clear that he intended for his contributors not merely to provide detailed information on every major topic but to do so within the framework of a distinctive architectonic of the sciences," an architectonic that, late in the nineteenth century, made no strong distinction between the physical and the human sciences and that was founded upon a strong belief in progress.[15] Hence these comments of the editor from the introduction to the first volume: "The available facts of human history, collected over the widest areas, are carefully coordinated and grouped together, in the hope of ultimately evolving the laws of progress, moral and material, which underlie them, and which will help to connect and interpret the whole movement of the race."[16] MacIntyre, reading only slightly between the lines, offers the following gloss on this passage:

> The Ninth Edition pointed the reader towards some future edition in which the *Britannica* would in an important way have displaced the Bible by offering a more comprehensive overview, within which the writings of the Bible, duly scrutinized by the relevant scholars, would be understood as sources of data both for particular sciences and for the overview afforded by the architectonic ordering of the sciences. The Encyclopaedia would have displaced the Bible as the canonical book, or set of books, of the culture.[17]

The Ninth Edition, then, embodied perfectly the wish of the Enlightenment that all humanity would one day be unified in the name of reason. The task of the Encyclopaedia was to record and map, in one grand architectonic, this unified world. The Encyclopaedia, as it was conceived by the editor of the Ninth Edition, was the visible proof that the world is organized around and unified by a single reason (which, in the wake of Kant, also implied a single morality): Everything in the world has a proper place within the grand scheme of this new canonical book. The particularities and differences that up to this point had divided peoples from one another would one day fall away and, as Kant had it, be dismissed as exercises in "self-incurred tutelage" to unnecessary authorities.

As I noted earlier, this dream of radical freedom, universal truths, autonomous individuals, and unstoppable progress was, in the wake of centuries of religious wars, attractive. But slowly, as this enterprise attempted to pour the whole world into its encyclopaedic mold, it became apparent that such notions had different names when they became practices: colonialism, imperialism, racism, war, torture, death, madness, genocide. As it turned out, the success of this "encyclopaedic enterprise" and the universal moral imperatives of the Enlightenment depended upon the help of guns and capitalism.

Put into practice Enlightenment liberalism became a morality that locked us into notions of individual preferences that can be secured the one against the other only by an ever growing state bureaucracy and regulated by the market. Thus individual freedom is bound now to an always more absolute state power and an increasingly invasive market that begins to regulate all aspects of life. Life in the nineties, as it were, is life squeezed out between the two "successes" of the Enlightenment: the nation-state and international corporations.[18] As moral visions (which, after all, is what the Enlightenment was) these successes are abject failures. Hence liberalism is dead (even though, like the saint in *Zarathustra* with regard to God's death, not every one knows it yet): It died of the madness expressed in the body count of a century steeped in tens of millions of corpses from the ravages of war alone.

Even a cursory look at the daily newspaper is proof enough that the dreams of unity, so central to Enlightenment assumptions about the progressive unfolding of the world, lie shattered. And if Enlightenment liberalism and the encyclopaedic enterprise were one and the same, then the failure of one should be reflected in the failure of the other. Indeed, as MacIntyre points out, Encyclopaedias are not what they used to be:

> In the Ninth Edition the editor's overall standpoint and scheme was widely, if not universally, shared by his contributors. . . . But with the Fifteenth Edition it is quite otherwise. Heterogeneous and divergent contributions, which recognize the diversity and fragmentation of standpoints in central areas, are

> deeply at odds with the overall scheme, insofar as that scheme presupposes any real unity to the work, rather than merely providing some organization for a massive work of reference. Mortimer J. Adler, chairman of the board of editors of this edition (Chicago, 1974), recognizes this when he allows at the close of his introductory account that what the Encyclopaedia embodies is no more than "faith in the unity of knowledge."[19]

"The encyclopaedic mode of enquiry," concludes MacIntyre, "has become one more fideism and a fideism which increasingly flies in the face of contemporary realities."[20] These realities are what MacIntyre calls the "accomplished fact" of the failure of the Enlightenment. And the discovery of this fact, if we want to give credit where credit is due, belongs to Nietzsche, who, as MacIntyre notes (with some qualification) is "*the* moral philosopher of the present age" not only because he recognized the fideistic nature of the encyclopaedic enterprise long before we as a culture did but also because he understood "more clearly than any other philosopher" the full implications of this fact. Indeed, Nietzsche understood that once the Enlightenment is exposed as one more fideism, then the cultural vertigo that we have come to think of as nihilism "stands at the door."[21]

MacIntyre's Response to Nietzsche

Without Aristotelian teleology and its embodiment in the great medieval cosmic worldview and without the unfettered and universal reason that was to be the replacement for such superstitious and outdated views of the world, all that remains are heterogeneous, diverse, divergent, and different perspectives. We are, as MacIntyre put it, all engaged partisans of certain commitments always already at war with the partisans of other, rival commitments. What MacIntyre hopes to gain with his recourse to Aquinas is, so to speak, a set of rules for how this war will be fought. Nietzsche, on the other hand, simply declared that the war was on—and left it at that.

In arguing against a universal reason that becomes the neutral judge of differences and the vehicle for a universal good, and in arguing for the idea that whatever we call 'good' is finally but an expression of the will to power, Nietzsche concludes that morality is forever grounded beyond reason in power. Reason is but the edifice that obscures the real fount of our action: the nonrational will to power.[22] According to MacIntyre's reading of Nietzsche, this collapse of universal reason yields two similar possibilities with regard to moral philosophy: relativism and perspectivism.

The relativist makes claims of 'truth', while acknowledging that such claims are contingent upon a particular historical tradition; thus reasoned judgments are possible within a tradition, but no objective measure exists by which rival traditions can adjudicate their differences. Rational debate between rival traditions is thus impossible. Perspectivists draw a similar but more radical conclusion from the acknowledgment of contingency: They jettison 'truth' altogether. The assertion that 'reason' can be defined only with criteria internal to a tradition implies that you cannot judge a different reason internal to a different tradition to be false—but this is only the converse of being unable to claim 'truth' for your own tradition. Both perspectivism and relativism, then, deliver us into a colosseum-like world, where conflict ends in senseless death.[23]

And so, according to MacIntyre, Nietzsche gives to the twentieth (or more aptly, the twenty-first) century one of its possible courses: an increasingly conflictual and violent world in which either truth is relative and we carry guns to settle inevitable disputes or truth has left the world altogether, which just leaves the guns—and our inability to offer any reasons at all for using them, though use them we will. With his notion of the will to power Nietzsche captures this post-Enlightenment moment perfectly. However, MacIntyre is not content to conclude with Nietzsche that the world is simply a world at war with itself: enter Aquinas.

The dialectical reason that MacIntyre finds embodied in the works of Aquinas stands as his answer to Nietzsche's sweeping dismissal of reason, in whatever form, as a ruse of power. MacIntyre acknowledges that Nietzsche's critique has devastating results when leveled at the Enlightenment. When pressed, Enlightenment universalism cannot offer reasons for its claims, since such claims no longer carry with them the context of the argument that made them reasonable in the first place. Hence, as MacIntyre puts it, "modern moral utterance and practice can only be understood as a series of fragmented survivals from an older past," such that "the deontological character of moral judgments is a ghost conception of divine law . . . [and] the teleological character is similarly the ghost of conceptions of human nature and activity" that originated with Aristotle.[24]

It was Nietzsche's insight, says MacIntyre, that the attempt of "the Enlightenment project to discover rational foundations for an objective morality" was doomed to fail.[25] For without rich arguments about such things as "the function of man" (to use Aristotle's phrase) and the commands of God, the purportedly objective and universal could not help but appear to be, just beneath the surface, simply a reflection of particular interests. Nietzsche's mistake, however, was to export this insight beyond the realm of the Enlightenment and make of it a grand claim not just about Enlightenment reason but reason as such.

As MacIntyre puts it in *After Virtue,* the efficacy of Nietzsche's export in this regard depends upon the question of whether it was right in the first place to reject Aristotle (and Aquinas). By using Aristotle and Aquinas to answer Nietzsche's charge that all reason is but a ruse of power, MacIntyre hopes to display the fact that the dialectical reason embodied in the *Summa* can withstand the Nietzschean critique.

Dialectical reason is reason embodied in certain virtues, which themselves are embodied in the living out of particular narratives. Dialectical reason makes no claims to be an ahistorical foundation that grounds the universality of truth and goodness. Rather dialectical reason always commences at some particular historical juncture and is contingent upon a host of historical particularities: a set of authoritative texts, a particular geographical location, neighboring communities with rival interpretations of the world, and so forth. Here reason emerges not as an abstract universal but as a dialectical enterprise always already underway—as individuals and communities engage with one another, with texts, and with the world. Dialectical reason emerges concretely, in the midst of historically contingent events, and is from the beginning not a blanket assertion of universal truth but an argument. As this argument is extended in time it becomes what MacIntyre calls a tradition, and the reason it embodies is thus tradition-constitutive and tradition-constituted: No tradition existed before the argument began, nor was there reason, until parts of the argument were settled. As long as the argument continues, reason will never become universal because it will always find itself challenged. Were it not to find itself challenged, then the argument would be over, and the tradition would, by definition, cease to be reasonable: Most likely it would have become fascist.

Dialectical reason is at once an alternative to the Enlightenment and to Nietzsche because it absorbs and affirms the Nietzschean critique of universal, foundational reason and yet does not cease to talk of reason altogether. MacIntyre contends that this Nietzschean critique of reason, which is so effective against the Enlightenment, loses all its force against dialectical reason. In facing up to its contingency, dialectical reason carries with it an openness that counters the Nietzschean claim that all rational legitimation of morality conceals the nonrational will to power. Indeed, dialectical traditions can offer reasons for their moral commitments, and when pressed they can point to the embodiment of these reasons in narratives and practices that make assertions about the good life and about the truth of the world. These assertions are offered not abstractly and in isolation but as embodied reasons that the tradition has developed across time in the course of its engagement with other traditions and the world. This concreteness of reason as an endless engagement with difference, as a truth that, by definition, exposes itself to the critique of ceaseless argument, gesturing always to other traditions and to the world, is an assurance that reason is not reducible to power.

By MacIntyre's account, to opt wholly for the Nietzschean critique of reason is to give in to the unreasoned violence of an increasingly conflictual world. MacIntyre hopes to recover via recourse to Aquinas another possibility, one where conflict can be rationally adjudicated. Not that MacIntyre counters the violence of the Nietzschean worldview with pacifism. Rather he exhorts that violence be justified with reasons that emerge only after long argument: That is what dialectics is all about.[26]

The University and the Moral Life

This framing of violence in dialectical argument is perhaps exemplified best in the last chapter of *Three Rival Versions,* where MacIntyre offers his version of what a university should be as we move toward the close of the twentieth century. If the new dark ages that MacIntyre refers to in the final paragraph of *After Virtue* are depicted in *Three Rival Versions* as the death throes of the encyclopaedic enterprise, then the local forms of community that MacIntyre gestures toward in *After Virtue* are depicted in the closing pages of *Three Rival Versions* not as Benedictine monasteries but as a new kind of university, whereby the university no longer aspires to the Enlightenment dream of "unconstrained agreement" but becomes instead "a place of constrained disagreement, of imposed participation in conflict, in which a central responsibility of higher education would be to initiate students into conflict."[27]

MacIntyre goes on to ask, as he thinks through his proposal for a university of constrained disagreement: "If within one and the same university arena modes of enquiry would have to develop in . . . very different ways, so that not only was thesis matched against thesis and argument against argument but genre against genre, the subversion of authority against the re-creation of authority, how could the university achieve a genuinely shared conversation?"[28] MacIntyre answers his own question with the reply that such a university could not in fact achieve a genuine conversation, and so "surely a set of rival universities would result. . . . And thus the wider society would be confronted with the claims of rival universities, each advancing its own enquiries in its own terms. . . . But then also required would be a set of institutionalized forums in which the debate between rival types of enquiry was afforded rhetorical expression."[29]

This account of the university supplies, it seems to me, the perfect picture of the moral life as MacIntyre envisions it, which is to say as a life lived amidst endless conflicts that are, nonetheless, refereed by dialectical reason. If we allow rival universities to stand in for rival traditions, and we then cast this image on a large scale, we arrive quickly at Nietzsche's description of the world as a place of radically incommensurable perspectives. Obviously, MacIntyre has no interest in denying that the world is so divided; in fact, he seems to celebrate such a world. For dialectics would have no place in a world of "unconstrained agreement."[30] On this note it is not surprising that MacIntyre is highly critical of the contemporary university, where as a matter of institutional and cultural habit everything still operates "*as if* we still did believe much of what the major contributors to the Ninth Edition believed. So we often still behave as if there is some overall coherence to and some underlying agreement about the academic project."[31]

In contrast to the habits of the contemporary university (and, of course, contemporary culture as well—since the one reflects the other), MacIntyre argues for a more openly conflictual world in which we no longer pretend to have enough in common with our rivals to have even "genuinely shared conversation." However, although MacIntyre makes conflict central to the moral life in a way unimaginable for the encyclopaedic enterprise of the Enlightenment, he does not assume with Nietzsche that conflict pushes the moral life beyond the pale of rational debate. Hence his insistence, with regard to the university, upon an institutionalized forum in which rivals would debate their differences. Here we see MacIntyre's Thomistic departure from Nietzsche's perspectivism.[32]

It is perhaps too easy to miss the import and radical nature of MacIntyre's vision of the university because we tend to read it as just another proposal among dozens about the future of this troubled institution; it almost reads as an addendum tacked on at the end of an interesting book about Augustine and Aquinas, Nietzsche and Foucault. However, MacIntyre's account of a university as a place of constrained disagreement is, it seems to me, a concrete proposal for the construction of precisely the new form of local community that MacIntyre placed his hopes in at the end of *After Virtue.* Of course we might see this connection and still miss the radical nature of MacIntyre's proposal simply because we fail to take him seriously, choosing instead to suggest that MacIntyre has waxed utopian, just as in *After Virtue* he was, in the words of Jeffrey Stout, "terminally wistful."

But if we choose to dismiss MacIntyre in these terms, then we must bear the brunt of the following tirade, which MacIntyre lets fly shortly before the end of *Three Rival Versions:*

> Those most prone to accuse others of utopianism are generally those men and women of affairs who pride themselves upon their pragmatic realism, who look for immediate results, who want the relationship between present input and future output to be predictable and measurable, and that is to say, a matter of the shorter, indeed the shortest run. They are the enemies of the incalculable, the skeptics about all expectations which outrun what *they* take to be hard evidence, the deliberately shortsighted who congratulate themselves upon the limits of their vision. Who were their predecessors?
>
> They include the fourth-century magistrates of the types of disordered city which Plato described in Book VIII of the *Republic,* the officials who tried to sustain the pagan Roman Empire in the age of Augustine, the sixteenth-century protobureaucrats who continued obediently to do the unprincipled

> bidding of Henry VIII while Thomas More set out on a course that led to his martyrdom. What these examples suggest is that the gap between Utopia and current social reality may on occasion furnish a measure, not of the lack of justification of Utopia, but rather the degree to which those who not only inhabit current social reality but insist upon seeing only what it allows them to see and upon learning only what it allows them to learn, cannot even identify, let alone confront the problems which will be inscribed in their epitaphs. It may be therefore that the charge of utopianism is sometimes best understood more as a symptom of the condition of those who level it than an indictment of the projects against which it is directed.[33]

This scathing critique of all those who attempt to secure the status quo is certainly every bit as much a rejection of the modern ethos as was MacIntyre's comment about the new dark ages at the end of *After Virtue*. These words should dispel the misreadings of MacIntyre, whereby his critics suggest that his later works take a step back from his radical assertions in *After Virtue*.[34] Lest there be any doubt about the extent to which MacIntyre has held his course from the beginning to the end of the "single project" upon which he embarked in 1977, consider the following comment that he made in an interview in 1993, where we see the final paragraphs of *After Virtue* flash before our eyes.

> I think the great disaster has already happened. I think the West is already gone. What we have to do is find means of constructing and sustaining local forms of community through which we can survive this age. When I was a Marxist, I devoted time and energy to thinking about how one might overthrow the political and economic order. I now see that this was not merely misdirected and wrongheaded energy; in fact, the existing order is so good at destroying itself, it doesn't need any help. What we have to do is withdraw from it, and not get involved in its disasters.[35]

MacIntyre's words here recall not only his claim in *After Virtue* that the new dark ages are already upon us but also the accompanying assertion that we should have something of a monastic response to this fact. What are we to make of MacIntyre's counsel that we should "withdraw from" and "not get involved in" the disaster of the current order? In order to explore this question and to begin to steer my discussion of MacIntyre back toward the question concerning the practical character of staging *Godot* in Sarajevo, let's consider MacIntyre's treatment of Sophocles' *Antigone*.

Antigone and MacIntyre Against the Imperium

First recall both the story that sets up the play and the story of the play itself. After Oedipus is exiled from Thebes, his two sons by Jocasta, Eteocles and Polynices (who were also, of course, his brothers—but that is another story), agree to rule the city in alternate years, with the nonruling brother to spend the year in exile. This arrangement does not sit well with Polynices (who spent the first year in exile while Eteocles ruled Thebes) and so, with the help of the Argive army, he attacks Thebes. The attack is a failure, and in the course of the battle Polynices and Eteocles kill each other in hand-to-hand combat, at which point Creon, Jocasta's brother, assumes the throne of Thebes. It is in the immediate wake of these events that Sophocles begins his play.

Creon's first act as the King of Thebes is to outlaw the burial of Polynices on the grounds that he was a traitor to the city. Antigone, sister to both Polynices and Eteocles, decides to bury Polynices in defiance of Creon's order. For this act, Creon orders that Antigone be sealed in a tomb to die (we suppose) of starvation. As the play draws to an end, Antigone hangs herself only moments before Creon's son, Haemon, to whom she had been engaged, comes to save her. Upon finding her dead body, Haemon kills himself, too. All of this happens as Creon is on his way to release Antigone, having relented from his judgment against her.

MacIntyre uses this play to hone his account of the virtues and to make the point that different communities will have different and often conflicting accounts of the virtues; hence the virtues of Homer's Greece are not the same as those of Sophocles' Greece. What MacIntyre finds particularly fascinating about Sophocles is that in his tragedies he exhibits for us precisely such conflicting accounts of the virtues. In fact, the tragic character of Sophocles' plays is rooted in this conflict of virtues. Thus, in the *Antigone* Creon, as the ruler of Thebes, embodies and represents the virtues of the Greek city-state, whereas Antigone, in defying the orders of the state to bury her fallen brother, represents the virtues as they were embodied in the Greek clan or family. And all of this represents the very real conflicts between differing accounts of the virtues in fifth-century B.C. Athens.

According to MacIntyre's somewhat Hegelian reading of the play, the conflict between Creon and Antigone is "tragic" because, at least from a certain perspective, both Antigone and Creon are "right." Sophocles forces us to recognize the authority of both sets of claims, those of the state and those of the clan, as they are embodied in the characters Creon and Antigone. Through this tragic conflict, Sophocles raises important questions for us about the nature of the virtues. What Sophocles does not do, in the play itself, is make any attempt to resolve the conflict.

MacIntyre wants us to see

> that what is at stake in Sophoclean dramatic encounter is not simply the fate of individuals. When Antigone and Creon contend, the life of the clan and the life of the city are weighed against each other. . . . It is the individual in his or her role, representing his or her community, who is as in epic the dramatic character. Hence in some important sense the community too is a dramatic character which enacts the narrative of its history.[36]

Cast this way, though, it is not enough, when standing outside the play, to say that both Creon and Antigone are right. Insofar as Antigone and Creon represent different communities with different accounts of the virtues, then we must take sides between Creon and Antigone, which is to say, between two conflicting accounts of the virtues. Sophocles himself does not resolve the conflict, but it is incumbent upon us to do so. If we cast Creon as not just the representative of a fifth-century B.C. Greek city-state but the representative of the state generally, and we cast Antigone not simply as the representative of ancient Greek clans but of small communities generally who stand in opposition to the state, then MacIntyre, I think, would recognize Antigone as the true hero of this play. Antigone is the predecessor to all those "men and women of good will" who refused "the task of shoring up the Roman *imperium* and ceased to identify the continuation of civility and moral community with the maintenance of that *imperium*." Although I do not mean to push this too far, Antigone is a Greek Benedict. She is the exemplar of a moral life lived outside of and in opposition to the imperium. And it is to a life so lived that MacIntyre calls us.

After asserting that every political tradition in our culture is exhausted, MacIntyre poses the question of whether this conclusion commits him or "anyone else who accepts [his analysis] to a generalized social pessimism."[37] After all, the story of Antigone is not exactly optimistic. However, MacIntyre's answer to his own question is an unequivocal no; and he justifies this answer by suggesting that insofar as a few local communities exist where the life of virtue has not been lost, then we have every reason to hold out hope.

But can we not ask of MacIntyre what the journalist asked of Sontag after learning of her decision to stage a play in Sarajevo: With the massive problems facing the modern world, is not the construction of a few virtuous local communities a bit like fiddling while Rome burns? MacIntyre, it seems, would answer that the construction of a few local communities amidst the current disaster is exactly like fiddling while Rome burns, and so is the staging of a play in a war zone. Indeed, what MacIntyre hopes to convince us of, I think, is that fiddling might just be the perfect and *practical* response to the burning of Rome. It is my task in the pages that follow to offer an account of politics that explains why Sontag's staging of *Godot* and MacIntyre's call for new forms of local community are profoundly practical and political acts.

Waiting for Godot in Sarajevo

So far I have suggested that to wait for Godot in Sarajevo serves not only to remind us of the suffering that belies the optimism of Enlightenment dreams but also to pose a question about the kind of politics adequate to the task of living the good life at the end of a century such as ours. I have suggested further that the backdrop to both suffering and a possible politics as we meet them in Sarajevo is the fragmented, post-Enlightenment world that Nietzsche attempted to describe by speaking of nihilism. Indeed, my discussion of MacIntyre added some depth to a description of the conflict-ridden world that Nietzsche, at the end of the nineteenth century, recognized as the coming future of Europe. My discussion of MacIntyre also led us toward the possibility that the failure of the Enlightenment does not lead inevitably to nihilism—that is, to a world bereft of meaning. We might yet discover a response to nihilism other than the tired and increasingly violent attempts to shore up the imperium. We might yet, as MacIntyre sees it, salvage from the disaster that surrounds us the possibility of meaningful, moral lives. As it happens, it is just this possibility that Beckett explores in *Waiting for Godot*. Hence, before I begin to explore this possibility in detail—and in order to explain why my reflections fall into the tripartite division of the subtitle—let me turn briefly to Beckett's play.

In Act I of *Waiting for Godot*, two men, Estragon and Vladimir, meet on a road, near a tree, in the evening, to wait for Godot. While they wait, Estragon complains of ill-fitting boots and reports that he had been beaten the night before, as usual, and Vladimir, the more reflective of the two, muses over their lot. The opening exchange is typical: After giving up the attempt to remove his boot, Estragon proclaims, "Nothing to be done." And Vladimir replies, "I'm beginning to come round to that opinion. All my life, I've tried to put it from me, saying, Vladimir, be reasonable, you haven't yet tried everything. And I resume the struggle. So there you are again."[38]

The play is filled with such exchanges: Estragon complains of hunger, continues to struggle with his boots, and proposes that they hang themselves (but concludes that the tree might not bear their weight), while Vladimir feeds Estragon a carrot to quiet his hunger, and continues to muse (wondering for instance about the two thieves who were crucified with Jesus, and why it is that only one of the four Gospels tells us that one of the thieves was saved). When Estragon proposes that they leave, Vladimir reminds him (and us) that they can't leave because they are waiting for Godot: "Let's wait and see what he says," remarks Vladimir. "Let's wait till we know exactly where we stand."

In the midst of this seemingly interminable waiting, where, as Estragon says, "Nothing happens, nobody comes, nobody goes," two men arrive on stage: Pozzo and Lucky. Lucky arrives first, with his arms full of bags and suitcases and with a rope around his neck. Holding the other end of the rope and walking a few paces behind Lucky is Pozzo. It appears in the events that follow that Lucky is Pozzo's slave. The action of the play now changes as Estragon and Vladimir become, in a sense, spectators to the master/slave routine of Pozzo and Lucky, whereby Pozzo frequently bellows at Lucky to do this or that, always jerking on the rope when Lucky is too slow to respond. When this routine has reached an end, Pozzo and Lucky exit. Shortly thereafter a young boy arrives on stage to inform Vladimir and Estragon that Mr. Godot won't be coming this evening but will surely come tomorrow.

In Act II the events of Act I repeat themselves, as Estragon and Vladimir arrive at the same spot at the same time on the next day to await Godot's arrival once again. There are, however, at least two significant differences between Act I and Act II: The tree, which in Act I had been completely bare of foliage, has now sprouted a few leaves; and when Pozzo and Lucky arrive they are in sorry shape: Pozzo has become blind and Lucky dumb. Shortly after arriving on stage, Pozzo falls, and Estragon and Vladimir then have a protracted debate about whether or not to help him up. When they finally do help him, Pozzo and Vladimir have an exchange that is one of the most striking moments in the entire play.

Vladimir has been questioning Pozzo incessantly about how it is that he became blind and Lucky dumb, given that just yesterday they were both fine. When, Vladimir asks, did all of this come to pass? Pozzo finally answers Vladimir with this tirade: "Have you not done tormenting me with your accursed time! It's abominable! When! When! One day, is that not enough for you, one day he went dumb, one day I went blind, one day we'll go deaf, one day we were born, one day we shall die, the same day, the same second, is that not enough for you. They give birth astride a grave, the light gleams an instant, then it's night once more."[39]

A few lines later, Vladimir utters something of a response, which serves as a good summary of the entire play:

> Was I sleeping while others suffered? Am I sleeping now? To-morrow, when I wake, or think I do, what shall I say of to-day? That with Estragon my friend, at this place, until the fall of night, I waited for Godot. That Pozzo passed with his carrier, and that he spoke to us? Probably. But in all that what truth will there be? He'll know nothing. He'll tell me about the blows he received and I'll give him a carrot. Astride a grave and a difficult birth. Down in the hole, lingeringly, the grave digger puts on the forceps. We have time to grow old. The air is full of our cries. But habit is a great deadener. At me, too, someone is looking, of me too someone is saying, he is sleeping, he knows nothing, let him sleep on.[40]

Immediately after this soliloquy, a boy arrives to say again that Mr. Godot will not come today but surely tomorrow. As the play ends, Estragon proposes again that they hang themselves, but the plan comes to naught because they don't have any rope, and Estragon's belt proves to be too weak. They decide to bring rope when they come back the next day and hang themselves, unless, of course, Mr. Godot arrives, in which case, says Vladimir, "We'll be saved."

What are we to make of this play, especially as we imagine it staged amidst much enthusiasm in Sarajevo in the summer of 1993? It might help to begin by noting that Beckett himself referred to the play as a "tragicomedy." Recalled with such brevity, and confronted as a text and not a performance, it is perhaps hard to see either the tragedy or comedy in this play. Thus with *Godot* in mind, consider these words from Schopenhauer:

> The life of every individual, viewed as a whole and in general, and when only its most significant features are emphasized, is really a tragedy; but gone through in detail it has the character of a comedy. For the doings and worries of the day, the restless mockeries of the moment, the desires and fears of the week, the mishaps of every hour, are all brought about by chance that is always bent on some mischievous trick; they are nothing but scenes from a comedy. The never-fulfilled wishes, the hopes mercilessly blighted by fate, the unfortunate mistakes of the whole life, with increasing suffering and death at the end, always gives us a tragedy. Thus, as if fate wished to add mockery to the misery of our existence, our life must contain all the woes of tragedy, and we cannot even assert the dignity of tragic characters, but, in the broad detail of life, are inevitably the foolish characters of a comedy.[41]

Beckett's play abounds in the mockeries and mishaps of comedy: Estragon's struggle with his boot; the decision about who should hang himself first being decided by who weighs the most, lest the branch break and leave one person stranded alone; the breaking of Estragon's belt, which they hope will work for a hanging rope, when they each tug on an end (not to mention that with his belt gone, Estragon's pants fall to his knees). All of these mishaps and mockeries, when combined with the timed taking on and off of bowler hats, suggest not only comedy but vaudeville. On the other hand, the fate of Pozzo and Lucky, certainly, and of Estragon and Vladimir, perhaps, is in some sense tragic, insofar as tragedy involves "increasing suffering and death at the end."

Why was this strange mix of tragedy and comedy such a success in Sarajevo? Why did this play stun the audience into silent tears? One answer, the one Sontag herself suggests, is obvious. The characters on the stage and the people in the audience shared lives that had been all but reduced to the task of waiting for a salvation that had been promised but had never arrived. Put simply, the people of Sarajevo who flocked to see performances of *Godot* fell into stunned silence because the drama on the stage was simply a mirror in which they saw themselves, as if for the first time: a suffering people awaiting the arrival not of Godot but of NATO or the UN.

I would like to at least imagine, however, that the success of *Godot* rested on something more profound, something that, although rooted in the particular circumstances of Sarajevo in 1993, nonetheless transcended these circumstances. After all, the play itself, first performed in 1953, was Beckett's response to a world still reeling from the reality of the Holocaust and World War II. It seems possible that the truly stunning thing about watching a performance of *Godot* in Sarajevo would have been the realization that what one was witnessing was not only the plight of a besieged city in 1993 but also the summary of a century that began in the trenches of World War I, passed through Auschwitz, and was now gathered on the hills outside the city. I can imagine that to witness a performance of *Godot* in Sarajevo in 1993 would have been to meet head-on the question of what such a century might mean—or rather, the question of whether *meaning* itself could possibly have survived a century such as this.

Indeed, *Waiting for Godot* is in part an exhibit of life in a world without meaning; and yet the play is also an exhibit of something else: the possibility that even in a world full of suffering, there might still be reason to go on.[42] In the play this reason is tied most obviously to the arrival of Godot and thus, by implication, to God. However, to the extent that Vladimir and Estragon do go on without Godot, the play also suggests, but only suggests, another possibility—namely, that even in the absence of God and in the presence of suffering life might be meaningful. This twofold possibility of meaning projected against a background of meaninglessness accounts, I think, for the profoundly suggestive character of Beckett's play, particularly when staged amidst the events in Sarajevo in the summer of 1993. And what Beckett suggests, Nietzsche articulates.

Nihilism, Tragedy, Apocalypse

Near the end of those notes published posthumously as *The Will to Power,* in a note dated March–June 1888, we read:

> Dionysus versus the "Crucified": there you have the antithesis. It is *not* a difference in regard to their martyrdom—it is a difference in the meaning of it. Life itself, its eternal fruitfulness and recurrence, created torment, destruction, the will to annihilation. In the other case, suffering—the "Crucified as the innocent one"—counts as an objection to this life, as a formula for its condemnation.—One will see that it is a problem of the meaning of suffering: whether a Christian meaning or a tragic meaning.[43]

According to Nietzsche, the nihilism that was to describe the coming century—our century— was the product of Christianity. "Nihilism stands at the door," declared Nietzsche, "whence this uncanniest of guests?"[44] And he concluded that nihilism is rooted in the Christian interpretation of the world. Nietzsche did not, however, imagine that nihilism was a permanent condition, but rather, "a pathological transitional stage."[45] Nietzsche's own hope seems to have been that we would (or at least some of us would) emerge on the other side of nihilism. To emerge on the "other side" of nihilism would be, for Nietzsche, to emerge into the Dionysian world that stands on the other side of Christianity. In the contest between Dionysus and the Crucified, then, Nietzsche not only has a favorite, he has declared a winner. But this seems premature, or rather, this seems a misconstrual of the rivalry itself.

Perhaps I see more substance in Nietzsche's opposition than even he did, but it seems to me that both Dionysus *and* the Crucified stand as alternatives to nihilism, alternatives that I will reconfigure in the following pages as tragedy and apocalypse. What I propose to do, then, is to reinhabit what Nietzsche understood toward the end of his working life as *the* crucial opposition, an opposition thoroughly rooted in his understanding of nihilism, and then to both work with and move beyond Nietzsche in an attempt to delineate the descriptive power for our times of these three terms—nihilism, tragedy, and apocalypse.

In sum so far, I can say that to wait for Godot in Sarajevo is to be reminded of suffering; it is to entertain questions about the political significance of seemingly futile acts; and it is, as Vladimir and Estragon remind us, to conclude that these questions concerning politics and action stand in the shadows of much larger, finally metaphysical, questions concerning the meaning of suffering.

On a stage in a poorly lit theater, with the intermittent sounds of a war going on outside, Estragon and Vladimir, and with them the audience—cold, hungry, and exhausted—await Godot, which is to say in part that they await a decision on the character of the universe. Is nihilism the last word? Does it all come to naught in the end? Is suffering, and with it the whole of existence, meaningless? "They give birth astride a grave, the light gleams an instant, then it's night once more." Is that the definitive description of the way of the world—the sum of our life? Or can we hope for more? Might we describe things differently, not in the hope of alleviating suffering (we cannot do that) but in the hope of rendering it meaningful? Might we say not that suffering is meaningless but that it is tragic, which is to say that when we arise to the occasion and meet suffering with dignity, we somehow transfigure the world? Do declarations of tragedy better describe the world than declarations of meaninglessness? And what of that other possibility, namely, that the world is neither meaningless nor tragic but apocalyptic, such that suffering not only finds meaning in dignity but comes to rest in the life of God?

After all, maybe Godot is God; maybe he will arrive, if not today or tomorrow, then one day, maybe even one day soon; maybe he will save us, as he saved one of the thieves on one of the crosses, at least in one of the four accounts we have of the crucifixion. On the other hand, maybe "Godot" is a play on the French word for "boot"; maybe there is no Mr.

Godot; maybe we wait in vain. But maybe, too, it doesn't matter; maybe, like Vladimir and Estragon at their best, we aspire to go on anyway. Or maybe we'll take that chance on the strength of the tree branch—if only we can remember to bring some rope. Maybe. Perhaps. But as Estragon declares, "Nothing is certain."

Yet we must act in the meantime, and how we describe the world in which we act is crucial. And just here the full power of Beckett's play becomes evident. For somehow he manages to keep all of these questions in the air at once. Is it all for naught? Then let's find some rope. But how can we be sure it's all for naught? What if we counter despair with dignity and turn that into hope—a thin thread, I know, but maybe it's worth the risk, given that the rope stands as our alternative. And what if Godot not only exists but arrives, what then? Do we abandon both the rope and the thin thread, or does the thread, at least, remain?

Nihilism, tragedy, apocalypse: three possible descriptions of the world (and three possible courses of action?) that arrive as suggestions from the staging of Godot in Sarajevo. My task in the coming pages is to explore at some length, and in turn, each of these suggestions. Thus, this book will unfold in three parts, one part for each of the three terms: nihilism, tragedy, apocalypse. Because the terms frequently mingle, particularly early on, I have not formally divided the book. But speaking roughly, I can say that Chapters Two and Three focus upon nihilism as we find it described in the works of Nietzsche and his critics (although the third chapter is in fact much broader than that); Chapters Four, Five, and Six turn to the works of both Nietzsche and Foucault for an account of tragedy; and Chapters Seven and Eight then focus upon both the New Testament and the work of John Howard Yoder, as I work toward an account of apocalypse.

2

From Out of the Abyss: Nihilism According to Nietzsche and His Critics

At the beginning of *The Will to Power,* Nietzsche says that nihilism concerns "the radical repudiation of value, meaning, and desirability."[1] Elsewhere—not speaking specifically of nihilism but espousing a thought related to the concept—Nietzsche says, echoing Dostoyevsky, that if "nothing is true, everything is permitted."[2] Such definitions of nihilism are a likely place to begin thinking about the term, if for no other reason than that they stand the closest to the meaning of the term in ordinary usage.

In this chapter, I explore nihilism as we find it in the works of Nietzsche and three of his critics, and although at times it might seem otherwise, we will never be far from these summary definitions of the term. The task of the first part of this chapter is to work toward what we might call the self-understanding of nihilism. This task demands that we consider at some length Nietzsche's understanding of the term, for, as Michael Gillespie notes: "When it comes to our understanding of nihilism, we are almost all Nietzscheans. . . . The great wars and totalitarian experiments of our century have borne an all too faithful witness to Nietzsche's prescience and we have consequently come to accept his explanation of the origin and meaning of nihilism."[3] As we will see later, Gillespie thinks that Nietzsche was wrong about nihilism. Nonetheless, Nietzsche's understanding of the term holds sway, such that even his most trenchant critics find they can discuss nihilism only after first paying some kind of tribute to Nietzsche.

After I have established Nietzsche's understanding of nihilism, I then turn to three of Nietzsche's critics—John Milbank, Martin Heidegger, and Michael Gillespie—in an attempt to add both depth and breadth to the term. Note, however, that my account of Nietzsche's account of nihilism is not meant to be a definitive exploration either of his use of the term or of the term generally. Such an exploration is not necessary for the purposes of my narrative, nor would it be particularly helpful in the big scheme of things, since several good expositions of Nietzsche's understanding of nihilism already exist.[4] Rather, by exploring the conflicts between Nietzsche and his critics, I hope to arrive at an overview of both the descriptive power of this term and the inherently political character of the conflicts rooted in precisely this descriptive power.

Although Nietzsche's account of nihilism is less than clear and far from systematic, a summary display of his understanding of the concept is not far out of reach, in spite of his own varied and at times confusing use of the term. Most of what Nietzsche has to say about nihilism is found in Book One of *The Will to Power,* a collection of posthumously published selections from Nietzsche's notebooks of the years 1883 through 1888. Indeed, almost all of Nietzsche's seemingly sustained reflection upon nihilism occurs in the first twenty-five pages of *The Will to Power.* However, since the editors are responsible for placing these particular notes together, these reflections only appear to represent a sustained effort. In fact, the majority of Nietzsche's comments about nihilism are little more than random if insightful thoughts, which have the appearance of being recorded on the run.

Let me place one of these thoughts here at the head of my account of Nietzsche on nihilism, since in my view it stands as the perfect summary of the complexities of Nietzsche's understanding of nihilism: "A nihilist is a man who judges of the world as it is that it ought *not* to be, and of the world as it ought to be that it does not exist. According to this view, our existence (action, suffering, willing, feeling) has no meaning: the pathos of the 'in vain' is the nihilist's pathos."[5] From this definition of a nihilist, it should be clear that nihilism is a term that describes the condition whereby the world and our lives within it appear to us as meaningless—hence Nietzsche's definition of nihilism as "the radical repudiation of value, meaning, and desirability"; or his reference to nihilism as "the agony of the 'in vain'," by which he means the agony of the thought that this world, with all of its attendant beauties and horrors, "aims at *nothing* and achieves *nothing*," that our lives, with all of their joys and sufferings, come to nothing.[6]

But what are we to make of the relationship between this conclusion that the world is meaningless and the judgments Nietzsche refers to concerning both the world as it is and the world as it ought to be. To sort out this "is" and "ought" we need to consider, if not the full breadth of Nietzsche's philosophical musings, at least a sizable swath, beginning with an early fragment of Nietzsche's writing, published posthumously and titled "Homer's Contest."[7]

The Pre-Homeric Abyss and the Question of Suffering

In this fragment, Nietzsche begins by asserting that nothing fundamental separates humanity from nature, which means that humanity is "wholly nature and embodies its uncanny dual character."[8] In other words, human beings are capable of both great beauty and terrifying violence. Nowhere is this fact clearer than in the ancient Greeks, who gave the world some of its most prized works of art, and yet who also were, like the great hero Achilles of Homer's *Iliad*, capable of "a tigerish lust to annihilate."[9] "Why," Nietzsche asks,

> must the Greek sculptor give form again and again to war and combat in innumerable repetitions: distended human bodies, their sinews tense with hatred or with arrogance of triumph; writhing bodies, wounded; dying bodies, expiring? Why did the whole Greek world exult over the combat scenes of the *Iliad*? I fear that we do not understand these in a sufficiently "Greek" manner; indeed, that we would shudder if we were ever to understand them "in Greek."[10]

Nietzsche thinks that we would shudder before the Greeks because behind the art of the classical age, and behind the reverence for Homer, stood an acceptance of a world filled with violence and suffering. Homer and other artists—and even the philosophers—Nietzsche argues, channeled this violence into the various contests that were a central aspect of Greek life and thereby in some sense tamed it. This emphasis on the contest is evident throughout Homer's *Iliad*, where elaborate rituals circumscribe much of the violence on the battlefield and where battle itself is converted into an Olympic competition in the penultimate book of the poem. Even though he tempers the pure horror of war with the beauty of his art, and in this art displays the movement from the pure violence of annihilation to the circumscribed violence of the contest, Homer still depicts for us a world where violence and suffering are not only accepted but celebrated. As Nietzsche reads him, Homer's great achievement is that in his poetic celebration of this world, he somehow makes such a world palatable to us. "But," asks Nietzsche, "what do we behold when, no longer led and protected by the hand of Homer, we stride back into the pre-Homeric world? Only night and terror and an imagination accustomed to the horrible. . . . When we remove the contest from Greek life we immediately look into the pre-Homeric abyss of a terrifying savagery of hatred and the lust to annihilate."[11]

To put it perhaps a bit too crudely, to step into the abyss of the pre-Homeric world is for Nietzsche to step into something akin to a state of nature; and what we find there are not exactly the Lotus-Eaters that Odysseus encounters on his way home from Troy, wandering around in an unreflective bliss. Instead, we find something quite like the battle of Troy itself—only here the battle never ends, Achilles does not withdraw from the field to reflect upon the meaning of courage and glory, and Andromache, with their infant in her arms, does not plead with Hector to forgo honor and fight from behind the walls, where he can better protect them. In the pre-Homeric world, no one has yet asked about the point of all the violence and suffering. The world somehow just *is* this way, and pre-Homeric humans reveled in the blood and the guts.

Such revelry could not sustain itself, however. Hence Nietzsche notes: "After the wave of that bloody age comes a trough that cuts deep into Hellenic history. The names of Orpheus, Musaeus, and their cults reveal the consequences to which the uninterrupted spectacle of a world of struggle and cruelty was pressing: toward a disgust with existence, toward the conception of existence as a punishment and penance, toward the belief in the identity of existence and guilt."[12]

Once violence and cruelty reigned supreme. But over time, certain questions began to interrupt the previously "uninterrupted spectacle of struggle and cruelty," just as the questions of Achilles interrupted the battle of Troy. Among these questions, Nietzsche suggests, was "why man at all?"[13] This question emerged from the sense that "something was *lacking*, that man was surrounded by a fearful void—he did not know how to justify, to account for, to affirm himself; he suffered from the problem of his meaning. He also suffered otherwise, he was in the main a sickly animal: but his problem was *not* suffering itself, but that there was no answer to the crying question, 'why do I suffer?'"[14] It is this question that interrupts the spectacle of violence and creates a distance between the humans who pose it and the abyss—with the result that what was once a spectacle now becomes a problem and a fearful void. Nietzsche suggests that the initial reaction to this problem was disgust, since a world so bent on violence and its havoc must be in some way defective.

This disparaging of existence was not, however, the only response to the question of suffering. As Nietzsche notes, "The Hellenic genius was ready with yet another answer to the question, 'What is a life of struggle and victory for?' and it gave that answer through the whole breadth of Greek history."[15] This response, which Nietzsche understands as the dominant response of the ancient Greeks to the question of suffering, does not assume that the world is defective but instead assumes that violence and suffering are simply a part of the way the world works; they are, in other words, "justified." Thus, Homer's Achilles may challenge the pre-Homeric identification of virtue and honor with courage amidst slaughter, but in the end he does join the battle and his heroism remains that of a warrior, even if he is now a reflective warrior who has posed in a new way, or maybe even for the first time, the question of what a life of struggle and victory is for. And the great tragedians, who do nothing but reflect upon the meaning of suffering, do not conclude that suffering stands as a judgment against the world but rather that the world is so designed that we must, in the words of Aeschylus, "suffer into truth."

At this point it is important to note that "Homer's Contest" is one of Nietzsche's early writings: It was written the same year he published *The Birth of Tragedy* and some fifteen years before he published *The Genealogy of Morals*. And yet already present is a sketch of much of Nietzsche's later thought, including his thought about nihilism. Thus, with this sketch from "Homer's Contest," and with reference to several of Nietzsche's other works, let me begin to explain Nietzsche's riddle-like definition of a nihilist as someone "who judges of the world as it is that it ought not to be, and of the world as it ought to be that it does not exist."

The World as It Is and the Birth of Nihilism

When Nietzsche says in "Homer's Contest" that human beings are "wholly nature" and that as such we embody nature's penchant for both beauty and violence, he has begun to describe what he will later call "the will to power," which is also, for Nietzsche, to describe "the world as it is." In the last of the notes collected under the title *The Will to Power,* Nietzsche describes this world with characteristic flare and eloquence:

> And do you know what "the world" is to me? Shall I show it to you in my mirror. This world: a monster of energy . . . a play of forces and waves of forces, at the same time one and many, increasing here and at the same time decreasing there; a sea of forces flowing and rushing together, eternally changing, eternally flooding back, with tremendous years of recurrence, with an ebb and a flood of its forms; out of the simplest forms, striving toward the most complex, out the stillest, most rigid, coldest forms toward the hottest, most turbulent, most self-contradictory, and then again returning home to the simple out of this abundance, out of the play of contradictions back to the joy of concord . . . a becoming that knows no satiety, no disgust, no weariness: this is my *Dionysian* world of the eternally self-creating, the eternally self-destroying. . . . Do you want a name for this world? . . . *This world is the will to power—and nothing besides!* And you yourselves are also this will to power—and nothing besides![16]

This, for Nietzsche, is the world as it is; this is the world of the pre-Homeric abyss; this is the world, "bloody and insatiable," in the midst of which emerged the question of what suffering might mean. And with this question what Nietzsche calls "the first nihilism" becomes possible.[17] For, as Nietzsche suggests the very posing of the question of suffering brings with it the possibility that our suffering has no meaning, that it serves no purpose, that we are surrounded by a void, and that it all comes to nothing in the end. To accept this answer would be, by Nietzsche's account, to become a nihilist in the most radical sense, to become, in other words, someone who accepts the "radical repudiation of value, meaning, and desirability," someone who lives at the mercy of a will to nothingness.

Interestingly, however, although radical nihilism emerges as a possible course when the question of suffering itself emerges from the pre-Homeric abyss, this course is not embarked upon until the nineteenth century. Instead, nihilism of a different sort develops precisely as a response to the threat of meaninglessness and in effect delays the arrival of radical nihilism for more than two millennia.

This second form of nihilism—which, as we will see, eventually turns full circle and becomes something like the originary and radical nihilism that first accompanies the question of suffering—is the kind of nihilism Nietzsche gestures toward in "Homer's Contest," when he invokes the name of Orpheus and the Orphic cult and that, later, he comes to identify with both Judaism and Christianity. Indeed, in Nietzsche's later work, nihilism in this guise is essentially synonymous with what Nietzsche designates "slave morality," the exemplars of which are the Jews and Christians.

To understand the role both Jews and Christians play in Nietzsche's account of nihilism, we have to understand one further thing about the origination of the question concerning suffering, a question that, at least on one path of its unfolding, led to the judgment that the world is not as it *should* be, led, in other words, to the very notion of morality, insofar as morality is dependent upon a distinction between the way things are and the way things ought to be. According to Nietzsche, it was the invention of morality

> that protected life against despair and the leap into nothing, among men and classes who were violated and oppressed by *men:* for it is the experience of being powerless against men, not against nature that generates the most desperate embitterment against existence. Morality treated the violent despots, the doers of violence, the "masters" in general as the enemies against whom the common man must be protected. . . . Morality consequently taught men to hate and despise most profoundly what is the basic character trait of those who rule: their will to power.[18]

Hence the question of suffering opens from out of the pre-Homeric abyss not as a consequence of suffering generally but as a consequence of that suffering inflicted by the violence one group of human beings levels at another.

"Let us admit to ourselves," says Nietzsche,

> without trying to be considerate, how every higher culture on earth so far has *begun.* Human beings whose nature was still natural, barbarians in every terrible sense of the word, men of prey who were still in possession of unbroken strength of will and lust for power, hurled themselves upon weaker, more civilized, more peaceful races.[19]

To Nietzsche's notion that the opening of the question of suffering is what marks off the pre-Homeric abyss from everything that comes later, we now need to add that this question arose specifically among those human beings who found themselves suffering at the hands of other human beings, which is why the Jews and Christians play a pivotal role for Nietzsche. From slavery in Egypt to the persecutions of Rome, first the Jews and then the Christians found themselves to be the victims of the power of empire. From this position of victim, which as Nietzsche describes it is a position of "weakness," Jews and Christians did a novel thing. To make sense of their suffering they concluded that those in power, like Pharaoh and the emperors of Rome, were evil and represented everything that was wrong with the world. On the other hand, as those who stood against evil, Jews and Christians concluded both that they must somehow embody the good and that their suffering at the hands of evil must therefore in some way count toward the betterment of a world out of whack. In this way, Jews and Christians came to resent and judge the power of empire, while at the same time staking their hopes and their lives on a different power: the power of Yahweh.[20]

Of Slaves and Nobles

As Nietzsche tells the tale, such judgments of good and evil stand at the heart of "slave morality," which amounts to an inversion of the values that had reigned supreme hitherto, values that originated not from the cries of the slaves but from the self-affirmation of the masters or "nobles." What Nietzsche calls "noble morality" does not emerge, as does its counterpart among the "slaves," from negative judgments about the other but from positive judgments about the self. Hence, as Nietzsche says,

> egoism belongs to the nature of noble soul—I mean that unshakable faith that to a being such as "we are" other beings must be subordinate by nature and have to sacrifice themselves. The noble soul accepts this fact of its egoism without any question mark, also without any feeling that it might contain hardness, constraint, or caprice, rather as something that may be found in the primordial law of things.[21]

From the perspective of this unshakable faith, "good" is a term that applies "in advance and spontaneously"[22] to the noble soul and its actions, whereas those who bear the brunt of these actions, the subordinate by nature, are not considered "evil" but "bad," which is to say that they are lesser, "weaker" souls who simply have not risen to the occasion of *life*, who have not, in other words, assented to the notion that "life itself is *essentially* appropriation, injury, overpowering of what is alien and weaker;

suppression, hardness, imposition of one's own forms, incorporation and at least, at its mildest, exploitation."[23]

Indeed, far from assenting to the notion that life simply is appropriation, injury, exploitation, and the lot, these "weaker" souls, as we have seen, conclude that such actions do not display the definitive characteristics of life itself but rather are perversions of life, indications of a world gone astray, are in other words "evil." Thus it is that the morality of the slaves inverts that of the nobles. And as Nietzsche tells the story, this inversion is a momentous event, for to condemn as evil the exploitive, injurious actions of the nobles is also to condemn that which the nobles embody: the will to power.

Of course, standing as they do on this side of the abyss, and therefore in the presence of the question of suffering, the nobles are not simply about appropriation and injury; for in their relationship with one another, the primal violence of the abyss, of the sheer unadulterated will to power, has been bottled up. As Nietzsche puts it: "Refraining mutually from injury, violence, and exploitation and placing one's will on a par with that of someone else—this may become, in a certain rough sense, good manners among individuals if the appropriate conditions are present (namely, if these men are actually similar in strength and value and belong together in *one* body)."[24] Nietzsche is then quick to add , however, that this body of men,

> if it is to be a living and not a dying body, has to do to other bodies what the individuals within it refrain from doing to each other: it will have to be an incarnate will to power, it will strive to grow, spread, seize, become predominant—not from any morality or immorality but because it is *living* and because life simply *is* will to power. . . . Exploitation does not belong to a corrupt or imperfect and primitive society: it belongs to the *essence* of what lives, as a basic organic function; it is a consequence of the will to power, which is after all the will to life.
>
> If this should be an innovation as a theory—as a reality it is the *primordial fact* of all history.[25]

As should now be apparent, this primordial fact of history is rooted in what Nietzsche called the "primordial law of things." At the bottom of both history and things is the will to power; and what the ancient Greek aristocracy embodied, and for this Nietzsche seems to praise them, is precisely this primordial will. The ancient Greeks, although "civilized," were never far from the abyss. On the other hand, what first the Jews and then the Christians did was to condemn outright not only the nobles but also, perforce, what the nobles embodied: nothing less than the will to life. Jews and Christians, and before them Orpheus, refused to live in such proximity to the abyss; but this refusal, at least as Nietzsche understands it, led to an outright denial of everything that makes the world work. For in a certain sense the world itself, no less than the question of suffering, is born from out of the abyss.

It seems when one reads Nietzsche's account of the inversion and eventual defeat of noble morality that he tells the tale with a profound sense of loss: Noble morality, where the "good" is equivalent with a strong affirmation of the will to power, was somehow more true to the way of things than the disparaging judgments of Jews and Christians, whereby "*precisely* the 'good man' of the other morality, precisely the noble, powerful man, the ruler, [is] dyed in another color, interpreted in another fashion, seen in another way by the venomous eye of *resentiment*."[26] One needs to be careful, however, in reading Nietzsche on this point, for although he wants us to escape the world-denying grip of the Jewish and Christian legacy, he does not want us to return to ancient Greece, which, we might say, remains too close to the abyss. Consider the following comments:

> Here there is one thing we shall be the last to deny: he who knows these "good men" only as enemies knows only *evil enemies*, and the same men who are held so sternly in check *inter pares* by custom, respect, usage, gratitude, and even more by mutual suspicion and jealousy, and who on the other hand in their relations with one another show themselves so resourceful in consideration, self-control, delicacy, loyalty, pride, and friendship—once they go outside, where the strange, the *stranger* is found, they are not much better than uncaged beasts of prey. . . . One cannot fail to see at the bottom of all these noble races the beast of prey, the splendid *blond beast* prowling about avidly in search of spoil and victory. . . . One may be quite justified in continuing to fear the blond beast at the core of all noble races and in being on guard against it.[27]

For Nietzsche, noble and slave moralities arise as two different courses that humans took when they stepped from the pre-Homeric abyss. As I read Nietzsche, both of these courses fail by his account: the former because it remains too close to the abyss (and therefore always on the edge of nihilism) and so in a certain sense does not fully appreciate the question of suffering; the latter because in the face of its full appreciation for the question of suffering it produces an answer that simply denies the presence of the abyss altogether. From the screams of the oppressed to the judgment that the world as it is ought not to exist is but a small step, and it is in this step that nihilism, in what we might call its second form, gets under way.

To avoid confusion, it is important to understand how nihilism of this sort is different from what we might call the originary and radical nihilism that emerges alongside the question of suffering in its initial appearance. The difference is simple. Originary and radical nihilism comes to be when one accepts as a fact that both suffering and the world in which it occurs are meaningless. The nihilism that Nietzsche associates first with Orpheus and Plato and then with the "slave morality" of the Jews and Christians is, on the other hand, a response to precisely this possibility of meaninglessness. The nihilist in this case refuses to accept as a fact that suffering is meaningless and instead attempts to establish the meaning of suffering. This is no easy task, however, because although such nihilists refuse to accept that suffering is meaningless, they cannot help but admit that suffering seems to be the way of the world; and the world therefore makes no immediate sense. In other words, the invention of slave morality is an uphill battle all the way. At this point it is necessary to explain in more detail exactly how slave morality works, for only with an understanding of this will we be able to understand the way in which slave morality transforms itself back into originary nihilism.

The World as It Ought to Be

Poised as they were, at least figuratively speaking, on the edge of the pre-Homeric abyss and faced therefore with the possibility that the suffering of which they were newly aware might be meaningless, certain factions of humanity developed the notion that any meaning that was to be found in suffering must be located elsewhere, since all that stood before them was what appeared to be an aimless, chaotic world. In their search for the meaning of suffering, these post-Homeric humans arrived in various ways at various times at the notion of what Nietzsche deems a "true world," which is simply to say they arrived at the notion of the world as it ought to be, whole and complete, without blemish and flaw, in a word, perfect. Although the descriptions of this world vary from one version of this tale to another, the tale accomplishes the same thing in any case: It lends a meaning to what otherwise seems to be a meaningless world full of meaningless suffering, and it does this in spite of the odds, which is to say at the expense of the world as it is.

Since Plato there has been a tendency in the West to give meaning to this world—the world of our daily lives, filled as they are with violence, suffering, injustice, deception, and so on—by invoking *another* world, a true world, on the basis of which we determine the aim, unity, and truth of *this* world. For Plato, this other world was the eternal and unchanging world of the Forms. For Christianity, this world is God's world as it stands in its perfection, the world as it was before the eating of the fruit and as it will be again at the end of things. Even Kant, as he reins in the metaphysical assumptions behind these Platonic and Christian claims, finds it necessary to posit another, "noumenal" world that, even though we cannot say anything about it, somehow makes this world possible. In short, the history of Western thought and morality has been, as Nietzsche describes it, the long history of an error, whereby this world, with all its suffering and "deficiencies" is explained and justified only with recourse to another, perfect world.

Indeed, it is in the name of this perfect world that the nihilist we met in Nietzsche's riddle-like definition with which I began makes the judgment that the world *as it is* should not exist. We have arrived, then—by a somewhat circuitous route, I admit—at an understanding of the first part of Nietzsche's definition of a nihilist: A nihilist is someone who judges of the world as it is that it ought not to be. Or to put it in the idiom that we have just learned, a nihilist is someone who, when confronted from out of the abyss with the question of suffering, concludes in one stroke both that suffering stands as a judgment against the world as it is and yet in some way is redeemed and given meaning by the invocation of another, perfect world. What remains before us now is the second part of Nietzsche's definition of a nihilist. You will recall that according to his riddle, a nihilist is not only someone who judges that the world as it *is* should not exist but also someone who concludes that the world as it *ought* to be does not exist. To understand this statement is to understand the way in which nihilism in its second form—the world-denying nihilism of slave morality that finds a meaning for suffering in another world—begins to slip toward something like radical and originary nihilism.

Most immediately, the attempt to understand this slip from one form of nihilism into another brings us to another riddle, the solution to which requires another detour. In one of the first notes collected in *The Will to Power,* Nietzsche says, "What does nihilism mean? That the highest values devaluate themselves. The aim is lacking; 'why?' finds no answer."[28] The solution to this riddle lies in what we might call the evolution of the notion of a true world. Or to put it in Nietzsche's terms, we will solve this riddle and arrive at nihilism in its third and contemporary (but also something like its original) form if we understand "how the 'true world' finally became a fable."[29]

The World as It Ought to Be Does Not Exist

As we have seen, when poised at the edge of the abyss it was not apparent immediately that the processes of life had a point. Or as Nietzsche puts it, it was not apparent that the question, which really belongs to Achilles, What is a life of struggle and victory for? had an answer. No goal or aim for the ceaseless becoming of the world presented itself. For that matter, it was not even clear that there was something called *a* world, insofar as the term itself suggests unity. Instead potential aimlessness and chaos, and thereby meaninglessness, beckoned from the abyss. We have already met the threat of this meaninglessness in the form of an originary and radical nihilism, which we can now say, with Nietzsche, arose as the possibility "that becoming has no goal and that underneath all becoming there is no grand unity."[30] With no aim and no overall unity or totality, no overarching order to events, only one escape from meaninglessness remained: "to pass sentence on this whole world of becoming as a deception and to invent a world beyond it, a *true* world."[31] What the true world supplied, then, that was otherwise lacking, were the notions that "something is to be *achieved* through the process" and that the process itself was but an expression of "some form of unity," some "organization in all events, and underneath all events."[32] This unity and aim that the true world supplies to the otherwise scattered events of this world are the roots of what Nietzsche calls the higher values: values, such as eternal peace, that seem to have no place in this world but that, if they exist in another world, make this world bearable.

The creation of these values led to an escape from the radical nihilism that first beckoned from the abyss. However, since after more than two millennia these values remained out of reach, remained, that is, part of another world and not *this* world, they began, by at least the end of the nineteenth century, to lose their value. They were not robbed but lost value on their own accord. People simply stopped staking their lives on these values, since they remained, even after thousands of years, out of reach; the higher values simply failed to fulfill their age-old promises. And when these values began to lose their value, then so, too, did the world, since it was only on the basis of these values that the world was judged to be anything more than an aimless wreck. Without the notion of a true world in place, the aim for this world is lacking. Why? finds no answer. What, then, in Nietzsche's words, "has happened, at bottom?":

> The feeling of valuelessness was reached with the realization that the overall character of existence may not be interpreted by means of the concept of "aim," the concept of "unity," or the concept of "truth." Existence has no goal or end; any comprehensive unity in the plurality of events is lacking: the character of existence is not "true," is false. One simply lacks any reason for convincing oneself that there is a *true* world.[33]

To say that "one simply lacks any reason for convincing oneself that there is a true world" or in Heidegger's words, that the "suprasensory world is without effective power"[34] is to describe the notion that the higher values have devalued themselves, which is also, of course, to describe nihilism in its final and contemporary form, at least as Nietzsche understands it. Heidegger's words here are in a way more helpful than Nietzsche's, since they point us toward the fact that nihilism can remain an apt description of our condition even though certain individuals, or even communities, continue to believe in another world. No doubt, huge portions of Nietzsche's society (not to mention our own) continued to believe in a suprasensory world of one sort or another. Nietzsche's point, however, is that no matter what many of us continue to believe, nihilism is a cultural fact because the notion of a "true world," although still present among us, has, again in Heidegger's words, suffered the loss of its "constructive force."

Lest this point remain obscure, just note the fact that we no longer build Gothic cathedrals; instead we spend comparable resources building research hospitals. And in the same manner, physicians have replaced priests as figures of authority. Although we may still profess belief in a suprasensory world, as a cultural force such a world commands little attention. Nietzsche's wonderfully succinct way of putting the matter is to say that "God is dead": "The greatest recent event—that 'God is dead,' that the belief in the Christian god has become unbelievable—is already beginning to cast its first shadows over Europe."[35] This, of course, is one of Nietzsche's most famous declarations, and again Heidegger is helpful:

> In the word "God is dead" the name "God," thought essentially, stands for the suprasensory world of those ideals which contain the goal that exists beyond earthly life for that life and that, accordingly, determine life from above, and also in a certain way, from without. . . . If God as the suprasensory ground and goal of all reality is dead, if the suprasensory world of the Ideas has suffered the loss of its obligatory and above all its vitalizing and upbuilding power, then nothing more remains to which man can cling and by which he can orient himself.[36]

Here we arrive, after another somewhat circuitous route, at the second part of Nietzsche's definition of a nihilist: The world as it ought to be does not exist. The notion of a suprasensory, true world has lost effective force.

In the most famous passage where Nietzsche declares that God is dead, he evokes eloquently the sense of disorientation that follows in the wake of this loss:

> How could we drink up the sea? Who gave us the sponge to wipe away the entire horizon? What were we doing when we unchained this earth from its sun? Whither is it moving now? Whither are we moving? Away from all suns? Are we not plunging continually? Backward, sideward, forward, in all directions? Is there still any up or down? Are we not straying as through an infinite nothing?[37]

Final Forms of Nihilism

We might say, then, that nihilism in its final form is for Nietzsche a kind of cultural vertigo with which we find ourselves afflicted when the descriptive power of narratives about the "true world" wanes. Because the aim of things, their meaning and value, was dependent upon conceptions of a true world, of a world as it should be, or will be, or once was, the failure of these narratives leads to "the radical repudiation of value, meaning, and desirability,"[38] and we find ourselves faced with "radical nihilism," which is to say with "the conviction of an absolute untenability of existence when it comes to the highest values one recognizes; plus the realization that we lack the least right to posit a beyond or an in-itself of things."[39]

In a certain sense, to find ourselves caught in the grips of radical nihilism is to have returned to precisely that place we have spent three thousand years trying to distance ourselves from: the edge of the pre-Homeric abyss. Of course, nihilism in its final form is like originary nihilism only in a certain sense, since the three thousand years of attempted escape, even though they have come to naught, still influence the way in which we can now imagine our options. For Nietzsche, all of our options involve nihilism; hence it has now become a "normal condition."[40] But nihilism as it now confronts us comes in two different types, the first of which is divided once more into two. Hence according to Nietzsche, nihilism is either complete or incomplete; and if it is complete, then it is either active or passive.

Incomplete nihilism is "an attempt to escape nihilism without reevaluating our values so far."[41] In his gloss on Nietzsche's thought at this point, Heidegger puts it well when he says that even though the realization of higher values has not been accomplished, such that the world begins to appear valueless, nonetheless,

> something else can still be attempted in the face of the tottering of the dominion of prior values. That is, if God in the sense of the Christian god has disappeared from his authoritative position in the suprasensory world, then this authoritative place itself is still always preserved, even though as that which has become empty. The now-empty authoritative realm of the suprasensory and the ideal world can still be adhered to. What is more, the empty place demands to be occupied anew and to have the god now vanished from it replaced by something else. . . .
>
> Incomplete nihilism does indeed replace the former values with others, but it still posits the latter always in the old position of authority. . . . Into the vanished authority of God steps the authority of conscience . . . obtrudes the authority of reason. . . . The flight from the world into the suprasensory is replaced by historical progress. The otherworldly goal of everlasting bliss is transformed into the earthly happiness of the greatest number. The careful maintenance of their cult of religion is relaxed through enthusiasm for the creating of a culture or the spreading of civilization. Creativity, previously the unique property of the biblical god, becomes the distinctive mark of human activity. Human activity finally passes over into business enterprise.[42]

In other words, rather than face the possibility that the death of God and the devaluing of higher values leads to meaninglessness, incomplete nihilists simply replace God with another god, namely, humanity itself.[43]

In this sense, incomplete nihilists produce new values to fill in the gaps left by the weakening of the old. But in fact, these values are not new at all, since they are generated from the same authoritative space as the old values. The only difference is that this space is now occupied by a new god. The same drive to escape meaninglessness, the same unwillingness to face the world as it is—a drive that Nietzsche deems "the will to truth"—remains operative in this incomplete form of nihilism. But once the will to truth is embodied in incomplete nihilism it becomes, as we will see later, vicious and destructive in ways unimaginable when the old God still held the throne.

Although incomplete nihilism rules the day, it is not the only contemporary option that Nietzsche identifies. Complete nihilism is another possibility. In this case, we meet the meaninglessness of the world in the wake of the diminished effective power of higher values not with denial and an overeagerness to revalue the world but with acceptance. A simple acceptance of this new vacuum delivers us into complete nihilism in its passive form, which in effect leaves us right at the edge of the abyss in a state of resignation. For Nietzsche this is a state in some way akin to Schopenhauer's pessimism. And this path is a dead end of despair.

However, complete nihilism also has an active form, in which the loss of the higher values is not only accepted but celebrated, and even more, this loss is accelerated by a willingness to actively destroy those values of old that yet remain a cultural force. It is nihilism in this form that Nietzsche refers to when he calls himself a nihilist, and when he says that "nihilism represents a pathological transitional stage."[44] It is a transitional stage, because the point of actively seeking the destruction of higher values is to clear the way so that one can replace those values with new ones, not in the way that incomplete nihilism proposes, but with a vigor that in fact leads not only to new values but to a whole new conception of value itself. Gone, in other words, are the structures of authority so deeply imprinted by the tales of the suprasensory world. This stage is pathological, however, because of "the tremendous generalization, the inference that there is no meaning at all."[45]

When Nietzsche refers to himself as a nihilist, he does not intimate that to have overcome higher values is to have arrived. Rather, this overcoming, this active destruction of any thought of the world as it ought to be, represents "the transition to new conditions of existence."[46] To get stuck in this transition, to fail to emerge on the other side of destruction, is pathological and in effect leaves one facing the resignation of passive nihilism. Active nihilism, although it cannot escape this pathology altogether, does not come to rest there. In Nietzsche's words:

> Such an experimental philosophy as I live anticipates experimentally even the possibilities of the most fundamental nihilism; but this does not mean

> that it must halt at a negation, a No, a will to negation. It wants rather to cross over to the opposite of this—to a Dionysian affirmation of the world as it is, without subtraction, exception, or selection.[47]

Of course to affirm the world as it is, without at the same time escaping the clutches of nihilism altogether, requires the positing of new goals. The question Why? which as long as nihilism reigns is without answer, does finally need an answer. Or as Nietzsche puts it, "the question 'for what?' after a terrible struggle, even victory. That . . . is a hundred times more important than the question of whether we feel well or not. . . . In sum, that we have a goal for which one does not hesitate to offer human sacrifices, to risk every danger, to take upon oneself whatever is bad and worst."[48]

With the prospect of new goals or, in any case, new values that allow for the Dionysian affirmation of the world as it is, that same world that has been explained away and denied for more than two millennia, we have arrived at the point in the story where we can no longer talk only of Nietzsche's account of nihilism but must instead begin to speak of his account of tragedy. For we have arrived, in a sense, back at the edge of the pre-Homeric abyss, where, you will recall, there arose a response to the question of suffering that was quite different from that of Orpheus, the Jews, or the Christians. In "Homer's Contest," Nietzsche refers to this response as that of "Hellenic genius." The genius he seems to have in mind is that of the great tragic poets. But to turn to Nietzsche on tragedy at this point would be premature, since before we leave nihilism behind we need to consider nihilism as we find it not in the works of Nietzsche but in the works of some of his critics.

Before turning in some detail to the criticisms John Milbank, Martin Heidegger, and Michael Gillespie level at Nietzsche, let me note that despite their differences, each of these critics adopts a similar method in their respective attempts to unseat Nietzsche's understanding of nihilism. This method involves two inextricably bound operations: In the first operation, each critic renarrates the intellectual history of the West in order to undermine Nietzsche's own narration of the development of nihilism; in the second, each critic writes Nietzsche into their narrative in such a way that he is portrayed not as a critic of nihilism, nor as someone who finally escapes nihilism, but as the ultimate nihilist. In other words, each of these critics attacks Nietzsche's account of nihilism by standing Nietzsche on his head, although they do not all do so in the same way.

Ethical Nihilism, Absolute Historicism, and Ontological Violence

To turn directly from Nietzsche on nihilism to Heidegger on nihilism would no doubt be the obvious course at this point. However, I have decided to begin instead with the work of the Anglican theologian John Milbank. Milbank's account of nihilism, as it appears in his book *Theology and Social Theory: Beyond Secular Reason*,[49] remains dependent on the thought of Nietzsche and Heidegger, and in part what he means by the term is precisely what Nietzsche means when he speaks of the repudiation of value and meaning. Nonetheless, Milbank brings to the discussion of nihilism a unique perspective that gathers nicely, I think, much of what is at stake in debates about the concept.

With the term "nihilism," Milbank attempts to capture certain assumptions shared by a diverse group of philosophers and social theorists: "I deliberately treat the writings of Nietzsche, Heidegger, Deleuze, Lyotard, Foucault and Derrida," he says, "as elaborations of a single nihilistic philosophy, paying relatively less attention to their divergences of opinion" (278). Lumping thinkers so subtle as these together in this way is no doubt problematic from the start, but Milbank's agenda is minimal. He wants simply to establish in broad scope that these thinkers (1) share an absolute historicism, which (2) rests upon a differential ontology of violence and (3) leads to an ethical nihilism. Milbank's critical account of nihilism unfolds along these three fronts. Let us take each in turn.

For Milbank the most prominent example of absolute historicism is Nietzsche's *Genealogy of Morals:* "Nietzsche's genealogy is a[n] . . . absolute historicism because it refuses to tell [the] Kantian and Hegelian (or sociological and Marxist) stories about a constant human subject. Instead it is only interested in disinterring the thresholds of emergence for many different fictions of subjectivity in the course of human history" (280). In other words, to narrate historical events genealogically, as Milbank understands it, is to speak of the arbitrary displacement of one cultural formation by another. History is not the unfolding of Spirit, nor the progressive resolution of societal conflicts. History does not progress but is instead "anarchic"; it is nothing more than "the possibly infinite series of self-transgressions on the part of humanity" (281).

The only constant in this series of self-transgressions is the arbitrary and hence violent nature of each subsequent displacement of one "power-constellation" with another. Milbank notes that the lesson contained in this understanding of history is that

> this state of affairs proper to 'life' is not to be condemned, but rather celebrated. Hence, genealogy is not an interpretation, but a new 'joyfully' nihilistic form of positivism which explains every cultural meaning-complex as a particular strategy or ruse of power. No universals are ascribed to human society save one: that it is always a field of warfare (281–282).[50]

After painting this picture of absolute historicism, Milbank asks the following question:

> How can the understanding of the *event as such*, of every event as a moment of combat, justify itself in merely historicist, genealogical terms? Supposedly, the genealogist is quite neutral with respect to different sorts of value promoted by different historical cultures: he should be equally suspicious of them all. Yet in fact, if the transcendental event, every possible event, is a military move of assertive difference over against 'the other', then cultures closer to realizing this truth will come to be celebrated as more 'natural', more spontaneous cultures. Hence Nietzsche celebrates a Homeric nobility delighting in war, trials of strength, spectacles of cruelty, strategies of deception. Unless it is clear that this really is a more 'natural' form of life, then the general thesis must fall into doubt, and Nietzsche's genealogy will appear as itself but another perspective: an account of the rise of Christianity, written from the point of view of the paganism which it displaced (282).

As these comments suggest, Milbank's answer to his own question is that the historicist narration of events as "a universal history of military manoeuvres" (282) cannot in fact be sustained on the grounds of historicism alone, which is to say that such a narrative rests upon a certain nonhistoricist assumption: namely, an ontology of violence. In order to explain what Milbank has in mind with this notion of an ontology of violence that stands behind both absolute historicism and an ethical nihilism, let me turn to the work of Jacques Derrida, who displays this ontology more clearly than any of the other so-called nihilists.[51]

"There is war," says Derrida, "only after the opening of discourse, and war dies only at the end of discourse. . . . There is no phrase which is indeterminate, that is, which does not pass through the violence of the concept. Violence appears with articulation."[52] In other words, the human capacity to speak and write—our unique talent for language—is, as Derrida understands it, irrevocably violent. "Speech is," he admits, "the first defeat of violence, but paradoxically, violence did not exist before the possibility of speech."[53] Speech is the first defeat of violence because it allows us to settle disputes with words instead of clubs. Nonetheless, the move from clubs to words does not simply end, but in fact originates, violence—that is, "if one wishes to determine violence as the necessity that the other not appear as what it is, that it not be respected except in, for, and by the same, that it be dissimulated by the same in the very freeing of its phenomenon."[54]

Derrida does wish to determine violence in this way, which is to say he wants to insist that when the other appears to us, whether the other is a tree, a wolf, or our own child, it does so only on our terms, in our arena, within our language—only, that is, as it ceases to be wholly other and in some way and to a certain degree enters the sameness of our lives, the similarities according to which our world hangs together. As Derrida puts it, "that the other appears as such only in relation to the same, is a self-evidence that the Greeks had no need to acknowledge."[55] Equally self-evident is the fact that the same appears as such only in relation to the other. Thus, in "effect, *either* there is only the same, which can no longer even appear and be said . . . , *or* indeed there is the same *and* the other."[56] And so the same and the other are locked in this dance, whereby the differences of one partner make the similarities of the other partner possible—but always this dance occurs at the expense of that partner deemed "other": "To return, as to the only possible point of departure, to the intentional phenomenon in which the other appears as other, and lends itself to language, *to every possible language,* is perhaps to give oneself over to violence, or to make oneself its accomplice at least, and to acquiesce—in the critical sense—to the violence of the fact; but in question, then, is an irreducible zone of facticity, an original, transcendental violence."[57]

It is this original, transcendental violence, "as the irreducible violence of the relation to the other," that for Derrida resides at the heart of speech, of discourse, and that leads, therefore, to the fact that speech does not simply end violence but also begins it: "A speech," he says, "produced without the least violence would determine nothing, would say nothing. . . . Nonviolent language would be a language of pure invocation, pure adoration, proffering only proper nouns in order to call to the other from afar."[58] All other language does determine things; it joins together nouns and verbs; it predicates; and "predication," declares Derrida, "is the first violence,"[59] the first appearance of the other within the realm of the same, where it ceases to be "what it is." "War, therefore," according to Derrida, "is congenital to phenomenality, is the very emergence of speech and appearing."[60] Derrida does not miss the implications of this account of discourse. For if our talent for language is *the* distinctive human trait, and if harbored within this trait is an irreducible violence, then we cannot escape but are rather condemned to live amidst and upon this violence. Indeed, by Derrida's account, "this infinite passage through violence is what is called history."[61]

Derrida's account of discourse as war, and history as violence, is a good display of the ontology of violence that, Milbank argues, lies at the root of nihilism. To suppose that the relationship between human being and all other being—not to mention Being itself—is in some way circumscribed by the violence of a rupture or break, what Heidegger calls an "ontological difference," is to assume that the relation between human language and the nonlinguistic world lacks the necessity of an order and is therefore arbitrary. Precisely the arbitrary character of this relationship defines the ethical nihilism that Milbank identifies as the third characteristic of the nihilist position. If everything is, in the last instance, arbitrary, then the words we choose, and the actions those words make possible, are without foundation and up for grabs. Meaning and value have, as Nietzsche describes it, been cut loose from any anchors; and the horizons, the natural confinements that limit and situate our world, have been washed away.

We can now take a bird's-eye view of Milbank's account of nihilism and see that what he has done, in effect, is work backward from the common—and in part at least, Nietzschean—understanding of nihilism as a kind of ethical free-for-all to the assumptions that make this stance possible. Hence Milbank shows us first, that nihilism as an ethical stance is rooted in an absolute historicism that grants no particular credence to one cultural formation over another, and second, that this historicism itself rests upon an ontology of violence. As Derrida has it, history is violent because discourse is violent, and discourse is violent because, at bottom, that's the way things "are."

Milbank wants to persuade us that this nihilist narrative is nothing more than a narrative and can therefore be challenged by another narrative, in particular by the Christian narrative. This is not to say that Derrida is wrong when he asserts that history is violence. Milbank does not want to dispute the presence of violence amidst, and even at the bottom of, all things human. He wants simply to remove the necessity of this violence by renarrating both its origins and its mechanisms.

Hence, history *is* violent; but "in the midst of history, the judgment of God has already happened. And either the Church enacts the vision of a paradisal community which this judgment opens out, or it promotes a hellish society beyond all terrors known to antiquity" (433). History *is* violent; but for Christians the story of Jesus is " a kind of climax, paradoxically in the 'middle' of history, for all other stories, so that all history before Christ can be narrated as 'anticipating' his story, and all history since as situated within it, such that everything which subsequently happens is nothing but the acceptance or the rejection of Christ" (383). History *is* violent; but the "*logic* of Christianity involves the claim that the 'interruption' of history by Christ and his bride, the Church, is the most fundamental of events" (388). History *is* violent; but Jesus and the Church have interrupted both history and its violence. History has been "wounded" (167), and in the wake of this wound, indeed as this wound, the Church makes possible a counterhistory, a history that does not rest on violence.

With this reference to a counterhistory, Milbank sets the stage for the contest between the Christian narrative and the narratives of nihilism. In the next chapter, I begin to look at this contest in some detail. But first let's consider nihilism as we find it in the works of Heidegger and Gillespie.

Heidegger on "Classical Nihilism"

Heidegger's genealogy of nihilism shares much with Nietzsche's. Hence, like Nietzsche, he understands nihilism not as a nineteenth-century phenomenon but as something bound to the unfolding of history itself. For Heidegger, as for Nietzsche, whatever nihilism is, it begins right at the edge of the abyss. As Heidegger puts it:

> Nihilism is a historical movement, and not just any view or doctrine advocated by someone or other. Nihilism moves history after the manner of a fundamental ongoing event. . . . Hence nihilism is not simply one historical phenomenon among others, not simply one intellectual current that, along with others, with Christendom, with humanism, and with the Enlightenment—also comes to the fore within Western history.
>
> Nihilism, thought in its essence, is, rather, the fundamental movement of the history of the West. It shows such great profundity that its unfolding can have nothing but world catastrophes as its consequence. Nihilism is a world-historical movement of peoples of the earth who have been drawn into the power realm of the modern age. Hence it is not only a phenomenon of the present age, nor is it primarily the product of the nineteenth century.[62]

In broad terms Heidegger and Nietzsche share this understanding of nihilism. To understand how Heidegger departs from Nietzsche, we must recall first how Nietzsche interprets nihilism as that which moves history, and how this interpretation allows him to build a case for moving beyond nihilism.

We saw earlier that Nietzsche's way of describing nihilism as a historical movement was to speak of "the highest values devaluing themselves," values that had originated just this side of the abyss. In whatever form, nihilism for Nietzsche is about this devaluation; and complete and active nihilism not only recognizes this devaluation but seeks to accelerate the process. Why? So that, with the highest values gone, the world can be reevaluated not now on the basis of another world but according to its own inner mechanisms: namely, the will to power, the will to life. Heidegger calls nihilism understood in this way "classical nihilism," which attempts, he says, to revalue the world according to a principle concerning "what is most alive." Nihilism itself is thus transformed into "the ideal of superabundant life."[63] Heidegger argues that since the new evaluative principle upon which Nietzsche's constructive, post-nihilist proposals rest is reducible to this notion of "superabundant life," it is crucial to understand what Nietzsche means by "life"; Heidegger then notes that Nietzsche's understanding of life hinges upon his understanding of value.

Nietzsche says of value that it "is the standpoint of conditions of the preservation and enhancement for complex forms of relative life-duration within the flux of becoming."[64] With this passage from Nietzsche in mind, Heidegger offers the following commentary on Nietzsche's understanding of the relationship between life and value:

> Preservation and enhancement mark the fundamental tendencies of life, tendencies that belong intrinsically together. To the essence of life belongs the will to grow, enhancement. Every instance of life-preservation stands at the service of life-enhancement. Every life that restricts itself to mere preservation is already in decline. . . . Anything that is alive is therefore something that is bound by the two fundamental tendencies of enhancement and preservation, i.e., a "complex form of life." . . . In that it posits the aims that are in view for whatever is alive, life, in its essence, proves to be value-positing.[65]

If to understand Nietzsche's notion of life, we must understand his notion of value, then it is equally the case that to understand what he means by both life and value we need to return to his notion of the will to power. For standing behind this superabundant, value-positing life is this will. As Heidegger puts it, the "will to power is, in its essence, the value-positing will. Values are the preservation-enhancement conditions within being of whatever is. . . . The will to power does not have its ground in a feeling of lack; rather it itself is the ground of superabundant life."[66]

Heidegger's exposition of "classical nihilism" helps to clarify what Nietzsche has in mind with the notion of active and complete nihilism, which, as we should now see clearly, brings to an end the last remnants of the meaning and value afforded by a true world, and then seeks to move beyond this purely negative exercise by revaluing the world as it is. What Heidegger helps us see is that this reevaluation calls not only for an affirmation of the will to power, that primal force that swirls in the abyss, but also for the appropriation of this will as something like a normative principle. Heidegger's exposition of Nietzsche at this point does more, however, than simply clarify Nietzsche's account of nihilism. It also sets up the beginning of Heidegger's critique of Nietzsche.

Nihilism as Insurrection: Heidegger's Critique of Nietzsche

In effect, Heidegger's critique rests in his attempt to follow through the logic of Nietzsche's identification of the will to power with "preservation-enhancement":

> The will to power, in that it posits the preservation, i.e., the securing of its own constancy and stability as a necessary value, at the same time justifies the necessity of such securing in everything that is. . . . The preservation of the level of power belonging to the will reached at any given time consists in the will's surrounding itself with an encircling sphere . . . that is immediately at the disposal of the will.[67]

What Heidegger describes here, in the context of a summary of Nietzsche's will to power, is the same process he describes elsewhere in the context of his reflections on the formative power of technology in the modern world. Hence, the shortest path to an understanding of Heidegger's critique of Nietzsche passes through at least a portion of his reflections on "the question concerning technology."[68]

Put all too briefly, in his essay "The Question Concerning Technology," Heidegger makes the straightforward point that technology has become the lens through which we view nature and its forces. Through this lens, forests are reduced to board feet, rivers to power plants, and entire mountains to a few ounces of gold or uranium. Heidegger's way of speaking of this lens is to say that modern technology is a particular "revealing"—which is to say that, when focused by the lens of technology, the world "shows up" or appears to us in this way rather than another. In a moment of unusually lucid prose, Heidegger describes the process in this way:

> The revealing that rules in modern technology is a challenging, which puts to nature the unreasonable demand that it supply energy that can be extracted and stored as such. . . . The earth now reveals itself as a coal mining district, the soil as a mineral deposit. . . . Agriculture is now the mechanized food industry. Air is now set upon to yield nitrogen, the earth to yield ore, ore to yield uranium, for example; uranium is set upon to yield atomic energy.[69]

Working toward a summary of this technological challenging forth and storing up of nature's energy, toward a summary, that is, of the peculiar way in which the world shows up for us, Heidegger says the following:

> The revealing that rules throughout modern technology has the character of a setting-upon, in the sense of a challenging forth. That challenging happens in that the energy concealed in nature is unlocked, what is unlocked is transformed, and what is transformed is stored up, what is stored up is, in turn, distributed, and what is distributed is switched about ever new. . . . Everywhere everything is ordered to stand by, to be immediately at hand, indeed to stand there just so that it may be on call for a further ordering. Whatever is ordered about in this way has its own standing. We call it the standing reserve.[70]

This notion of a world reduced to and revealed as "standing reserve" is not only an accurate description of the prevailing appearance of the world in our time; it is also a description of where Heidegger thinks Nietzsche has to arrive once he attempts to reevaluate a devalued world by invoking the will to power. Let me explain.

As we have seen, according to Nietzsche, the complete and active nihilist is someone who proves capable of revaluing a devalued world by affirming and appropriating as something like a normative principle the will to power, thereby avoiding both the trap of incomplete nihilism and the despair of passive nihilism. For Nietzsche, the person who accomplishes this feat ceases to be a nihilist and becomes what Nietzsche calls the "overman," which Heidegger describes memorably as "the executor of the unconditional will to power."[71] To be the executor of the unconditional will to power is not only to be the overman; it is to be "set before the task of taking over the dominion of the earth."[72] And to be set in this way before and over against the world is to become, in the language of modern philosophy, the ultimate *subject*. As Heidegger puts it:

> Man, within the subjectness belonging to whatever is, rises up into the subjectivity of his essence. Man enters into insurrection. The world changes into object. In this revolutionary objectifying of everything that is, the earth, that which first of all must be put at the disposal of representing and setting forth, moves into the midst of human positing and analyzing. The earth itself can show itself only as the object of assault, an assault that, in human willing, establishes itself as unconditional objectification. Nature appears everywhere . . . as the object of technology.[73]

Here we see Heidegger once again displaying for us the way in which human beings have objectified the whole of nature and turned it into standing reserve. However, this time Heidegger is talking only indirectly about technology. Nietzsche's account of the overman as the escape from nihilism is the true focus of these comments.

If the overman, by understanding fully and therefore embodying perfectly the logic of preservation-enhancement, becomes the ultimate subject as the world becomes nothing more than standing reserve, then Nietzsche's hero, by Heidegger's account, is in fact a villain. A villain who, far from escaping nihilism, is in fact the ultimate nihilist. Of course, no sooner has Heidegger leveled this charge against Nietzsche than he realizes that to make the charge stick he has to redefine nihilism. Or put differently, by calling Nietzsche's hero a nihilist, Heidegger has already begun to redefine nihilism:

> What is happening to Being in the age of dominion, now beginning, of the unconditional will to power?
>
> Being has been transformed into a value. The making constant of the stability of the constant reserve is a necessary condition of its own securing of itself, which the will to power itself posits. . . . Yet in that Being is accorded worth as value, it is already degraded to a condition posited by the will to power itself. . . . Value does not let Being be being, does not let it be what it is as being itself, [hence Nietzsche's] supposed overcoming is above all the consummation of nihilism.[74]

For Heidegger, nihilism is not, then, the result of the devaluing of the highest values but rather of the revaluing of a devalued world with recourse to the will to power. Heidegger does not exactly dispute Nietzsche's account of the self-devaluing of the highest values, particularly that part of the account that reads this devaluing as something that has been inevitable since the ancient Greeks first started to value this world with recourse to another one. What Heidegger does do, however, is redescribe, renarrate, this process, such that the focal point of his story is the way in which, almost from the beginning, Western metaphysics has "forgotten" Being. As he puts it, "metaphysics . . . is, in its essence, nihilism."[75] To make of Nietzsche the consummate nihilist, Heidegger simply gives him the main role in the last act of a long story about the tradition of Western metaphysics. In other words, Nietzsche is the ultimate nihilist because he is the ultimate metaphysician; and the will to power is the ultimate metaphysical concept.

There remains, of course, much more to both Heidegger's critique of metaphysics and his critique of Nietzsche as the consummate metaphysician. Further details of these critiques are, however, beyond the scope of my concern, which, you will recall, is simply to work toward a further understanding of Nietzsche's account of nihilism by subjecting it to critique. With two such critiques in place, let me take a moment to summarize them before moving on to Michael Gillespie's reading of Nietzsche.

We have now seen both Milbank and Heidegger describe Nietzsche as a nihilist in ways that Nietzsche himself would more than likely reject. For Milbank, Nietzsche is a nihilist because his work rests upon a historicist genealogy and an ontology of violence, which, taken together, reduce ethics to power. It seems at first glance that Heidegger, with his fixation upon the forgetting of Being, means something quite different when he calls Nietzsche a nihilist. Another look, however, finds Milbank and Heidegger arriving at similar conclusions. For Heidegger, Nietzsche is a nihilist because, like all the metaphysicians before him, he forgets Being. Nietzsche is the *consummate* nihilist, however, not simply because of his "forgetfulness" but because with his notions of the will to power and the overman he releases us into a world where this forgetfulness leads, for the first time, to a frontal assault upon Being and upon everything that is.

For all their differences, many of which are profound, Milbank and Heidegger finally agree, it seems to me, that nihilism is, in Heidegger's phrase, a "radical killing" rooted in an unconstrained will to power.[76] As the philosopher of the will to power, Nietzsche is the ultimate nihilist. The test for this reading of Nietzsche, as I have already intimated, lies not in Nietzsche's account of nihilism, per se, but in his account of tragedy, which I take up in Chapter Four. At this point, however, let me consider one more of Nietzsche's critics, in an attempt to bring my discussion of nihilism to a conclusion.

Nihilism Before Nietzsche

The title of Gillespie's book, *Nihilism Before Nietzsche,* is a succinct indication of what Gillespie sets out to do, which is to explore the origins of the term "nihilism" *before* Nietzsche begins to use the term late in the nineteenth century. What we learn in the course of his exploration is "that Nietzsche's definition of nihilism is actually the reversal of the concept as it was originally understood."[77] As this comment already suggests, Gillespie's story about the origins of the concept of nihilism is a story that, quite like the narratives of Milbank and Heidegger, turns Nietzsche on his head.

In the narratives of Milbank and Heidegger, to turn Nietzsche on his head involves the argument that Nietzsche was a nihilist because in the end he reduced the world to power and delivered this world into the hands of the overman. Gillespie in effect assents to these conclusions. He would, in other words, agree with both Milbank and Heidegger that nihilism is about the radical killing made possible by the unleashing of an unconstrained will to power, a will that is now in some way the possession of humanity. What Gillespie wants to understand, however, is not the relationship between this will and Being (Heidegger) nor the relationship between this will and the will of a charitable God (Milbank). Instead, Gillespie wants to know both where this notion of an unconstrained, all-powerful will comes from and how this will came to be identified as the possession of human beings. As he puts it when summarizing his argument:

> The history of nihilism is the history of the development of this notion of will. . . . It was this idea of an absolute will that gave birth to the idea of nihilism, for if the I is everything, then . . . God is nothing. Nihilism, as it was originally understood, was thus not the result of the degeneration of man and his concomitant inability to sustain a God [Nietzsche's version]. It was rather the consequence of the assertion of an absolute human will that renders God superfluous and thus for all intents and purposes dead.[78]

Here we see Gillespie's reversal of Nietzsche in summary fashion; it remains now to look at his narrative in more detail.

Gillespie's narrative starts in the fourteenth century with a review of nominalist theology, particularly that of Ockham. For, in Gillespie's view, the notion of an unbridled human will that becomes the centerpiece of nihilism begins, ironically enough, as the nominalist notion of an omnipotent God, a notion that was hatched in order to save the power of God from the undue constraints that had been placed upon this power by the marriage of theology and philosophy characteristic of medieval Scholasticism. The nominalist notion of an omnipotent God, completely without constraints, even those of reason, was an attempt to restore the importance of revelation, which had given significant ground to reason in Scholastic theology. As Gillespie describes it, the nominalist attempt to rescue God from Scholasticism produced the vision of

> a God of infinite power whose dark and incomprehensible form was as much an object of terror as of love and devotion. . . . Such an arbitrary and

> capricious God became increasingly plausible in a world devastated by plague and internecine political and theological strife. Historical circumstances thus gave a real substance and magnitude to this conception of God. Under such conditions it is little wonder that this God was a source of profound anxiety and insecurity in the succeeding centuries.[79]

According to Gillespie, we find the proof, as it were, of the extent to which this nominalist God influenced the succeeding centuries when we turn to the seventeenth century and the philosophical ruminations of René Descartes:

> Descartes' thought can thus be understood at least in part as the attempt to open up a space for man, a realm of freedom invulnerable to the powers of this God. The basis for this realm of human freedom is Descartes' *ego cogito ergo sum*. . . . This principle, however, is not merely a bastion or refuge—it is also the Archimedean point upon which Descartes stands in his attempt to move the world, the basis for the universal science with which he seeks to win back the earth for man by dethroning this arbitrary and irrational God and making man the master and possessor of nature. . . . Underlying the Cartesian project in a way that never becomes entirely explicit is the possibility that man is or at least can become God.[80]

According to Gillespie, what was not entirely explicit in Descartes becomes so in the course of the next two centuries, beginning with the work of Johann Gottlieb Fichte (1762–1814), who takes the notion of will present in Descartes (and even more prominently in Kant) and transforms it into "a world-creating will." If the history of nihilism is, as Gillespie suggests, the history of the notion of an infinite will, then Fichte is the pivotal figure. For at the center of Fichtean idealism is the notion of an Absolute I that is bound by none of the constraints that either Descartes or Kant placed upon the subject. Fichte is a pivotal figure in the story of nihilism not only because he begins to make explicit the notion of an infinite will but also because, interestingly enough, both his philosophy and that of his students attracted charges of "nihilism." Hence, Friedrich Jacobi in 1799, in a letter to Fichte, referred to Fichte's idealism as "nihilism" and concluded: "Man has this choice and this alone: nothing or God. Choosing nothing he makes himself God; that means he makes God an apparition, for it is impossible, if there is no God, for man and all that is around him to be more than an apparition. I repeat: God is and is outside of me, a living essence that subsists for itself, or I am God. There is no third alternative."[81]

Jacobi's student, Jean Paul, leveled a similar charge against the desire for absolute autonomy present in the works of the early German Romantics (many of whom were Fichte's students) when he called them "aesthetic nihilists." For Jean Paul, the early Romantics represented "the lawless, capricious spirit of the present age, which would egotistically annihilate the world and the universe in order to clear a space merely for free *play* in the void. . . . [I]n an age when God has set like the sun, soon afterwards the world too passes into darkness. He who scorns the universe respects nothing more than himself and at night fears only his own creations."[82]

At the heart of Gillespie's narrative about nihilism stands this relationship between the notion of an all-powerful human will and the charge of nihilism. From Fichte and the Romantics, Gillespie traces the development of this understanding of nihilism through Goethe and Hegel to the Russian nihilists, and from there to Nietzsche, with a detour through Schopenhauer, who was both a student of Fichte and a decisive presence in Nietzsche's early thought. This intricate history of nihilism is well worth recounting, but this is not the place to do it. Suffice it to say that by Gillespie's account, after Fichte and the early Romantics were criticized as "nihilists," the meaning of the term was well established, and until Nietzsche it would continue to designate the elevating and empowering of the human will at the expense of both God and the world.

Gillespie's narrative about nihilism before Nietzsche allows him, when he finally arrives at Nietzsche's own account of nihilism, to position Nietzsche in much the same way that Milbank and Heidegger do. Hence Gillespie declares that Nietzsche's

> interpretation of nihilism is a complete reversal of the earlier usage of the concept. Previously, nihilism was understood as the consequence of the hubristic magnification of man. In Nietzsche's view, it is the consequence of the democratic diminution of man. On the basis of this new understanding, Nietzsche argues that the solution to nihilism is a turn to the superhuman, that is, a turn to exactly that notion that previously was conceived to be the essence of nihilism.[83]

Here we see Gillespie performing exactly the same maneuver that both Heidegger and Milbank, each in their own way, performed in order to disarm Nietzsche. By renarrating the development of Western thought, each of these figures finds a way to describe nihilism as the ultimate evil and then to cast Nietzsche in the role of antihero. In the next chapter, as I turn back to the work of John Milbank, I will take an extended look at one of these counter-Nietzschean narratives. First, however, let me try to make some sense of what's at stake in these various accounts of nihilism, Nietzsche's included.

Nihilism and the Politics of Description

Interestingly, if we step back from the differing accounts of the origins of nihilism, we can see that each of these thinkers share, at bottom, a basic understanding of nihilism as the evacuation of meaning and value from the world, so that all that remains is unconstrained power erupting from the abyss. To return to the provisional definition of nihilism that I used in Chapter One: Nihilism simply bespeaks a world at war with itself, a world run amok with no bounds, no constraints, no guidance. Both Nietzsche and Heidegger refer explicitly to this world as one that is poised on the edge of catastrophe; and nothing in the works of Milbank and Gillespie suggests to me that either of them would disagree with this conclusion. Indeed, as we saw previously, Gillespie notes that one of the reasons Nietzsche's understanding of nihilism as the death of God is so compelling is that "the great wars and totalitarian experiments of our century have borne an all too faithful witness to Nietzsche's prescience" about the coming catastrophe whose proportions can be measured, as the recent events in Bosnia remind us, by the number of unmarked mass graves.

What is at stake, then, in the differences between these various accounts of nihilism is not so much the bottom-line definition of the term as it is the politics that stands behind the various narrative accounts of how it is that this term has come to carry such descriptive power. As we saw, Nietzsche declares that nihilism has become our "normal condition"; and the works of Milbank, Heidegger, and Gillespie do not dispute this fact. The disputes begin when each of these thinkers begins to offer an account of the causes of this condition. None of these thinkers, Nietzsche included, are content to live as normal nihilists. All of them want to escape nihilism. But a successful escape hinges upon an account of how we came to be stuck here in the first place. As an example of how political concerns influence these narratives about nihilism, take the politics that stands behind Gillespie's account.

A good deal of Gillespie's narrative about nihilism is devoted to an account not of the transformations in the meaning of the term per se but of the way in which nihilism moves from an "academic" notion to "a world-historical force." Hence, to trace the lineage all too briefly, Fichte and the early Romantics heavily influence both the Promethean character of Russian nihilism and, in a different vein, Hegelian dialectics. Left-Hegelianism and Russian nihilism then meet on the world stage in Russia and become the Russian Revolution. And, says Gillespie, in a comment that summarizes his story about nihilism *before* Nietzsche, "What we discover in the afterglow of this great event is that the fire this new Prometheus brings down to earth is not the hearth flame that is the center of the home but a conflagration that consumes civilization. . . . At the end of modernity, the dark God of nominalism appears enthroned within the bastion of reason as the grim lord of Stalin's universal terror."[84]

This positioning of the Russian Revolution indicates the extent to which Gillespie's account of nihilism serves political purposes, given that his account of the revolution carries an implicit critique of Marx. Gillespie indicates his political agenda more straightforwardly in the introduction to his book when he states the following intention: "I want to argue that Nietzsche's account of the origin and nature of nihilism has led us wrongly to devalue the modern world, especially in implicating liberalism in nihilism. In his view, liberalism is the final triumph of slave morality. . . . My argument suggests that this view is fallacious. Nihilism is not the result of liberalism but of a strain of modern thought that is largely at odds with liberalism."[85] Gillespie also refers to this strain of thought as "modern radicalism" and says that he wants to emphasize "the essentially negative and destructive character" of "modern radical thought," which "necessarily worships a dark god of negation."[86]

Gillespie thus constructs a narrative about nihilism in the hope of saving liberalism. And if we ask the question, Save it from what? the answer seems to be from the purely negative exercise of radical thought and its logical conclusion: for "where negation ends, tyranny and degeneration begin."[87] Even more tellingly, Gillespie in effect says that where negation *begins*, politics ends. Hence when speaking of the Russian nihilists, Gillespie says that they were not "politically effective . . . because neither was really interested in political reform. . . . The nihilists' neglect of politics, which they believed to be outdated, proved in this case to be their undoing."[88] What these statements indicate is that, for Gillespie, politics is always to be equated with the politics of liberal reform. Any radical departure from liberalism ceases to be politics and becomes a negative exercise, becomes in other words, nihilism. This delimiting of what counts for politics has profound implications, not the least of which is Gillespie's inability to see the inherently political, if radical, character of Nietzsche's move from nihilism to tragedy.

This inability to recognize the viability of a tragic politics is not unique to Gillespie's account of Nietzsche. Rather Gillespie seems simply to echo a common tendency among liberal political theorists. Radical departures from liberalism are often dismissed as nihilism. In Chapters Five and Six, I turn to the work of Foucault in an attempt to argue for a tragic politics that appears to be nihilism only when viewed through liberal lenses. Then in Chapters Seven and Eight, I make a similar argument concerning the conflict between liberalism and a Christian politics that is not tragic but apocalyptic.

In order to both prepare for the notions of a tragic and an apocalyptic politics and to display more fully the political character of narratives about nihilism, let me turn now to an extended consideration of John Milbank's theological project, which is an attempt to save not liberalism but the distinctiveness of a Christian politics that is opposed to *both* liberalism and nihilism.

3

Between Nihilism and Apocalypse: The Tragic Theology of John Milbank

In the course of developing his argument that ethical nihilism is founded upon the twin assumptions of an absolute historicism and an ontology of violence, John Milbank notes that Nietzschean genealogy, with its celebration of the heroic virtues, is in effect "an account of Christianity, written from the point of view of the paganism it displaced."[1] "Nihilism must," says Milbank, "discover a sufficient reason for Christianity. This is because Christianity, as Nietzsche brilliantly diagnosed, is the total inversion of any heroic identity of virtue with strength, achievement, or conquest. . . . [B]y devaluing the heroic, Christianity marks an epochal shift" (286).

Nietzsche's reading of this shift, as we saw, involves both his claim that life is the will to power and his claim that Christianity, in the reactionary spirit of *resentiment,* rejects this will, celebrates "weakness" in place of strength, and thus denigrates life. That at least, as Milbank sees it, is the story as told from the point of view of the paganism Christianity displaced, or rather, from the point of view of a Nietzschean "neopaganism" with a chip on its shoulder. However, Milbank argues that if this story is "to be defended as more than just an interpretation," then this "reading of Christianity has to be objectively correct" (288). But according to Milbank, it is neither clear that the virtues of "strength" really do display a more "natural" way of life nor that Nietzsche's reading of Christianity as a reactionary, resentment-bound, weak-willed cultural force is right:

> Clearly this is not how Christianity understands itself: for Christian self-understanding, the primary receptivity of 'weakness' is the relation not to the strong, but to God, the source of all charity. And this receptivity is a paradoxical, active reception, because the lover of God is authenticated by the love which she actively transmits to her neighbor. But then one may ask, why should the natural, active, creative will not be understood, as it is understood by Christianity, as essentially the charitable will, the will whose exer-

> cise of power is not a will to dominate, or to condescend, but rather to endorse, raise up, increase the capacity of, the human other? (288)

In the first part of this chapter I offer an extended exposition of what Milbank takes to be Christianity's self-understanding.[2] Milbank's theological project is an attempt to prove that Nietzsche is not "objectively correct" about Christianity. Nietzsche "was objectively right to the extent that Christianity is unique in refusing ultimate reality to all conflictual phenomena" (262), but he was wrong to think that this refusal runs counter to life and is therefore somehow "unnatural."

As Milbank sees it, Nietzsche's misreading of Christianity in this regard is the deathblow to Nietzsche's own constructive position, given that Nietzsche's philosophy emerges in direct opposition to his understanding of Christianity. Just as Augustine wrote "against the pagans," Nietzsche wrote against the Christians.[3] But if Christians are not who Nietzsche makes them out to be, then his whole case is in doubt. This, at least, is Milbank's argument. Attending to this argument is the primary task of this chapter. However, after attending to this argument I want to extend Milbank's logic and say that if it is incumbent upon Nietzsche to get Christianity right, then it is equally incumbent upon Milbank to get Nietzsche right, since he himself notes that Christianity "is the true 'opposite' of Nietzschean postmodernism" (262). And, as I will argue, Milbank does not get Nietzsche and the neo-Nietzscheans right. Toward the end of this chapter, I will take up again the task I started in the last chapter, insofar as there I was working toward something like the self-understanding of nihilism. Milbank's understanding of nihilism is certainly not Nietzsche's own, and so we should be able to say of Milbank's account of nihilism that "clearly, this is not how nihilism understands itself." In the latter part of this chapter and in all of the next one, I will display what we might call nihilism's self-understanding, in an attempt to offer a critique of at least a portion of Milbank's theological project.

In other words, I am now about to display some of the features of the contest I mentioned in the last chapter when Milbank spoke of a counterhistory to the history of violence that, for thinkers like Derrida, is history itself. As Milbank sees it, Jesus and the Church are the interruption of this history of violence, which is also to say that they transform history itself—they become, in a sense, the counterhistory upon which Milbank rests his entire narrative. In this regard, Milbank provides an initial indication of the role "apocalypse" will play in my narrative. For Milbank's thought is apocalyptic, insofar as he insists that the privileging of the Christian logos leads to a profound and revolutionary interpretation of all events—past, present, and future—as in some way a manifestation of the (often hidden) work of God.[4]

The task now is to recount how Milbank's privileging of the Christian narrative brings into view this apocalyptic counterhistory, which, to Milbank's mind, is *the* alternative to nihilism. The best way to begin this task is to turn briefly to Augustine's *City of God*. For Milbank's privileging of the Christian logos, together with his understanding that the Christian narrative provides a unique alternative to nihilism's narrative of power, amounts to nothing less than a recasting of Augustine's narrative in the *City of God*, where the paganism of Rome stands in stark contrast to the "Eternal City, on pilgrimage in this world."[5]

Milbank's Postmodern Augustinianism

Milbank himself calls our attention to the importance of Augustine when he says the following:

> In my view, a true Christian metanarrative realism must attempt to retrieve and elaborate the account of history given by Augustine in the *Civitas Dei*. . . .
>
> Augustine's philosophy of history appears more viable than that of either Hegel or Marx. These two provide 'gnostic' versions of Augustine's critical Christianity by giving us a story in which antagonism is inevitably brought to an end by a necessary dialectical passage through conflict. Augustine on the other hand, puts peaceful reconciliation in no dialectical relationship with conflict . . . but rather does something prodigiously more historicist, in that he isolates the codes which support the universal sway of antagonism, and contrasts this with a code of a peaceful mode of existence, which has historically arisen as 'something else', an *altera civitas*, having no logical or causal connection with the city of violence.[6] (389)

Perhaps the simplest way to elaborate upon Augustine's account of history and to display what Milbank has in mind when he says that Augustine isolates the pagan "code" of antagonism and contrasts it with the peaceful code of Christianity is to turn, as Augustine does, to the founding narratives of these respective communities:

> For this is how Rome was founded, when Remus, as Roman history witnesses, was slain by his brother Romulus. . . . Both sought the glory of establishing the Roman state, but a joint foundation would not bring to each the glory that a single founder would enjoy. Anyone whose aim was to glory in the exercise of power would obviously enjoy less power if his sovereignty was diminished by a living partner. Therefore, in order that the sole power should be wielded by one person, the partner was eliminated.[7]

Of course the elimination of the partner did not simply consolidate power but prevented the conflict that would have resided at the heart of things had both rivals remained alive. Hence, when the conflict between these two rivals ends with the violent death of Remus, an order, a kind of peace even, is secured, an order and a peace that is not only internal to the operation of Rome itself but that is then exported throughout the empire: the famous *Pax Romana*, a peace founded upon violence. Milbank explains it this way:

> In the story which Rome tells about its own foundations, the principle of a prior violence 'stayed' and limited by a single violent hand is firmly established. Romulus, the founder, is the murderer of his brother and rival Remus; he is also the enslaver of the *clienteles* to whom he offered protection against foreign enemies. In battle, Romulus invoked the staying hand of Jupiter, who then received the title *stator.* The supreme God, therefore, like the founding hero, arises merely as the limiter of a preceding disorder. . . . Mythical beginnings of legal order are therefore traced back to the arbitrary limitation of violence by violence. (391)

Augustine wants us to see in the story of Romulus and Remus that the cornerstone of Rome's foundation is, even as Rome itself tells it, an act of violence. And insofar as Rome's history and Rome's self-understanding are rooted in the story of this foundational act of violence, Rome cannot and will not cease to be about violence. Hence, as Milbank notes, "according to Augustine, the Romans continued to 'live out' [this] mythos: within the city gates, the goddess most celebrated was *Bellona* [war], the virtues most celebrated were the military ones. The statue of the goddess *Quies* [tranquillity], by contrast, stood outside the gates, as if to indicate that peace was a benefit brought through war by Rome to others" (391).[8]

As Augustine has it, then, "what would have been kept smaller and better by innocence [had Romulus not killed Remus] grew through crime into something bigger and worse."[9] That something bigger and worse was of course the Roman Empire itself, and by extension, not simply the Roman Empire but all empires, and with them, all of history—since the history of the world is, at least from Rome's perspective, the history of empires. Augustine proposes, however, that there is another way to understand history.

The story of Romulus and Remus does suggest, as Derrida would have it, that violence lies at the root of everything. But this is not the only story we can tell. And in fact, this story is but a later version of a similar, and yet radically different, story: the story of Cain and Abel in Genesis 4. The founding of the city of Rome upon the violent act of Romulus in fact repeats Cain's founding of the first city after he murders his brother Abel. According to Augustine, all earthly cities henceforth repeat and remain rooted in this primal act of violence. But the story of Romulus and Remus does not repeat the story of Cain and Abel exactly. For while Romulus and Remus represent the conflict over power that divides "the earthly city against itself," the story of Cain and Abel depicts the hostility between the earthly city and another city, which is not exactly a city—the City of God: "Cain founded a city, whereas Abel, as a pilgrim, did not found one . . . and did not aim at power in the city his brother was founding."[10]

Thus all earthly cities—and in Augustine's day, Rome was first among them—rest upon the legacy of Cain, whereas the City of God has as its foundation not murder but the murdered, or as Milbank puts it: "Whereas the *civitas terrena* inherits its power from the conqueror of a fraternal rival, the 'city of God on pilgrimage through this world' founds itself not in a succession of power, but upon the memory of the murdered brother. . . . Instead of a peace 'achieved' through the abandonment of the losers, the subordination of potential rivals and resistance to enemies, the Church provides a genuine peace by its memory of all the victims" (392).

This brief account of Augustine's reading of these two stories about fratricide should go some way toward explaining what it is that Milbank wants to retrieve from a rereading of the *City of God.* As Milbank sees it, Augustine realized that myth and ritual are the engines that drive the daily life of a community. Rome was what Rome was both because of the stories Rome told itself about itself and because of the rituals in which those stories were embodied. Thus, in a summary comment about Rome, Augustine declares: "Strange marriage rites, strange causes of war, strange conditions of fraternity, of alliance, and of divinity. In short, what a strange sort of life in a city under the protection of so many gods."[11] What he doesn't say here, but what he might have said and surely implies is, "What strange stories these people tell."

Milbank says that Augustine begins the great Western tradition of critique and that this critique is prodigiously historicist. What he means to suggest is that Augustine, in an almost postmodern way, realized that pagan Rome could be opposed successfully only by telling what was, from Rome's perspective at least, an equally strange but radically different story about how things came to be. Because the life of Rome was "so deeply inscribed at the level of myth and ritual," only at this level could that life be challenged. Hence Augustine opposes Roman myth with Christian myth, Roman ritual with Christian ritual, a Roman account of history—where history unfolds as the work of emperors and empires—with a Christian account of history—where history unfolds as the work of a God who, from Abel to Jesus, stands with the victims and against empire.[12]

Augustine does not suppose, like Hegel and Marx, that the inner drive of history is the progressive, dialectical working out of conflict but instead argues that conflict emerges from, in Milbank's idiom, a particular coding of the world, and from the clash between this code and its alternative. History is not the progressive resolution of conflict. Any alternative to conflict arrives not as something internal to the conflict itself but as something, as

Milbank puts it, "having no logical or causal connection with the city of violence." In an Augustinian scheme, neither conflict nor its resolution are built in to the way things are; the world has not been programmed to function dialectically. Rather, both conflict and peace arise historically as the contingent products of narrative codings. Thus, if peace arrives, it does so not by way of dialectics but as the result of what Milbank identifies as "a persuasion intrinsic to the Christian *logos* itself" (1). To say that peace rests upon persuasion is to say that the world has been programmed to function rhetorically. To adopt Augustine's account of history is, then, to grant that "a Christian understanding of the logos . . . [is] much closer to a rhetorical than a dialectical habit of mind" (328). Hence we might say that the *City of God* was Augustine's attempt to outnarrate pagan Rome, or more generally, that the task for Christians is to "persuade people—for reasons of literary taste—that Christianity offers a much better story" (330) than its competitors: To read the flow of history as in some crucial way related to the spilling of Abel's blood, rather than to the violent hand of Romulus, provides a more persuasive account of events.

To comprehend the implications of Milbank's Augustinian move from dialectics to rhetoric, with its attending emphasis on the power of narrative, we should look briefly at the difference between Milbank and MacIntyre, a comparison not only warranted because of the clarity it will bring to my exposition of Milbank's enterprise but also in some sense necessary, since Milbank himself says of his project that it is "a temeritous attempt to radicalize the thought of MacIntyre" (327).[13]

Revisiting MacIntyre: From Dialectics to Rhetoric

Just as MacIntyre's narrative contains a watershed moment, the moment in the thirteenth century after which everything somehow went wrong, Milbank's narrative, as we have seen, pivots upon a similar moment—the moment when history received its wound in an outlying part of the Roman Empire on the east end of the Mediterranean: "all history before Christ can be narrated as 'anticipating' his story, and all history since as situated within it, such that everything that subsequently happens is nothing but the acceptance or rejection of Christ" (383). Whatever difference exists between Milbank and MacIntyre, it rests, I think, in the difference between these pivotal moments in their respective narratives. Aquinas holds a central place in MacIntyre's narrative because his work embodies the dialectics that is so crucial to MacIntyre's project. Milbank, on the other hand, in a sense privileging Augustine's method over that of Aquinas, centers his narrative on the incarnation, twelve centuries earlier. And it is then on the basis of this starting point, on this pivotal event of the logos incarnate (filtered through an Augustinian lens), that Milbank bases his notion that a Christian understanding of the logos is a rhetorical rather than dialectical affair.

Milbank argues that MacIntyre's Thomistic narrative is too reliant upon the Greek logos, a reliance that leads MacIntyre's narrative into two serious problems: for one thing MacIntyre's "reason," although embodied in the *Summa* and in a tradition, is still not the logos incarnate, and thus MacIntyre's narrative is insufficiently theological and insufficiently Christian.[14] For another thing, it is not at all clear that MacIntyre, with his commitment to the Greek logos, has an answer for Nietzsche. As Milbank puts it, "antique thought . . . is deconstructible into 'modern' thought: a cosmos including both chaos and reason implies an ultimate principle, the 'difference' between the two, and enshrines a permanent conflict" (5).

Antique thought is deconstructible into modern thought because in both cases the founding assumption is that truth is founded upon the violence that comes with unceasing conflict. As we saw in Chapter One, with MacIntyre's notion of tradition as argument, this conflict, this dialectical sifting of "the world" through the sieve of reason, is what prevents the violence of the arbitrary—which, on MacIntyre's account, is another name for both modernity and its Nietzschean critique. However, in order to refute the arbitrary, MacIntyre must rely on two assumptions: first, that to be human is to be always already launched upon a "narrative quest" that assumes the form of an enquiry; and second, that the world exists not only as a linguistic construction displayed in narrative but also "as such," and that the telos of our enquiry is to disclose the truth of this "as such."[15]

Of course the narratives we use to display the world always mediate this "as such," and MacIntyre concedes that no simple correspondence between the world and our assertions about it is possible. Nonetheless, for MacIntyre our will to order the narratives in which we find ourselves and the world embedded is not finally the arbitrary will to power. Rather, this will is a reasoned will that seeks to enquire into the truth of the world—which is also the truth of being human. This truth, finally, is timeless, though never in practice is it universal—because it can be truth only when it is embodied historically in a tradition. What is universal for MacIntyre is the activity of enquiry, defined as the inherently reasoned quest for the truth of the world as it is displayed in narrative. This will to enquire is in the end a kind of transcendental reason that makes the notion of tradition-constituted and tradition-constitutive reason possible. And this transcendental reason is in turn guaranteed only by the further assumption of a variant of philosophical realism. For only if the world stands as a test for truth can one construe reason as dialectical.

Dialectical reason, then, which is MacIntyre's answer to Nietzsche, and which is supposed to guarantee that all allegiances are not arbitrary, rests upon the two arbitrary assumptions of "reason" and "the world." MacIntyre's mistake does not, according to Milbank, lie in these assumptions themselves. Rather his mistake is to use these assumptions to make claims that transcend the contingency of their origination.[16] MacIntyre is aware that to speak of "reason" in general and the world "as such" is reminiscent of the modernity he is seeking to refute, yet he claims to avoid the pitfalls of modernity by foregrounding the conflict that lies at the heart of claims about reason and the world. Milbank's response is to point out that this assumption of conflict is precisely what antiquity and modernity share. MacIntyre seeks to avoid the violence of the arbitrary by substituting for it the reasoned violence of dialectics. What MacIntyre fails to notice is that violence itself, as the product of an arbitrary difference between reason and the irrational, the world and chaos, is arbitrary. To step beyond both liberalism and Nietzschean nihilism requires more than a different account of violence; it requires the questioning of violence by way of an alternative account of difference itself.

From Plato to Kant to Nietzsche to MacIntyre runs the arbitrary path of the violence of a logos founded upon the fissure between reason and madness, order and chaos, presence and absence. Only a different logos, speaking differently of difference, can provide the alternative MacIntyre seeks. As Milbank puts it: "Poised between a permanent reason, and a permanent realm of unreason, one must live also in unreason, also under the rule of warfare. Therefore, the Platonic logos—dialectical truth itself—is *not* the logos that proclaims love for the enemy. Rather it still "makes war at the stranger's gate" (371).

Opposing MacIntyre's commitment to the dialectics of the Greek logos, Milbank exposes MacIntyre's philosophical realism, which, from Milbank's postmodern Augustinian perspective, is much too Greek, too modern, and too foundational. In place of this Greek "habit of mind," Milbank declares that "God can no longer be arrived at by dialectics, by the 'discipline of truth.' . . . Hence the relationship of God to the world becomes, after Christianity, a rhetorical one" (429–430), which is also to say, as we will see, an aesthetic one, as Christians seek to persuade others, as a matter of "literary taste," of the beauty of the Christian story. Like MacIntyre, Milbank is willing to accept and even celebrate a Nietzschean world of conflicting perspectives; but in a radical departure from MacIntyre, Milbank does not think that such conflicts can be adjudicated rationally. Instead, Milbank argues that the most we can expect is the possibility that we might persuade our rivals that our particular narrative is somehow more "true" than theirs because it is, quite simply, more beautiful. To speak of narrative and truth in this way is to begin to move toward the center of Milbank's theological project, an integral part of which is what Milbank himself calls "metanarrative realism," a version of realism that stands in stark contrast to the philosophical realism of MacIntyre that I have just described.

Metanarrative Realism

Put simply, metanarrative realism amounts to this: Our lives in the world emerge into meaning and become real only within the context of narratives. As Milbank says, "Without the story of the tree, there is no abiding tree" (358). Even scientific truth is but a narration of events.[17] Furthermore, in order that the myriad narratives that course the world do not yield confusion and disorientation, they must be ordered, such that we come to identify, as MacIntyre puts it, "the single history of the world within which all other stories find their place."[18] This single history of the world is a metanarrative: "a story privileged by faith, and seen as the key to the interpretation and regulation of all other stories" (386). In other words, whatever story we tell about the tree will be embedded in another, more comprehensive story about the world generally: It makes a difference whether you tell the story of the tree from the perspective of a druid, or from the perspective of a CEO of a wood-products corporation.

As it stands, this account of narrative is not unlike MacIntyre's, with the difference that on MacIntyre's account the druid and the CEO, if they were both speaking of a tree that occupied the same time and place, would finally be subject to "the discipline of truth," by which their accounts of the tree would be tested against the timeless truth of the tree as such. In Milbank's account, on the other hand, each could do no more than persuade the other of the beauty of their story about the tree. In fact, however, Milbank's account of narrative-dependent realism differs yet more markedly from MacIntyre's.

Narrative, says Milbank,

> is our primary mode of inhabiting the world, and it characterizes the way the world happens to us, not primarily, the cultural world which humans make. There is, therefore, no special 'human' sphere of narrative action, and no sphere of 'ethics' which uniquely characterizes human life. . . . Instead the question about what the whole of nature should look like, how even it would like to appear, impresses itself through all our apprehensions. (359)

Where MacIntyre would say of the tree that it is mediated in narrative and that the narrative, if it is to be truthful, must then be tested dialectically against both the tree as such and other accounts of the tree, Milbank says that the tree "happens" already and only as narrative. Nothing stands beneath nor behind the narrative that might hold it accountable; only an "incorporeal" aesthetic necessity, impressed persuasively in a narrative always already underway, can impress us to opt for one account of the tree over another. "Thus," says Milbank, "I am suggesting, against MacIntyre, that what makes an action is *not* the presence of a 'human' or 'cultural' motive or 'internal' reason [MacIntyre's "narrative quest" for the world "as such"]: all this is really still Cartesian and Kantian. What matters is the objective surface presence of a teleological ordering where intention of a goal shows up in visible structure" (359).

Milbank's notion of an "objective surface presence" is something he borrows from Gilles Deleuze, and it is rooted in a reversed or "overturned" Platonism, which "would preserve Plato's integration of the True, the Good and the Beautiful, and yet ground theory in the making, the original in the copy, the cause in the effect . . . [such that] the Platonic forms 'rise to the surface' as productions of space and time in their aspect of ideal repeatability and elemental latency of suggestion" (354).[19]

To understand more fully this Deleuzian notion, consider Milbank's claim that narrative is how the world happens to us. To say that there is no distinguishable abiding tree without the story of the tree, is to say that "nothing is first known to us as a mere indistinguishable continuum, nor as a sequence of cause and effect [or of original and copy]. Instead, relatively stable entities and isolatable sequences—facts and motions—always present themselves (as Deleuze argues) to us already as 'meanings' or as 'incorporeal' elements ('Platonic ideas on the surface')" (358). The tree "arrives," then, as one of these "meanings," which is also to say as a narrative, or as a character in a narrative—and not *my* narrative. In a sense, the world presents itself always and already as a story. And there is nothing beyond or behind this story. "Everything that happens," says Deleuze, "and everything that is said happens or is said at the surface. The surface is no less explorable and unknown than depth and height which are nonsense."[20] The surface is all we have. We cannot penetrate the surface to expose some deeper truth, nor lift the curtain of appearances to discover the essence of eternal ideas. To overturn Platonism is to give up on the notion of a distinction between reality and appearance and, instead, to approach the surface of the world with what Deleuze calls "a properly ideal or ghostly capacity for the apprehension of incorporeal transformations; an aptitude for grasping language as an immense indirect discourse."[21] This capacity or aptitude, as we will see, still involves an "idealism," but not in a Platonic sense.

Plato aspired to the height of ideas, to the depth of essences, and then developed a philosophy motivated by the need to discern which appearances were true pretenders (copies of the ideas) and which were false imitation (simulacra). Copies were identified according to their intrinsic relation to the model idea, according to criteria of resemblance and identity. Simulacra, on the other hand, as a (deficient) copy of a copy, mark their existence not by an internal resemblance to an idea, but by an external difference between themselves and the objects they copy. (You can tell this is a copy of that painting because the colors are dull, the brush strokes are lost, etc.) Again, Deleuze puts it this way: "The simulacrum is built upon disparity or upon a difference. It internalizes a dissimilarity. . . . Without doubt, it still produces an *effect* of resemblance; but this is an effect of the whole, completely external and produced by totally different means than those at work in the model."[22] Simulacra "subvert" resemblance and identity by not "passing through the Idea" and by embodying an "internalized dissemblance."

This distinction between copies and simulacra, which is Plato's distinction, now focused in a particular way by Deleuze, leads to

> two distinct readings of the world: one invites us to think of difference from the standpoint of previous similitude or identity; whereas the other invites us to think of similitude and even identity as the product of a deep disparity. The first reading precisely defines the world of copies or representations; it posits the world as icon. The second, contrary to the first, defines the world of simulacra; it posits the world itself as phantasm.[23]

A philosophy of Forms involves the task of "insuring the triumph of copies over simulacra," of good copies over bad. Bad copies are repressed as pretenders that have bypassed the notion of an internal resemblance to an idea, and so polluted similarity with difference. But what if the notion of transcendent ideas is discredited as nonsense? Henceforth, all copies bypass ideas; all copies are simulacra. And when ideas recede to the point of total obscurity, they take with them 'depth' and 'height', leaving only the surface: phantasms replace icons. Plato has been turned on his head. Nonetheless, in a certain sense, as "objective surface presences," "ideas" remain. Thus part and parcel of Milbank's metanarrative realism is what he calls "linguistic idealism."[24] To begin to get a sense of the relationship between narratives and "ideas," consider the Christian idea of God.

Linguistic Idealism

In part, Christians give content to the term "God," and thus to themselves and their world, with recourse to the biblical narratives. But these "narratives are difficult, hard to read, and one cannot abstract . . . a few simple rules about how to interpret them. . . . Narratives only identify God because they simultaneously invent the unpresentable 'idea' of God" (385). But "this invention is hesitating and uncertain" and always in "excess" of the narrative, even though the narrative itself calls us to such "radically inventive moments" of excess (384–385). Take, for instance, the doctrine of the incarnation.

"One has to recognize in the doctrinal affirmation of the incarnation a radically inventive moment, which asserts the 'finality' of God's appearance in a life involving suffering and violent death, and claims also in a certain sense God 'has to' be like this" (384). Milbank notes that nothing at the level of the narratives themselves justifies this extrapolation. "Thus the *idea* of a God-become-incarnate . . . is in some sense 'excessive' in relation to the stories about Jesus" (384). And yet this excess is justified in part because it gives force to existing Christian practice and, even more, because "of the inherent attractiveness of the picture of God thence provided: no other picture, save incarnation in 'a' joyful and suffering life, gives quite such an acute notion of divine love, and involvement in our destiny" (384). To speak of the incarnation as excessive in relation to the narrative is to remind ourselves that it does not simply rest with a certain obviousness in the opening pages of John's Gospel. What seems obvious to us now required centuries of debate: The invention of the unpresentable idea of God is no easy task.

Milbank's concept of an idea that in some sense is "excessive" in relation to the narrative is not unlike Kant's notion of an "aesthetic idea," a concept that Kant formulated while trying to account for "the powers of the mind which constitute genius" and that produce those great aesthetic works that lend spirit to our world and "quicken" our cognitive faculties, producing that state of vibration we experience as beauty.[25] Kant locates such powers of genius in an "animating principle" that quickens the soul. This principle, says Kant, "is nothing but the ability to exhibit aesthetic ideas: and by an aesthetic idea I mean a presentation of the imagination which prompts much thought, but to which no determinate thought whatsoever . . . can be adequate, so that no language can express it completely and allow us to grasp it." Or again, this presentation of the imagination prompts "so much thought as can never be comprehended within a determinate concept and thereby the presentation aesthetically expands the concept itself in an unlimited way . . . it makes reason think more." And finally, "an aesthetic idea is a presentation of the imagination . . . that makes us add to the concept the thoughts of much that is ineffable, but the feeling of which quickens our cognitive powers and connects language, which otherwise would be mere letters, with spirit."

Milbank acknowledges (almost explicitly) that what he has in mind with his linguistic idealism is something akin to Kant's notion here, with the exception that where Kant limits these ideas to aesthetics, as opposed to cognition, and further, attributes them only to genius, Milbank suggests that such ideas are part and parcel of all of our lives and that they embody an "aesthetic necessity" which is itself the basis for cognition.[26]

The world happens to us as narrative, yet rising to the surface of narrative, with the help of the imagination, are presentations ("objective surface presences") that "aesthetically expand" the narrative itself. These presentations make us add to the narrative the "thoughts of much that is ineffable, but the feeling of which quickens our cognitive powers and connects language, which otherwise would be mere letters, with spirit." The task, then, is to discover ideas for the mere letters of the narratives that happen to us, and to then, as Kant puts it, "hit upon a way that enables us to communicate to others" the aesthetic appeal these ideas lend to the narrative. This communication takes the form of persuasion, such that Christians offer to others a story charged with the power of ideas such as the doctrine of the incarnation: of a God-become-incarnate who dies on a cross so that he might save the world.[27]

Like Kant's aesthetic ideas, which add the ineffable to our thoughts and aesthetically expand our concepts, and somewhat akin to the Deleuzian notion that champions a "ghostly and ideal capacity for apprehending incorporeal transformations," Milbank's linguistic idealism is about reading the surface of the world in search of the "ideas," suggestions, and announcements that lie there. In this regard, "reading" is the most fundamental of activities. To

> read is not, as for hermeneutics, to 'redeem' the text, to put an end to its alien distance, or to discover its essentially 'human' reference, but simply to add to the text, to answer its indeterminacies with a particular new, written emphasis which itself, far from ending puzzlement or estrangement, merely indicates new and promising uncertainties. If there is a question here as to the 'true meaning' of the text, then this can only mean what is the truly desirable *order* of the text? (266)

This ordering of the text is precisely what Milbank's idealism is about, and since the world happens already as narrative, textuality is not limited to books but "is the condition of all culture," of "events, structures, institutions, tendencies as well as of lives," of the whole of creation (267).[28]

By Milbank's account, the world as text has a formal structure; all is not arbitrary; to add to the text does not mean that we can add anything we want. Rather, the world-as-narrative,

> if we are attentive, forms a loose and complex knot of resistance. . . . We register this resistance in a number of ways. We may place the pressure here or there, complicate the knot here, undo it a little there—yet, infuriatingly perhaps, we cannot undo the knot altogether. . . . Always we feel the resistance, although this is from elsewhere, and we cannot precisely place it, for it belongs, ultimately, to the whole wider network of resistances and counter-resistances, which we ourselves, by our intervention, are further adjusting and altering. (267)

In other words, "to understand is to encounter and reorganize a formal structure," and yet there is "an element of indeterminacy intrinsic to a structural formation itself" (266). Narratives structure the world, but always with an element of indeterminacy. This play between structure and indeterminacy is a play between the resistance of the "visible structures" of narrative and the invitation of the ineffable and "unpresentable ideas" that come "from elsewhere."[29]

In summary, then, ideas float to the surface of the world-as-narrative from the ineffable reaches of elsewhere, like some distant object that, as one walks along the beach, crests an ocean wave far out to sea: Suddenly, and from nowhere, it appears on a crest, but as a momentary suggestion, only to ride the next trough to obscurity, and then to rise again with a crest, and so on. The task is to string together enough glimpses of the crests to turn "latent suggestion" into "ideal repeatability" (354). Not "repeatability" in the sense that every glimpse of the object is the same (given the variabilities of wave size, distance, wind, lighting, and so forth, surely this is not the case), but rather in the sense of a "non-identical repetition," (306) such that certain glimpses produce what is recognizably the same object, although it looks quite different at sunrise than at sunset. The notion of non-identical repetition brings us to one additional aspect of Milbank's metanarrative realism and linguistic idealism: the "analogical code."

The Analogical Code

Non-identical repetition is Milbank's phrase for capturing the way narrative and ideas work together to form what he calls an "analogical code," as opposed to the "univocal code" of nihilist philosophy.[30] Deleuze's reversal of Plato delivers us into a world where difference, and not resemblance, is the ultimate principle. Where Plato ordered the world according to the participation of copies in the hierarchically ordered essences of ideas, Deleuze, according to Milbank, jettisons all hierarchy and speaks, like Duns Scotus, of the univocity of Being. Put simply, this univocal code asserts that Being is embodied in each being with the same meaning, or as Milbank puts it, "things 'are' in the same way" (303).[31] Such a code renders problematic, in the absence of something like a Platonic hierarchy, any but the most radical account of difference. If all things are the same according to their being, and yet obviously diverge enormously in other attributes, then whatever differences they have must be absolute, for Being is indifferent to the differences of beings. In other words, Being is not, in this account, something that adjudicates, or in any way accounts for, the relationship between fundamental differences. This conclusion leads to "a philosophy of pure heterogeneity" that can order the world only arbitrarily.

The Christian alternative to this code, says Milbank, is a recourse to analogy. Milbank thinks Deleuze is right to subvert Platonism and to arrive at the conclusion that difference is the ultimate principle. However, where he thinks Deleuze is wrong is in his assumption that Being is indifferent to the ordering of different beings. Rather, might we not conjecture with equal confidence that all things participate in divine Being and in divine creativity, such that Being "shows hierarchical preference amidst the differences of being." This would be a conception of Being not as univocal but as analogical.

To speak of an analogical coding is to presuppose a temporal infinity that—unlike the temporal infinity of nihilism, where the infinite equals the endless and arbitrary play of difference—is not indifferent to differences; it is to presuppose a "hierarchy of differentiation." In fact, this hierarchy "*is* this infinite process itself," so that what "we see as desirable, that which we choose to construct as sign or image, must 'already belong' to infinitude as non-identical repetition." In other words, analogy codes the world so that we confront "every temporal ontological arrangement" in aesthetic terms: "x and y may be different, yet they belong together in their difference in a specific 'exemplary' ordering." Unlike the Aristotelian ordering of genera and species, an analogical ordering is "not fixed once and for all." If the ordering of x and y into this exemplary relation lasts, it is because "of a 'Platonic' hierarchy, which accords to some particular cultural arrangement the privilege of an 'Ideal' status, and a generative productiveness in marking out the scope for new combinations and disposals."

If "things" persist it is because, as narratives, they are repeated. The task is always that of discovering which narratives to repeat. But, contra Plato, repetition cannot be a matter of copying preceding ideas; rather, "we have to discover the content of the infinite through labor, and creative effort"; ideals must be produced, even though in one sense they are discovered, and even as they in turn generate new productions. Such creative effort is not as rote as copying an idea but requires "genuine innovations, genuine additions"; it requires that we participate in God's creativity as well as in God's Being.

And God here is "not substance" but rather "power-act": an infinite power in which nothing is unrealized, and yet no realization exhausts the power: "Infinite realized act and infinite unrealized power mysteriously coincide in God" (423). The creaturely task of discovering the content of the infinite via creativity and innovation is a matter of participating in this power-act:

> Creation is therefore not a finished product in space, but is continuously generated *ex nihilo* in time. To sustain this process, the monads, seeds or ratios also self-generate, but in this they do not "assist" God, who supplies all power and all being, but rather participate in God. For if God is internally creative power-act, then he can only be participated in by creatures who do not embody an infinite coincidence of act and power [else there would be no

> distinction between God and creation], but a finite oscillation between the two, yet are themselves thereby radically creative and differentiating. (425)

To speak of genuine innovations, which is to say "preferred" additions, is to posit precisely, in addition to a temporal infinite, a God who, as "a plentitudinous supra-temporal infinite," "has 'already realized' in an eminent fashion every desirable effect. . . . Thus a historicism upon which one superimposes an analogical, rather than univocal coding, requires the positing of transcendence." Having said this, Milbank then insists, however, that "no attempt need be made (by Christian faith) to claim that this transcendentalism is any more than the effect of a linguistic code."[32]

This linguistic code, recalling the function of Kant's aesthetic ideas, is about the linking of ideals (which "already belong" to an infinite process and have been "already realized" in infinite Being) to the yet-to-be-created ordering of narratives. To code the world in this way is to say that certain narratives bear repeating at certain times and in certain places, others at other times and other places, and still others should never be repeated—and all according to the ideals of a linguistic code. To say of this repetition that it is "non-identical" is to acknowledge that the fit between ideals and narratives is never exactly the same.[33]

To begin to put all of this together, I can say in summary that the world happens to us as narrative. Inscribed upon the surface of narrative are the latent suggestions of ideas that, speculatively produced and imaginatively presented, crest the surface with enough consistency to constitute a repetition. This repetition in turn, as something new, as something added, rearranges the "look" of the entire surface, just as, after long observation, that distant object turned out to be the foam produced by waves crashing into a reef—which, once I say the word, incorporeally transforms the sea into a harbor. This reconstitution of the surface occurs when ideas are infused back into the narrative, reordering the world according to an analogical code and an aesthetic necessity.

Cast in these terms, theology, both as Milbank envisions it and as he does it, is a speculative task that generates, in radically inventive moments, the narrative excesses of unpresentable ideas. If these ideas are worthy, if they are compelling in their picture of God and carry with them an aesthetic necessity, then not only will they end up infused back into the narrative but their very nature demands that they return here: "If Jesus really is the word of God, then it is not the mere 'extrinsic' knowledge of this which will save us, but rather a precise attention to his many words and deeds and all their historical results" (385). Thus the narrative calls us outside its bounds into the excess of an idea; the idea in turn propels us, with new force, back into the narrative, and this entire movement culminates as a concrete historical difference that has rearranged the surface of the world: Speculative theology becomes "a variant of pragmatism" (5). "The idea helps to confirm *that* God is love, the narrative alone instructs about *what* love is" (385), and together idea and narrative produce real historical churches that exist as peaceable havens in a world of violence.

We should not misunderstand, either in its speculative or its pragmatic guise, Milbank's allegiance to the notion of nonviolence; for he does not mean to deny that "we are locked in a world of deep-seated conflict which it would be folly to deny or evade" (411). But if we root our thought in Abel, and not Cain or Romulus, we should be able to "unthink the necessity of violence" through the indication "that there is a way to act in a violent world which assumes the ontological priority of non-violence" (411). Put simply, the world is violent, but Christians don't have to be.

Augustine and Heidegger on Being

This possibility of unthinking the necessity of violence rests for Milbank upon Augustine's ontology, which, to make the point, Milbank contrasts with the ontology of Heidegger, since as Milbank sees it, all of the nihilists share, in some way, Heidegger's notion of a "rupture" or "fall" of Being that creates the "ontological difference" between Being and beings. We saw something of this rupture displayed in Derrida's account of discourse as war. Milbank affirms something like this difference and agrees with Heidegger about its implications: "if beings are *constituted* by their relationship to Being, then this is not a relationship we can survey, and Being remains forever absent, forever concealed behind its presentation in the temporal series of beings" (300). Milbank disagrees, however, with the nihilist tendency "to give this concealment the overtones of dissimulation, of violence, of a necessary suppression" and suggests that one might say instead "that as much as a being is a particular existence and not Being itself, it yet exhibits in its sheer contingency the inescapable mystery of Being" (300).

Heidegger, too, thinks that the sheer contingency of our existence as beings suggests something more than being. But, as Milbank notes, for Heidegger, "our present existence is a basis for something else, not because it is lacking, but because it might be otherwise" (301). Hence for Heidegger, what beings suggest in their presence is not the negativity of a mysterious divine "reserve" but rather a "nullity" that arises from the realization that to be this is not to be that: "Every being which has inevitably lapsed into 'presence' precludes, through its arbitrary and groundless insistence on some preferences and some values, the sublime perspective of infinite difference which is the (non) point of view of Being itself" (301). In other words, I exist as this presence only because an infinity of other things do not exist here at this time and this place. But my presence here and now is arbitrary, and thus any one of those different things might have happened just as easily. "I am" only at the expense of the infinity of different things I am not, and this expense suggests a sort of violence inherent in my being present at all, as well as a sense of guilt for being the cause of this violence, or so Heidegger has it. Augustine puts it differently.

For Augustine, violence and guilt do not come about in this way at all. Violence and guilt are not tied to the occlusion of difference in presence but to rebellion against God. With a notion almost the precise opposite of Heidegger's, Augustine says that were beings to forgo violence and its accompanying guilt, they would embody the full presence of divine Being. Violence results when something that should be present is not present, not from the fullness of presence itself. Violence, then, is not, as it is for Heidegger, the result of the nullity of a particular presence in relation to the infinity of Being but is instead the product of the lack of right desire.

The difference between violence as misdirected desire and violence as part and parcel of the very "presence" of beings is the same difference that Milbank notes between a world that is divinely ordered and one that is ordered arbitrarily. Both Augustine and Heidegger understand Being as in some sense temporal becoming, but only "Augustine admits a hierarchy of values and a teleological ordering into his view of becoming" (302), such that existence is the series of particular presences ordered according the infinite presence of divine love. If guilt arises here, it does so out of the awareness that the order is confused, that, strictly speaking, something that should exist does not, that at the heart of presence is an absence violence has wrought—a wound. This wound, however, is not simply a matter of course but is the result of a misplaced desire, which is to say of sin. Contra Heidegger, Augustine has no notion of the necessity of the fall. The fall is not ontological; it conveys none of the necessity incumbent upon the Heideggerian view that the fall is caught up with "the way things are." For Augustine, the fall is historical; right desire is always possible.

The implications of this opposition between the ontologies of Heidegger and Augustine surface in Milbank's appropriation of this opposition for the construction of his own ontology of nonviolence, an appropriation that leads, as Milbank understands it, to the incommensurability between nihilism and Christianity. At this point it is worth turning again to a comparison of Milbank and MacIntyre, since this opposition between Christianity and nihilism is central to both of their projects (although as MacIntyre casts it, it is an opposition between Thomism and Nietzschean genealogy).

Dismantling MacIntyre's Castle

As I noted in the first chapter, MacIntyre's project begins as a critique of Enlightenment liberalism. This critique brings him unavoidably into close proximity with Nietzsche. Thus it is not surprising that in the middle of *After Virtue* MacIntyre poses the question, Nietzsche or Aristotle?[34] MacIntyre has, in a sense, never ceased to ask this question, even if he has rephrased it. Nor has he ceased to suggest that Nietzsche's position is inherently flawed. Although he says that it is not yet "due time" to declare Aristotle (as incorporated into Aquinas) the victor, he does suggest that Nietzsche and his heirs (principally Foucault) face seemingly insurmountable problems.[35]

The evolution of MacIntyre's relation to Nietzsche is interesting in its own right, but here it suffices to note that Nietzsche is an incessant presence in MacIntyre's thought. And MacIntyre's response to this presence is illuminating. MacIntyre's philosophy is every bit as much a response to Nietzsche as it is a critique of liberalism, and he responds by first building a distance between himself and Nietzsche and then topping this distance with ramparts behind which he can withstand a Nietzschean siege. It is as if dialectical reason were a castle upon a hill, the world "as such" a vast open field sloping down from the castle to the edge of a forest, and Nietzsche the chaotic outlaw lurking behind the trees and beyond the reach of the castle's archers. MacIntyre stands on the castle wall, safe in the distance, and throws taunts to the forest's edge: "Stay in the forest," he yells, "and you are no threat to me. Emerge from the forest and you will be caught by the arrows of reason. Either way, I am safe in my castle." In this way, MacIntyre acknowledges that, in the wake of liberalism, Nietzsche is his only rival and, in the same stroke, disposes of his rival as a serious threat.

To keep with the metaphor, Milbank makes the simple case that most of us no longer live in castles. No dialectical guarantees stand, like castle walls, between the Christian and the nihilist. Whatever distance we create between ourselves and Nietzsche is a mirage that vanishes the instant we open our mouths to explain what we mean when we say "as such." Milbank's theological project is at once his response to that same incessant presence of Nietzsche and his way of dismantling MacIntyre's castle.

Unlike MacIntyre, Milbank does not think that Nietzschean nihilism borders upon incoherence but instead respects "the possibility of nihilism as an intellectual stance . . . which could even become a guide for practice" (217, 304). Milbank's recognition of the viability of nihilism yields a radically different view of the contemporary terrain, vis-à-vis MacIntyre. Milbank tears down MacIntyre's antique castle by disclosing that its foundations are modern after all, thus it does not provide that refuge of distance that comes with open hillsides and moats. Unlike MacIntyre, Milbank's response to nihilism is to collapse the distance between his theology and nihilist philosophy, not so much standing against Nietzsche as moving beyond him: "To pass critically beyond Nietzsche is to pass into the recognition of the necessity and yet ungrounded character of some sort of metanarrative, some privileged transcendent factor. . . . At this new critical juncture, which is postmodern, yet also post-Nietzschean, one recognizes that suppositions of transcendence are ungrounded and mutually incommensurable, although necessary for the slightest cultural decision" (2–3).

Milbank cannot oppose Nietzsche, as MacIntyre does, with "the discipline of truth" because he affirms the Nietzschean and postmodern insight that all "truths" are "fictions," that beneath the "real" is always myth. However, to pass critically beyond Nietzsche is to recognize that the final truth of nihilism is that even the violence inherent in the nihilist position has its origin in myth; even the will to power is but a fiction. According to Milbank, as we stand in the wake of liberalism and in the rubble of MacIntyre's failed attempt to restore antiquity, we face a choice between two myths. Both myths are postmodern metanarratives: They are "postmodern" because they recognize the contemporary challenge as that of "thinking difference"—indeed, they root the very possibility of thought itself in "difference"; they are "metanarratives" because at bottom both myths tell a story about the way the world "is"; both narratives presuppose an ontology. This connection between narrative and ontology is for Milbank "the postmodern moment," where Christian and nihilist alike meet at a new critical juncture and face "the challenge of thinking difference." "Such a challenge," says Milbank, ". . . arise[s] from a fundamental ontology which fixes its gaze on difference as the condition of possibility for thought and action" (260).[36]

Heretofore such an ontology was the possession of nihilism alone; and, so possessed, this ontology placed violence at the foundation of the world. Milbank argues that, as the sphere of the conflictual ordering of difference through power and violence, the secular was the invention of this ontology as it was embodied in pagan and heretical myths. But, he asks, cannot there be an alternative myth, an alternative ontology, "cannot there be an alternative invention of a social and linguistic process that is not the dominance of power (that is to say, power as violence)? Obviously, such a concept is itself problematic" (320). And yet, says Milbank, the Church—if theology is to have anything interesting to say—must be construed as precisely the invention of this alternative.

What Milbank hopes to show is that for Christian theology, no less than nihilism, "an ontological questioning is 'always already begun'"(388). Hence, the narration of "Christian difference" requires a "doctrinal-ontological effort to interpret that difference of setting which the [Christian] narrative has always presupposed" (388). In this way, "narrative and ontology reinforce each other" (430). Unlike the nihilist narratives, however, Christian narratives do not presuppose an ontology of violence but rather an "ontological God . . . who is, who includes difference," and who "must be known both as the speaking of created difference, and as the inexhaustible plenitude of otherness." This God who is difference, "and yet is unified, . . . speaks in the harmonious happening of Being" and provides the nonviolent "ontological background" to the Christian narratives (430).

At stake in this battle of ontologies is an alternative to the narrative of power: Where the aesthetic and the ethical are arbitrary, "then, indeed, only power rules. . . . If, however, the ethical and the aesthetic are ontologically objective realities, then there is an alternative to the narrative of power" (275). However, as the connection between narrative and ontology suggests, the narrative of power, which is the more prominent narrative of our time, can be opposed only "at the level of its ontological assumptions" (261).

Charity and Forgiveness

At the root of Milbank's ontological assumptions lie the notions of charity, sin, and forgiveness. As we have seen, for Milbank the Christian God is an analogical/ontological God who as Being is the "infinity of differences" and as "a power within Being" is "the God who differentiates." We can now say further that the existence of these differences is the work of charity: "charity is originally the gratuitous, creative positing of difference, and the offering to others of the space of freedom, which is existence" (416). Hence charity, as "the infinite serial emanation" of difference, becomes the defining term of ontology (416). Insofar as the emanation of difference flows without interruption, the world is the product of a loving God who speaks both created difference and the harmonious happening of difference. If, on the other hand, the emanation of difference is interrupted or diverted, then sin, not charity, is at work:

> There is a way of acting that inhibits the flow [of the serial emanation of difference], which prevents the infinitely more being done in the future. This is the failure to 'refer' our desire to God [who is 'the infinity of differences']. . . . To 'refer' things to the infinite is to arrange them in their proper place in a sequence, and hence 'privation' implies not just inhibition of the flow, but also a false, ugly, misdirection of the flow. Although evil is negative, it can be 'seen' in an ugly misarrangement. All the same, nothing is positively wrong here, for every scene can be adjusted by rearrangement, omission, and recontextualization. (430–431)

Were this not a fallen world, then sin would never interrupt the work of a charitable God; misdirected desire would never inhibit or divert the flow of difference; and God's first speech—that of the proliferation of difference—would resonate as the unceasing harmony of some grand ontological symphony, as it does when God speaks from the whirlwind in the

Book of Job and describes the wonder of a creation that contains not only the mountain goat and the wild ox but also the "monsters" Behemoth and Leviathan, which in their wildness somehow still coexist with the rest of creation.[37] "Nothing that properly is, by nature, resists other natures" (410). Hence ontology, by definition, reflects "a peaceful order that is a pure consensus" (410). But this *is* a fallen world: We live amidst conflict and violence; and ugliness abounds. Even without an ontological purchase these facts tend to obscure that original, creative positing of difference that is existence. If the world only "is" as love and harmony, then how does one exist in a world at war? How does one exist amongst all this nonexistent, yet visible, horror?

The answer comes as forgiveness. Forgiveness is charity after charity has passed through sin. There is a way to act that inhibits and diverts the flow of charity into an ugly misarrangement of violence; this way is called sin. But there is also "a way to act in a violent world" that unstops and redirects the flow, "and this way is called the forgiveness of sins" (411). Christianity is "a sphere for the operation of charity" (97–98), which means, in a world of violence, for the operation of forgiveness.

In the beginning, God spoke the world as created difference. These differences were harmonized through the analogical mediation of love. In fact, only the work of charity is capable of joining differences into a series of beings called Being. Before this synthesis "is" nothing. Hence, "the meaning of the series itself is love. . . . There are only the mediating links," only the incorporeal phantasms of meaning (215). When sin broke these links and threatened the series, God spoke a second time: This time "God speaks in the world in order to redeem it" (422). Charity becomes forgiveness; the God of creation becomes the God of redemption; "God" can now mean only "Trinity."[38]

> If what holds the monads and the chain in being is love, then the love expressed here must be perfect [which is to say reciprocal], the world must offer itself back to the Father, on the pain of ceasing to be the World. . . . Before the fall, humanity might have collectively made this perfect return. But after the fall, all human action is impaired by sin, and therefore if God's action is not to be denied and the world to collapse, there must somewhere be a perfect return still made. (216)

"On the pain of ceasing to be the World," the world needs the Son, who restores the love that sustains the link between God and the world. Of course, for Christians the order of knowledge here is important. Christians know of the ontological God who sustains the world in love only because they first know of the Son who defined love on the cross. Only in the early evening shadows of Golgotha "does one construe reality in terms of the need for the perfect offering of love" (217). We know the love of the Father only "with and through" the love of the Son, and we can know of this love only "because we can be incorporated into the community which he founded, and the response of this community to Christ is made possible by the response of the divine Spirit to the divine Son, from whom it receives the love that flows between Son and Father" (387).[39]

In moments of conflict, when surges of resistance obscure the work of love, when the world teeters on the edge of collapse, and when love has met with sin, then charity is refracted through the cross and becomes forgiveness. The flow of charity is a reservoir that buoys the world into existence; existence is threatened when charity is drained and diverted through the channel of sin. Jesus redirects this misdirected channel back to the Father, renews the circulation of charity, conceived of now as forgiveness, and saves the world. The cross not only points the way to a world beyond argument, where absolute consensus reigns, but also allows the world to continue to exist. Salvation is "the restoration of being," which is to say, of charity, through the practice of forgiveness, which is to say, after the cross, through the Church (402).

This Augustinian account of the Trinity provides a nice summary of Milbank's theology, with its stress upon an ontology of nonviolence, which stands as an alternative to the ontology of violence characteristic of nihilism. It remains to be asked, however, whether or not Milbank's ontology—or more importantly, his strong distinction between his own theological speculation and the nihilist narrative—is convincing. As it happens, Milbank's text contains contradictions that raise questions about this distinction between Christianity and nihilism; and these questions in turn raise further questions not simply about nihilism but about tragedy and apocalypse. These questions are the beginning of a critique of both Milbank's account of nihilism and his own theological speculation. Let me turn now to this critique, beginning with questions about Milbank's ontology.

The Logos Crucified

What can we make of the notion of an evil that we can see and yet that has no positive ontological purchase? The image conveyed here is that of a substantively good ontological world that, in its density, is immune from surface disturbances of evil. Evil may scratch and scar the surface of the world, but it is incapable of reaching into Being itself and altering anything there, and always the power of Being can burst forth and heal whatever deed evil has done. And yet, as we have seen, Milbank's own account of the world does not allow for this image of surface and depth.

Recall that the world happens to us already as meaning, and Milbank does not construe "meaning" only as human intention. The world "is" only with and through the incorporeal phantasms of meaning that course the surface. If we can see evil, if the world happens to us as conflict and violence, then this happening holds no less of a purchase on our being than the purchase of good. We cannot draw back into some depth and allow evil to pass us over. We can, of course, do the work of an incorporeal transformation and perhaps speak the world into a different arrangement, into a different surface presentation, but not always and never unfailingly. And where we fail, we reside, perforce, in an ugly and evil arrangement that defines, for the moment at least, our being. To speculate that conflict has no ontological purchase, although it may make for neat distinctions, does not allow us to account for the extent to which conflict captures and determines us. Milbank, of course, is simply reciting Augustine's account of the origins of evil; and it is, therefore, worth looking at a thoughtful critique of this Augustinian theodicy. Fredrick Bauerschmidt, I think, puts it well:

> The wound of violence is characterized by presence not absence. It is the nail which pierces the flesh and fills it with its own presence. . . . Too often we think of evil exclusively as *privatio boni*, an absence of good, as non-being. A theodicy which seeks to understand evil exclusively in terms of an absence of good fails to do justice to the character of evil. . . . [W]e are left without symbols or concepts to articulate the way in which evil seems to grasp hold of our lives in an active way.[40]

In Milbank's idiom, we might say a theology that accounts for evil exclusively as absence fails to work speculation back into the first-order level of narrative and devotion. Remember that Milbank, when speaking of the doctrine of the incarnation, says of theological speculation that its ungrounded and excessive nature is justified only when such speculations return to the first-order level of narrative and devotion, only, that is, when they enhance Christian practice. To deny evil "the hard, unyielding presence of the nail, the knife, the bullet" that "inflicts the wound of violence" is to underestimate the meaning of the crucifixion.[41] Granted, the rending of the veil of the temple, the centurion's proclamation that Jesus was the Son of God, and the words of the angel at the tomb—"you seek Jesus who was crucified. He is not here; for he has risen"—each of these events rearrange the meaning of the crucifixion: Evil did not win at Golgotha. Still from the first nail until the third day, incapable themselves of effecting an incorporeal transformation, the followers of Jesus were caught in a web of events that, as an ugly arrangement of surface presentations, gripped their very beings.

Milbank's mistake finally, I think, is to stress the incarnation of the logos as the decisive moment and not to stress even more that the logos incarnate passed through the cross. Bauerschmidt distinguishes wounds of violence from wounds of love: Wounds of violence are a presence that obliterates the other, the sorts of wounds made by bombs and bullets. The wound of love is an absence, "a clearing amid the violence of presence," a clearing that "struggles to stay open so that life might flow out of it." Milbank defines being as the nonviolent flow of an incarnate logos, when in fact Being, since the cross, flows from the wounds of Christ, from an incarnate but *crucified* logos.

An incarnate but uncrucified logos all too easily flows as pure presence. Our participation in the incarnation alone suggests that we always have the power, as Milbank all too often says, to arrange and rearrange the flow of being into a nonviolent one. In fact, though, in between the cross and the eschaton, we participate in a slain logos that is always caught in violence and that does not provide us with the sort of transformative powers Milbank speaks of. Jesus' life was nonviolent, but his death was not, and as Milbank does note, it is his death too that we have to imitate. Participation in a crucified logos cannot be what Milbank makes of it. The decisive moment is not that with the incarnation of the Word Christians learn to speak of nonviolence but rather that with the crucifixion Christians learn to identify the violence which, on this side of the eschaton, now resides with the logos.

The fact that an "alien moment" of violence, like a centurion's sword, is part and parcel of a crucified logos throws into question the persuasive power of Milbank's attempt to unthink the necessity of violence. As we will see, even Milbank seems to sense as much when, in the climactic moments of his story, he makes concessions to at least a certain necessity that violence carries in our world. Before I expand upon this point, however, I want to first begin the second aspect of what amounts to a twofold critique of Milbank. For Milbank's project is thrown into question not only because of its inability to offer a persuasive account of nonviolence but also because he offers a less than convincing portrayal of nihilism as somehow fixated upon and bound to violence. The possibility that nihilism is not simply about violence throws Milbank's narrative further off balance. That what Milbank calls nihilism is not simply about violence becomes apparent with a closer look at Milbank's misreading of Gilles Deleuze.[42]

Misreading Deleuze

"As Gilles Deleuze has stressed," notes Milbank, "the will to power . . . is the pure affirmation of difference"; and "for a Nietzschean philosophy, difference is defined as oppositional difference, a difference which enters the common cultural space to compete, displace or expel. Yet if the objective effect of affirmative difference is aggression and enmity . . . then there is a transcendental assumption of a negative relation persisting between all differences" (289). But if this is so, then what are we to make of these words from Deleuze?

> Heretofore it was only a question of knowing how a particular thing can decompose other things . . . or, on the contrary, how it risks being decomposed by other things. But now it is a question of knowing whether relations (and which ones?) can compound directly to form a new, more 'extensive' relation. . . . It is no longer a matter of utilizations and captures, but of sociabilities and communities. How do individuals enter into composition with one another in order to form a higher individual, ad infinitum? How can a being take another being into its world, but while preserving or respecting the other's own relations and world? . . . Now we are concerned not with a relation of point to counterpoint . . . but with a symphony of Nature, the composition of a world that is increasingly wide and intense.[43]

Obviously, Deleuze has not made, as Milbank suggests, a transcendental assumption about the negative relation existing between all differences. Milbank's misreading of Deleuze is particularly interesting because of all the so-called nihilists, Deleuze is the one who clearly has had the deepest influence on him. Milbank relies so heavily on Deleuzian metaphors and notions that the reader familiar with Deleuze will be able to mark his entrance into the text, even, and especially, when Milbank does not. In fact, Milbank's text ends with an allusion to Deleuze: "And the absolute Christian vision of ontological peace now provides the only alternative to a nihilistic outlook. Even today, in the midst of the self-torturing circle of secular reason, there can open to view again a series with which it is in no continuity: the emanation of harmonious difference, the exodus of new generations, the path of peaceful flight . . . (434; the ellipsis is Milbank's). The image "path of flight" belongs to Deleuze. No doubt, the qualification "peaceful" is to drive home as the text ends the opposition between Christianity and nihilism, the implication being that Deleuzian "flight" is violent. But is it? Or rather is there a subtlety here that disrupts Milbank's account of nihilism?

Consider Milbank's account of charity and sin in the light of the following distinction Deleuze makes between the "connection" and "conjugation" of "flows":

> We must introduce a distinction between the two notions of *connection* and *conjugation* of flows. 'Connection' indicates the way in which decoded and deterritorialized flows boost one another, accelerate their shared escape, and augment the stoke of their quanta; the 'conjugation' of these same flows, on the other hand, indicates their relative stoppage, like a point of accumulation that plugs or seals the lines of flight.[44]

Milbank's appropriation of Deleuze here is obvious: The unrestricted flow of charity is akin to what Deleuze calls "the plane of consistency" and involves the proper "connection" of flows, so that difference proliferates without interruption. Once stoppage occurs (and for Deleuze it has always already occurred, as it has for Milbank with the ineliminable presence of sin), once evil has inhibited, captured, and "conjugated" the flow into an ugly misarrangement, then the task is to seek the paths of escape, routes of exodus, lines of flight, through which to reroute, reconnect, reinstitute the flow as charity. Having already suggested mistakenly that Deleuze conceives of differences only as oppositional, Milbank apparently misunderstands Deleuze here as well. As the distinction between "conjugation" and "connection" implies, Deleuze is not uninterested in the harmonious flow of difference. Milbank's mistake, once again, is to interpret Deleuzian flight as violence, when in fact Deleuze, too, is interested in peaceful flight, while recognizing, like Milbank, the risks along the way.

Lines of flight, says Deleuze, "always risk abandoning their creative potential and turning into a line of death, being turned into a line of destruction pure and simple (fascism)."[15] The qualification "pure and simple" is important. According to Deleuze lines of flight destroy, certainly, but to read this destruction as violent and fascist (as Milbank does) is a mistake. Lines of flight unstop, rearrange, and destroy "ugly" conjugations. But one need not conclude that this destruction is violent, any more than Milbank's rearrangement of evil is violent. Violence, and of the worst sort, is always the risk where flight is concerned, always a danger according to which all others pale by comparison. Milbank almost acknowledges this when he says of the task of rearranging the flow that "finding the right perspective on the infinite is a matter . . . of being open to the *risks* of new and unexpected beauty" (431, emphasis added). Milbank says that aesthetic declarations of "new and unexpected beauty" incorporeally transform dissonance into harmony. But nothing guarantees that flight, as the manipulation of flows, will result in the desired connections. What Milbank knows but does not say here is that the risk is equally that of new and unexpected ugliness—and always the danger is present that this ugliness, as the sheer destruction of fascism, will obliterate all arrangements. Fascism is the risk of all flight, even, and perhaps especially, peaceful flight. But if fascism exists as a risk within Milbank's theological speculation, and if peaceful flight is put forth as a possibility within Deleuze's narrative, then the opposition between Christianity and nihilism cannot be what Milbank makes of it.

Indeed, Deleuze, with both his notion of "symphony" and his account of the play between "connection" and "conjugation," disrupts Milbank's narrative. It seems little is left of the "celebratory" nihilism that Milbank posits as his enemy: The series that knows only violence does not exist nor does, once the "necessity" of violence is admitted, the series that knows only peace. We arrive, then, at what Milbank himself refers to as a moment of "undecidability," a moment I can describe by returning to Milbank's notion of the analogical code.

Baroque Risks of Harmony and the Moment of Undecidability

You will recall that it is the analogical ordering of differences that allows the Christian to avoid nihilism's arbitrary and conflictual alternative. The ontological God who speaks "created difference" as "harmonious happening" is the God who grounds this analogical character of the Christian coding of the world; in fact, this God is "but simply the infinite realization of this quality in all the diversity and unity of its actual/possible instances" (304). In other words, God is the "infinite capacity for analogizing," and our participation in both God's Being and God's creativity is a matter of probing this capacity by ceaselessly drawing particular analogies, showing how differences belong together in "a certain sort of convergence, a certain commonality" (304). Note, however, that this "belonging together is only a 'kind of' likeness; in the notion of analogy, the meaning of alike is itself stretched almost to the breaking point" (304).

Milbank compares the harmony that results from this stretching of likeness through analogy to baroque music, where

> the individual lines become increasingly distinct and individually ornamented: there is an increasing 'delay' of resolutions, and an increasing generation of new developments out of temporary resolutions. The possibility of consonance is stretched to the limits, and yet the path of dissonance is not embarked upon. To say (with Deleuze) that dissonance and atonality are 'held back' or 'not arrived at', would be a mistake of the same order as claiming that nihilism is evidently true in its disclosure of the impossibility of truth. Instead, one should say, it is always possible to place dissonance back in 'Baroque suspense'; at every turn of a phrase, new, unexpected harmony may still arrive. Between the nihilistic promotion of dissonance, of differences that clash or only accord through conflict, and the Baroque risk of a harmony stretched to the limits—the openness to musical grace—there remains an undecidability. (429)[46]

Here Milbank confesses in some detail, it seems to me, the problematic nature of his theological enterprise, which before he mentioned only in passing. The problem is twofold: First, when you live in a world where "the Baroque risk of harmony is stretched to the limit," you have no way of distinguishing for sure, from moment to moment, dissonance from harmony—thus the "suspense." You have no guarantee that harmony will in fact arrive, that you have not just embarked upon a path of dissonance from which you may not return. Second, we do not always possess the power that will allow us to place dissonance in the baroque suspense that resolves into harmony. It is not always possible to rearrange ugly misarrangements.[47]

Milbank's entire narrative happens in this moment of undecidability, which is one of the reasons that his narrative is so valuable to my account not only of nihilism but also of tragedy and apocalypse. The moment of undecidability into which Milbank delivers us is, I think, not unlike the moment in which Vladimir and Estragon wait for Godot, and as Estragon reminds us, in this moment, what Milbank refers to as the postmodern moment, "nothing is certain."

Nothing is certain, even less so, now that we have arrived at the end of a long excursion into the complexities of Milbank's narrative both about nihilism and a distinctive Christian response to the nihilist narrative. But let me at least attempt to be clear about the nature of this uncertainty, which is even more complex than I have indicated so far. For not only does Milbank's undecidability throw into question his account of nihilism—and hence his theological project—but in the space of this question emerges the further question of whether both the nihilist and Christian narratives, as Milbank understands them, are not, in the last analysis, "tragic" depictions of the world. In other words, both Milbank's Augustinian and apocalyptic casting of the Christian narrative and his depiction of nihilism seem in the end to come together, blur, and emerge as tragedy.[48] Let me explain.

The fact that Milbank invokes the language of tragedy at crucial moments in his final chapter, when speaking both of life "within" the Church and, more generally, of life in a violent world, may seem to be nothing more than a matter of semantics.[49] But this slip into the language of tragedy is more than a simple matter of a perhaps arbitrary choice of words, since Milbank uses this language to gain descriptive power when speaking of the issues that are the most central to his narrative. For example, after arguing in an apocalyptic vein that Jesus and the Church have interrupted, and thereby reinterpreted, history, Milbank goes on to say that "one should recognize that this interruption has tragically failed. . . . Insofar as the Church has failed, and has even become a hellish anti-Church it has confined Christianity, like everything else, within the cycle of the ceaseless exhaustion and return to violence" (432–433).

In part what we see in this comment is an admirable confession, much needed within the Church, of the extent to which Christianity itself is responsible—by way not only of its failure to be a paradisal community but also of its success in coming to the aid of imperialism—for the violence of our world, from Cortez to Auschwitz to Sarajevo. But the designation of this violence as "tragic" leads Milbank beyond confession to more sweeping conclusions:

> The Church, to be the Church, must seek to extend the sphere of socially aesthetic harmony—'within' the state where this is possible; but of a state com-

> mitted by its very nature only to the formal goals of *dominium*, little is to be hoped. A measure of resignation to the necessity of this *dominium* can also not be avoided. But with, and beyond Augustine, we should recognize the tragic character of this resignation: violence delivers no dialectical benefits, of itself it encourages only further violence, and it can only be 'beneficial' when the good motives of those resorting to it are recognized and recuperated by a defaulter coming to his senses. The positive content of the benefit flows only in the quite different series of purely positive acts, a series that knows only conviviality, and seeks to escape, forever, all tragic profundity. (422)

Placed in the overall context of Milbank's narrative, which is meant to persuade us that violence does not carry the power of necessity, this resignation to just such a necessary violence is odd, even if we grant a distinction between an ontological and a historical necessity. Even more glaring in its oddity, though, is the gesture here concerning how we should think about violence within the Church.

Even granting a level of resignation to the violence of the world, the Church at least remains a place, as Milbank notes, where we can seek "to escape, forever," the "tragic profundity" that would be our lot if the Church did not exist. Why Milbank finds the meaning and profundity of violence in tragedy remains a serious question; but at least by placing the Church in opposition to this tragic profundity, Milbank seems to be making the apocalyptic point that the Church stands as a peaceful alternative to a world of violence. However, as soon as Milbank proposes the possibility of an escape from tragic profundity, he cuts us off at the pass, when he admits that even within the Church the need exists "for some measures of coercion":

> Such coercive action remains in itself dangerous, as it risks promoting resentment, but this risk is offset by the possibility that the recipient can later come to understand and retrospectively consent to the means taken. Such action may not be 'peaceable', yet can still be 'redeemed' by retrospective acceptance, and so contribute to the final goal of peace. And Christianity has traditionally seen peace as a comprehensive eschatological goal, and *not* as the name of a virtue. (418)[50]

After offering this Augustinian account of coercion within the church, Milbank takes a step beyond Augustine:

> In any coercion, however mild and benignly motivated, there is still present a moment of 'pure' violence, externally and arbitrarily related to the end one has in mind. . . . Thus though a punishment may be subordinate to essentially persuasive purposes which are at variance with worldly *dominium*, Augustine fails to see that the duration of punishment has to be an interval of such *dominium*, for the lesson *immediately* and intrinsically taught must be the power of one over another, and it is always possible that the victim will

> learn only this lesson, and build up a resentment which prevents him from seeing what the punishment was really trying to point out. Punishment is always a tragic risk. (420)[51]

As Milbank understands, punishment is a risk not only because in some cases it may not be retrospectively redeemed but also because as a crossing over of *dominium* into *ecclesia* it is always a possibility, as critics of Augustine have noted, that the "precariously upheld tragic distinction of 'state' from Church [*dominium* from *ecclesia*] will simply disappear" (419). For all that, Milbank still concludes that such risks are "tragically necessary" (421), which should force us to wonder whether or not any meaningful line between tragic profundity and any other possibility has been erased from Milbank's text.

The proof, it seems to me, that this line has been at least put in jeopardy arrives when Milbank says that even when retrospective consent redeems an act of coercion, it is still not the case that we can call such coercion "peaceable." Almost as if to apologize for this admission, Milbank then notes that "Christianity has traditionally seen peace as the comprehensive eschatological goal, and *not* as the name of a virtue." This assertion seems to contradict Milbank's own claim that what makes the Church the Church is an alternative, concrete, and peaceable social practice (388). In any event, to oppose peaceableness as a virtue to peaceableness as an eschatological goal is to depart from an apocalyptic eschatology and an apocalyptic politics.

It may be wrong to say that with his recourse to the notion of tragic profundity, Milbank ceases altogether to be an apocalyptic thinker. But it is certainly right to note that by invoking the descriptive power of tragedy in order to come to terms with the profound character of violence, Milbank in some sense falters and, as he does so, returns us to the stage in Sarajevo, as Estragon and Vladimir and the Sarajevans, surrounded now by even more corpses, await a decision on the character of the universe, which is why Milbank's recourse to the language of tragedy is not simply a matter of semantics.

At stake in Milbank's use of the language of tragedy at the expense of his otherwise apocalyptic project is the power of two competing descriptive possibilities. And behind or within, or in any case dependent upon, these descriptions stand the day-to-day lives of suffering human beings. Not that a decision for or against tragedy or for or against apocalypse as the most apt description of events will somehow change the course of the war in the Balkans. Serbia will march on. But for those who stand in the path of the Serbs, as well as for those of us who watch the slow march of genocide and the even slower response of the world, everything in the end depends upon what they, and we, can make of the suffering that seems only to escalate day by day.[52] For before Serbia, there was El Salvador; and before El Salvador, Cambodia; and before Cambodia, Algeria; and before Algeria, Poland; and before Poland, the Americas; and before that—well, as Hegel had it, before that was "the slaughterbench of history," all the way back to the Athenians, who, shortly before they slaughtered and enslaved the Melians in the fifth century B.C., said to the inhabitants of Melos, "Nature always compels gods (we believe) and men (we are certain) to rule over anyone they can control. We did not make this law, and we were not the first to follow it; but we will take it as we found it and leave it to posterity forever."[53]

If, as Socrates would have it, the most important thing is not life but the good life, then how we live—and how we die—in the face of suffering is the only equation that matters. And it makes a difference, then, whether the world is a tragic place, condemned forever to the legacy of the Athenians, or an apocalyptic place—not condemned but loved by the God on the cross. If the violence of *dominium* is present within the Church, if peace is the name of some possible future but not a concrete practice here and now, if Godot, in other words, never arrives, or if he does, arrives too late, after they find the rope, then tragedy indeed wins the day.

Without the more detailed account of apocalyptic thought that I will offer in Chapters Seven and Eight, it is too soon to make a definitive statement about the character of Milbank's work. What matters at this point is that we see clearly how Milbank simply recasts at a different level the uncertainty, the undecidability, that plagues Vladimir and Estragon.

Does Godot exist? Will Godot arrive? Is it really but a short burst of light between the womb and the grave? What is our fate? Can we make a life of waiting for Godot? What would it mean to make a life of *not* waiting for Godot? What would our suffering mean then? As it stands, Milbank's work delivers us into a world of both tragedy and apocalypse. And for now, like Vladimir and Estragon, we will simply have to wait and see what such a world means—if such a world is even possible. However, while we wait, we have to attend to one other matter. For Milbank's moment of undecidability concerns not only, and perhaps not even primarily, tragedy and apocalypse but rather nihilism and Christianity. In the final analysis, the difference between nihilism and Christianity remains an open question in Milbank's text—in spite of his rhetoric to the contrary.

Adjusting Milbank's Christology

Recall that Milbank says at the beginning of *Theology and Social Theory* that if his narrative is persuasive it will be because of a "persuasion intrinsic to the Christian *logos* itself." This is, of course, the logos incarnate, the pivot of all history, the event that determines the meaning of all other events. We now know, however, that this logos is not simply the logos incarnate but also the logos crucified. The problem that accompanies this knowledge is that the image of a crucified logos makes the notion of nonviolence, so central to Milbank's narrative, much more difficult to understand. Or put another way, the image of the logos crucified seems naturally conducive to the language of tragedy and somewhat resistant to the language of apocalypse—insofar as "apocalypse" indicates not only a way of reading history but a way of reading history whereby the operative phrase is "victory for the victims." When faced with the image of a crucified logos we are inclined to side with the disciples on the way to Emmaus, who saw in the crucifixion only the sign of defeat. Once the emphasis is placed on the crucifixion,[54] Milbank's opposition between nonviolence and violence is not particularly persuasive. In fact, both the nihilist and the Christian are caught up in the naming of violence; neither, in this fallen world, escapes completely the violence they try to name. However, because of the example of both Jesus' life and death, the Christian has learned a particular way to name violence. The promise of Christian nonviolence is inseparable from this naming.

Put this way, the persuasion intrinsic to the Christian logos is not simply an offer of nonviolent practice, for, as the term "nonviolence" itself suggests, no such simplicity exists. Whatever nonviolence is, it is not separable from an account of violence. Even more, the account of violence determines the shape of nonviolence. Hence the seduction of the Christian logos is, first and foremost, its account of violence: not the logos but the logos crucified.

The danger of an uncrucified logos, to borrow words again from Fredrick Bauerschmidt, is that "without the death on the Cross of the Logos, one cannot distinguish the wound of love from the wound of violence."[55] Because the incarnation reaches a crescendo with the crucifixion, Christians learn how to name, but not escape, violence. The crucifixion is the definitive example of both love and sin, nonviolence and violence, and Christians are forever nailed to the center of the cross where love and sin intersect. This intersection of violence and nonviolence, and not the nonviolence of an original charity, composes the seduction intrinsic to the Christian logos. Hence persuasion is not harbored in a Word that promises the charitable rearrangement of every scene but rather comes in the form of a promise to grant us the words with which to name the violence that pierces our love.

At stake in the distinction between logos and logos crucified, between charity and forgiveness, an original Word and wounded words, is the seductive nature of an image of the power of the God in which we participate. Milbank tends to portray the creative potential of our participation as limitless: "every scene can be rearranged"—thus the image of our participation in an all-powerful, unstoppable, unscathed God. This is the image of the incarnate God, we might say with Bauerschmidt, we have all had since childhood: "robed in white, hair hanging loosely upon his shoulders, face unlined, hands tender. The very confidence and power of God."[56] However, Bauerschmidt speaks of another image that evokes the very confidence and power of God: ". . . his robe is purple, not white, and it is stained with his own blood. His face is darkened by bruises, and on his head is a crown of thorns," and in his side—a "wound, externally fresh; the blood glistens."[57] Milbank's image of God is all too often the former: God incarnate; the Word become flesh; the same Word that said at the 'beginning,' "Let there be . . ." and "there was." The God whose power speaks of limitless arrangements and rearrangements, of an original and transparent flow of charity. It is perhaps this image of God that leaves Milbank muttering about tragedy in the end, when such limitless rearrangement falls short.

But what of the second image of God crucified? Is not this image more persuasive, which is to say a speculation more apt to be infused into the first-order level of narrative and devotion, an image perhaps more apt to make sense in Sarajevo? Is it perhaps this image that makes apocalyptic thought possible and that prevents us from invoking the language of tragedy when we discover that we have to make concessions to violence after all? The transparent flow of an original charity, transformed by the thrust of a spear, now has the opacity of blood. And is not this the flow in which we participate? Is not this flow the path of peaceful flight? Are not our words, as moments in the crucified logos, themselves wounded words, drops of blood, flowing from the wound? And as blood, do they not signal, equally, the possibility of life and of death, nonviolence and violence?

As moments in the crucified logos, our words are forever implicated in violence. Tracing them to their origin we find both the heart of Jesus and the centurion's sword. Violence cohabits the logos.[58] Jesus interrupts history. But history is vengeful. The Church as history's wound is itself born of a wound that history inflicts. The Church is born where spear and heart meet to form the flow of a wounded Word.

The challenge now is to discover whether or not such images as these carry with them descriptive power. Do they offer compelling accounts of the meaning of suffering? When put in this way, you should now see that we have come full circle and returned to the problem as Nietzsche described it at the end of the first chapter. What is at stake is the meaning of suffering; that meaning depends upon how we describe the world; and, for Nietzsche, when faced with this task of description, we have two choices: Dionysus or the Crucified.

You should now be able to see that Milbank recasts this choice as a choice between nihilism and Christianity, although in an odd way both nihilism and Christianity become "tragic" in Milbank's narrative, hence the final fuzziness of the boundaries between them. You should also be able at least to begin to see, in the wake both of Milbank's theological project and my critique of this project, what it might mean to view suffering through the lens of the Crucified. The task now is to consider the other side of the equation and to turn to both nihilism and Dionysus—which is also to say, to tragedy—as they exist not in Milbank's account of things but within the complexities of Nietzsche's own narrative.

4

Toward a Metaphysics of Tragedy: Justifying the World as Art

"It is only as an aesthetic phenomenon that existence and the world are eternally justified."[1] In spite of the fact that this declaration exists as a parenthetical comment in *The Birth of Tragedy,* it is, and rightly so, one of the most famous things Nietzsche wrote. To comprehend Nietzsche's understanding of Dionysus, tragedy, and the link between the one and the other is to understand what Nietzsche means when he says, in effect, that only as a work of art does the world have meaning. The task of this chapter is to work toward an understanding of Nietzsche's words to this effect and thereby to arrive at an understanding of his account of tragedy. This task will involve a close reading not only of Nietzsche's *Birth of Tragedy* but also of Euripides' *Bacchae* and, finally, of Norman Maclean's book *Young Men and Fire,* the tragic story of thirteen young men who were killed by a forest fire in a remote gulch in Montana in the summer of 1949.

Aesthetic Justification and Musical Dissonance

Nietzsche makes the parenthetical comment about the world as an aesthetic phenomenon in the middle of a discussion about the origins of art, and the declaration is framed most immediately in the following way:

> The entire comedy of art is neither performed for our betterment or education nor are we the true authors of this art world. On the contrary, we may assume that we are merely images and artistic projections for the true author, and that we have our highest dignity in our significance as works of art—for it is only as an *aesthetic phenomenon* that existence and the world are eternally *justified*—while of course our consciousness of our own significance hardly differs from that which the soldiers painted on the canvas have of the battle represented on it.[2]

Here we have both a remarkable notion and an equally remarkable image. According to Nietzsche, human beings attain their highest dignity as works of art. What is remarkable here is not simply Nietzsche's aesthetic view of the world but his sense that only in such a world do human beings have dignity. In other words, Nietzsche's declaration is profoundly moral, even if his equation of aesthetics and ethics violates our modern sensibilities.

The image of the soldiers in the painting is equally remarkable. Only as an aesthetic phenomenon is the world justified and do humans thereby attain dignity. Most of the time, however, we are not conscious of either ourselves or the world as works of art. And it follows that most of the time the world is not justified and we have no dignity. Like the soldiers in the painting with regard to the battle, we are not conscious of our own significance as art—as figures painted on the canvas of the world. Only the artist and the spectator, from the distance of their particular vantage, can see the relationship between the soldiers and the battle, can see, that is, the significance of the whole scene as it unfolds on the canvas. To be a figure on the canvas is to be but a few brush strokes whose significance is apparent only, in the first instance, to the artist who put them there. According to Nietzsche, to understand both the significance of the world and our own dignified presence in that world is in some way to align ourselves with the "primordial artist" who paints us in scene after scene. Only by way of such an alignment will we be able to appreciate the beauty of our lives in a world of suffering.

The primordial artist is, of course, Dionysus. As Nietzsche puts it much later in *The Birth of Tragedy,* "the Dionysian is seen to be . . . the eternal and original artistic power that first calls the whole world of phenomena into existence."[3] To recognize the world as an aesthetic phenomenon and to align ourselves with the primordial artist is, then, to celebrate the power of Dionysus. Greek tragedy was precisely such a celebration; and the great tragedies, as Nietzsche understands them, therefore caused the audience to become conscious of their significance as art in a way the soldiers in the painting are not. The mechanisms through which tragic drama instills in the spectators a sense of their own aesthetic dignity are complex. After all, it is far from obvious that the act of watching other people suffer will lead us to a sense of our own dignity. Nietzsche himself poses the problem in this way: "how can the ugly and disharmonic, the content of tragic myth, stimulate aesthetic pleasure?"[4] Nietzsche then proceeds to answer his own question:

> It is precisely the tragic myth that has to convince us that even the ugly and disharmonic are part of the artistic game that the will in the eternal amplitude of its pleasure plays with itself. But this primordial phenomenon of Dionysian art is difficult to grasp, and there is only one direct way to make it intelligible and grasp it immediately: through the wonderful significance of *musical disso-*

> *nance.* Quite generally, only music, placed beside the world, can give us an idea of what is meant by the justification of the world as an aesthetic phenomenon. The joy aroused by tragic myth has the same origin as the joyous sensation of dissonance in music. The Dionysian, with its primordial joy experienced even in pain, is the common source of music and tragic myth.[5]

With this notion of "the wonderful significance of musical dissonance" in mind, it is worth pausing to remember that in his own attempt to justify the world as an aesthetic phenomenon, John Milbank also invokes the analogy of music; and, what's more, he does so just at the moment in which he admits the undecidability that exists between "the nihilistic promotion of dissonance" and the Christian "risk of harmony stretched to its limits." Although I discussed this aspect of Milbank's work in the last chapter, it will be fruitful, I think, to return to Milbank for a moment before continuing on with Nietzsche's account of tragedy.

You will recall that according to Milbank, nihilism is characterized by an ontology of violence and that this ontology is part and parcel of the view that all differences between particular things are finally arbitrary, since no overarching universals exist that in any way unify differences. Milbank's Christian alternative to nihilism, so construed, is to attempt to speak of the unity of all differences and thereby to argue that differences are not arbitrary. In a decidedly postmodern fashion, however, Milbank refuses to look toward an *essential* ordering of the world. Rather, Milbank argues that unity

> in this Christian outlook, ceases to be anything hypostatically real in contrast to difference, and becomes instead only the 'subjective' apprehension of a harmony displayed in the order of differences, a desire at work in their midst, although proceeding beyond them (as the Holy Spirit). . . . This entirely reinvents the idea of order. Order is now more purely an aesthetic relation of the different, and no longer primarily self-identity or resemblance.[6]

Milbank's notion of "aesthetic relation of the different" causes him to invoke first architecture and then music as examples of what he has in mind:

> In aesthetic terms, there is something 'Baroque' here. . . . In the perspective of infinitude, ornamentation overtakes what it embellishes. . . . Structural supports are consequently overrun by the designs they are supposed to contain, and massive architectural edifices appear merely 'suspended' from above, by aery, celestial scenes. This hierarchy is not an antique natural order, but nor is it a postmodern 'plateau' where all is 'indifferent'. Baroque hierarchy . . . is instead divine self-realization in finitude. . . . Here the analogy switches from architecture to music. . . . In Baroque music, the individual lines become increasingly distinct and individually ornamented; there is an increasing 'delay' of resolutions, and an increasing generation of new devel-

> opments out of temporary resolutions. The possibility of consonance is stretched to its limits, and yet the path of dissonance is not embarked upon. . . . Instead, one should say, it is always possible to place dissonance back in Baroque 'suspense'; at every turn of a phrase, new, unexpected harmony may still arrive. Between the nihilistic promotion of dissonance, of differences that clash or accord only through conflict, and the Baroque risk of harmony stretched to the limits—the openness to musical grace—there remains an undecidability.[7]

We visited some of these words in the last chapter. But with Nietzsche's recourse to musical dissonance in mind, it is worth revisiting them, since Milbank, too, places music next to the world in an attempt to talk about what it might mean to view the world as an aesthetic phenomenon.

According to Milbank, in baroque music the path of dissonance is never embarked upon. However, to say that the path of dissonance is never embarked upon is not to say, as Milbank himself implies, that dissonance plays no role in baroque music, or, to use an example a little closer to home—in jazz. Indeed, certain kinds of music might best be described as exercises in dissonance, but exercises whose goal is, in Milbank's words, to "place dissonance back in Baroque 'suspense'." In this sense, dissonance never becomes a path in its own right, since it is always placed within some more elaborate harmonic structure. Nonetheless, such music cannot be interpreted as harmony gone astray but rather as dissonance forever suspended.

Along these lines, consider what Wynton Marsalis, the great American jazz musician, says about the difference between classical music and jazz. Classical music is, he says, "harmony through harmony"; jazz is "harmony through conflict."[8] Note that Milbank does not use classical music as an example of his Christian aesthetics. Classical music would better serve as an example of that ordering of the world that depends on notions of self-identity and resemblance, an ordering that Milbank dismisses. The question that lurks in Milbank's appropriation of baroque music is whether we should say that in baroque music "consonance is stretched to its limits" or that, as in jazz, dissonance can always be placed back in "Baroque suspense." Milbank says *both* of these things, and in saying them both he arrives at the undecidability that haunts both his own characterization of the contest between nihilism and Christianity and, as we will see, my own rendering of this contest as that between tragedy and apocalypse.

There is, I think, a remarkable affinity between Nietzsche's declaration about "the wonderful significance of musical dissonance" and Milbank's notion of "the risk of a harmony stretched to its limits." For Milbank, only if harmony is stretched to its limits can the world accommodate the profusion of difference that is, finally, God's charity. The tragic risk of this stretch, however, lies in the ever present possibility that harmony may not, in fact, arrive, but instead a path of dissonance will be embarked upon. In *The Birth of Tragedy,* Nietzsche seems to be thinking about the same problem. He, too, is interested in the play between dissonance and harmony, between proliferating difference and the unity of all differences in some grand order. We have seen already that for Nietzsche this play between dissonance and harmony is the play of the world itself, insofar as the world is an aesthetic phenomenon. In *The Birth of Tragedy,* Nietzsche attempts to analyze this play not by speaking of dissonance and harmony, per se, but of Dionysus and Apollo.

Vultures Are No Reproach to the World

Dionysus, as we have seen, is the original and eternal artistic power that first calls the world into existence. After having been so called, the world requires for its continued existence another artistic power, the power of Apollo:

> It is only in the midst of this [Dionysian] world that a new transfiguring illusion becomes necessary in order to keep the animated world of individuation alive.
>
> If we could imagine dissonance become man—and what else is man?—this dissonance, to be able to live, would need a splendid illusion that would cover dissonance with a veil of beauty. This is the true artistic aim of Apollo in whose name we comprehend all those countless illusions of the beauty of mere appearance that at every moment make life worth living at all and prompt the desire to live in order to experience the next moment.[9]

Nietzsche notes that he borrows the terms "Apollo" and "Dionysus" from the ancient Greeks,

> who disclose to the discerning mind the profound mysteries of their view of art, not, to be sure, in concepts, but in the intensely clear figures of their gods. Through Apollo and Dionysus, the two art deities of the Greeks, we come to recognize that in the Greek world there existed a tremendous opposition, in origin and aims, between the Apollinian art of sculpture and the nonimagistic, Dionysian art of music.[10]

For Nietzsche this opposition between Apollo and Dionysus contains the secret not only to the Greek view of art but to the world itself, insofar as it can be justified only as art. Hence Apollo and Dionysus are not for Nietzsche simply the names of ancient Greek gods but instead designate the "artistic energies which burst forth from nature herself."[11]

Together the Apollinian and the Dionysian create the world. The Dionysian is the original primal energy that calls the world into existence, and then in the midst of this world the Apollinian surges forth "in order to keep the animated world of individuation alive." Indeed, for Nietzsche, Apollo stands first and foremost for the principle of individuation without which we would not experience the world as a plethora of different things. Without Apollo, we would be awash in the "intoxicated reality" of the Dionysian, we would never experience the world as world but, to risk borrowing a Kantian image, would be caught in the extra-experiential din of the chaotic manifold.

As the principle of individuation, Apollo is fittingly the god of sculpture, the god who forms the things of the world out of the formless reality of the Dionysian. Just as fittingly, Apollo is the god of light, the god who shines on things and makes them show up in our world. Apollo is also the god of dreams and, by extension, the god of mere appearances and illusion. Hence the world crafted from the intoxicated reality of the Dionysian by the "measured restraint" of the sculptor god is a world of mere appearance, and beneath the appearances lurks the abyss, which we can now designate not only as "pre-Homeric" but also as "Dionysian."

In Chapter Two, when discussing Nietzsche's account of nihilism, I relied on Nietzsche's short essay "Homer's Contest" to paint a picture both of the pre-Homeric abyss and of Homer's initial answer to the question of suffering—which, when placed in Achilles' mouth in the *Iliad,* is the question "What is a life of struggle and victory for?" Homer's poetic rendering of the question of suffering is itself, as Nietzsche sees it, also already an answer. In "Homer's Contest," Nietzsche puts it this way:

> But what lies *behind* the Homeric world? For *in* that world the extraordinary artistic precision, calm, and purity of the lines raise us above the mere contents: through an artistic deception the colors seem lighter, milder, warmer; and in this colorful warm light the men appear better and more sympathetic. But what do we behold when, no longer led and protected by the hand of Homer, we stride back into the pre-Homeric world? Only night and terror and an imagination accustomed to the horrible.[12]

The conceptual work that Nietzsche does in *The Birth of Tragedy* allows us to see more clearly exactly what separates Homer from the abyss. According to Nietzsche, Homer is a "monument" to the victory of the Apollinian artistic impulse at a particular stage in Greek culture. Prior to Homer, the Dionysian reigned supreme. In Greek myth, this age is depicted in the wars of the Titans. Thinking historically and not mythically, the age of the Titans is the age when armies ripped one another to shreds without yet questioning the meaning of that activity, as Achilles does in the *Iliad.* Put another way, we might say that before Homer transformed the Trojan War into a work of art, war in its raw state was but an indication of the character of life in the abyss.

As Nietzsche sees it, the ancient

> Greek knew and felt the terror and horror of existence. That he might endure this terror at all, he had to interpose between himself and life the radiant dream-birth of the Olympians. . . . It was in order to be able to live that the Greeks had to create these gods from the most profound need. Perhaps we may picture the process to ourselves somewhat as follows: out of the original Titanic divine order of terror, the Olympian divine order of joy gradually evolved through the Apollinian impulse toward beauty, just as roses burst from thorny bushes. How else could this people, so sensitive, so vehement in its desires, so singularly capable of *suffering,* have endured existence, if it had not been revealed to them in their gods, surrounded with a higher glory?[13]

The Greek gods, then, transfigure suffering so as to make it bearable. And as with gods, so with the Apollinian artistic impulse. For Nietzsche, it is the same impulse that calls both the gods and Homer into being. Both Homer and the gods make suffering not only bearable but beautiful. The great Homeric image that captures, I think, what Nietzsche has in mind lies in Book VII of *The Iliad,* when Hector challenges one of the Achaeans to single-handed combat, and the two armies pause on the field to prepare for this contest:

> [The Trojans] all sat down, and Agamemnon made the Achaean soldiers do the same. Athene and Apollo of the Silver Bow also sat down, in the form of vultures, on the tall oak sacred to the aegis-bearing Zeus. They enjoyed the sight of all these Trojan and Achaean warriors sitting there on the plain, rank upon rank, bristling with shields, helmets and spears, like the darkened surface of the sea when the West Wind begins to blow and ripples spread across it.[14]

Walter Kaufmann offers a priceless comment upon this scene from *The Iliad:*

> In a large part of the Western World today one sees no vultures; and death, disease, and old age are concealed. In Calcutta, vultures still sit in trees in the city, waiting for death in the streets; and sickness, suffering, and the disintegration of age assault the senses everywhere. But it is only in Homer that, while death is ever present to consciousness, the vultures in the tree are experienced as Athene and Apollo, delighting in the beautiful sight of a sea of shields, helmets, and spears. In this vision death has not lost its sting; neither has life lost its beauty. The very vultures are no reproach to the world.[15]

Kaufmann's comment reflects perfectly Nietzsche's understanding of Homer and the Apollinian artistic impulse. Homer's ability to turn vultures into gods and the gore of battle into beauty, and thereby to transfigure suffering, is his great accomplishment and represents the Apollinian triumph over the abyss. Nietzsche does not mean to disparage the accomplishment; however, he does want us to see that there is something "naive" and "illusory" here.

> Where we encounter the "naive" in art, we should recognize the highest effect of Apollinian culture—which always must first overthrow an empire of Titans and slay monsters, and which must have triumphed over an abysmal and terrifying view of the world and the keenest susceptibility to suffering through recourse to the most forceful and pleasurable illusions. . . . The Homeric "naivete" can be understood only as the complete victory of the Apollinian illusion . . . and as a monument of its victory, we have Homer, the naive artist.[16]

If it is true that the world can be justified only as an aesthetic phenomenon and if it is also true that the world is full of suffering, then it seems we can do nothing other than applaud Homer's artistic rendering of this world. For, in Nietzsche's own words, Homer "redeems" the world for us. And yet Nietzsche considers Homer's poetry to be naive and illusory; and these are not exactly words of praise. What purpose do they serve in Nietzsche's characterization of Homer? Put simply, they convey to us that neither *The Iliad* nor *The Odyssey* are tragedies and that Homer, as a monument to the triumph of the Apollinian artistic impulse, was not a tragic poet. Homer allowed the Greeks to exist in the presence of the abyss but only by shielding the abyss in a veil of illusory beauty. Tragedy, by contrast, and in spite of the fact that it retains an Apollinian moment, immerses us in the beauty of the abyss itself. This immersion is a thoroughly Dionysian exercise. What then is the Dionysian? We have seen that Nietzsche contrasts the Dionysian with the Apollinian—and this contrast is perhaps the place to begin to answer that question.

Dionysus, Apollo, and the Birth of Tragedy

If Apollo, as the sculptor god, represents the individuating power of a measured restraint that dams up becoming and maintains the being of individuals amidst the flux, then Dionysus represents the flux itself. The Dionysian is therefore the primordial unity of a world whose individuating differences have been washed away in the flood of an intoxicated reality. This reality itself is not free from suffering in Nietzsche's view, for he refers to it repeatedly as "eternally suffering and contradictory."[17] To experience the Dionysian is not, then, to escape suffering, but it is to experience a redemption or reconciliation that is somehow more "true" than the Apollinian redemption of Homer—more true because despite the beauty and moderation of Homeric redemption, the existence of the ancient Greek still "rested on a hidden substratum of suffering and of knowledge, revealed to him by the Dionysian."[18] Homeric redemption, says Nietzsche, "paled before an art that, in its intoxication, spoke the truth."[19] And the truth in question is not a truth that arrives by way of moderation and measured restraint but as excess. To the Greeks of the tragic age, "*excess*," says Nietzsche, "revealed itself as truth. Contradiction, the bliss born of pain, spoke out from the very heart of nature."[20]

If we were to ask how such pain spoke from out of the heart of nature, the answer, says Nietzsche, is to be found in the music of the Dionysian dithyramb. The Dionysian artist

> has identified himself with the primal unity, its pain and contradiction. Assuming that music has been correctly termed a repetition and a recast of the world, we may say that he produces the copy of this primal unity as music. . . . The plastic artist, like the epic poet who is related to him, is absorbed in the pure contemplation of images. The Dionysian musician is, without any images, himself pure primordial pain and its primordial re-echoing. . . . Language can never adequately render the cosmic symbolism of music, because music stands in symbolic relation to the primordial contradiction and primordial pain in the heart of the primal unity, and therefore symbolizes a sphere which is beyond and prior to all phenomena.[21]

This symbolic relationship between a particular kind of music and "the primordial contradiction and primordial pain in the heart of the primal unity" is the source of the redemptive, reconciling power of tragic drama, which Nietzsche refers to elsewhere as the power of "metaphysical comfort."[22] Indeed, the role of "the spirit of music" in tragic drama is that upon which Nietzsche rests his entire case for the birth of tragedy: Tragedy was born from the music of the Dionysian dithyramb. Put this way, Nietzsche's whole argument is simply an attempt to explain Aristotle's comment in his *Poetics* that tragic drama originated "with the authors of the dithyramb."[23] As Nietzsche puts it, the tradition "tells us quite unequivocally *that tragedy arose from the tragic chorus,* and was originally only chorus and nothing but chorus. Hence we consider it our duty to look into the heart of this tragic chorus as the real proto-drama."[24]

What Nietzsche finds when he looks into the heart of the tragic chorus is the satyr—the fictional creature from Greek mythology that, as the embodiment of both man and goat, gestures toward the boundary between culture and nature. "The satyr," says Nietzsche, "is the offspring of a longing for the primitive and the natural. . . . Nature, as yet unchanged by knowledge, with the bolts of culture still unbroken—that is what the Greek saw in the satyr."[25] The tragic chorus, as Nietzsche understands it, would have been dressed up as a group of satyrs. And Nietzsche imagines that this strange being beckoned to the Greeks from the edges of the abyss, recalling with its physical features the primal, natural, intoxicated energies of the Dionysian:

> The Greek man of culture felt himself nullified in the presence of the satyric chorus; and this is the most immediate effect of the Dionysian tragedy, that

> the state and society and, quite generally, the gulfs between man and man give way to an overwhelming feeling of unity leading back to the very heart of nature. The metaphysical comfort—with which, I am suggesting even now, every true tragedy leaves us—that life is at the bottom of things, despite all the changes of appearances, indestructible powerful and pleasurable—this comfort appears in incarnate clarity in the chorus of satyrs, a chorus of natural beings who live ineradicably, as it were, behind all civilization.[26]

The tragic chorus, with the suggestive power both of its music and its physical appearance as a group of singing and dancing goat-men, mimics the primal unity at the heart of the world. At this point, we must remind ourselves that the primal unity is a contradictory, suffering unity. Hence insofar as the tragic chorus draws us into the intoxicated reality of the Dionysian it also draws us into the depths of the abyss and the suffering that lives there. In this way, says Nietzsche, in some of his most famous words,

> the Dionysian man resembles Hamlet: both have once looked truly into the essence of things, they have *gained knowledge,* and nausea inhibits action. For their action could not change anything in the eternal nature of things; they feel it to be ridiculous or humiliating that they should be asked to set right a world that is out of joint. Knowledge kills action; action requires the veils of illusion: that is the doctrine of Hamlet, not that cheap wisdom of Jack the Dreamer who reflects too much and, as it were, from an excess of possibilities does not get around to action. Not reflection, no—true knowledge, an insight into the horrible truth, outweighs any motive for action, both in Hamlet and in the Dionysian man. . . . Conscious of the truth he has once seen, man now sees everywhere only the horror or absurdity of existence.[27]

At this point, says Nietzsche, which is precisely that point at which two roads diverge in a wood, just west of the abyss, the danger to the human will is severe. For little prevents the will from ceasing to will at all, or if continuing to will, then doing so in such a way as to will only that the world did not exist. In other words, it is at precisely this point that nihilism, in both its original and classical forms, is born. Nihilism, however, is only one of the two roads in the wood. The other road, the one that overcomes the danger, is the road that leads from the tragic chorus to tragic drama.

As Nietzsche describes it, tragic drama emerges from the chorus the way the world itself emerges from the Dionysian artistic impulse: "the choral parts with which tragedy is interlaced are, as it were, the womb that gave birth to the whole of the so-called dialogue, that is, the entire world of the stage, the real drama. In several successive discharges this primal ground of tragedy radiates this vision of the drama which is by all means a dream apparition and to that extent epic in nature."[28] In other words, the world of the stage may come into being through the powers of the Dionysian impulse, but the drama that takes place on that stage, like the drama of the world generally, requires the efforts of the Apollinian impulse as well. To understand this relationship between the birthing power of the Dionysian chorus and the radiating of an Apollinian vision that *is* the drama, we need to understand something of the architecture of ancient Greek theaters.

The spectators were seated stadium-style in stair-stepped seats that formed a semicircle around the stage. In front of the stage was the orchestra; and it is here that the chorus would have danced and sung their part. As Nietzsche imagines it, the Dionysian energies of the chorus served as something of a projector, whereby the choral songs and dances would have cast onto the stage each scene in the drama. These scenes, obviously, are no longer music but, like scenes in a modern film, are dramatic images—and are therefore the work of the Apollinian impulse. It is as if the Dionysian energies of the chorus project themselves onto the screen, but the Apollinian artistic impulse must then bring these energies into focus. In its earliest forms, Nietzsche supposes that the projections of tragic drama were always meant to be depictions of Dionysus himself, just as the earliest choral odes were essentially songs of Dionysian worship—and just as the drama of the Mass is meant to depict the life, death, and resurrection of Jesus. However, as tragic drama developed, a tragic hero replaces the depictions of Dionysus, even though the hero, in his or her suffering, would have nonetheless represented Dionysus. To understand this aspect of Greek tragedy, we should perhaps turn to the one surviving tragedy in which Dionysus remains the central character: Euripides' *Bacchae.*[29] This play will help us see not only the mechanisms of tragedy as Nietzsche understands them but also the reason Nietzsche associates those mechanisms with Dionysus.

Euripides' *Bacchae*

The play begins as Dionysus and his followers—an all women contingent called the Maenads—enter the city of Thebes. Legend had it that Dionysus was the son of Semele, who was the daughter of Cadmus (once-king of Thebes) and Zeus. While giving birth to Dionysus, Semele was consumed by a flash of lightning, and her grave is now in Thebes. In the opening scene of the play, Semele's tomb is in the center of the orchestra; and we see Dionysus arrive in the city. He has come, he says, "to refute that slander spoken by mother's sisters" (25–26). The slander in question involved the claim that Zeus was not in fact Dionysus' father, which implied that Dionysus was not, therefore, divine.

Dionysus' first response to this slander upon arriving in Thebes is to begin to punish not only Semele's sisters but all the women of Thebes by driving them away from the city and into the mountains, mad and frenzied. Dionysus' immediate agenda is to initiate the city of Thebes into his mysteries. Standing in the way of any citywide appreciation of Dionysian mysteries, however, is the grandson of Cadmus and the current king of Thebes, Pentheus—who harbors no affections for Dionysus whatsoever. Jan Kott offers a memorable summary of Pentheus' first encounter with Dionysus:

> Pentheus looks at the Stranger the way a sheriff in Arizona would at a bearded guru who has invaded the town with a gang of tattered girls. He counters the arrogance of mysticism with the arrogance of pragmatic reason, cuts off the Stranger's tresses and orders him to be locked in a stable. The god has been offended. Sacrilege has been committed. The Chorus cries to heaven for revenge.
>
> No sooner have the Bacchants completed their threnody than the earth shakes, flames burst from Semele's tomb and a wing of the royal palace falls down. The god has emerged from darkness into light. He has returned to his women. They touch his hands from which the fetters have fallen. He is alive.[30]

Not surprisingly, after the miraculous, earthshaking events of Dionysus' escape, Pentheus loses the self-confidence that accompanied his first meeting with Dionysus. Shortly after the palace collapses, Pentheus meets Dionysus again and begins to question him about his escape. At this moment a messenger arrives from the mountain where he has just seen the crazed women of Thebes, including Pentheus' mother and sisters. The messenger is a cowherd and had come upon the women as they were awaking from a nap on the mountainside. He describes the scene to Pentheus:

> *First they let their hair fall loose, down*
> *over their shoulders, and those whose straps had slipped*
> *fastened their skins of fawn with writhing snakes*
> *that licked their cheeks. Breasts swollen with milk,*
> *new mothers who had left their babies behind at home*
> *nestled gazelles and young wolves in their arms,*
> *suckling them. Then they crowned their hair with leaves,*
> *ivy and oak and flowering bryony.* (695–702)

Thinking perhaps that he and his fellow cowherds and shepherds might gain the favor of Pentheus if they captured Agave, Pentheus' mother, and returned her to Thebes, the cowherd and his fellow herders decided to set an ambush for Agave. Agave discovered the ambush, however, and instructed the women to attack the men:

At this we fled
and barely missed being torn to pieces by the women.
Unarmed, they swooped down upon the herds of cattle
grazing there on the green of the meadow. And then
you could have seen a single woman with bare hands
tear a fat calf, still bellowing with fright,
in two, while others clawed the heifers to pieces.
There were ribs and cloven hooves scattered everywhere,
and scraps smeared with blood hung from the fir trees.
And bulls, their raging fury gathered in their horns,
lowered their heads to charge, then fell, stumbling
to the earth, pulled down by hordes of women
and stripped of flesh and skin more quickly, sire,
than you could blink your royal eyes. . . .
Some god, I say, was with them.
The Bacchae then returned where they had started,
by the springs the god had made, and washed their hands
while the snakes licked away the drops of blood
that dabbed their cheeks.
Whoever this god may be,
sire, welcome him to Thebes. (734–769)

In the wake of this report, Pentheus does not in fact welcome Dionysus to Thebes but orders his troops to stand ready to march against the Bacchae. Dionysus, however, suggests another plan: He could go to the mountains and lead the women back to Thebes without bloodshed. With images of bellowing and shredded cattle still in his head, Pentheus is uninterested in this plan and calls for his army. Dionysus then switches tactics: "Wait," he exclaims, "would you like to *see* their revels on the mountain?" (811). Without hesitation, led on it seems by the erotic thoughts of voyeurism, Pentheus replies that he would like very much to see that sight.

Dionysus then suggests that Pentheus go to the mountain disguised as a bacchant, lest the women recognize him. Pentheus is skeptical about putting on a wig and a woman's dress and playing the part of a bacchant. But Dionysus convinces him that it is necessary. A short time later, Dionysus leads Pentheus, who now looks remarkably like the effeminate Dionysus, out of the city to the mountain. The next time we see Pentheus, he is dead and dismembered, having met the same fate as the cattle had at the hands of the frenzied women of Thebes. The audience does not witness Pentheus' death, just as we did not witness the revelry of the women on the mountain. Instead, as before, we hear of the events on Mount Cithaeron from a messenger.

The messenger describes how Dionysus had helped Pentheus into the top of a fir tree, so that he could see more clearly "the shameless orgies" of the bacchants, and how, as he was huddled in the top of the tree, the women discovered him and, almost at the same time, heard a voice from above commanding them to seek revenge against the one who had mocked Dionysus. After tearing the tree from its roots and toppling Pentheus, "sobbing and screaming" to the ground, the women converge upon him as they had converged upon the cattle:

> *His own mother,*
> *like a priestess with her victim, fell upon him*
> *first. But snatching off his wig and snood*
> *so she would recognize his face, he touched her cheeks,*
> *screaming, "No, no, Mother! I am Pentheus,*
> *your own son, the child you bore to Echion!*
> *Pity me, spare me, Mother! I have done a wrong,*
> *but do not kill your own son for my offense."*
> *But she was foaming at the mouth, and her crazed eyes*
> *rolling with frenzy. She was mad, stark mad. . . .*
> *Then Autonoë and the whole horde*
> *of Bacchae swarmed upon him. Shouts everywhere,*
> *he screaming with what little breath was left,*
> *they shrieking in triumph. One tore off an arm,*
> *another a foot still warm in its shoe. His ribs*
> *were clawed clean of flesh and every hand*
> *was smeared with blood as they played ball with scraps*
> *of Pentheus' body.* (1114–1136)

Euripides' play does not end quite here, although it might have. Instead, we witness Agave enter Thebes, bearing Pentheus' head impaled on the end of her wand. And we watch, horrified, as she struts around in the delusion that the head is not that of her son but of a lion that she killed up on the mountain. We look on as she calls for Pentheus so that she might show him her prize. And then, in the ensuing scene, we watch as Cadmus, the old king, coaxes Agave out of her delusion and forces her to see that it is no lion's head she bears but the head of her own son. As the play draws to a close, Cadmus has pieced Pentheus' body together for burial; and Dionysus returns to the stage just long enough to speak of the fate that will now fall upon Agave and her sisters, as well as Cadmus and his wife, because of the blasphemy of Thebes.

When I decided to turn to the *Bacchae,* I noted that the play would help us comprehend not only Nietzsche's understanding of the mechanisms of tragedy but also his understanding of the relationship between tragedy and Dionysus. Let me turn now to two readings of the *Bacchae* in an attempt to display the relationship between this play and Nietzsche's understanding of tragedy and Dionysus.[31] Taken together, these readings will not only allow me to summarize Nietzsche's tragic philosophy but will begin to set the stage for my discussion of Michel Foucault's tragic politics in the next chapter. Let me turn first to Jan Kott's essay on the *Bacchae* which appears as the title essay in his book, *The Eating of the Gods*.[32]

Visions of Dionysian Apocalypse

Kott notes that the "climax of the Dionysian rite in Euripides' *Bacchae* is the *sparagmos* and the *omophagia*, tearing wild animals to pieces and consuming their raw flesh, still warm with blood."[33] In the play we witness this rite when the frenzied women of Thebes attack the herd of cattle, a scene that serves as a forecast of the play's climactic moment, when the same women tear apart Pentheus (although in the second event we witness only *sparagmos*: They do not eat Pentheus). Euripides takes care on three different occasions in the play to let us know that these two events are but repetitions of an earlier event: the death of Pentheus' cousin, Acteon—which also occurred on Mount Cithaeron. Acteon "had watched Artemis bathing in a mountain brook. The offended goddess turned him into a stag and set his own dogs on him. Acteon climbed a tree, but the dogs got at him and tore him to pieces."[34] The death of Pentheus, then, is like the death of his cousin Acteon. And the death of Acteon is in turn like yet another death.

In one version of the story about the birth of Dionysus, Zeus sends the infant Dionysus to live with King Athamas and Queen Ino in an attempt to shield him from Hera, who was angry that Zeus had slept with Semele and fathered Dionysus. Ino was not only Semele's sister but also a sister to both Agave (the mother of Pentheus) and Autonoë (the mother of Acteon). Hera discovers the whereabouts of Dionysus and in her anger drives Athamas and Ino mad. In their madness, they kill their own son, mistaking him for a deer. Hence the three sons of the three sisters die similar deaths. What are we to make of the repetitive nature of these stories, which are in fact but three of a whole group of such stories in Greek myth? Kott offers the following suggestion:

> If we put these accounts one on top of the other, like cutout drawings, certain common elements in them emerge. These are: madness, the divine frenzy, sent most commonly by Dionysus; the murder of a child, most commonly a son; murder effected by tearing to pieces (*sparagmos*); murder connected with the eating of raw flesh; . . . the son torn apart and eaten by the mother. This pattern in its bare structure is not a myth. . . . It is an image of the same ritual, a ritual which repeats and commemorates events that happened, in Mircea Eliade's

> words, "at the beginning of time".... The sacral offering is the repetition of the first sacrifice. It is told in the ur-myth, the original Dionysian myth.[35]

In the original Dionysian myth, Hera compels the Titans to kidnap and kill Dionysus. For a time, Dionysus eludes the Titans by taking on the form of various animals. But then, while he is in the form of a bull, the Titans catch him, tear him apart, and eat him. In retaliation, Zeus kills the Titans and then miraculously resurrects the dismembered Dionysus. Kott continues the tale:

> The resurrected Dionysus descended into Hades in order to free his dead mother, Semele. Then he ascended to Olympus with her and was admitted to the company of the immortal ones. Semele became Persephone, who, at the advent of winter, descends to the underworld, leaving it toward the close of the season to rejoin the spring Dionysus. The dismembering and reunification of Dionysus is the cosmic myth of the eternal renewal, death and rebirth, chaos and cosmos.[36]

Pentheus, Acteon, and the unnamed son of Ino each meet the same kind of death as that of their now immortal cousin Dionysus. By centering upon the death of the last of these four cousins, while at the same time alluding to the deaths of the other three, Euripides' *Bacchae* both draws us into the heart of a cosmic myth and shows us that myth in ritual practice. In keeping with Nietzsche's understanding of Greek tragedy, Kott suggests that the Chorus serves to draw us into both myth and ritual by projecting the climactic scenes with the pure energy of its song and dance: "The sacral *sparagmos* and agony of Pentheus in *The Bacchae* takes place offstage, and the audience learns about it from messengers. But the Chorus of bacchants is present on the stage from the first to the last scene. The Chorus, as in Aeschylus, not only witnesses events but participates in them."[37] This participation takes the form of both song and dance until, as Kott puts it, "the song becomes a dance.... The Chorus of bacchants from Lydia dances the madness sent by Dionysus on the women of Thebes.... The dance to the beat of drums, punctuated by the wailing of flutes and high tones of pipes, leads into a holy trance. When, at the climax of the tragedy, the Messenger speaks about Pentheus' torn body, the dance becomes a spasm."[38]

The Chorus draws us into myth and ritual, and at one level the *Bacchae* certainly seems to supply something of a record of what worship in the Dionysian cult might have been like. Kott warns us, however, that this final spasm is not to be mistaken for a Dionysian victory dance.

We would be wrong, says Kott, to see in this final frenzied dance the ritual that recalls the cosmic myth of eternal renewal—the never-ending reunification of a dismembered Dionysus. In the *Bacchae,* says Kott,

> the eating of the god, the rite of death and renewal, becomes in the end a cruel killing of son by mother. The ritual turns into ritual murder. . . . The death and resurrection of the god are in *The Bacchae* a symbolic sign, but the agony and death of man are real. The *sparagmos* of animals on the slopes of Cithaeron is described as rite and as liturgy. Bulls humbly bow their heads when the Maenads approach to tear them apart. But Pentheus calls in despair: "Mother! I am Pentheus, your own son!" The passion and death of Pentheus are shown deliberately in all their cruel realism:
>
> *One tore off an arm,*
> *another a foot still warm in its shoe. His ribs*
> *were clawed clean of flesh and every hand*
> *was smeared with blood as they played ball with scraps*
> *of Pentheus' body. (1133ff)*
>
> In a foot torn off with a shoe there is nothing left of sacral offering. Ritual has become slaughter.[39]

Kott reminds us that at the end of the *Bacchae* the stage is not empty, even though the actors have left. For Pentheus' dismembered corpse, pieced together such as it is, remains: "the only great unburied corpse in all Greek tragedy."[40] There will be no resurrection. What has been torn apart in the course of the play remains flung far and wide. Dionysus, who came to initiate Thebes into his mysteries, in fact destroyed it—and with it, any hope that it might worship him. As Kott notes, there is an odd reversal here, or maybe it would be better termed a contagion. For Dionysus comes to Thebes a stranger; and by the end of the play Thebes has become a stranger to itself. Hence,

> Cadmus and Agave the filicide are now strangers. The frenzied women of Thebes, who fled to the mountains and tore their own king apart, are also strangers to the city. The bacchants, who came to Thebes with Dionysus from Asiatic Lydia, have already gone away. They were strangers from the outset. But it is the massacred body of Pentheus, covered in mockery with the wig of long blond tresses in which the god entered Thebes—it is this body that is the most strange to gods and men. . . . Eating of the gods—the Dionysian ritual and the Easter rite—is the victory of life over death, a triumphant feast of rebirth, fertility and abundance. *The Bacchae* ends with the defeat of order and life by sterility, negation and decay. . . . God has departed. Thebes is empty. All that remains in it is the unburied body of the King.[41]

What are we to make of this unburied body of the king, if what we want from the *Bacchae* is a comment not only on the character of Dionysus but the character of Nietzsche's Dionysus? Kott himself has something to say on this note, and he leads into it speaking of what he calls the "two

Dionysian Apocalypses" that Euripides presents in the *Bacchae:* "The first is a return to the lost paradise, where milk and wine flow from the earth, honey drips from trees, and all will again be innocent and naked."[42] This of course is the scene on Mount Cithaeron as we see it for the first time when the messenger describes it for us:

> *Breasts swollen with milk,*
> *new mothers who had left their babies behind at home*
> *nestled gazelles and young wolves in their arms,*
> *suckling them. Then they crowned their hair with leaves,*
> *ivy and oak and flowering bryony. (698–702)*

"The second Dionysian apocalypse," says Kott, "is always deadly. . . . The green slopes of Mount Cithaeron are stained with blood. Dionysus' second call is the throb of death."[43] The reference here is, of course, to the murder of Pentheus.

Having marked the difference between these two apocalypses, Kott then turns to describe, in this poignant paragraph, the final moments of Nietzsche's life in sanity:

> Nietzsche signed his last legible letters, before he succumbed to incurable madness, "Dionysus" and "The Crucified." In January 1889, when he saw a cabman beating a horse, he threw himself forward and embraced the horse. When later he was sane for a short time, he sent his friend a letter containing just one sentence: "Sing me a new song. The world is transfigured and all the heavens are full of joy." In this desperate cry of Nietzsche's there is a vision of the same apocalypse, which Euripides' Maenads saw on Mount Cithaeron. But after it came the other Dionysian apocalypse—the *omophagia*, first of animals, then of man.[44]

As Kott sees it, one apocalypse leads inevitably to the other. For you can arrive at the paradise of the first apocalypse only by succumbing to the intoxication of the bacchic dance. However, "the price of the intensification of all the senses is the loss of control. . . . Dionysus promises liberation from alienation and freedom from all ties, but he grants only one ultimate freedom: the freedom to kill. The girls decked out in flowers turn into beautiful murderesses."[45]

Kott has given us here a wonderful commentary not only on Euripides' *Bacchae* but also on Nietzsche's Dionysus, at least as he appears to Nietzsche's critics. In order to see the way in which Kott's reading of the *Bacchae* supports the views of Nietzsche's critics, remember first Nietzsche's own account of what Kott calls the first Dionysian apocalypse:

> Under the charm of the Dionysian, not only is the union between man and man reaffirmed, but nature which has become alienated, hostile, or subju-

gated, celebrates once more her reconciliation with her lost son, man. Freely, earth proffers her gifts, and peacefully the beasts of prey of the rocks and desert approach. The chariot of Dionysus is covered with flowers and garlands; panthers and tigers walk under its yoke. . . . Now the slave is a free man; now all the rigid, hostile barriers that necessity, caprice, or "impudent convention" have fixed between man and man are broken. Now in the gospel of universal harmony, each one feels himself not only united, reconciled, and fused with his neighbor, but as one with him.[46]

These words recall the scene of the women frolicking with the beasts on Mount Cithaeron; and for Nietzsche they convey an image of what he calls the "mysterious primordial unity."[47] Like Nietzsche's critics, Kott sees an inextricable link between this Dionysian paradise and catastrophe. Kott suggests that we can experience this primordial unity only at the price of a loss of control, as we subject ourselves to the powers of this strange divinity. But with this loss of control comes the blurring of the fine line between the killing of cattle, which as Kott notes is clearly a sacral ritual, and the killing of Pentheus, which is simply slaughter.

Milbank, Heidegger, and Gillespie say the same thing differently. To concede the world to Dionysus is to concede the world to power and violence; and to concede to this is, finally, to place freedom and reconciliation in the hands of the crazed women of Thebes: They are beautiful, even stunning, as they frolic on the mountainside. But they are in the end, as the first apocalypse gives way to the second, beautiful murderesses—and so, perforce, is the overman.

Kott presents what I take to be a persuasive reading of the *Bacchae,* and his distinction between the two Dionysian apocalypses illuminates Nietzsche's understanding of Dionysus, or, more accurately, it illuminates the Dionysian as it appears to Nietzsche's critics: the affirmation of an unconstrained power that can end only in radical killing. There is another way to read the *Bacchae,* however, that is equally persuasive and that not only alters Kott's view of the Dionysian apocalypses but also and accordingly challenges the reading of Nietzsche proffered by his critics. Interestingly, at the end of his essay on the *Bacchae,* Kott himself lays the foundation for this reading when he sets the play in its historical context:

The Bacchae was written in the third decade of the Peloponnesian War; less than two years after its first performance, Athens fell. History . . . had been unleashed. Greek civilization was undergoing the greatest of its upheavals, from which it never fully recovered. *The Bacchae* is the tragedy of the madness of Greece, the madness of rulers and of people. "You are mad, beyond the power of any drugs to cure, for you are drugged with madness" (326ff). On this occasion, pitiful blind Teiresias has cried out the truth.[48]

In the play, Teiresias levels these words at Pentheus as a warning against his treatment of Dionysus. But one need only read Thucydides to see that

Kott's suggestion that Euripides is leveling these words at Athens itself is well founded. Like Thebes, Athens had, by the end of the Peloponnesian War, become a stranger to itself. Kott notes that history often writes the final interpretations of the great tragedies. It strikes me that the *Bacchae,* too, would have played well in Sarajevo. But once we begin to read the *Bacchae* as social commentary about the madness of empire, then what are we to make of its portrayal of Dionysus? To explore this question, let me turn to Jean-Pierre Vernant's reading of the *Bacchae.*[49]

The Dionysian Subversion of the Polis

Vernant points out that when Dionysus, the stranger from the east, enters Thebes at the beginning of the play, he has not come to Thebes to found a foreign cult. Rather he

> demands to be fully accepted in the ranks of the gods of the civic community. His ambition is to see his cult officially recognized and unanimously practiced in all the different forms it may assume. The polis as such must be initiated.... The religious status claimed by Dionysus is not that of a marginal, eccentric deity with a cult reserved for the brotherhood of sectarians.... Dionysus demands from the city official recognition for a religion that in a sense eludes the city and is beyond it. He is out to establish at the very heart and center of public life practices that, either openly or covertly, present aspects of eccentricity.[50]

Note the difference here between a sectarian Dionysian cult at the margins of the polis and that instantiation of practices "at the very heart and center of public life," practices that effect a change in the very nature of the polis. Indeed, "the polis as such must be initiated." It is for this reason that Dionysus comes to Thebes; and it is because of this assault upon the very nature of the polis itself that Thebes in general and Pentheus in particular resist Dionysus—and therein lies the tragedy:

> The tragedy of the *Bacchae* shows the dangers that are involved when a city retrenches within its own boundaries. If the world of the same refuses to absorb the element of otherness that every group and every human being unconsciously carry within themselves, just as Pentheus refuses to recognize that mysterious, feminine, Dionysian element that attracts and fascinates him despite the horror that he claims to feel for it, then all that is stable, regular, and the same tips over and collapses.[51]

Like Kott, Vernant recognizes that the *Bacchae* is in part a commentary on the stranger or, to choose another idiom, the other. Vernant would agree that in the end Thebes has become a stranger to itself, has in fact become other—and in the most drastic way. Vernant, however, does not see this particular ending as inevitable; he does not think, in other words, that Dionysus, as such, is a destroyer of cities. Rather, the tragedy of the *Bacchae* lies in the fact that Thebes (or Athens, or the Serbs of Sarajevo) might have done otherwise; they might have welcomed the other and its polis-altering otherness: "The victorious eruption of Dionysus is a sign that otherness is being given its place, with full honors, at the center of the social system."[52]

The *Bacchae* is a tragic drama precisely because Thebes does not give otherness a place of honor at the center of the polis and, like Athens at the peak of its power, suffers the consequences, which are dire indeed. Of course part of the tragedy also lies in the fact that Pentheus was at least in part right to resist Dionysus, insofar as he was a threat to the polis. For to grant Dionysus the place of honor he seeks is inevitably to subvert the status quo:

> What the vision of Dionysus does is explode from within and shatter the "positivist" vision that claims to be the only valid one, in which every being has a particular form, a definite place, and a particular essence in a fixed world. . . . To see Dionysus, it is necessary to enter a different world where it is the "other," not the "same" that reigns. . . . [Dionysus] blurs the frontiers between the divine and the human, the human and the animal, the here and the beyond. He sets up communion between things hitherto isolated, separate. His eruption into nature, the social system, and each individual human being . . . is a subversion of order.[53]

This blurring of frontiers and communion between things hitherto isolated is, of course, what Kott refers to as the first Dionysian apocalypse—and it is what Nietzsche—and following him Foucault, as we will see—has in mind when he calls us to celebrate a Dionysian world: a world where otherness is not marginalized but welcomed into the heart of things. This apocalyptic vision has a different appearance for Vernant than for Kott, however, because Vernant emphasizes the fact that this is, in the end, a *social* vision.[54]

It is at this point that Vernant's reading of the *Bacchae* allows us to see an aspect of Nietzsche's understanding of Dionysus that is blurred by both Kott and Nietzsche's critics: Nietzsche's appeal to Dionysus is not simply (and some would say *not at all*) a metaphysical proposal but is in fact a practical one.[55] To celebrate Dionysus is to blur the hard edges of our world in order to unite in communion those things hitherto separate—whether these things are different "races" of human beings or different "species" of animals. Dionysus subverts all order, but not with the intention of leaving behind ruins. Rather the subversion is itself a reordering, one that always privileges the presence of the other.

What this reordering means, of course, is that from Vernant's perspective, the first Dionysian apocalypse does not lead, as it does for Kott, inevitably to the second. Instead, for Vernant the two apocalypses present two different possibilities. Vernant puts it this way: The mania or madness through which Dionysus works "takes two very different forms, one for his initiates who are united with him . . . another for his enemies whom frenzy strikes as punishment."[56] When the women of Thebes tear apart Pentheus they are in the grips of a "frenetic rage" that arrives as punishment. However, the "picture is quite different where followers of Dionysus are concerned. . . . Not only are they never seen demented or seized by mania, but when, in the *parados,* they recall their wanderings and dances on the mountainside, at the beck and call of the god and in his company, all is purity, peace, joy, supernatural well-being."[57] Vernant seems to suggest that the second Dionysian apocalypse does not arrive inevitably as an extension of the first but is a different path altogether—a path that both Thebes and Athens embarked upon when they refused to welcome the stranger, when they refused to take the risk required of all those who seek the communion of things characteristic of the first apocalypse. I do not mean to underplay the risk involved in avoiding the fate of both Athens and Thebes, and to understand this risk we need to leave behind the *Bacchae* and return to Nietzsche and *The Birth of Tragedy.*

Tragic Drama and the Artistic Taming of the Horrible

I introduced my discussion of the *Bacchae* by noting that, among other things, the play would help us make sense of Nietzsche's claim that the tragic hero represents Dionysus himself. We are now in a position to understand this claim. For as Nietzsche sees it, the power of tragedy lies not simply in the spirit of the Dionysian dithyramb but also in the way this music projects a drama that is, at its core, a ritual reenactment of the death and dismemberment of Dionysus. Kott called our attention to the presence of that ritual in the *Bacchae,* but Nietzsche wants us to understand that the same ritual is present in every tragedy:

> It is only through the spirit of music that we can understand the joy involved in the annihilation of the individual. For it is only in particular examples of such annihilation that we see clearly the eternal phenomenon of Dionysian art, which gives expression to the will in its omnipotence, as it were, behind the *principium individuationis,* the eternal life behind all phenomena, and despite all annihilation. The metaphysical joy in the tragic is a translation of the instinctive unconscious Dionysian wisdom into the language of images: the hero, the highest manifestation of the will, is negated for our pleasure, because he is only phenomenon, and because the eternal life of the will is not affected by his annihilation.[58]

Tragedy, then, dramatizes for us the way of the world—or, more accurately, the way of the cosmos—as it recasts the great cosmic myth of Dionysus' death, dismemberment, and eventual resurrection. As I noted earlier, in tragedy as Nietzsche sees it, the dialogue and the actors are projections, and therefore images, of the choral energy. They are the individuated, Apollinian moment of an otherwise Dionysian affair. And even though the drama would not be possible without this Apollinian impulse, tragedy belongs to Dionysus in the end. For it is precisely in the destruction of the Apollinian illusions and masks that we are allowed to peer into the Dionysian abyss. Or put differently, and more accurately, the Apollinian images are the necessary result of a glance into the abyss. Nietzsche makes this point by drawing an analogy to what occurs when we stare into the sun:

> When after a forceful attempt to gaze on the sun we turn away blinded, we see dark-colored spots before our eyes, as a cure, as it were. Conversely, the bright image projections of the Sophoclean hero—in short, the Apollinian aspect of the mask—are necessary effects of a glance into the inside and terrors of nature; as it were, luminous spots to cure eyes damaged by gruesome night.[59]

Not only tragic heroes but the whole of tragic drama itself is the effect of this glance into "gruesome night"; and according to Nietzsche this effect of a "forceful attempt" to glance into the abyss generates the further effect of stimulating in us a joyful affirmation of this Dionysian universe—an affirmation justified only in aesthetic terms. As Nietzsche puts it, "Here, when the danger to the will is the greatest, *art* approaches as a saving process, expert at healing. She alone knows how to turn these nauseous thoughts about the horror or absurdity of existence into notions with which one can live."[60]

Nietzsche stresses repeatedly that as the artistic taming of the horrible, tragic drama is not to be confused with a similar taming accomplished by Apollo—as, for example, in epic poetry or classical sculpture. The calm of the sculptor god overcomes suffering by rendering it beautiful, but the beauty is illusory: "Apollo overcomes the suffering of the individual by the radiant glorification of the *eternity of the phenomenon:* here beauty triumphs over the suffering inherent in life; pain is obliterated by lies from the features of nature."[61] The artistic taming of the horrible accomplished by tragic drama is of a different order:

> Dionysian art, too, wishes to convince us of the eternal joy of existence: only we are to seek this joy not in phenomena, but behind them. We are to recognize that all that comes into being must be ready for a sorrowful end; we are forced to look into the terrors of the individual existence—yet we are not to become rigid with fear: a metaphysical comfort tears us momentarily from the bustle of the changing figures. We are really for a brief moment primordial being itself, feeling its raging desire for existence and joy in existence; the struggle, the pain, the destruction of phenomena, now appear necessary to us, in view of the excess of countless forms of existence which force and push one

> another into life, in view of the exuberant fertility of the universal will. We are pierced by the maddening sting of these pains just when we have become, as it were, one with the infinite primordial joy in existence, and when we anticipate, in Dionysian ecstasy, the indestructibility and eternity of this joy.[62]

To say that tragic drama teaches us the necessity of the destruction of phenomena, and to say further that this lesson is embodied in the fate of the tragic hero, is, of course, to say that we all, at one time or another, are called to be a tragic hero because we all must realize, as Oedipus finally does, that our final calling is to relinquish control of our existence. Like the tragic hero, we must learn to succumb to events and bear ourselves with grace and dignity.

We are now in a position to see the brilliance of Nietzsche's account of tragedy, which lies precisely in this displacing of the hero. For Nietzsche the role of the hero in tragic drama is but a secondary effect, a blur in our vision after we have glanced at the abyss. For Nietzsche it is this glance, and not the hero, that matters in the last analysis. As Nietzsche sees things, heroes are not tragic, cultures are—and by extension so is the cosmos. In fact it was Nietzsche's intent, at least in the energy of his youth, to inaugurate "a tragic culture." To fully appreciate the novelty of Nietzsche's insight into the nature of tragedy, perhaps it would be helpful to situate briefly his account of tragic drama in the context of two of the more prominent accounts of tragedy that Nietzsche had inherited, those of Aristotle and Schopenhauer.

Tragedy According to Aristotle and Schopenhauer

Nietzsche himself contrasts his understanding of tragedy with that of both of these figures on several occasions, perhaps most tellingly in these words from *Twilight of the Idols:*

> Tragedy is so far from providing evidence for pessimism among the Helenes in Schopenhauer's sense that it has to be considered the decisive repudiation of that idea and the *counter-verdict* to it. Affirmation of life even in its strangest and sternest problems; the will to life rejoicing in its own inexhaustibility through the sacrifice of its highest types—*that* is what I called Dionysian, that is what I recognized as the bridge to the psychology of the *tragic* poet. *Not* so as to get rid of pity and terror, not so as to purify oneself of a dangerous emotion through its vehement discharge—it was thus Aristotle misunderstood it—: but beyond pity and terror, *to realize in oneself* the eternal joy of becoming—the joy which also encompasses joy in destruction.[63]

As Nietzsche notes, Aristotle argued that tragic drama acted as a catharsis, purging the audience of two emotions that are particularly dangerous as extremes: pity and terror. Hence the polis was a healthier place because of the performance of tragedies, during which the audience gave themselves over so thoroughly to these two emotions that in the wake of the performance their capacity for both pity and terror had been spent. It is in these terms that Aristotle attempts to explain why it is that people actually enjoy watching the suffering of others on stage. Nietzsche obviously was not satisfied with this explanation because in a sense it does not do enough: Tragedy is in some way *beyond* pity and terror. We enjoy tragic drama not because it purges us of these emotions but because it delivers us into one of those rare moments in our lives when the meaning of the universe stands clear of the fog—and it is in these moments that we experience the profound joy of existence, even as we realize the transience of our own place amidst things.

For Nietzsche, then, *the* tragic emotion is neither fear nor pity, but joy; and such joy stands in the way of all "pessimistic philosophy." Most immediately for Nietzsche, this reference to pessimism is a reference to Schopenhauer. Aristotle misunderstood the mechanics of the emotions central to the viewing of tragic drama. Schopenhauer's understanding of tragic drama, however, is even further off the mark. To understand both Schopenhauer's account of tragedy and the way in which Nietzsche's understanding of tragedy develops as a "counterverdict" to Schopenhauerian pessimism, we have to have at least a basic sense of Schopenhauer's philosophy.[64]

Schopenhauer had an immense impact on Nietzsche's own philosophy, particularly as we find it in early works such as *The Birth of Tragedy.* Nietzsche himself noted, in the "Attempt at Self-Criticism" that he added to *The Birth of Tragedy* in 1886, that in that work he remained far too dependent on "Schopenhauerian formulas," even as he attempted to delineate an account of tragedy that was at odds with "Schopenhauer's spirit and taste."[65] The Schopenhauerian formulas in question are numerous. For example, Nietzsche's account in *The Birth of Tragedy* of both music in particular and aesthetics generally owes much to Schopenhauer. However, most prominently it is Schopenhauer's understanding of the will that Nietzsche borrows.

Schopenhauer understood his own philosophical project as the logical extension of Kant. Kant leaves unexplained the relationship between the noumenal thing-in-itself and the phenomenal realm of our experience. In some mysterious way, the thing-in-itself "gives" representations to us, which we then form into experience. But Kant never offers an account of the activity by way of which we receive these gifts. Schopenhauer sets out to make up for Kant's silence on this subject, and he does so by arguing that the thing-in-itself is best understood as the will that underlies all phenomena. Everything in the phenomenal world is an expression of this will, or rather, *is* this will as it manifests itself in the world of our experience. According to Schopenhauer, Kant was right, the will itself harks from the noumenal realm and so is inaccessible to us. However, unlike Kant's notion of the thing-in-itself, the will as Schopenhauer conceives of it does not remain beyond our knowledge altogether, since we can in effect see this will in our own inner passions and desires. As Michael Gillespie notes, Schopenhauer imagines that each individual has access to this will: "I discover in the immediate intuition of my own feelings, drives, and so on, the concealed essence of all things, a will that governs the motions of all things, from the motion of my hand to the motion of the stars in the most distant galaxy."[66]

For Schopenhauer the central characteristic of this will that we discover at the heart of things is its aimlessness. Although at any given point in our own day-to-day willing our actions have a goal or a purpose, "willing as a whole has no end in view."[67] To conceive of an aimless general will that manifests itself in a host of individual wills, each with its own self-interested aim, is to imagine a world in endless and inevitable conflict:

> Thus everywhere in nature we see contest and struggle, and the fluctuation of victory. . . . Every grade of the will's objectification fights for the matter, the space, and the time of another. . . . This contest can be followed through the whole of nature; indeed only through it does nature exist. . . . Thus the will-to-live generally feasts on itself, and is in different forms its own nourishment, till finally the human race, because it subdues all the others, regards nature as manufactured for its own use.[68]

Put simply, then, Schopenhauer imagines that we live in a world that in the last instance is governed by an aimless world-will and that our lot as subjects in this realm is to feast on one another. We act; we will; we live only at the expense of the suffering of others, as we compete with them for a place in the world. Gillespie summarizes Schopenhauer's conception of the will by saying that it "is a monstrous inhuman force that through its blind and aimless activity makes this world into hell . . . [and renders life] a constantly prevented dying."[69]

What, then, according to Schopenhauer, are we to do in such a world. We have, he says, two options. The first option is in some way to bow out of the contest by ceasing to be an individual, since only as an individual do we find ourselves feasting on the suffering of others. We cannot, of course, cease to be individuals altogether without dying, but what we can do, as an imaginative exercise, is lose ourselves in something that transcends our individual concerns: And this "something" is art. When Nietzsche says that art saves life, he is in effect simply quoting Schopenhauer.

Salvation through art is one of our options, but it does not represent our highest calling when faced with the aimlessness of a world at war with itself. We might also opt for asceticism, which is an attempt not to cease to be an individual but to cease to will altogether. Our involvement in the cause of the suffering of others is a result of our willing. Hence if we cease to will, then we cease to participate in the feast, which is not to say that we cease to participate in the world altogether. Those who walk the ascetic path have a unique capacity for identifying with the suffering of others, and this capacity, as Gillespie summarizes it, allows them to "bear the pain and suffering of their fellow human beings and thus recognize the futility and immorality of willing."[70] The ascetic path is the path to what Schopenhauer calls "resignation."

Let's move now from Schopenhauer's philosophy generally to his philosophy of tragedy. Tragic drama elevates us, according to Schopenhauer, precisely to the extent that it teaches us to resign from the senselessness of our suffering world.

> [In] tragedy the terrible side of life is presented to us, the wailing and lamentation of mankind, the dominion of chance and error, the fall of the righteous, the triumph of the wicked; and so that aspect of the world is brought before our eyes which directly opposes our will. At this sight we see ourselves urged to turn away from life, to give up willing and loving life. But precisely in this way we become aware that there is still left in us something different . . . that which does not will life. . . . At the moment of the tragic collision, we become convinced more clearly than ever that life is a bad dream from which we have to awake . . . [and] that the world and life can afford us no true satisfaction, and are therefore not worth our attachment to them. In this the tragic spirit consists; accordingly, it leads to resignation.[71]

Even as he depends on Schopenhauer for much of what he says in *The Birth of Tragedy,* Nietzsche opposes both Schopenhauer's pessimism and the accompanying notion that what the great tragedies teach us is to resign from willing. To so resign is, for Nietzsche, to resign from living and to become a thoroughgoing and radical nihilist. Our task is not, as Nietzsche describes it, to resign from the world once we realize that the world is full of suffering; rather our task is to grab hold of this suffering and claim it as our own. Not resignation, says Nietzsche, but compassion; and not pity and terror, but joy—these are the lessons of tragedy. Lessons that for Nietzsche had profound implications.

Toward a Tragic Culture

Although Nietzsche's recourse to the notion of "metaphysical comfort" perhaps fogs the issue, his account of tragedy, like Vernant's account of Euripides' *Bacchae,* has social and political intentions. Nietzsche after all speaks hopefully in *The Birth of Tragedy* of the coming of a new tragic culture—and even if he recanted later from the claim that Germany would be the home of this culture, in general terms his hope, I think, remains. In a "tragic culture," Nietzsche says, the "most important characteristic is that wisdom takes the place of science as the highest end—wisdom that, uninfluenced by the seductive distractions of the sciences, turns with unmoved eyes to a comprehensive view of the world, and seeks to grasp, with sympathetic feelings of love, the eternal suffering as its own."[72]

To relinquish the control that is the dream of science and to grasp eternal suffering as its own, that is the goal of a tragic culture. I do not think we can understand Nietzsche's tragic philosophy unless we see that his notion of the overman, whose task it is to inaugurate this culture, exists within the confines of this tragic vision, something that Milbank, Heidegger, and Gillespie, in varying degrees, seem unwilling to consider.[73] As I read it, the whole of *Zarathustra* is an extended reflection on exactly the consequences of the inherently tragic character of the overman. Consider, for instance, these words from the section titled "On Self-Overcoming":

> Where I found the living, there I found the will to power; and even in the will of those who serve I found the will to be master.
>
> That the weaker should serve the stronger, to that it is persuaded by its own will, which would be master over what is weaker still: this is the one pleasure it does not want to renounce. And as the smaller yields to the greater that it may have pleasure and power over the smallest, thus even the greatest still yields, and for the sake of power risks life. That is the yielding of the greatest: it is hazard and danger and casting dice for death.[74]

What can it mean to risk life for the sake of power? If we think about these words in the context of a tragic culture whose sole motivation is to grasp eternal suffering as its own, it can mean only that power does not lie where we imagine it does—in control—but in the Dionysian abandoning of all such control—even if, in such abandon, tragic characters lose their lives. And where are we most likely to meet such tragic risks, where are we most likely to be called away from control and into suffering? Just in those instances when and where we meet the other.

This thought returns us, of course, to the lesson of Thebes, which was really the lesson of Athens and may well be the lesson of Sarajevo. And it is a lesson that concerns not simply the other but the source of otherness itself. Vernant puts it this way:

> Men must accept their mortal condition, recognize that they are nothing compared with the powers that are beyond them on every side and that are able to crush them utterly. Dionysus is no exception to the rule. His devotee must submit to him as to an irrational force that is beyond his comprehension and that can dispose of him at will. The god has no need to explain himself. He is alien to our norms and customs, alien to our preoccupations, beyond good and evil, supremely sweet and supremely terrible. His pleasure is to summon us to the multiple aspects of otherness around us and within us.[75]

Neither Thebes nor Athens, of course, learned this lesson. "Rendering oneself unarmed when one had been the best-armed, out of a height of feeling—that," says Nietzsche, "is the means to real peace, which must always rest on a peace of mind."[76] Such a peace of mind, a height of feeling, Athens itself, as the center of an empire, never attained. But apparently there were those within Athens, the tragic poets foremost among them, who did reach such heights, or so Nietzsche imagines it:

> One feels ashamed and afraid in the presence of the Greeks, unless one prizes truth above all things and dares acknowledge even this truth: that the Greeks, as charioteers, hold in their hands the reins of our own and every other culture, but that almost always chariot and horses are of inferior quality and not up to the glory of their leaders, who consider it sport to run such a team into an abyss which they themselves clear with the leap of Achilles.[77]

Nietzsche's vision of a tragic culture asks us to climb into the chariot, such as it is, and to make a headlong run toward the abyss; and then, when the sheer speed of the team makes any other course impossible, to steal a glance into the abyss in an attempt to claim eternal suffering as our own. If we can rise to the occasion, then the inertia of our mad race will launch us across the abyss and into the metaphysical comfort produced by the joyful glow of a Dionysian sunrise. On the other hand, if the team proves too slow or if our skills as charioteers prove insufficient, then we will plunge into the abyss and be forever lost in nihilism. If all this sounds like a dream or if the notion of "metaphysical comfort" lacks appeal (as it did even for Nietzsche in his later years), then let me attempt to make Nietzsche's tragic vision more compelling by turning to Norman Maclean's remarkable book, *Young Men and Fire.*[78]

The Story of Mann Gulch: Courage Struggling for Oxygen

In *Young Men and Fire,* Maclean tells the story of the Mann Gulch fire, a relatively small wildfire that burned out of control for a short time on August 5, 1949, in a gulch along the Missouri River in Montana. This story can be reduced, in Maclean's words, to the story of "a race with fire to death" (182), or as he puts it in another place, the story of "courage struggling for oxygen" (301). At its most fevered pace, the fire swept up the north side of the gulch at about 660 feet per minute, or 11 feet per second, with flames reaching forty feet in height. In front of the fire sixteen young men—fifteen of whom had parachuted into the gulch just minutes before—ran for their lives. Thirteen of them lost the race; two made it to the top of the ridge and safety just seconds before the fire did. One man, the foreman of the fire-fighting crew, survived in the ashes of an escape fire he had started just in front of the wall of flame racing up the hillside.

The elapsed on-the-ground time for the smoke jumpers who died was about fifty-six minutes. The elapsed time of the actual race with fire to death was probably under fifteen minutes. In *Young Men and Fire* Maclean attempts to tell the story of that race, which is also, he suggests, to tell the story of the thirteen crosses that now stand where each man fell. Maclean notes that the story of Mann Gulch is "a mystery story" because "it left unexplained what dramatic and devastating forces coincided to make the best of young men into bodies, how the bodies got to their crosses and what it was like on the way" (143). In the course of his narrative, Maclean tries to solve the mystery and to tell us "what it was like on the way." Maclean never ceases to inform us about the challenges of this task: "I have had to learn a good many things to tell this story—one is how it might feel to die in the heat of an Inferno. Since the Inferno is also a pit, I have had to learn how to die in the Inferno always falling down, and always falling down I now know is a terrible way to die—it destroys the confidence before it destroys the body, and it must be terrible to die with nothing left but the body" (205). Such is one of the lessons Maclean has to learn to tell the story of the Mann Gulch fire. But we should note, because Maclean does, that the lesson here is not simply about the story of death by fire but about the very art of storytelling itself:

> If a storyteller thinks enough of story telling to regard it as a calling, unlike a historian he cannot turn from the suffering of his characters. A storyteller, unlike a historian, must be able to accompany his characters, even into smoke and fire, and bear witness to what they thought and felt even when they themselves no longer knew. This story of the Mann Gulch fire will not end until it feels able to walk the final distance to the crosses with those who for the time being are blotted out by the smoke. They were young and did not leave much behind them and need someone to remember them. (102)

There can be little doubt that for Norman Maclean storytelling was a calling. However, it is not storytelling (or not simply so) that makes *Young Men and Fire* a remarkable book.

The book is remarkable because as he follows these young men into smoke and flames and death, Maclean pauses frequently, as in the passage above, to comment on what is at stake in storytelling. Although later I will emphasize this commentary, I do not mean to do so at the expense of the story, for there seems to be a particular affinity between Maclean's commentary on storytelling and the story itself. It is as if just *this* story enables the eloquence and wisdom of Maclean's commentary on the practice of storytelling. Maclean himself is at least peripherally aware of this affinity between story and commentary:

> It should be clear now after nearly forty years that the truculent universe prefers to retain the Mann Gulch fire as one of its secrets—left to itself, it

> fades away, an unsolved, violent incident grieved over by fewer and fewer still living who are old enough to grieve over fatalities of 1949. If there is a story in Mann Gulch, it will take something of a storyteller at this date to find it, and it is not easy to imagine what impulses would lead him to search for it. He probably should be an old storyteller, at least old enough to know that the problem of identity is always a problem, not just a problem of youth, and even old enough to know that the nearest anyone can come to finding himself at any given age is to find a story that somehow tells him about himself. (145)

Maclean's story about Mann Gulch is, then, in some way a story about himself—an old man in his own race with death. But Maclean is not content to be alone in this race. He knows that more than simply *his* identity is at stake. For in his attempt to reclaim from the universe the secrets of the Mann Gulch fire, he hopes to find a story not only about his own life and death but also about the universe itself. Maclean's book is an attempt not only to give meaning to the defeat of thirteen young men but in so doing to restore justice, and thereby meaning, to the world as a whole.

In the act of both telling the story of the Mann Gulch fire and commenting upon that telling, Maclean, it seems to me, seeks to impart to us the secret of the universe. To the extent Maclean divulges that secret with any success, it appears to be the same secret that Nietzsche found in Greek tragedy. Hence to understand Maclean's literary efforts, we have to imagine him as one of Nietzsche's Greek charioteers, who considered it sport to run a team into the abyss as they themselves jumped clear. The race into the abyss and the race with fire to death are, in the end, the same race. The time has come to look at this race more closely by following Maclean as he follows thirteen young men the final distance to their crosses:

> We enter now a different time zone, even a different world of time. Suddenly comes the world of slow-time that accompanies grief and moral bewilderment trying to understand the extinction of those whose love and everlasting presence were never questioned.
>
> Things moved rapidly to the end after the crew left the foreman at his escape fire. It makes no difference whether the crew could not understand in the roaring of the main fire what Dodge was trying to say to them or whether they thought his idea of lying down in the hot ashes of his own fire was crazy. Either way they were entering No Man's Land, lonely in the boiling semi-darkness of the main fire, which by now must have been less than fifty yards behind them.
>
> Their loneliness loomed up suddenly—they were young and not used to being alone, and as Smokejumpers they were not allowed to be alone, except in that perilous moment after they jumped from the sky and before they landed on earth.

To project ourselves into their final thoughts will require feelings about a special kind of death—the sudden death of the young, elite, unfulfilled, and seemingly unconquerable. . . . One thing is certain about these final thoughts—there was not much size to them. Time and place did not permit even superior young men dying suddenly "to see their whole lives pass in review." . . . Everything . . . gets smaller on its way to becoming eternal. It is also probable that the final thoughts of elite young men dying suddenly were not seeing or scenic thoughts but were cries or a single cry of passion, often of self-compassion, justifiable if those who cry are justly proud. The two living survivors of the Mann Gulch fire have told me that, as they went up the last hillside, they remember thinking only, "My God, how could you do this to me? I cannot be allowed to die so young and so close to the top." They said they could remember hearing their voices saying this aloud.

The most eloquent expression of this cry was made by a young man who came from the sky and returned to it and who, while on earth, knew he was alone and beyond all other men, and who, when he died, died on a hill.

Although we can enter their last thoughts and feelings only by indirection, we are sure of the final act of many of them. Dr. Hawkins, the physician who went in with the rescue crew the night the men were burned, told me that, after the bodies had fallen, most of them had risen again, taken a few steps, and fallen again, this time like pilgrims in prayer, facing the top of the hill, which on that slope is nearly east.

The evidence, then, is that at the very end beyond thought and beyond fear and beyond even self-compassion and divine bewilderment there remains some firm intention to continue doing forever and ever what we last hoped to do on earth. By this final act they had come about as close as body and spirit can to establishing a unity of themselves with earth, fire, and perhaps the sky.

This is as far as we are able to accompany them. When the fire struck their bodies, it blew their watches away. The two hands of a recovered watch had melted together at about four minutes to six. For them, that may be taken as the end of time. (143, 296–297)[79]

Such is Maclean's rendition of that final distance, which I quote here at some length not simply because excerpting Maclean's prose is as perilous as excerpting poetry. The extended quotation also contributes to what is in fact a theoretical claim of the same sort that Nietzsche makes in *The Birth of Tragedy.*

Remember that Nietzsche speaks of tragedy as "the artistic taming of the horrible" and that he argues that in Greek tragedy the "profound Hellene, uniquely susceptible to the tenderest and deepest suffering, comforts himself, having looked boldly right into the terrible destructiveness of so-called world history as well as the cruelty of nature."[80] This susceptibility to the deepest suffering, together with the bold looks into the abyss, left the Hellene in danger of longing for a negation of the will, for a negation of life. As Nietzsche sees it, art, however, saves the Hellene from this danger—and most decisively not art as such but art in the form of tragic drama. In both their susceptibility to suffering and their daring glances into the abyss, the profound Hellene and Norman Maclean are one and the same. And if it is art that saved the Hellene, then it is just as surely art that saves Maclean, as he struggles through the sheer power of his prose to accomplish an artistic taming of the horrible—a taming that, as for the Greeks, has something to do with tragedy, which will become clear if we move from Maclean's telling of the story of Mann Gulch to his commentary on the practice of storytelling.

From Catastrophe to Tragedy: Wonder-Altered Grief

Two days after the fire, an investigator returned to the scene and composed a report of what he found there. Early in his book, Maclean refers to the investigator's description of the scene:

> He found the perfectly balanced body of a young grouse, neck and head "still alertly erect in fear and wonder," the beak, feathers, and feet seared away. Within a few yards was a squirrel, stretched out at full length. "The burned-off stubs of his little hands were reaching out as far ahead as possible, the back legs were extended to the full in one final, hopeless push, trying like any human, to crawl just one painful inch further to escape this unnecessary death." (37)

Pushed, it seems, by these images, Maclean begins to speak about the impulses that led him to search for the story of the Mann Gulch fire:

> Although young men died like squirrels in Mann Gulch, the Mann Gulch fire should not end there, smoke drifting away and leaving terror without consolation of explanation. . . . Probably most catastrophes end this way without an ending, the dead not even knowing how they died but "still alertly erect in fear and wonder," those who loved them forever questioning "this unnecessary death," and the rest of us tiring of this inconsolable catastrophe and turning to the next one. This is a catastrophe that we hope will not end where it began; it might go on and become a story. . . . This story is a test of its own belief—that in this cockeyed world there are shapes and designs, if only we have some curiosity, training, and compassion and take care not to lie or be sentimental. It would be a start to this story if this catastrophe were found to have circled around out there somewhere until it could return to itself with explanations of its own mysteries and with the grief it left behind, not removed, because grief has its own place at or near the end of things, but altered somewhat by the addition of something like wonder—wonder, for

> example, because now we can say that the fire swirl which destroyed was caused by three winds on a river. If we could say something like this and be speaking both accurately and somewhat like Shelley when he spoke of clouds and winds, then what we would be talking about would start to change from catastrophe without a filled-in story to what could be called the story of a tragedy, but tragedy would be only part of it, as it is of life. (37–38)

Once again, I have quoted Maclean at some length in order to contribute to the theoretical claim about the redemptive powers of art. The proof that art does indeed save the world lies not in argument but in the art itself. Maclean's intention is through the very act of storytelling itself to turn a catastrophe into a tragedy, and thereby both to lend meaning to the deaths of thirteen young men and to restore justice to a cockeyed world. The reference to Shelley makes it clear that Maclean knows he can succeed only if the beauty of his prose in some way captures and mimics the beauty of the universe, even as it destroys young men. Hence, I offer Maclean's prose as proof that Nietzsche is right when he says that the world is justified only as an aesthetic phenomenon. Maclean brings a specificity to this claim when, speaking like Shelley, he suggests that the transformation of a catastrophe into a tragedy occurs when art alters grief by exposing us to wonder. I can think of no more precise summary of Nietzsche's understanding of the metaphysical comfort of Greek tragedy than this notion of wonder-altered grief.

For Nietzsche the source of wonder is the "world-building" force of the Dionysian abyss. Insofar as tragedy enables us to withstand a glance into this abyss, "again and again it reveals to us the playful construction and destruction of the individual world as the overflow of a primordial delight."[81] For Maclean the source of wonder is this same world-building force, this same overflow of primordial delight, but embodied now in the blowup of a wildfire and in the winds that made that fire possible.

Before expanding upon the Nietzschean character of Maclean's account of the Mann Gulch fire, let me pause for a moment to confront the charges of one of Maclean's critics. Richard Manning argues that, far from portraying the fire as an overflow of primordial delight, Maclean demonizes the fire that destroyed thirteen young men in Mann Gulch, thus perpetuating the myth of American forest-fire policy—a policy of almost total fire suppression that has led to ecological disaster by ignoring the role of fire in maintaining the long-term health of forests.[82] Manning says that throughout Maclean's book, "the fire is demonized. It is evil. It is a monster. It is death generalized to the point that by the end of the book it is transformed to nuclear fire, in that 'it looked much like an atomic explosion in Nevada on its cancerous way to Utah.' Ultimately, the story is cast in religious metaphor, the struggle between good and evil as prosecuted by young men." Maclean "was simply not capable," Manning says, "of seeing the fire as something other than evil." Hence, as literature Maclean's book "succeeds, but as an account of nature it is myopic and negligently incomplete." Had Manning been attuned to the subtle and profound character of Maclean's efforts to transform a catastrophe into a tragedy, he could not have arrived so easily at this harsh judgment of Maclean's work, the profundity of which lies precisely in its account of nature.

Maclean knows that to demonize the forces of nature leaves us in a world of "terror without consolation," where we simply tire of this inconsolable catastrophe and then turn to the next. To turn catastrophe into tragedy and to escape from sheer terror requires precisely that we do not demonize nature but rather stand before it in wonder—even as it destroys us. Admittedly, Maclean does not meet this requirement unfailingly. But in a sense Maclean's failures contribute to the strength of his narrative. Let me explain.

From Scientific Instinct to Tragic Insight

In several lengthy sections of the book, Maclean attempts to atone for the deaths of the men in Mann Gulch by turning them into martyrs for the science of fire: Through their deaths, we learned a technical lesson about fire; they died so that later firefighters might live. The Mann Gulch fire taught scientists who study fire behavior something about "blowups"—those situations in which a small fire can, in the space of little more than an instant, become an uncontrollable conflagration. Maclean points out that in the wake of the Mann Gulch fire this better understanding of fire behavior led to new procedures and orders pertaining to fire-fighting methods and precautions. These new administrative orders, says Maclean, saved future lives—and yet would not have existed if it were not for the tragic deaths of the young men in Mann Gulch. Hence Maclean arrives at a place quite late in his narrative where he offers these words of consolation:

> Their crosses are quiet and a long way off, and from this remove their influence is quiet and seemingly distant. But quietly they are present on every fire-line, even though those whose lives they are helping to protect know only the order and not the fatality it represents. For those who crave immortality by name, clearly this is not enough, but for many of us it would mean a great deal to know that, by our dying, we were often to be present in times of catastrophe helping to save the living from our deaths. (222)

Although Maclean's eloquence does not falter here, something else does. For to argue that advances in fire science and administrative procedure somehow atone for these deaths in fact does *not* "mean a great deal." In this aspect of his narrative, Maclean seems to be following what Nietzsche deems "Socratic insight," which is also the insight that lies at the heart of science.

For Nietzsche, Socrates and science share "the unshakable faith that thought, using the thread of causality, can penetrate the deepest abysses of being, and that thought is capable not only of knowing being but even of *correcting* it. This sublime metaphysical illusion accompanies science as an instinct and leads science again and again to its limits at which it must turn into art."[83] Although no doubt part of what drives Maclean's search for the story of Mann Gulch is the Socratic/scientific instinct or insight, Maclean himself, it seems, was not satisfied finally with this attempt at consolation. And how could he be? For in this account of the lessons of Mann Gulch there is no place for grief-altering wonder. Without wonder, there is no tragedy. And the absence of tragedy leaves Maclean where he began—awash in the storyless terror of catastrophe. And so, Maclean continues to write, aware, it seems to me, that whatever might finally atone for the deaths of Mann Gulch, it will not be a scientific explanation but one that lurks in the "shapes and designs" that exist at the edges of science, at the edges of what we normally take to be real. Maclean voices something like this thought as he tries to reconstruct the final race in Mann Gulch, a race whose finish line is now marked by two tiers of crosses: an upper tier, marking the deaths of those within a minute of reaching the top; and a lower tier, standing where another group of young men simply ran out of strength.

> All of us have the privilege to choose what we wish to visualize as the edge of reality. Either tier of crosses allows us to picture the dead as dying with their boots on. On some of the bodies all but the boots were burned off. If you have lived a life that has thrown you in contact many times with nature, you have already discovered that sometimes you can deal with nature only by allowing it to push back what until now you and others thought were its edges. (277)

Here Maclean has, I think, discovered the limits at which the scientific instinct must relinquish its hold on reality and turn into art. That Maclean struggles throughout his narrative with the promise of this instinct in an attempt to find consolation in the shapes and designs of scientific explanation is not surprising. Indeed, this pursuit of scientific explanation even may have been necessary—a kind of prelude to the artistic impulse that triumphs in the end. Certainly this is how Nietzsche understood the relationship between Socratic and "tragic" insight:

> Anyone who has ever experienced the pleasure of Socratic insight and felt how, spreading in ever-widening circles, it seeks to embrace the whole world of appearances, will never again find any stimulus toward existence more vi-

> olent than the craving to complete this conquest and weave the net impenetrably tight. . . . But science, spurred by its powerful illusion, speeds irresistibly toward its limits where its optimism, concealed in the essence of logic, suffers shipwreck. For the periphery of the circle of science has an infinite number of points; and while there is no telling how this circle could ever be surveyed completely, noble and gifted men nevertheless reach, e'er half their time and inevitably, such boundary points on the periphery from which one gazes into what defies illumination. When they see to their horror how logic coils up at these boundaries and finally bites its own tail—suddenly the new form of insight breaks through, *tragic insight* which, merely to be endured, needs art as a protection and remedy.[84]

Maclean finds in the events of the Mann Gulch fire precisely one of these boundary points from which one gazes beyond the edges of reality into the abyss. From this point and in this gaze, Maclean finds the wonder that alters grief and changes catastrophe into tragedy. And it is worth noting that nature as we find it here, beyond logic and beyond scientific instinct, is not, as Maclean renders it, demonic:

> It would be natural near the end to try to divest the fire of any personal liability to those who died in it and to become for a moment a distant and detached spectator. It might be possible then, if ever, to see fire in something like total perspective as it became total conflagration. . . . Viewing total conflagration is literally blinding, as sight becomes sound and the roar of the fire goes out of the head of the gulch and away and beyond, far away. The last you saw of the ground was a mole coming out of the smoke, a little more terrified than you, debating which way to go and ending the argument with itself forever by turning back into the impenetrable fire. So it is, when you cannot see the fire because of the smoke, sight becomes sound. You hear the fire as a roar of an animal without the animal or as an attacking army blown up by the explosion of its own ammunition dump. . . .
>
> After its deranged military front has passed, pieces of the main fire remained burning fiercely in clutches of timber. Dead standing trees . . . became giant candles burning for the dead. Then one would explode, disappearing from the air where it stood, detonated by its own heat. The disappearance of the tree would not be visible; it would be a theological disappearance; immediately after the explosion, its falling would be transubstantiated into spreading waves of earth generated by its own earthquake, and after its waves had swelled and broken and passed over and under and on, it would return as sound and terminate in echoes of its earthquake rumbling out of the sides and head of the gulch. The world then was more than ever theological and the nuclear was never far off. (293–294)

Earlier, Maclean used his literary skills to take us the final distance to the crosses, as young men fell and then rose again, only to fall again, just before their watches were blown up the hill ahead of them. Here Maclean uses these same skills to recreate for us not the final steps of young men but the fire that chased them down. And as I read him, this is an exercise in wonder—even a theological wonder—and not in the making of demons. In his imaginative rendering of both the final steps of young men and of the fire itself, Maclean succeeds, I think, in turning a catastrophe into a tragedy. He succeeds in presenting to us, even if only fleetingly, the horror of a glance into the abyss, even as he renders both the forces of the abyss and its victims beautiful.

Pausing to Take Pictures of the World as Art

As we have seen, Maclean says early on that his story is "a test of its own belief—that in this cockeyed world there are shapes and designs." For a while his story unfolds along the path of Socratic insight, and he leads us to believe that these shapes and designs will produce something like a scientific explanation. But in the end, as his prose makes clear, Maclean follows a different path, the path of a tragic insight that reveals the shapes and designs in question to be not of a scientific but rather an artistic sort:

> A story that honors the dead realistically partly atones for their sufferings, and so instead of leaving us in moral bewilderment, adds dimensions to our acuteness in watching the universe's four elements at work—sky, earth, fire, and young men. . . .
>
> Far back in the impulses to find this story is the storyteller's belief that at times life takes on the shape of art and that the remembered remnants of these moments are largely what we come to mean by life. The short semihumorous comedies we live, our long certain tragedies, and our springtime lyrics and limericks make up most of what we are. They become almost all of what we remember of ourselves. (144)

Life takes on the shape of art, which is to say, as Maclean does when speaking of that different world of time in which young men died while trying to outrun a fire, "It is in the world of slow-time that truth and art are found as one" (146). In a sentence, that is the secret of the universe that Maclean discovers in Mann Gulch. It is, of course, the same secret that Nietzsche discovers in Greek tragedy and summarizes with equal brevity when he says that only as an aesthetic phenomenon is the world justified.

When Maclean first confronted the Mann Gulch fire, he found it a catastrophe. Later, says Maclean, after discovering a crucial part of the story, it became a poem. "Finding it a poem," he says, "I hoped I could next complete it as a tragedy, more exactly as the story of a tragedy, more exactly still as a tragedy of this whole cockeyed world that probably makes its own kind of sense and beauty but not always ours" (207–208). With these words, Maclean has once again aligned himself with Nietzsche. For Maclean finds in the story of Mann Gulch not just the tragedy of thirteen sudden deaths at the hands of the "explosive power of the universe." He finds as well the shapes and patterns of a universe that is itself tragic. Hence to write the story of the Mann Gulch fire was at the same time to map the tragic designs of the universe—a thought that returns us to the reason I took this foray into *Young Men and Fire.*

I turned to Maclean's narrative suggesting that it would make Nietzsche's tragic vision more compelling. And I hope it has; but no doubt a question persists, since in the end we are left with the seemingly amorphous notion of metaphysical comfort. Such a notion does not seem satisfying—and yet this is precisely the catch. Just when we most want something substantial, both Maclean and Nietzsche gesture beyond logic and beyond the edges of the real toward the place where truth and art meet—and what they find there is tragedy. They try to show us the beauty of the world as they see it—and because the written word is the medium of their own artistic impulses, everything in the end rests upon their prose. In the works of both Nietzsche and Maclean there is an inextricable link between what they say conceptually and the way they say it.[85] My hope is that because Maclean's narrative is rooted in a particular event that it provides a compelling display of Nietzsche's account of tragedy. In any case, both men have given us works of art that struggle to atone for the suffering of the world by somehow rendering both the world and its suffering beautiful. With this thought in mind, let me turn to Maclean one last time:

> The atomic mushroom has become for our age the outer symbol of our inner fear of the explosive power of the universe. It is the symbol of a whole age, and it took an artist to express the meaning the mushroom has for us. [Henry Moore's] bronze atomic mushroom, with its hollow eyes, is intentionally bivisual from every point of view. Wherever you stand, the bronze looks like both an atomic mushroom and a skull, and is meant to.
>
> When the blowup rose out of Mann Gulch and its smoke merged with the jet stream, it looked much like an atomic explosion in Nevada on its cancerous way to Utah. When last seen . . . [it] had stretched out and was on its way, far, far, far away, looking like death and looking back at its dead and looking forward to its dead yet to come. Perhaps it could see all of us.
>
> No one could know the power of it. It stretched until it became particles on the horizon, where it might have joined the company of Sky Spirits as particles, knowing what we do not know, probably something nuclear.
>
> Now almost forty years later, small trees have just started to grow along the bottoms of dry finger gulches on the hillside in Mann Gulch, where moisture from rain and snow are retained underground. Since even now these little evergreens are only six or eight inches high, the grass has to be parted to find them, but I look for such things. I see better what happened in the grass than on the horizon. Most of us do, and probably it is just as well, but what's found buried in the grass doesn't tell us how to get out of the way. (295–296)

This is, of course, the passage Manning singles out when he makes his case for the notion that Maclean demonizes the Mann Gulch fire. But is this in fact a portrayal of fire as a demon, or is it something much more profound? The answer lies back in the gulch with the young men and the race.

Maclean reports that even after the young men of Mann Gulch realized they were in a race with death and were traveling at top speed up the steep hillside, one of them stopped along the way to take pictures. In the Colorado fire in the summer of 1994 that killed fourteen smoke jumpers in circumstances that bear an eerie resemblance to those of Mann Gulch, one of the men also stopped to take photographs.

Maclean says that in the race with fire to death, one passes all the stations of the cross, and one of these stations is "the aesthetic one." "On forest fires," remarks Maclean, "there are moments almost solely for beauty" (69)—a beauty so compelling that it can even cause men in a race with death to stop and take pictures. In the last analysis the beauty of the fire is no different from the beauty of the young trees buried in the grass that have come to repopulate Mann Gulch. These two instances of beauty are of a piece. The lesson here is that the world is a work of art and that we are caught invariably, like the men on that hillside, in the path of the beauty of the world as it sweeps up the hill as fire on its way to transforming itself into the beauty of young trees. Nothing in this lesson tells us how to get out of the way, and it might be the case that the recognition of beauty will cause us to stop and take pictures, even if that means we lose the race to the top. We don't want to lose the race, of course. So when we fall, as Maclean describes it, we rise again, only to fall again—like pilgrims in prayer—harboring "some firm intention to continue doing forever and ever what we last hoped to do on earth." But this firm intention does not get us out of the way, although it may contribute to our dignity.

Speaking of Greek tragedy, Jan Kott says that to "the end, the dead do not want to die; the living are still their ultimate nourishment. The succeeding generations must satisfy the demands of the dead, give meaning to their defeat and restore justice to the world. But this mediation through time and through history only ends in tragedy, with new corpses filling the stage."[86] These are not particularly happy thoughts; but such are the shapes and designs of the world as an aesthetic phenomenon and of a universe deemed tragic. Just because these thoughts lack the cheerfulness we have come to expect from a world that seems set upon ignoring the accumulation of corpses does not mean, however, that they should not be pursued. And to pursue them is to move from what we might call the metaphysics of tragedy to the politics of tragedy. Such a move requires a turn to the works of Michel Foucault.

5

From a Metaphysics to a Politics of Tragedy: Michel Foucault and the Lyricism of Protest

Let me begin this chapter with a confession, which is that the work of the previous four chapters has been an extended attempt to prepare for both the reading of Foucault I will offer in this chapter and the next one, and the reading of Yoder and the New Testament that follows in Chapters Seven and Eight. I have now arrived, in other words, at what has been my destination all along. With that thought in mind, let me offer something of a summary of how the first four chapters have prepared the way for, in the current instance, a reading of Foucault.

Recall first the fact that I began in Sarajevo and that Sarajevo both *is* and metaphorically *represents* a world of suffering. Recall, too, that in the particular instance of Sarajevo, this suffering is simply another instance of the unfolding of nihilism that Nietzsche declared would be the distinguishing mark of both the twentieth and the twenty-first centuries. Note, however, that I began not simply in Sarajevo but on a dimly lit stage there, while awaiting the arrival of Godot. And, as I remarked near the end of the first chapter, to wait for Godot in Sarajevo is to await a decision on the character of the universe.

To the extent the screams and sobs amidst the mortar-torn bodies in the marketplace suggest that the universe is without character—which is to say, without meaning—then Sarajevo depicts for us the despair of radical nihilism and nothing more. Sarajevo depicts, in other words, both the question of suffering as it first arose from the abyss—and the abyss itself. And having heard the screams and seen the limbs scattered on the pavement, having looked, that is, into the abyss, we are left, like Hamlet, only with the paralysis of horror and its subsequent despair. If we are left with anything more than this, it can be only the overwhelming sense of the depths of this despair, since it is a despair that arrives not solely from a glance into the abyss but also as the result of an awareness of the failure of more than two thousand years of attempted escape, or so we saw Nietzsche argue. In other words, it is the contrast between our highest hopes—which most immediately are the hopes of the Enlightenment—and the tattered and bleeding bodies of Sarajevo that leads to the full depth of our despair.

As it takes the stage in Sarajevo, then, nihilism is not, properly speaking, radical nihilism but radical nihilism multiplied exponentially by the failure of a particular course that history has taken for more than two thousand years. Such at least was the lesson of Chapter Two—a lesson that both Nietzsche and his critics, for all their differences, seem intent upon teaching us when they invoke the language of nihilism—even if this lesson tends to be lost in their attempts to outnarrate one another and accuse one another of having become the ultimate nihilist.

As they await Godot, however, Vladimir and Estragon suggest that it *might* be otherwise, that nihilism might *not* be the final word. But if not nihilism, then what? The simple reply is, if not nihilism, then tragedy or apocalypse. As it turns out, however, this reply is far from simple. In Chapter Three, we saw that even as Milbank marches toward apocalypse, he invokes the language of tragedy and arrives at a moment of undecidability between his own Christian rendering of the world and that Nietzschean rendering of the world that he deems nihilist.

Milbank begins to map the course of the journey from nihilism to apocalypse, but the accuracy of his map is suspect. In the end it is not clear whether his map leads us to apocalypse, tragedy, or both—and besides that, his mapping of nihilism itself leaves us confused, since what he designates nihilism bears a resemblance to what he calls tragedy. My account of Nietzsche and the metaphysics of tragedy in Chapter Four was the beginning of an attempt to redraw Milbank's map by trying to display more clearly than he does the path from nihilism to tragedy. As I turn now to Foucault, I am simply extending the work of the last chapter.

Although I hope this summary of the argument so far is a helpful reminder of where we are, I realize it still does not explain, at least not in any obvious way, how the work of the last four chapters prepares the way for a reading of Foucault. To understand how I have arrived at Foucault, you need to recall another aspect of my discussion in Chapter One about waiting for Godot in Sarajevo. If what it means to wait for Godot in Sarajevo is to await a decision on the character of the universe, and if one aspect of the waiting is itself the staging of a performance of *Waiting for Godot*, then what is at stake is how to make sense of the profoundly practical character of this act. In the last chapter, I offered an account of tragedy that goes some way, I hope, toward giving Vladimir and Estragon one possible answer to their question about the character of the universe; but that answer is not sufficient.

What Vladimir and Estragon need is not simply a metaphysical account of the world in which they wait but an account of how, as they wait, they can face suffering with dignity, which is, I think, what Susan Sontag and the people of Sarajevo were doing when they staged a performance of *Godot*. The fact that in this act they blurred the lines between the art of the theater and the reality of the world outside simply helps us to see that dignity is finally, as Nietzsche would have it, an aesthetic phenomenon. After my account of the metaphysics of tragedy in the last chapter, we should now have some sense of what it means to say that the staging of a play in the middle of a war is an exercise in dignity. Nonetheless, our understanding of such dignity at this point remains partial; and therefore we cannot appreciate fully the significance of Sontag's staging of *Godot* unless we move from the metaphysics to the politics of tragedy.

What Foucault will do that Nietzsche does not is give us a detailed and suggestive account of the practical and political character of what otherwise seem small and insignificant acts—acts relegated at best to artistic performance and at worst simply dismissed as frivolous and nonpolitical. Note, however, that we should not divorce Foucault's politics from the metaphysics of tragedy I outlined in the last chapter. Foucault's politics is finally *tragic* because he calls us to a dignity in the face of suffering that makes sense only against the backdrop of something like a metaphysics of tragedy. The necessity of this relationship between Foucault's politics and the metaphysics of tragedy will become clear as I proceed, but let me at least begin to offer an explanation of the link between metaphysics and politics by returning to two of Nietzsche's critics.

Toward a Metaphysics *and* a Politics of Tragedy

Remember Gillespie declares at the beginning of his account of nihilism that his intent is to show that Nietzsche's understanding of nihilism is fallacious and therefore so is his critique of liberalism. The stated aim of Gillespie's narrative is to save the politics of liberalism from its Nietzschean critique. Gillespie's text is thus an exercise in political theory. Gillespie does not, however, attempt to delineate Nietzsche's political theory (such as it is) in any detail but instead seeks to expose Nietzsche's metaphysics. Hence Gillespie argues that Nietzsche's notion of the Dionysian is simply the nominalist notion of an omnipotent God revisited. Gillespie concludes his critique of Nietzsche in this way:

> Even in his most radical incarnation as the world-game or pure music, Dionysus remains within the horizon of the philosophy of will that had its

> origins in the omnipotent God of nominalism. . . . Dionysus in this sense is not a new God who rises up to replace the old God who has died, but the old God who appears under a new mask. Dionysus, for Nietzsche, was the solution to nihilism, which he saw as the final form of Christianity. We have seen that Nietzsche was mistaken about the origins of nihilism, and we see here that he was equally mistaken about its solution, for his Dionysus is not the great antagonist of the Christian God but only his most recent incarnation.[1]

The crux of Gillespie's critique here is evident perhaps only if we remember that for Gillespie the omnipotent God of nominalism is a dark, incomprehensible, irrational, capricious, arbitrary, terrifying God, who, when he becomes human centuries later, arrives as Stalin. With this image in mind, the implications of Gillespie's critique of Nietzsche's notion of Dionysus are clear: To the extent Nietzsche offers us anything like a politics, it can be only "a politics of terror and destruction,"[2] since it is a politics founded upon metaphysical assumptions about the Dionysian will to power. Liberalism, says Gillespie, "may in some instances produce banality and boredom," but it will never lead us to Stalin.[3]

Gillespie's critique of Nietzsche's nihilism and politics unfolds, then, as a critique of his metaphysics. This relationship between metaphysics and politics is, of course, exactly what Milbank wants to expose for us when, echoing Gillespie, he suggests both that the politics of the so-called nihilists is a politics of fascism and that this politics rests upon ontological assumptions about the necessity of violence.[4] Where Milbank differs from Gillespie, of course, is that he does not limit his critique to Nietzsche but speaks in sweeping terms of "a single nihilist philosophy." In this sweeping critique, one of the figures Milbank charges with nihilism and convicts of fascism is Michel Foucault. As the accusation of "fascist" indicates, the focus of Milbank's concern is Foucault's politics; but like Gillespie, Milbank launches his attack primarily upon metaphysical terrain.

Unlike Gillespie's critique of Nietzsche, Milbank's politically motivated critique of Foucault's nihilism is not an attempt to save liberalism. Many of Foucault's critics, however, are out to save liberalism; and it is worth noting that although they might not share Milbank's politics, they do seem to share his understanding of Foucault. Hence Michael Walzer says that Foucault's politics is not anarchist, as some have suggested, "so much as nihilist. For on his own arguments, either there will be nothing left at all, nothing visibly human; or new codes and disciplines will be produced, and Foucault gives us no reason to expect that these will be any better than the ones we now live with. Nor, for that matter, does he give us any way of knowing what 'better' might mean."[5] Walzer suggests here that because Foucault refuses to construct a politics that champions certain values over others, values that finally would have to be rooted in certain metaphysical assumptions about the world, Foucault delivers us into a world without meaning, which is also a world where the very notion of politics loses all sense. Like Gillespie and Milbank, then, Walzer launches a political critique at the level of metaphysics.

According to Walzer, Foucault's refusal to delineate constructive positions and thereby risk exposing his metaphysical assumptions leaves him unable to make a distinction between fascism and liberalism, a distinction that requires, says Walzer, "some positive evaluation of the liberal state."[6] In the absence of any metaphysical commitments, Foucault is unable to make this distinction.[7] And, as Walzer sees it, the absence of this distinction desensitizes Foucault's "readers to the importance of politics; but politics matters."[8] Walzer thus shares Gillespie's notion that "politics" is synonymous with "liberal politics" and that any radical departure from the politics of liberalism is to be dismissed as nihilism.

It seems to me the best way to defend Foucault against these criticisms is to redescribe the terrain. In the myopic vision of critics such as Walzer, Foucault appears as a nihilist because such critics fail to see the tragic character of Foucault's politics. In a partial concession to Foucault's critics, however, I admit that the best way to display Foucault's politics is to do something he himself refused to do—and that is to set his politics against the background of something like the metaphysics of tragedy I outlined in the last chapter.

What does it mean to set Foucault's politics within the context of a metaphysics of tragedy that is itself rooted in Nietzsche? Well, certainly it means that Foucault's works in some way embody the Dionysian impulse. Of course this is exactly what Foucault's critics argue. Invariably they see Foucault as a direct descendent of Nietzsche. They then argue that to the extent Foucault's works embody an affirmation of Dionysus they lead us into nihilism and, worse, the horror of what Jan Kott identifies as the second Dionysian apocalypse—a politics of terror.

Remember, though, that Jean-Pierre Vernant offers us a different understanding of the link between an affirmation of Dionysian metaphysics and a subsequent politics. To place Foucault's politics against the background of a metaphysics of tragedy is, I think, to explore this link between an affirmation of Dionysus and a politics that ends not in terror but in the initiation of the *polis* into the practices of welcoming the other into the very heart of public life. It is this link between Dionysus and the *polis*, between metaphysics and politics, that supplies the key to the tragic politics of Michel Foucault.

The task at hand, then, is to explore this link, first by considering, in this chapter, both the metaphysical and political character of Foucault's early works—from *Madness and Civilization* (1961) to *The Archaeology of Knowledge* (1969)—and then by looking closely, in the next chapter, at the decidedly more political but still metaphysical character of his later works—from "The Order of Discourse" (1970) to the three-volume *History of Sexuality* (1976; 1984). This division between Foucault's "early" and "late" works is somewhat arbitrary. Nonetheless, as a matter of emphasis and in the name of schematic clarity, it makes sense to divide his works in this way for the following reason: It will allow us to read his early works as already anticipating his later politics; and conversely, it will allow us to see that the politics of his later works makes sense only against the background of the metaphysics that lurks in the early works. Hence, although I have divided Foucault's works in two, I have done so in order to unite his work along a single trajectory. Because sensitive critics, at least, will object immediately to my attempt to unite Foucault's works in this way, before I turn directly to Foucault's works, let me say a few words about how I intend to read Foucault.

Waiting for Godot in Paris

In the first chapter, I noted that Sarajevo provides a striking focal point for a summary of the twentieth century. After all, little more than a decade into the century the assassination of Archduke Ferdinand turned the eyes of the world toward Sarajevo and the subsequent unfolding of World War I. Now just a few years before the end of that same century—the bloodiest in history—the eyes of the world are once again fixed upon events in Sarajevo, events that in their immediacy have come to symbolize for our time what the Holocaust symbolized for an earlier generation. An unlikely conjunction of events across the course of a century have, then, made Sarajevo a uniquely symbolic place, which makes Susan Sontag's decision to stage a performance of *Waiting for Godot* in Sarajevo all the more remarkable—and all the more powerful.

For surely when Sontag says that *Waiting for Godot* "seems written for, and about, Sarajevo" and that it was the "one obvious play" for her to stage in that besieged city, she cannot be unaware that Beckett's play has the same focusing power for an understanding of the twentieth century as does the city of Sarajevo itself. Certainly it is more than coincidence that Foucault, one of the centuries greatest intellectuals, traces the roots of his own thought back to a winter night in Paris in 1953, when he went to see *Waiting for Godot*. It was, he remarked, "a breathtaking performance," one that led him to break with what had been the horizons of both his life and his thought until then.[9]

The horizons of his thought were those shared by "all other students of philosophy at that time" in France: Marxism, phenomenology, and existentialism.[10] The horizons of his life were those created by the events of World War II. In an interview from 1983, Foucault speaks about the horizons of someone growing up, as he did, in a small town in France in the 1930s and 1940s:

> What strikes me now when I try to recall those impressions is that nearly all the great emotional memories I have are related to the political situation. I think that boys and girls of this generation had their childhood formed by . . . great historical events. The menace of war was our background, our framework of existence. Then the war arrived. Much more than the activities of family life, it was these events concerning the world which are the substance of our memory.[11]

In another interview, Foucault mentions the relationship between this memory of a world at war and the possibilities of a meaningful postwar politics:

> For anyone who was twenty right after the World War, for anyone who had endured rather than participated in that tragedy, what on earth could politics represent when it was a matter of choosing between the America of Truman or the U.S.S.R. of Stalin? . . . The very experience of the war had shown us the necessity and the urgency of creating a society radically different from the one in which we had lived; a society that had accepted Nazism, had prostituted itself before it, and then had come out of it *en masse* with De Gaulle. In the light of all that, many young people in France had had the reaction of total rejection. One not only wanted a different world and a different society, one also wanted to go deeper, to transform oneself and to revolutionize relationships to be completely "other."[12]

Of course as a political enterprise, to become "completely other" was to break with the politics of Marxism and the politics of liberal democracy. But what would such a break entail, given that what was needed was not simply a different politics but one that could confront Hitler and Stalin? As Foucault puts it, the "gigantic shadows of fascism and Stalinism" darkened all the possible horizons of the postwar period.[13] Even in the early 1950s, decades before he would begin to think in a direct way about politics, Foucault seems to have had a sense that after Auschwitz and the Gulag the very notion of politics itself stood in question.

It is not hard to imagine the impact that a performance of *Waiting for Godot* might have had on a young Parisian intellectual living in the gloom of the great shadows of Hitler and Stalin, just as it is not hard to imagine the captivated audience sitting in the dim light of a theater in Sarajevo. Years after he wrote the play, Beckett commented that the world of *Godot* is a world where "it is not even possible to talk about truth, that's part of the anguish."[14] The world of *Godot* is, then, an impossible world, a world of dead ends and interminable waiting. And yet, says Beckett, it may be that "the artist can find a possible way out."[15] By his own account, Foucault's work in some important way began on that winter night in Paris in 1953 amidst the musings of Vladimir and Estragon. Hence we can imagine, I think, that all of Foucault's works depart from this moment and represent his attempt to find "a possible way out."

Of course, to say that all of Foucault's works depart from a single moment is to artificially unite the diverse corpus of his writings; and to unite his works in this way is to work against the grain of much of what Foucault was about.[16] Such a unifying account succumbs to what Gary Gutting calls the temptation of a "general interpretation" of Foucault.[17] Such an interpretation, says Gutting,

> is guaranteed to distort his thought. Interpretation typically means finding a unifying schema through which we can make overall sense of an author's works. Interpretations of Foucault, accordingly, single out some comprehensive unity or definitive achievement that is thought to provide the key to his work. They claim to have attained a privileged standpoint that provides the real meaning or significance of his achievement.
>
> Interpretation distorts Foucault because Foucault's work is at root ad hoc, fragmentary, and incomplete. . . . General interpretations of Foucault . . . deny two things that . . . are most distinctive and valuable about his voice: its specificity and its marginality.[18]

Gutting is right, I think, about the distorting powers of all attempts to force Foucault's works to gather around a single point. Nonetheless, this is exactly what I intend to do as I try to delineate Foucault's tragic politics. Such a reading of Foucault is justified, I think, in two ways, both of which Gutting identifies when he says the following: "General interpretations of Foucault are tempting because, for all their distortion, they can put us on to some important truths. My suggestion is not that we renounce them but that we regard them as nonunique and developed for specific purposes."[19] By imagining that Foucault's works both emerge from his encounter with *Godot* and, taken together, form something of a guide to a politics of tragedy, I do arrive, I think, at some important truths about Foucault. Note, however, that to arrive here is not the same as arriving at *the* truth about Foucault; rather, I enlist these truths not for the general purpose of offering a definitive interpretation of Foucault but, to use Gutting's word, for the more "specific" purpose of constructing my own narrative about nihilism, tragedy, and apocalypse.

Note, as well, that I say we can "imagine" such a reading of Foucault. The choice of the word is deliberate and draws upon Foucault's own words about the task of criticism—words that I quoted in the Preface but that are worth quoting again:

> I can't help but dream of a kind of criticism that would not try to judge, but to bring an oeuvre, a book, a sentence, an idea to life; it would light fires,

> watch the grass grow, listen to the wind, and catch the sea-foam in the breeze and scatter it. It would multiply, not judgments, but signs of existence; it would summon them, drag them from their sleep. Perhaps it would invent them sometimes—all the better. All the better. Criticism that hands down sentences sends me to sleep; I'd like a criticism of scintillating leaps of the imagination. It would not be sovereign or dressed in red. It would bear the lightning of possible storms.[20]

In what follows I do not mean to make any sovereign declarations about the meaning of Foucault's work; rather, my hope is that I can bring his works to life by imagining, for instance, that his suggestion at the end of *Madness and Civilization* that the world must now justify itself before the artistic works of madness is related in a decisive way both to Nietzsche's understanding of tragedy and to the notion of an "aesthetics of existence" that occupies Foucault's last books. To begin to imagine that this might be the case, let me turn now to Foucault's first major work.

Madness and Civilization

To the extent Foucault did find a way out of the world in which Vladimir and Estragon are confined, we should probably not be surprised that it was Nietzsche who led him there and that what he found when he arrived was tragedy. Foucault noted on numerous occasions that no single author influenced him more than Nietzsche.[21] Nowhere is Nietzsche more present in Foucault's work than in his first major book, *Madness and Civilization*, which bears a remarkable resemblance to Nietzsche's *Birth of Tragedy*.

For Nietzsche, what "we call culture" is the result of an ongoing competition between the Dionysian and Apollinian impulses, as each seeks to respond to the terror of the abyss and its accompanying questions of suffering. Both Dionysus and Apollo are present in any cultural complex; however, it is also the case that at any given moment one or the other of these impulses will be dominant. For example, Nietzsche argues that during the Homeric period, Apollo reigned over Greece like Pentheus reigned over Thebes—with a certain "measured restraint." But then into this Apollinian world marched Dionysus. And

> wherever the Dionysian prevailed, the Apollinian was checked and destroyed. But, on the other hand, it is equally certain that, wherever the first Dionysian onslaught was successfully withstood, the authority and majesty of the Delphic god exhibited itself as more rigid and menacing than ever. For to me the *Doric* state and Doric art are explicable only as a permanent military encampment of the Apollinian.[22]

As we saw in the last chapter, in the contest between Apollo and Dionysus, Nietzsche exhibits a preference for the latter, and hence tragedy is, as

Nietzsche sees it, finally a Dionysian phenomenon. If we turn to *Madness and Civilization* with both this contest and Nietzsche's preference in mind, we recognize immediately that in this work Foucault has moved the contest between Apollo and Dionysus forward into the seventeenth and eighteenth centuries and recast the characters as Reason and Madness.

We can imagine a time, says Foucault, in the Middle Ages and before, when madness did not exist, a "zero point" when "madness is an undifferentiated experience."[23] Then, late in the fifteenth century, madness as a distinct phenomenon appears in Europe. Indeed, madness displaces death as the main source of cultural "uneasiness." "Up to the second half of the fifteenth century, or even a little beyond," says Foucault, "the theme of death reigns alone. The end of man, the end of time bear the face of pestilence and war."[24] However, late in the fifteenth century, "the mockery of madness replaces death and its solemnity"[25] as the eschatological and apocalyptic figure of the day. Sometime during the fifteenth century in Europe, madness stepped from the abyss much as suffering itself did in the time of Homer.

Reason's initial response to the presence of madness was to engage it in dialogue. As Foucault puts it, in "the Middle Ages and until the Renaissance, man's dispute with madness was a dramatic debate in which he confronted the secret powers of the world."[26] According to Foucault, we discover something of the nature of this debate in the image of "the Ship of Fools." This ship appeared in "the imaginary landscape of the Renaissance,"[27] most notably in the painting of Bosch. However, this ship also

> had a real existence—for they did exist, these boats that conveyed their insane cargo from town to town. Madmen then led an easy wandering existence. The towns drove them outside their limits; they were allowed to wander in the open countryside, when not entrusted to a group of merchants or pilgrims. . . . Often the cities of Europe must have seen these "ships of fools" approaching their harbors.[28]

As Foucault sees it, the Ship of Fools provides us with an image of the dialogue between reason and madness in those initial moments when the latter first stepped from the abyss. Apparently what was at stake in this dialogue were "the limits rather than the identity of a culture."[29] Or to put it another way, the existence of the Ship of Fools—both as an image and a reality—indicates that for a time at least medieval Europe recognized in madness a legitimate questioning of its cultural identity; and thus the mad were not confined and excluded but were instead free to wander from city to city. As they wandered on the margins of the city, the mad existed as a questioning presence in medieval Europe, that is, as others who existed not to affirm a culture's identity but to remind it of its absolute limits. Such was the momentary dialogue between reason and madness.

In the matter of a few decades or perhaps a century, however, this dialogue first faltered and then ceased altogether. This dialogue faltered in the middle of the seventeenth century, when the cities of Europe began to intern and confine the mad, along with a host of other souls—the poor, the criminal, the sexually deviant. With the advent of what Foucault calls "the great confinement," the dialogue between reason and madness changed. As Foucault puts it, "Compared to the incessant dialogue of reason and madness during the Renaissance, the classical internment had been a silencing. But it was not total: language was engaged in things rather than really suppressed. Confinement, prisons, dungeons, even tortures, engaged in a mute dialogue between reason and unreason—the dialogue of struggle."[30]

Although at this point the dialogue between reason and madness had only faltered, by the end of the eighteenth century it would cease altogether—as the prison that had replaced the "madship" of fools became a "madhouse" and madness lost altogether its "dramatic seriousness" and "its tragic reality."[31] Foucault argues that with this loss the

> classical experience of madness is born. The great threat that dawned on the horizon of the fifteenth century subsides. . . . Madness has ceased to be—at the limits of the world, of man and death—an eschatological figure. . . . Madness will no longer proceed from a point within the world to a point beyond, on its strange voyage; it will never again be that fugitive and absolute limit. Behold it moored now, made fast among things and men. Retained and maintained. No longer a ship but a hospital.[32]

Once the ship becomes a hospital, the dialogue between reason and madness ceases. Whatever voice madness might have had as the limit of a culture is now silenced, as the mad are institutionalized and "inscribed in the sacred circle" of cultural identity.[33] Within this circle, madness no longer "refers elsewhere, and to *other things*"; the mad no longer bear the "stigmata" of another world but become instead the signs of cultural abnormality.[34] In short, the mad become the "mentally ill" and "rank among the problems of the city."[35] Foucault argues that it is precisely this understanding of madness as mental illness that we have inherited from the eighteenth and nineteenth centuries:

> In the serene world of mental illness, modern man no longer communicates with the madman: . . . the constitution of madness as a mental illness, at the end of the eighteenth century, affords the evidence of a broken dialogue, posits the separation as already effected, and thrusts into oblivion all those stammered, imperfect words without fixed syntax in which the exchange between reason and madness was made. The language of psychiatry, which is a monologue of reason *about* madness, has been established only on the basis of this silence.[36]

Foucault goes on to remark, famously, that the purpose of *Madness and Civilization* is to write not a history of psychiatry but "rather the archaeology of that silence."[37] For "in our era, the experience of madness remains silent in the composure of a knowledge which, knowing too much about madness, forgets it."[38]

Madness and Tragedy in the Classical Age

Between our own forgetting of madness and the Renaissance debate with it lies the classical age.[39] Hence it is to this age Foucault turns in order to discover the origins of what remains silent in the knowledge of psychiatry. And as he digs through the archives of the seventeenth and eighteenth centuries, Foucault discovers at the heart of the classical age "an extremely abstract law, which nonetheless forms the most vivid and concrete opposition, that of *day and night* . . . [an] absolutely divided time of brightness and darkness":[40]

> a law which excludes all dialectic and all reconciliation; which establishes, consequently, both the flawless unity of knowledge and the uncompromising division of tragic existence; it rules over a world without twilight, which knows no effusion, nor the attenuated cares of lyricism; everything must be either waking or dream, truth or darkness, the light of being or the nothingness of shadow. Such a law prescribes an inevitable order, a serene division which makes truth possible and confirms it forever.[41]

What we find, then, in the classical age, is a great division between reason and unreason, truth and darkness. This division is absolute. There is no twilight here. No margins exist at the edges of night and day. And given that the mad, as we find them early in the Renaissance, were marginal figures, what place might they have in a world without margins? Of course, we know already that they had no place and so were locked away. But what else might we say about the place of madness in the "inevitable order" of a "serene division"? According to Foucault, we might say also that madness, not content with its caged silence, "bears witness" to the "extremities where [this order] can be transgressed."[42] In "the confused murmur of madness," says Foucault, "the great law of the division has been violated; shadow and light mingle in the fury of madness."[43] Madness bears witness to the possibility of transgressing the stark boundaries of the classical division between day and night, reason and unreason. Indeed, it is precisely this transgressive and threatening power of madness that leads to its confinement. Hence madness was both a witness to a possible transgression of the classical order and, at the same time, a witness to "what degree it is essential not to transgress it."[44] To the extent madness did transgress the classical order, it was imprisoned. In the classical age, says Foucault,

> a sensibility was born which had drawn a line and laid a cornerstone, and which chose—only to banish. The concrete space of classical society reserved a neutral region, a blank page where the real life of the city was suspended; here order no longer freely confronted disorder, reason no longer tried to make its own way among all that might evade or seek to deny it. Here reason reigned in the pure state, in a triumph arranged for it in advance over a frenzied unreason.[45]

Foucault's account of the triumphant reign of reason over madness recalls Euripides' *Bacchae*. We can imagine that the Ships of Fools sailed into the cities of Europe in the same way that Dionysus entered Thebes, hoping that eccentricity might find a home in the polis. For a time, the cities of Europe, not knowing quite what to do with the phenomenon of madness, gave it a place—but only for a time. Before long, these cities came to see madness as a threat to their order, and so they banished the mad from the city, not now by sending them to wander on but by locking them up, just as Pentheus locked away Dionysus.

At this point, Foucault's script departs radically from that of the *Bacchae*, however, for in Foucault's account of the confinement of "frenzied unreason," the palace does not come tumbling down and Dionysus does not escape. Instead the Apollinian powers of reason win the day, and the intoxicating powers of Dionysian madness remain caged and silenced, still a witness, no doubt, to the limits of reason, but a witness reduced to an "indifferent murmur."

According to Foucault, madness does not stand alone as a witness to the possibility of transgressing the serene division of the classical age; another figure, standing apart from madness and yet complicit with it, also bears witness against reason—the figure of tragedy: "for tragedy is ultimately nothing but the confrontation of two realms," as the "tragic man . . . flings in the face of the pitiless sun all the secrets of the night."[46]

Foucault's tragic man, as he bears the secrets of the night and flings truths at the sun, is, of course, Nietzsche's Dionysus erupting into Apollo's camp, which at the time in question had taken on the guise of classical reason. Foucault says, however, that in the classical age the tragic man was not a madman:

> We understand that the tragic hero—in contrast to the baroque character of the proceeding period—can never be mad; and conversely madness cannot bear within itself those values of tragedy, which we have known since Nietzsche and Artaud. In the classical period, the man of tragedy and the man of madness confront each other, without a possible dialogue, without a common language; for the former can utter only the decisive words of being, uniting in a flash the truth of light and the depth of darkness; the latter endlessly drones out the indifferent murmur which cancels out both the day's chatter and the lying dark.[47]

Foucault notes that in the sixteenth century it was otherwise; hence King Lear was both a tragic figure and also a madman. In the seventeenth century, however, tragedy and madness are without a common language and stand as "two symmetrical, inverse figures" that bear witness against the triumph of classical reason.[48] Standing alone, neither madness nor tragedy can challenge reason's permanent military encampment. Without the stature of tragic heroes, the mad are condemned to their murmurs. Conversely, as heroes who can speak only with the concision of reason's words, classical heroes bear something less than the full measure of the world's secrets. If the transgression of the great division that empowers reason is to be more than a possibility, then madness and tragedy must once again find a common language, which, as it turns out, will be a language caught up in "the attenuated cares of lyricism." According to Foucault, at the end of the eighteenth century something occurs that creates the opening for this "possible dialogue" between madness and tragedy. However, before we can understand this event and its significance, I must first clarify a distinction that Foucault makes between "unreason" and "madness."

Madness as the Truth of Confinement

With the term "unreason" Foucault marks everything that opposes the order of reason. "Unreason" is thus an all-encompassing term. When in the seventeenth century Europe began to imprison those who threatened the order of the day, not only the mad found themselves incarcerated but so did "innumerable major and petty criminals . . . the poor and disabled, the elderly poor, beggars, the work-shy, those with venereal diseases, libertines of all kinds, people whose families or the royal power wished to spare public punishment, spendthrift fathers, defrocked priests; in short, all those who, in relation to the order of reason, morality, and society, showed signs of 'derangement.'"[49]

In the classical age, madness was but one of various manifestations of unreason; and

> it was in relation to unreason and to it alone that madness could be understood. Unreason was its support; or let us say that unreason defined the locus of madness's possibility. For classical man, madness was . . . unreason's empirical form; and the madman, tracing the course of human degradation to the frenzied nadir of animality, disclosed that underlying realm of unreason which threatens man and envelops—at a tremendous distance—all the forms of his natural existence.[50]

We see here why Foucault says that in the classical age the silencing of madness is not total, for a "dialogue of struggle" persists between reason and madness. Even after its confinement madness remained, for the classical age, a peculiarly fascinating and suggestive phenomenon—suggestive, in particular, because even in its muted voice and from behind the bars madness retained something of the apocalyptic character it had had in the Renaissance.[51] In other words, as the "empirical form" of unreason, madness, more than anything else, indicated the limits of reason's power.

By the end of the eighteenth century, however, madness no longer had even this role, for the mad were recognized now as distinct from their companions in prison, and in an effort of reform, critics of confinement argued that the incarceration of the mad was a scandal. Subsequently, as we've seen, the mad were transferred from the hands of prison guards to the hands of doctors; they ceased to be prisoners and were now patients. According to Foucault, here the silencing of madness is complete because what appeared to be a more humane treatment of the mad in fact separated madness from its truth:

> When, in the years that followed, this great experience of unreason, whose unity is characteristic of the classical age, was dissociated, when madness, entirely confined within a moral intuition, was nothing more than disease, then . . . psychology was born—not as the truth of madness, but as a sign that madness was now detached from its truth which was unreason and that it was henceforth nothing but a phenomenon adrift, *insignificant* upon the undefined surface of nature. An enigma without any truth except that which could reduce it.[52]

In the company of all the other marginal figures of classical unreason, madness was in an odd way at home, for in its cage it stood as both the face and the voice of unreason and thus represented to reason the truth of its own mad practice of locking away everything that, in its difference, threatened reason's triumphant reign. As long as the truth of madness was rooted in unreason, it retained its apocalyptic character and made apparent another truth: the truth of confinement. Or as Foucault puts it: "The presence of the mad among the prisoners is not the scandalous limit of confinement, but its truth; not abuse, but essence. The polemic instituted by the eighteenth century against confinement certainly dealt with the enforced mingling of the mad and the sane; but it did not deal with the basic relation acknowledged between madness and confinement."[53]

Because madness was the truth of confinement, the freeing of madness from its shackles had two enormous consequences: On one hand, it could no longer serve as the empirical form of unreason; on the other, without this association with unreason, madness itself was set adrift from its own truth as a manifestation of unreason and was reduced to an illness and a disease, a "surface" phenomenon that could be scientifically catalogued, treated, and perhaps cured.

The Lyricism of Protest

With the details of Foucault's story of the complex relationship between unreason and madness now in place, we are in a position to understand the crucial event at the end of the eighteenth century that will eventually open a space for the possible dialogue between madness and tragedy, a dialogue that in turn will lend itself to the transgression and contestation of the great division that empowers reason:

> In the disparity between the awareness of unreason and the awareness of madness, we have, at the end of the eighteenth century, the point of departure for a decisive movement: that by which the experience of unreason will continue, with Hölderlin, Nerval, and Nietzsche, to proceed ever deeper toward the roots of time—unreason thus becoming, *par excellence,* the world's *contratempo*—and the knowledge of madness seeking on the contrary to situate it ever more precisely within the development of nature and history. It is after this period that the time of unreason and the time of madness receive two opposing vectors: one being unconditioned return and absolute submersion; the other, on the contrary, developing according to the chronicle of a history.[54]

From the end of the eighteenth century until now, madness has lived within the confines of a science that, as it seeks to situate madness within its biological and social causes, has reduced it to "mental illness." According to Foucault, this approach to madness is an exercise that treats only surface phenomena and fails to consider that madness might emerge from the depths of time, that it might stand, as it did in the Renaissance—and even in the classical age—as a sign of the limits of reason and its order, that it might, in other words, be the product and the truth of a world without shades, which chooses to divide itself into the absolutes of day and night. To say that madness is the truth of confinement is to say that its existence is the result of a cultural choice to banish the other. But once science categorizes madness as an illness, the relationship between madness and this truth is lost. The truth, however, has not disappeared; it is now a truth born by unreason—the other vector that Foucault refers to above.

Although psychology and psychiatric medicine effectively silence madness, unreason persists as "the world's contratempo" and announces itself in what Foucault calls "the lyricism of protest."[55] The "lyrics" of unreason are not exactly the voice of the mad but of artists like Hölderlin, Nerval, and Nietzsche, who lurk on the margins of reason. Although not always imprisoned and not, in some instances, exactly mad, these figures bear an affinity nonetheless with the mad as we found them caged in the classical period:

> What the classical period had confined was not only an abstract unreason which mingled madmen and libertines, invalids and criminals, but also an

> enormous reservoir of the fantastic, a dormant world of monsters. . . . One might say that the fortresses of confinement added to their social role of segregation and purification a quite opposite cultural function. Even as they separated reason from unreason on society's surface, they preserved in depth the images where they mingled and exchanged properties. The fortresses of confinement functioned as a great, long silent memory; they maintained in the shadows an iconographic power that men might have thought was exorcised; created by the new classical order, they preserved against it and against time, forbidden figures that could thus be transmitted intact from the sixteenth to the nineteenth century. . . . Confinement allowed, indeed called for, this resistance of imagery.[56]

The new voice of unreason is not the voice of the mad but that of the artists, who nonetheless inherit across the centuries and in the lyricism of their protest the iconographic power and resistance of imagery that stands as the silent memory of confinement. Out of this reservoir of the fantastic, these new voices now speak where madness cannot and challenge the tyranny of reason, as if madness had transmitted

> to those able to receive it, to Nietzsche and to Artaud—those barely audible voices of classical unreason, in which it was always a question of nothingness and night, but amplifying them now to shrieks and frenzy . . . [and] giving them for the first time an expression, a *droit de cité,* and a hold on Western culture which makes possible all contestations, as well as *total* contestation.[57]

In what way do the works of Nietzsche and Hölderlin, Nerval and Artaud, Goya and Sade, make possible all contestation? And what is it that these figures contest? To answer this question is to return to the notion of a possible dialogue between madness and tragedy. For what these figures contest is precisely the great division of the classical period. These figures protest reason's permanent military encampment, a protest that once belonged to both madness and tragedy, before madness was progressively silenced and before tragedy was cleansed of its madness. According to Foucault, "in the lightning flash of works such as those of Hölderlin, of Nerval, of Nietzsche, or of Artaud—forever irreducible to those alienations that can be cured, resisting by their own strength that gigantic moral imprisonment which we are in the habit of calling . . . the liberation of the insane" the transgressive powers of madness and tragedy are reunited.[58]

The decisive event that takes place at the end of the eighteenth century, just as madness disappears and becomes an illness, is the emergence of this new voice of unreason that will now sound out from works of art. Art, and not madness, will now contest the totalizing power of reason; art will now bear witness to the possibility of transgressing the classical division between day and night, reason and unreason. Indeed, precisely as this witness, art makes possible all contestation, as it unites in a lightning flash the contesting powers of both tragedy and madness. Foucault says it this way: "Through Sade and Goya, the Western world received the possibility of transcending its reason in violence, and of recovering tragic experience beyond the promises of dialectic. After Sade and Goya, and since them, unreason has belonged to whatever is decisive, for the modern world, in any work of art."[59]

Unreason belongs to the work of art; and the work of art shatters the military-like powers of reason; but this is not to say that in the work of art unreason finds a long awaited home, that madness has regained its voice and is suddenly free of all confinement. For as Foucault notes, "where there is a work of art, there is no madness,"[60] for madness "can manifest itself only by departing from itself, by assuming an appearance in the order of reason and thus becoming contrary to itself. . . . Madness is always absent, in a perpetual retreat where it is inaccessible . . . and yet it is present."[61] According to Foucault, in its absence, madness is present as a question:

> By the madness which interrupts it, a work of art opens a void, a moment of silence, a question without answer, provokes a breach without reconciliation where the world is forced to question itself . . . [where] the world is made aware of its guilt. Henceforth, and through the mediation of madness, it is the world that becomes culpable . . . in relation to the work of art; it is now arraigned by the work of art, obliged to order itself by its language, compelled by it to a task of recognition, of reparation, to the task of restoring reason from that unreason and to that unreason. The madness in which the work of art is engulfed is the space of our enterprise.[62]

And what exactly is our enterprise, as Foucault conceives of it? Well, in the wake of our history from the middle of the seventeenth century until now, our enterprise can be nothing less than to contest a reason and an order whose very existence depends upon the exclusion of the other. In *Madness and Civilization* that other carries the face and the name of those who are mad; and although in subsequent works Foucault will explore in some detail a host of figures that have been, and continue to be, excluded in order to confirm the truth of reason, the mad seem to represent all others for Foucault, just as they were once the primary voice of unreason.[63] Consider the closing words of *Madness and Civilization:*

> Ruse and new triumph of madness: the world that thought to measure and justify madness through psychology must justify itself before madness, since in its struggles and agonies it measures itself by the excess of works like those of Nietzsche, of Van Gogh, of Artaud. And nothing in itself, especially not what it can know of madness, assures the world that it is justified by such works of madness.[64]

I said earlier that *Madness and Civilization* is remarkably similar to Nietzsche's *The Birth of Tragedy,* insofar as Foucault's account of the struggle between reason and the "frenzied unreason" of madness is simply a recasting of the struggle Nietzsche identifies with the names of Apollo and Dionysus. Hence we need to see that the ruse and new triumph of madness is a victory for Dionysus, since in these works of art madness comes storming out of the abyss and launches an attack upon reason's encampment. This similarity between the two narratives is amplified when Foucault interprets this resurgence of madness as the recovery of tragedy. But what does it mean to recover tragedy? What does it mean to declare a new triumph for Dionysus? Like Nietzsche in *The Birth of Tragedy,* all Foucault seems capable of saying at this point is something about the relationship between art and the justification of the world. And although Foucault does not invoke the language of "metaphysical comfort," he does, in the closing words of *Madness and Civilization,* remain bound to something like a metaphysics of tragedy, insofar as madness is but a manifestation of the intoxicating powers of Dionysus as they bear witness against the blinding light of Apollo's reason.

Let me pause for a moment to consider the status of Foucault's recourse to metaphysics, since my overall argument depends upon the link between the kind of metaphysical gestures Foucault makes in *Madness and Civilization* and the decidedly less metaphysical, and more obviously political, character of his later works.

From the Necessity of Metaphysics to the Real Work of Writing History

In a later work, Foucault comments on the metaphysical tendencies of his earlier book: "*Madness and Civilization* accorded far too great a place, and a very enigmatic one too, to what I called an 'experience,' thus showing to what extent one was still close to admitting an anonymous and general subject of history."[65] This retrospective comment echoes Nietzsche's attempt at self-criticism, in which he disparaged his own metaphysical tendencies in *The Birth of Tragedy.* And indeed, as Foucault moved forward from *Madness and Civilization* into his subsequent works, he attempted to leave behind the notion of an anonymous subject of history, or as one interviewer called it, the "diffuse naturalism" that haunts his early works.[66] And yet even as he leaves behind his metaphysical tendencies, Foucault does not dismiss them. Witness this exchange in the interview where his interlocutor brings up the issue of Foucault's "diffuse naturalism":

MF: What you call "naturalism" designates two things, I believe. A certain theory, the idea that underneath power with its acts of violence and its artifice we should be able to recuperate things themselves in their primitive vivacity: behind the asylum walls, the spontaneity of madness; through the penal system, the generous fever of delinquence; under the sexual interdiction the freshness of desire. And also a certain aesthetic or moral choice: power is evil, it's ugly, poor, sterile, monotonous, dead; and what power is exercised upon is right, good, rich.

Q: Yes. And finally the theme common to the orthodox Marxist and to the New Left: "Under the cobblestones lies the beach."

MF: If you like. There are moments when such simplifications are necessary. Such a dualism is provisionally useful to change the scenery from time to time and move from pro to contra.[67]

If we use these words to comment upon both *The Birth of Tragedy* and *Madness and Civilization,* then we find ourselves proclaiming that both Nietzsche's narrative about Dionysus and Apollo and Foucault's recasting of this narrative with the characters of reason and madness are necessary, metaphysically-bound simplifications, or what Gary Gutting calls, in the case of Foucault, "myths":

> The power of Foucault's writing is due not only to his carefully wrought histories and theories; it also derives from the much less consciously developed, deeply emotional myths that inform many of his books. These myths take the traditional form of a struggle between monsters and heroes. *The History of Madness,* for example, is built upon the struggle between the terrors inflicted on the mad by moralizing psychiatrists and the dazzling transgressions of mad artists.[68]

In what way are such "myths" necessary? Later in the same interview, Foucault identifies this necessity quite clearly:

> This reversal of values and of truths, which I was speaking about a while ago, has been important to the extent that it does not stop with simple cheers (long live insanity, delinquency, sex), but it permits new strategies. . . . One must pass to the other side—the "good side"—but in order to extract oneself from these mechanisms which make two sides appear, in order to dissolve the false unity, the illusory "nature" of this other side with which we have taken sides. This is where the real work begins, that of the historian of the present.[69]

These words are crucial if we are to understand Foucault's simultaneous dependence upon and transcendence of metaphysics, which is also to understand the relationship between his metaphysics and his politics.

Insofar as the metaphysics of tragedy involves first the bifurcation of the world into the same and the other and then the championing of the other over against the imprisonments of the same, then Foucault's myths are strategic necessities that serve to disturb the comfort of familiarity and provoke an awareness of the other's existence. This metaphysical, mythical bifurcation of the world into the forces of good and evil, however, is not where "the real work begins." For the real work involves what Foucault refers to here and elsewhere as the task of mapping "the history of the present"—and this work is not the work of metaphysics but of politics.[70]

At the end of *Madness and Civilization,* Foucault has not yet arrived at the real work of politics but has accomplished only a provisional, and largely metaphysical, change of scenery. Against the backdrop of this new scenery, the real work must now begin. To the extent *Madness and Civilization* accomplishes more than a change of scenery and at least gestures toward, for instance, the real work of protest, it is worth noting the character of this gesture. For in the closing words of the text, protest does not have the character of an agenda for political reform, nor is it a call for revolution. Rather, "the space of our enterprise," the locus of our work, is in some crucial way linked to art. For Foucault, as for Nietzsche, the political is also the aesthetic. Indeed, the final words of *Madness and Civilization* are an odd twisting of Nietzsche's declaration that the world is justified only as an aesthetic phenomenon.

As we saw in the last chapter, to justify the world as an aesthetic phenomenon is to affirm the Dionysian impulse that first calls the world into being. Foucault's narrative in *Madness and Civilization* depicts for us a world in which this impulse has been locked away and all but eliminated. What remains of the Dionysian impulse resides in works of art, works that serve a double purpose: On one hand, they represent the only hope we have of recovering a sense of "the great tragic powers of the world"[71] and, therefore, of justifying both the world and our existence within it; on the other hand, the fact these works exist at all is a sign that with the imprisonment of the Dionysian, we may have crafted a world that is beyond justification, for the caging of Dionysus separates the world from its aesthetic character.

Still, although we continue in the absence of any assurance that the world *is* justified—and that, therefore, politics is possible—we must, as Foucault sees it, continue nonetheless. The problem Foucault faces now, however, is how to speak with more clarity and in some detail about the powers of Dionysian art in the face of a triumphant reason, to speak, in other words, about the "real work" of a politics that in some way involves the task of writing a history of the present. Not until Foucault writes *Discipline and Punish* in the early 1970s does he begin to speak with any success about how it is that artists and their art might contest the oppressive powers of reason—and by then Foucault will no longer speak of transgression and contestation but of the strategies, tactics, and techniques of resistance. The real work of Foucault's tragic politics, in other words, although rooted in the kind of work he did in *Madness and Civilization,* does not really come to light until the 1970s and 1980s. This is not to say, however, that the works in between *Madness and Civilization* (1961) and *Discipline and Punish* (1975) do not contribute to Foucault's politics. In fact, they are vital, because in these works we learn why Foucault aligns politics with a particular way of reading and writing history.

It turns out that even though changing the scenery is a mythical, metaphysical enterprise, these myths are not exactly fairy tales, and they are linked to Foucault's politics by more than simple association.[72] Indeed, the link between myth and politics passes straight through history—or rather, the relationship between Foucault's metaphysics and his politics is to be found in his historiography. Before we can understand the importance of Foucault's historical method, however, we need to take a detour into his account of language as we find it in *The Birth of the Clinic* and *The Order of Things.*

A Pure Gaze That Would Be Pure Language

In his preface to *The Order of Things,* Foucault offers his own account of the relationship between *Madness and Civilization* and his next two major works. This account is a helpful guide to the path Foucault's work takes between 1961 and 1966, and beyond:

> It is evident that the present study is, in a sense, an echo of my undertaking to write a history of madness in the Classical age; it has the same articulations in time, taking the end of the Renaissance as its starting point, then encountering, at the beginning of the nineteenth century, just as my history of madness did, the threshold of a modernity that we have not yet left behind. But whereas in the history of madness I was investigating the way in which a culture can determine in a massive, general form the difference that limits it, I am concerned here with observing how a culture experiences the propinquity of things, how it establishes the tabula of their relationship and the order by which they must be considered. . . . The history of madness would be the history of the Other—of that which, for a given culture, is at once interior and foreign, therefore to be excluded (so as to exorcize the interior danger) but by being shut away (in order to reduce its otherness); whereas the history of the order imposed on things would be the history of the Same—of that which, for a given culture, is both dispersed and related, therefore to be distinguished by kinds and collected together into identities.[73]

We might say, then, that there is a difference between writing about *what* reason excludes and silences in order to confirm its truth and writing about *how* reason accomplishes this silencing. To write about the former is to write about the muted voice of the other; to write about the latter is to observe how difference is invariably situated within the order of the same. The task now is to write not the history of madness but the history of reason, a task that Foucault begins not in *The Order of Things* but in an earlier work, *The Birth of the Clinic,* which displays something of a transition from a history of the other to a history of the same.

In *The Birth of the Clinic,* the other is not madness but disease and death; and standing opposite this other, representing the same, is not the discipline of psychiatry but that of medicine. In the details, this work tells the story of a remarkable event that occurs as the eighteenth century gives way to the nineteenth: the birth of what Foucault calls the medical "gaze." The character of this gaze is quite familiar in our time, when x-rays, MRIs, and other such technological devices allow physicians to render visible even the darkest recesses of our bodies. However, in the first decades of the nineteenth century, when, for instance, the field of anatomy came into its own, this relationship between the diagnosis of disease and the visibility of the body was entirely new. For, according to Foucault, only at the end of the eighteenth century does the notion that the truth of disease lies in the depths of our bodies begin to emerge.

The birth of the gaze is the birth of a new kind of "light." Just a few decades before the end of the eighteenth century, the existence and truth of things required light, of course. But this light was "anterior to the gaze"; it shone from behind things, and through them, rendering them transparent. It was the light either of the world itself or of the divine; and in both cases, it came from elsewhere. Foucault notes that at

> the end of the eighteenth century, however, seeing consists in leaving to experience its greatest corporal opacity; the solidity, the obscurity, the density of things closed in upon themselves, have powers of truth that they owe not to light, but to the slowness of the gaze that passes over them, around them, and gradually into them, bringing them nothing more than its own light. The residence of truth in the dark center of things is linked, paradoxically, to this sovereign power of the empirical gaze that turns their darkness into light. All light is passed over into the thin flame of the eye, which now flickers around solid objects and, in so doing, establishes their place and form.[74]

Because this gaze was embodied in a new power of description, it was a gaze linked inextricably to language. The more doctors could see, the more they could say. Hence Foucault argues that this new medical knowledge rested on "a formidable postulate that all that is *visible* is *expressible,* and that it is *wholly visible* because it is *wholly expressible.*"[75] Complete visibility and total description together defined this new medical knowledge. Or as Foucault puts it, hovering over the whole enterprise was "the great myth of a pure Gaze that would be pure Language."[76]

Although both this Gaze and this Language are mythical, they are nonetheless the driving force behind the realities of what has become modern medicine. More importantly, at least for my purposes, this myth serves as a metaphor not only for a particular kind of medical perception but also for the entire edifice of reason as Foucault finds it both in the classical age and in the modern era. For the world of a pure Gaze that would be pure Language is the world of pure Reason—and in such a world as this, nothing is unexplained, nothing is out of sight, nor out of order. Nothing, finally, remains of the other, since the other is now inscribed in the sacred circle of the same.

If *The Birth of the Clinic* displays the transition in Foucault's work that takes place in between *Madness and Civilization* and *The Order of Things*, it is for the reason that here Foucault begins to analyze both the totalizing character of reason and the fact that the net reason casts over the world is a net composed of words. We should not be surprised, then, to find that the French title of Foucault's next work was *Les Mots et les choses—Words and Things*—and that in this work he would be preoccupied with language.

The Confinement of Language

As with *Madness and Civilization, The Order of Things* is a complex and intricate work. However, if our task is simply to chase down amidst the density of this text the primary object of Foucault's concern, then we can reduce the intricate nature of his argument to a certain level of simplicity. I have noted already that Foucault identifies this text as a history of the same, "a history of the order imposed on things." And yet in many ways the driving concern of this work remains the troubling status of the other. But here the other is neither madness nor disease but language. And insofar as this text is a history of language, it parallels Foucault's earlier history of madness.

Hence prior to the advent of the classical age in the seventeenth century, language, like madness, "was present everywhere and mingled with every experience";[77] words and things were inextricably linked, and language was a part of the world, a strange phenomenon in need of ceaseless decipherment. As Foucault notes, this understanding of language was possible because of the kinship between language and the divine:

> In its original form, when it was given to men by God himself, language was an absolutely certain and transparent sign for things, because it resembled them. The names for things were lodged in the things they designated. . . . This transparency was destroyed at Babel as a punishment for men. . . .
>
> But though language no longer bears an immediate resemblance to the things it names, this does not mean that it is separate from the world; . . . it is no longer nature in its primal visibility. . . . It is rather the figure of a world redeeming itself.[78]

Language and redemption are bound to one another because after Babel the task is "to uncover a language which God had previously distributed across the face of the earth" and thereby "to reconstitute the order of the universe."[79] This reconstitution of order is possible because everything in the world bears a mark, a signature "stamped upon things since the beginning of time."[80] As Foucault notes, in "the sixteenth century, signs were thought to have been placed upon things so that men might be able to uncover their secrets," and in so doing to restore "the great unbroken plain of words and things."[81] This task of redeeming the world bears an affinity with the practice of commentary, which assumes that

> below the language one is reading and deciphering there runs the sovereignty of an original Text. And it is this text which, by providing a foundation for the commentary, offers its ultimate revelation as the promised reward of commentary. . . . One speaks upon the basis of a writing that is part of the fabric of the world; one speaks about it to infinity, and each of its signs becomes in turn written matter for further discourse; but each of these stages of discourse is addressed to that primal written word whose return it simultaneously promises and postpones.[82]

According to Foucault, then, the relationship between words and things in the sixteenth century "enabled language to accumulate to infinity, since it never ceased to develop, to revise itself, and to lay its successive forms one over another. Perhaps for the first time in Western culture, we find revealed the absolutely open dimension of a language no longer able to halt itself."[83]

Unable to halt and accumulating to infinity, language in the sixteenth century lost itself in an "enigmatic density"[84] and had a status not unlike that of madness—insofar as, like madness, it was something full of secrets that beckoned from beyond. With the advent of the classical age in the seventeenth century, however, language left its home in the thickness of the world and entered what in effect was a period of confinement: "From an extreme point of view, one might say that language in the Classical era does not exist. But that it functions: its whole existence is located in its representative role, is limited precisely to that role and finally exhausts it. Language has no other locus, no other value, than in representation."[85]

Language did not, of course, literally cease to exist in the classical age. In fact, it was all-important. Foucault calls our attention, however, to the fact that its importance did not rest in its enigmatic character, in its intriguing existence, but in its ability to function as a device designed to gather the whole of the world into a system of representations. In the classical age, language exists

> only in order to be transparent; it has lost that secret consistency which, in the sixteenth century, inspissated it into a world to be deciphered, and interwove it with all the things of the world . . . ; in the Classical age, discourse is

> that translucent necessity through which representation and beings must pass—as beings are represented to the mind's eye, and as representation renders beings visible in their truth.[86]

With this understanding of the representative power of language was born "the great utopia of a perfectly transparent language in which things themselves could be named without any penumbra of confusion."[87] Words are no longer enigmatic, but "sovereign," and they capture, "without residium and without opacity," the things of the world.[88] As we know from Foucault's earlier work, one of the "things" captured in this age was madness, but what we can now see perhaps more clearly than before is that the confinement of madness was simply part of a general imprisonment in the classical age, an imprisonment that extended, oddly enough, even to words themselves, as they were reduced to the transparency necessary for their representative function.

To recall *The Birth of the Clinic,* we should see clearly now that the classical utopia of a perfectly transparent language and a perfectly transparent world outlived the classical age and became the founding myth of the modern period, where this utopia is transformed into the hope of a pure Gaze that would be pure Language. There is a difference, however, between the classical utopia and the modern myth. For as Foucault describes it in *The Birth of the Clinic,* the modern myth of the pure Gaze is, paradoxically, born not of transparency but of a new density and opacity that both things and words gather around themselves. Thus at the end of the classical age, "things in their fundamental truth have now escaped from the space of [representation]. . . . They turn in upon themselves, posit their own volumes, and define for themselves an internal space."[89] And as with things, so, too, with words: "From the nineteenth century, language began to fold in upon itself, to acquire its own particular density, to deploy a history, an objectivity, and laws of its own. It became one object of knowledge among others."[90] Compared with the rich, fertile, and primal character of language during the Renaissance, language in the nineteenth century experienced a "demotion . . . to the mere status of an object."[91] According to Foucault, this demotion is not, however, without compensation.

The Madman and the Poet

Foucault notes that "at a time when language was burying itself within its own density as an object and allowing itself to be traversed, through and through by knowledge, it was also reconstituting itself elsewhere, in an independent form, difficult to access, folded back upon the enigma of its own origin and existing wholly in reference to the pure act of writing."[92] This reconstitution elsewhere takes place, as Foucault sees it, in literature:

> Literature is the contestation of philology . . . : it leads language back from grammar to the naked power of speech, and there it encounters the untamed, imperious being of words. . . . At the moment when language, as spoken and scattered words, becomes an object of knowledge, we see it reappearing in a strictly opposite modality: a silent, cautious deposition of the word upon the whiteness of a piece of paper, where it can possess neither sound nor interlocutor, where it has nothing to say but itself, nothing to do but shine in the brightness of its being.[93]

Language may have been demoted to an object, but at the same time it had "resumed the enigmatic density it possessed at the time of the Renaissance," as if from within the folds of its new found opacity it had discovered the path of an escape not only from the "colorless," representative functions it had served in the classical age but also from the renewed efforts of a penetrating Gaze that had not given up hope of a pure Language and total description. Like the silent memory and the dormant world of monsters that arose in the fortresses of confinement and that came later to haunt reason, language, as it was subjected to its confinement as an object of knowledge, formed its own reservoir of the fantastic in literature. Indeed, opposite the penetrating Gaze that turns even language into an object and "at the other extremity of our culture,"

> the question of language is entrusted to that form of speech which has no doubt never ceased to pose it, but which is now, for the first time, posing it to itself. That literature in our day is fascinated by the being of language is neither the sign of an imminent end nor proof of a radicalization: it is a phenomenon whose necessity has its roots in a vast configuration in which the whole structure of our thought and our knowledge is traced.[94]

Foucault consistently traces the beginning of this "vast configuration" of our thought to the middle of the seventeenth century, to the division between reason and unreason, and to the confinement not only of the mad but of words and things generally within the sovereignty of representation. And even though this age came to an end less than two centuries after it began, it nonetheless bestowed upon its descendants its hopes and dreams. Hence the classical utopia of a perfectly transparent language that captures perfectly and without remainder all the things of the world becomes, at the end of the eighteenth century, the myth of a pure Gaze that would be pure Language—and that myth lives among us still. That's the bad news.

The good news, according to Foucault, is that already in the sixteenth and seventeenth centuries, even before it was fully formed, there were those who stood as witnesses against this myth. For in their stammered, imperfect words "without fixed syntax," the mad contested the notion of a transparent language. Recall that Foucault suggests in *Madness and Civi-*

lization that this contestation, preserved as a silent memory in the fortresses of confinement, was transmitted across the centuries and emerged, intact, in the works of nineteenth- and twentieth-century artists. In *The Order of Things,* Foucault speaks more specifically about this link between the mad of the sixteenth and seventeenth centuries and the artists of our own time.

On one end of the vast configuration that is our thought, says Foucault, stands the madman and at the other the poet—and both bear witness against the confining powers of language-become-rational discourse, a discourse that depends upon the division between the same and the other, identity and difference. The madman, says Foucault,

> is the disordered player of the Same and the Other. He takes things for what they are not, and people for one another. . . . In the cultural perception of the madman that prevailed up to the end of the eighteenth century, he is Different only in so far as he is unaware of Difference; he sees nothing but resemblances and signs of resemblance everywhere; for him all signs resemble one another, and all resemblances have the value of signs.[95]

Much nearer us, says Foucault, and brought close by "symmetry" to the madman, is the poet:

> he who, beneath the named, constantly expected differences, rediscovers the buried kinships between things, their scattered resemblances. Beneath the established signs, and in spite of them, he hears another, deeper, discourse, which recalls the time when words glittered in the universal resemblance of things. . . . The poet brings similitude to the signs that speak it, whereas the madman loads all signs with a resemblance that ultimately erases them. They share, then, on the outer edge of our culture and at the point nearest to its essential divisions, that "frontier" situation—a marginal position and a profoundly archaic silhouette—where their words unceasingly renew the power of their strangeness and the strength of their contestation.[96]

At the end of *The Order of Things,* Foucault pins his hope for contestation on the rebirth of language as literature. More concretely, he pins his hope on the poets. It would appear, then, that we have arrived back at the end of *Madness and Civilization,* knowing a little more perhaps about the classical age and about words and things, but knowing very little still about exactly how it is that poets might effectively challenge the hegemony of reason. At best, Foucault has made it clear that the contest between reason and unreason, between order and all those things that do not fit into that order without residium, is a contest that plays itself out upon the terrain of language. But of the details concerning a politics of poetry, for instance, Foucault says nothing. Despite appearance, however, Foucault has in fact moved much closer to what, in the space of the next ten years, will become his politics. If this is not apparent, it is because in my attempt to reduce *The Order of Things* to a history of language that bears some resemblance to the history of madness, I have left out a crucial part of Foucault's story, the part that concerns not the history of language but the history of history itself.

Enslaved Sovereignty and the Homeland of History

Although language is a pivotal character, it is in fact only one of three main characters in *The Order of Things.* For Foucault did not set out to write a history of language but, as the subtitle indicates, "An Archaeology of the Human Sciences." The human sciences are those sciences that focus upon human beings as objects of knowledge, sciences that concern, when they first emerge in the nineteenth century, life, labor, and language (biology, political economy, and philology) and that later are joined by anthropology, psychology, sociology, and so on. Such sciences have not existed forever, which is to say that human beings have not always been in the curious position of being at once objects of knowledge and subjects that know. Thus in the classical period we do not find the sciences of biology, economics, and philology, but natural history, the analysis of wealth, and general grammar: "When natural history becomes biology, when the analysis of wealth becomes economics, when, above all, reflection upon language becomes philology, and Classical *discourse,* in which being and representation found their common locus, is eclipsed, then, in the profound upheaval of such an archaeological mutation, man appears in his ambiguous position as an object of knowledge and as a subject that knows."[97] From this ambiguous position human beings enter into an entirely different relationship with things:

> It is no longer their identity that beings manifest in representation, but the external relation they establish with the human being. The latter, with his own being, with his power to present himself with representations, arises in a space hollowed out by living beings, objects of exchange, and words, when, abandoning representation, which had been their natural site hitherto, they withdraw into the depths of things and roll up upon themselves in accordance with the laws of life, production, and language.[98]

Not just words and things, then, regain their enigmatic density at the end of the classical era, but human beings as well. For in their ambiguous position as objects of knowledge and subjects that know, human beings become what Foucault calls "enslaved sovereigns."[99] Insofar as we are subjects who command a knowledge of both the world and ourselves, we are sovereigns; we have finally received the dominion that was given to us so long ago. And yet because as objects we are composed of the very things we study, when life, labor, and language withdraw into the depths we find ourselves curiously trapped in the vacancy they leave behind. In keeping with the paradoxical and simultaneous birth of a pure Gaze and opaque things, just as human beings locate themselves within this gaze as objects to be known, they, too, roll up upon themselves. In an extension of the paradox, human beings arrive at a new relationship with their finitude. Prior to the nineteenth century, an awareness of finitude was rooted in an awareness of human inadequacy. As Foucault puts it, human beings experienced a "negative relation to infinity."[100] We knew that we were finite because we were inherently limited and not, therefore, infinite. However, according to Foucault:

> The experience taking form at the beginning of the nineteenth century situates the discovery of finitude not within the thought of the infinite, but at the very heart of those contents that are given, by a finite act of knowing, as the concrete forms of finite existence . . . : if man's knowledge is finite, it is because he is trapped, without possibility of liberation, within the positive contents of language, labour, and life; and inversely, if life, labour, and language may be posited in their positivity, it is because knowledge has finite forms. . . . Thus, in the very heart of empiricity, there is indicated the obligation to work backwards—or downwards—to an analytic of finitude, in which man's being will be able to provide a foundation in their own positivity for all those forms that indicate to him that he is not infinite.[101]

We are trapped in positivity because, paradoxically, the very things that compose us and indicate to us our finite nature appear themselves, as they retreat before the gaze of our knowledge, to be infinite. Or to put it in Foucault's words, "Heralded in positivity, man's finitude is outlined in the paradoxical form of the endless."[102] Kant declared that only on the basis of our finitude, only on the basis of our finite knowledge, can we provide the foundations of our thought. Foucault wants us to see the paradoxical and "ultimately unworkable" character of this enterprise.[103] The knowledge we have of ourselves is possible only if we are, indeed, finite beings composed of finite things; and yet as we stake everything on the finite character of our life, our work, and our words, we discover that this finitude cannot "contemplate itself" and, in fact, promises instead "that very infinity it refuses":[104]

> When he tries to define himself as a living being, he can uncover his own beginning only against the background of a life which itself began long before him; when he attempts to re-apprehend himself as a labouring being, he cannot bring even the most rudimentary forms of such a being to light except within a human time and space which have been previously institutionalized, and previously subjugated by society; and when he attempts to define his essence as a speaking subject, prior to any effectively constituted language, all

> he ever finds is the previously unfolded possibility of language, and not the stumbling sound, the first word on the basis of which all languages and even language itself became possible. It is always against a background of the already begun that man is able to reflect on what may serve him as origin.[105]

Foucault's narrative in *The Order of Things* is a story not only about the progressive imprisonment of words and things but also of the imprisonment of those beings who, standing amidst words and things, occupy the ambiguous position of the modern subject, whose ceaseless task to render both the world and itself visible is met with the endless retreat of the objects locked within its gaze, a retreat that is in turn met with an ever renewed search for origins. In fact, it is precisely this search for origins that defines the vocation of modern human beings; thus the discipline of history holds a unique place, since to apprehend ourselves is now to write the history of the positivities that simultaneously compose us and yet escape our knowledge. This search for the historicity of life, labor, and language brings with it, and in tow, something else: a "more radical" history,

> that of man himself—a history that now concerns man's very being, since he now realizes that he not only "has history" all around him, but is himself, in his own historicity, that by means of which a history of human life, a history of economics, and a history of languages are given their form. . . . History constitutes, therefore, a favourable environment. . . . To each of the sciences of man it offers a background, which establishes it and provides it with a fixed ground and, as it were, a homeland.[106]

As Foucault tells the tale, the modern discipline of history is born at that point where the positivities that compose us folded up upon themselves and escaped into obscurity, leaving us oddly homeless in the hollow left behind by their retreat. The writing of history is an attempt to run past these positivities in retreat, to get behind them, to stand in their way and stop their escape. If they themselves refuse to yield to us the mysteries of our origin, then history will reveal what they will not; it will become their fixed ground and our homeland.

This account of the relationship between the human sciences and history is, I think, *the* discovery of *The Order of Things*—a discovery that Foucault will carry with him into the rest of his works and that will become the central preoccupation of the work that follows most closely upon this one. It is not fair to say, therefore, that between the obscure gestures toward art at the end of *Madness and Civilization* and the appearance of the poet in *The Order of Things,* Foucault fails to move any closer to delineating a politics. In fact, as it will turn out, Foucault's narrative about the birth of the modern subject as an enslaved sovereign, who tries to escape the trap of its finitude in the act of writing history, both makes possible and makes sense of Foucault's politics as we find it displayed in his later works. For it is in the light of his discoveries about the human sciences that Foucault declares the need to rewrite "the history of History,"[107] that he discovers, in other words, that what we might call the politics of the other will involve a novel historiography. This historiography attempts to outline a way to write history that counters that writing of history which serves only to shore up the sovereignty of the same. To varying degrees, Foucault employed this historiography in each of his first three major works—and as early as *Madness and Civilization* had designated it, if somewhat tentatively, "archaeology." In *The Archaeology of Knowledge*, Foucault sets out to define this method in some detail.

Murdering History

Archaeology is *counterhistory*—insofar as *history* is an attempt to ground the sovereignty of the subject. Foucault calls the latter sort of history "total history" and notes that its project "is one that seeks to reconstitute the overall form of a civilization, the principle—material or spiritual—of a society, the significance common to all the phenomena of a period, the law that accounts for their cohesion."[108] Like the myth of a pure Gaze that would be pure Language, total history works toward the possibility of "total description"; it "draws all phenomena around a single center—a principle, a meaning, a spirit, a world-view, an overall shape."[109] To write history in this way is to assume that beneath the panoply of events lies "a network of causality" that can bind disparate events together and thus spin a tale of the coherence and the continuity of the human enterprise.[110] Where total history champions themes of cause and effect and continuity, the counterhistory of archaeology focuses upon the notions of chance, discontinuity, and the singularity of the event.

The task of formulating what Foucault calls the "general theory of discontinuity" appears, he says, to be "particularly difficult"; it is as "if we were afraid to conceive of the Other in the time of our own thought."[111] Here we see the link Foucault makes between archaeology as a historical method and the championing of the other that was so central to his first three works. Archaeology, then, depends upon the ability to discern the presence of the other within the fortress of the same. For traditional history, this discernment proves difficult; and according to Foucault,

> there is a reason for this. If the history of thought could remain the locus of uninterrupted continuities, if it could endlessly forge connexions . . . if it could weave, around everything that men say and do, obscure syntheses that anticipate for him, prepare him, and lead him endlessly toward his future, it would provide a privileged shelter for the sovereignty of conscious-

> ness. Continuous history is the indispensable correlative of the founding function of the subject: that guarantee that everything that has eluded him may be restored to him; the certainty that time will disperse nothing without restoring it in a reconstituted unity; the promise that one day the subject—in the form of historical consciousness—will once again be able to appropriate, to bring back under his sway, all those things that are kept at a distance by difference, and find in them what might be called his abode.

Here we see perhaps more clearly than we did in *The Order of Things* both that the modern subject and total history are twins, born of the same desire for total description and complete visibility, and that history serves the function of restoring to this subject all those words and things that elude it in the distance of their opacity. History, then, contributes in a vital and foundational way to the sovereignty of the same. Against this sovereignty and against this history, Foucault places the counterhistory of archaeology, which, not surprisingly, given Foucault's previous work in *The Order of Things,* looks at first glance more like a theory about language than a historical method. Indeed, *The Archaeology of Knowledge*—which is Foucault's self-professed attempt to delineate and refine the method that had been, perhaps surreptitiously, at work in his first three books—extends the discussion of language that had been particularly prominent in *The Order of Things*—or rather, it extends the analysis of discourse, which is not synonymous with the analysis of language.

"The question posed by language analysis of some discursive fact or another," Foucault notes, "is always: according to what rules has a particular statement been made, and consequently according to what rules could other similar statements be made? The description of the events of discourse poses a quite different question: how is it that one particular statement appeared rather than another?"[112] Foucault's answer to this question involves the notion of a "discursive practice": "a body of anonymous, historical rules, always determined in the time and space that have defined a given period, and for a given social, economic, geographical, or linguistic area, the conditions of operation of the enunciative function."[113] James Bernauer offers a helpful gloss on Foucault's notion of a discursive practice: "The practice of discourse is a 'violence' done to things, not by virtue of men's ideas nor through the grammatical systems of language, but by a set of rules that determine what can be stated at a particular time and how these statements are related to others."[114] In the intricacy of its details, *The Archaeology of Knowledge* is Foucault's attempt to delineate these rules of discourse. What anonymous, historical rules, for instance, lurking in silence beyond the grammar of language, indeed beyond language itself, produced the statements that unified the diverse phenomena of madness into an object called "mental illness"? Or what rules determine that something said by a doctor will count and become a statement, when the same thing, or something different, said by someone else will not?

In *The Order of Things,* Foucault discovered the importance of the relationship between words and the confining power of reason; in *The Archaeology of Knowledge,* with his analysis of discursive practices, he attempts to display, in more detail and with more precision, how words achieve this kind of power. Of course, to arrive at a description of how words empower imprisonment is also to describe how words might lead to an escape from that imprisonment. Foucault suggests as much early in *The Archaeology of Knowledge* when he speaks of the procedure that enables his new approach to the analysis of discourse, a procedure at odds with the narratives of continuity that draw "all phenomena around a single center—a principle, a meaning, a spirit, a world-view, an overall shape":

> We must renounce all those themes whose function is to ensure the infinite continuity of discourse. . . . Once these immediate forms of continuity are suspended, an entire field is set free. A vast field, but one that can be defined nonetheless: this field is made up of the totality of all effective statements (whether spoken or written), in their dispersion as events and in the occurrence that is proper to them. Before approaching with any degree of certainty, a science, or novels, or political speeches, or the *oeuvre* of an author, or even a single book, the material with which one is dealing is, in its raw, neutral state, a population of events in the space of discourse in general.[115]

This setting free of the field of effective statements, such that statements are not prematurely drawn into the continuity of a narrative about an author's work or a historical epoch, is of a piece with the writing of the counterhistory that *is* archaeology. Foucault puts the matter this way:

> We must ask ourselves what purpose it ultimately served by this suspension of all accepted unities. . . . In fact, the systematic erasure of all given unities enables us first to restore to the statement the specificity of its occurrence, and to show that discontinuity is one of those great accidents that create cracks not only in the geology of history, but also in the simple fact of the statement; it emerges in its historical irruption.[116]

To analyze discursive practices is to map the anonymous rules according to which, at a given time and location, the world is ordered in one way rather than another. However, one can map these rules for a given group of statements, indeed, one can determine what qualifies as a statement and what kind of group it belongs to, only if one first frees statements from all assumptions of unity. Precisely this liberation of statements makes possible a counterhistory. Archaeology, therefore, "seeks . . . to untie all those knots that historians have patiently tied."[117] Foucault says that by freeing statements from "all the groupings that purport to be natural, immediate, universal unities, one is able to describe other unities, but this time by a group of controlled decisions," that is, strategically.[118] Thus the analysis of discursive practices goes hand in hand with the writing of counterhistory because both involve the freeing of words and events from all previous assumptions of unity. In this way, as Thomas Flynn puts it,

> archaeology is both counter-history and social critique. It is counter-history because it assumes a contrapuntal relationship to traditional history, whose conclusions it more rearranges than denies and whose resources it mines for its own purposes. . . . [As] social critique . . . [i]t radicalizes our sense of the contingency of our dearest biases and most accepted necessities, thereby opening up a space for change.[119]

Such counterhistory meets resistance among historians, however. As Foucault says:

> The cry goes up that one is murdering history whenever . . . one is seen to be using in too obvious a way the categories of discontinuity and difference. One will be denounced for attacking the inalienable rights of history and the very foundations of any possible historicity. But one must not be deceived: what is being bewailed with such vehemence is not the disappearance of history, but the eclipse of that form of history that was secretly, but entirely, related to the synthetic activity of the subject. . . . What is being bewailed, is that ideological use of history by which one tries to restore to man everything that has unceasingly eluded him for over a hundred years.[120]

With its focus upon discontinuity and rupture, archaeology has absolutely no interest in restoring to humans all that eludes them, since it works from the assumption that this task of restoration is rooted in a fear of the other. Rather, archaeology seeks to explain both how discourse functions to construct the world of the same and how the rules of discourse might be evaded and breached, allowing for the possibility of contestation. Given Foucault's account of discursive practices, however, the possibility of the latter is not apparent immediately. In other words, the problem that existed at the end of *Madness and Civilization* and in *The Order of Things* remains: Given the hegemony of a particular order and a particular rational discourse, how can it be that the madman or the poet can effectively contest anything?

As if still thinking about the mad artist, Foucault, at the end of *The Archaeology of Knowledge*, confronts precisely this problem in his work in the form of questions from an imaginary interlocutor:

> Are you forgetting the care with which you enclosed the discourse of others within systems of rules? Are you forgetting all those constraints that you described so meticulously? Have you not deprived individuals of the right to

> intervene personally in the positivities in which their discourse is situated? . . . You make revolution very easy for yourself, but very difficult for others. It might be better if you had a clearer awareness of the conditions in which you speak, and a greater confidence in the real action of men and in their possibilities.[121]

To these self-imposed questions, Foucault replies that they emerge from a misunderstanding both of his account of discursive practices and, more generally, of human freedom. "I have not," he says, "denied—far from it—the possibility of changing discourse: I have deprived the sovereignty of the subject of the exclusive and instantaneous right to it."[122] Foucault then turns the tables and begins to ask questions of the imaginary questioner:

> What political status can you give to discourse if you see in it merely a thin transparency that shines for an instant at the limit of things and thoughts? Has not the practice of revolutionary discourse and scientific discourse in Europe over the past two hundred years freed you from this idea that words are wind, an external whisper, a beating of wings that one has difficulty in hearing in the serious matter of history? . . . What is that fear which makes you seek, beyond all boundaries, ruptures, shifts, and divisions, the great historic-transcendental destiny of the Occident?
>
> It seems to me that the only reply to this question is a political one. But let us leave that to one side for today. Perhaps we will take it up again soon in another way.[123]

All along, Foucault's narratives have led us to ask about the status of those marginal figures who contest confinement. And all along, what we have wanted to hear about is the "real action" of such figures, since it is just this sort of action that characterizes our understanding of politics. Instead, Foucault offered us the murmurs of the madman and the lightning flashes embodied in works of art; and now, just when his thought has achieved an unparalleled rigor, it seems we are left with only some vague sense of the possibilities that emerge when we free statements from narratives of continuity.

In fact, though, we are left with a good deal more than this. For we know now that the path to politics passes straight through the contested ground of history; and we can count on the fact that Foucault, even though he leaves it to the side for now, will return to the political character of his proposal for a counterhistory. We also know, or at least can guess, how Foucault will take up again "in another way" the relationship between history and politics. For standing just inside the limits of Foucault's peripheral vision in *The Archaeology of Knowledge* is the whole question of the relationship between discursive and *nondiscursive* practices. Indeed, words are not wind, but Foucault must now prove that this is so by analyzing what he will come to call the "material reality" of discourse.[124] In the details of this analysis, Foucault will begin, as Gilles Deleuze says, "to outline his conception of a political philosophy"[125]—a political philosophy that does not lead, as Gillespie, Milbank, and others would have it, to a politics of terror. It will be the task of the next chapter to follow Foucault as he picks up where he left off in *The Archaeology of Knowledge* and begins to outline a politics. However, before we move on, let me summarize the path of Foucault's thought so far.

As I have imagined it, Foucault's thought departs from his encounter with *Waiting for Godot* on a winter night in Paris in 1953. It then follows a trajectory of escape that, from the beginning, was an attempt to think about "what on earth" politics could be after Hitler and Stalin. As if following Beckett's suggestion that only the artist might find a way out of this impossible postwar world, Foucault makes the artists, and more particularly the poets, the heroes of his early works. The poets are heroes because, as the inheritors of the silent memory of all those excluded from the order of reason, they stand as the last line of defense against a world founded upon the confinement and the exclusion of the other. Indeed, in the lyricism of their protest they contest this world and call it to account; they refuse to allow the myriad voices of the other to be reduced to silence. In the attenuated cares of their lyricism, the poets keep open the possibility that we might yet face suffering with dignity and thus avoid the radical despair of nihilism. This attempt to answer Hitler and Stalin—and to avoid the pathetic fate of Vladimir and Estragon—with recourse to poetry may seem doomed from the start. But that continuing sense of doom is the reason that the promise of the poet involves a recovery of tragedy. As we will see in the next chapter, the politics of the poet, though it may not make sense to the liberal mind, makes perfect sense against the mythical background of a tragic universe.

6

On the Borders of Heaven and Earth: The Tragic Politics of Michel Foucault

At the end of the last chapter, I noted that the next stage of Foucault's attempted escape would involve linking discursive practices to their nondiscursive counterparts. In fact, Foucault had begun to make this link already in *The Archaeology of Knowledge.* Archaeology, says Foucault, is not only the analysis of discursive practices, it

> also reveals relations between discursive formations and non-discursive domains (institutions, political events, economic practices and processes).... In other words, the archaeological description of discourses is deployed in the dimension of a general history; it seeks to discover that whole domain of institutions, economic processes, and social relations on which a discursive formation can be articulated; it tries to show how the autonomy of discourse and its specificity nevertheless do not give it the status of pure ideality and total historical independence.[1]

As the 1960s gave way to the 1970s, Foucault continued to think about the paradoxical notion of an autonomous discourse that is yet not historically independent; and these thoughts carried him away from the analysis of discursive practices into the analysis of nondiscursive domains—or rather, into the analysis of the relationship between discourse and the institutional, material conditions that are the field of its operation. Without this analysis, any claims Foucault might want to make about artistic and poetic challenges to the constraints of discourse would remain unconvincing. If such claims were to be convincing, then Foucault needed to support them with a more precise account of how poetry might change the world. As it stood, one of the limits of archaeology was its inability to account for change.[2]

Archaeology was, as Foucault described it, a purely descriptive enterprise.[3] Although it could record that change had occurred, it could offer no account of change itself—even if it did have something to say about how change does *not* occur: hence the challenge it leveled both at the idea that change is rooted in the actions of sovereign subjects and at the notion that history can be narrated according to a linear series of cause and effect. These attacks upon traditional accounts of history seem to leave Foucault in a world where discourse has cast its seamless net over things and where any account of political action is precluded from the start. In fact, though, even if Foucault had yet to explain how change is possible, he had identified quite precisely where that possibility rests. Hence at the end of *The Archaeology of Knowledge,* he suggested both that his critics underestimated the power of words and that clearly the power of words was linked to an entire domain of nondiscursive practices. What Foucault had to do next was continue to emphasize that words are not wind, while at the same time proving that this is so by connecting them to the "material reality" of nondiscursive practices; in other words, he had to supplement his archaeological method with a new approach, which, borrowing from Nietzsche, he deemed "genealogy."

Foucault's first full-scale attempt to think further about the relationship between discursive and nondiscursive practices takes place in *Discipline and Punish.*[4] Before we turn to this work, however, it will be helpful to look at two of Foucault's essays. One of the essays, "The Order of Discourse," served as Foucault's inaugural lecture at the Collège de France in 1970; the other, "Nietzsche, Genealogy, History," was published the following year.[5] Taken together they display the transition in Foucault's thought that occurred between the publication of *The Archaeology of Knowledge* in 1969 and of *Discipline and Punish* in 1975.

The Material Reality of Discourse and Effective History

According to Foucault, one of the indications that words are not wind is that we pay far too much attention to them. Why, if words are of no consequence, do we focus so intently upon them? In "The Order of Discourse," Foucault works from the dual assumption that lurking beneath our interest in words is "a certain fear" concerning their power and that our response to this fear, like our response to madness, is to fix discourse tightly within the confines of the sacred circle of an order. Unlike the case of madness, however, our fear of discourse does not originate in the seventeenth century but is rooted in what Foucault, following Nietzsche, deems a "will to truth," whose origin is at least as old as Plato. In fact, Foucault now argues, echoing both Nietzsche and Heidegger, that the great division between madness and unreason is simply a later manifestation of the founding division of Western culture: the division between true and false discourse, the division that begins when the sophists are banished, and with them, an acknowledgment of the link between discourse and power. After the banishment of the sophists, says Foucault, "all that appears to our eyes is a truth conceived as a richness, a fecundity, a gentle and insidiously universal force."[6] But this conception of truth is blind to the fact that truth does not simply arrive, of its own accord and from elsewhere, but rather is something discourse itself produces. Once the sophists were banished, all awareness of the relationship between discourse and truth, between truth and power, was lost. Or as Foucault puts it, we became "unaware of the will to truth, that prodigious machinery designed to exclude."[7]

Foucault sets out in "The Order of Discourse" to renew our awareness of the relationship between discourse and power; he sets out to expose the mechanisms of exclusion that exist within discourse itself and that are the result of the will to truth. Hence, in a comment that resonates with the portrait he painted of discourse in *The Order of Things*, Foucault declares that "all those who, from time to time in our history, have tried to dodge this will to truth and to put it into question against truth, at the very point where truth undertakes to justify the prohibition and define madness, all of them, from Nietzsche to Artaud to Bataille, must now serve as the . . . signs of our daily work."[8] Following these signs, Foucault now expands the work he had begun in earnest in *The Archaeology of Knowledge* and describes with a new clarity how we came to confine not only the mad but discourse itself.

Early in "The Order of Discourse" Foucault announces the hypothesis of his work in progress: "In every society the production of discourse is at once controlled, selected, organized and redistributed by a certain number of procedures whose role is to ward off its powers and dangers, to gain mastery over its chance events, to evade its ponderous, formidable materiality."[9] Foucault goes on to argue that we can locate within our society procedures, some external and some internal to discourse, that exist

> in order to master, at least partly, the great proliferation of discourse, in order to remove from its richness the most dangerous part, and in order to organize its disorder according to figures which dodge what is most uncontrollable about it. It is as if we had tried to efface all trace of its irruption into the activity of thought and language. No doubt there is in our society, and, I imagine, in all others, but following a different outline and different rhythms, a profound logophobia, a sort of mute terror against these events, against this mass of things said.[10]

As if echoing the objections of those who equate words with wind, who suppose that words "never put anything at stake except signs,"[11] Foucault poses a rhetorical question: "What is so perilous in the fact that people speak, and that their discourse proliferates to infinity? Where is the danger in that?" Answering his own question, Foucault suggests that the danger (and hence also the promise) of discourse lies "in its material reality as a thing pronounced or written."[12] It is, to paraphrase Foucault, in their material reality that words found struggles, attain victories, injure, dominate, and enslave. Hence "discourse is not simply that which translates struggles or systems of domination, but is the thing for which and by which there is struggle, discourse is the power which is to be seized."[13]

Of course words are not "material" in an ordinary sense. Foucault attempts to describe the material reality of discourse with recourse to the notion, so important in *The Archaeology of Knowledge,* of the statement as an event. An

> event is not of the order of bodies. And yet it is not something immaterial either; it is always at the level of materiality that it takes effect, that it is effect; it has its locus and it consists in the relation, the coexistence, the dispersion, the overlapping, the accumulation, and the selection of material elements. It is not the act or the property of a body; it is produced as an effect of, and within, a dispersion of matter. Let us say that the philosophy of the event should move in the at first sight paradoxical direction of a materialism of the incorporeal.[14]

Discourse is not itself material, which is why it can appear that words are wind. Nonetheless, discourse takes effect at "the level of materiality"; it is not "the property of a body," and yet it exists only among bodies. If all this seems paradoxical, it is because what's missing is an analysis of nondiscursive practices, an analysis Foucault refers to already in "The Order of Discourse" as "genealogy."

Genealogy, like archaeology, remains an exercise in counterhistory. Hence in the essay "Nietzsche, Genealogy, History," which appeared shortly after "The Order of Discourse," Foucault notes that genealogy "is situated within the articulation of the body and history. Its task is to expose a body totally imprinted by history."[15] Not until *Discipline and Punish* will we see the exact nature of this relationship between the body and history. What matters at this point is that we understand how Foucault's new focus on nondiscursive practices and the material reality of discourse remains committed to the archaeological enterprise of opening up the possibility of a counterhistory. In "Nietzsche, Genealogy, History," Foucault, borrowing from Nietzsche, refers to this enterprise as "effective history":

> History becomes "effective" to the degree that it introduces discontinuity into our very being—as it divides our emotions, dramatizes our instincts, multiplies our body and sets it against itself. "Effective" history deprives the self of the reassuring stability of life and nature, and it will not permit itself to be transported by a voiceless obstinacy toward a millennial ending. It will uproot its traditional foundations and relentlessly interrupt its pretended continuity.[16]

In "The Order of Discourse" Foucault suggests that to introduce discontinuity into our being is to introduce chance into history: "We must accept the introduction of the *alea* [chance] as a category in the production of events."[17] In "Nietzsche, Genealogy, History" Foucault expands upon this suggestion: "The forces operating in history are not controlled by destiny or regulative mechanisms, but respond to haphazard conflicts. They do not manifest the successive forms of a primordial intention and their attraction is not that of a conclusion, for they always appear through the singular randomness of events."[18] Formed as we are, from grade school on, by traditional history, we "want the historians to confirm our belief that the present rests upon profound intentions and immutable necessities. But," says Foucault, "the true historical sense confirms our existence among countless lost events, without a landmark or a point of reference."[19]

The task of genealogy is in part to sacrifice the traditional truths of history upon the altar of chance and thereby to open us up to the "jolts" and "surprises" of countless lost events that belie the facade of continuity and comfort put forth by standard historical narratives. However, as an exercise in counterhistory, the task of genealogy is also to reconnect us to landmarks and points of reference and to build a "countermemory."[20] Because genealogy involves the articulation of history and the body, this construction of a countermemory is not limited, as it was for the most part in *The Archaeology of Knowledge*, to the freeing of discursive events from the tyranny of continuity but now involves in a fundamental way the memory of the body. This emphasis upon history and the body brings us to *Discipline and Punish.*

The Panopticon, Disciplinary Power, and the Carceral City

In "Nietzsche, Genealogy, History," Foucault had written of a body totally imprinted by history. "The body," he said, "manifests the stigmata of past experience. . . . [It] is the inscribed surface of events."[21] In *Discipline and Punish,* Foucault, in effect, sets out to explain these curious statements by engaging in the genealogical enterprise of analyzing the relationship between history and bodies, between discourse and its material reality.

Early in *Discipline and Punish,* Foucault notes, "Historians long ago began to write the history of the body."[22] However, with their attention turned toward demography, disease, needs, and appetites, what these historians missed is that "the body is also directly involved in a political field; power relations have an immediate hold upon it; they invest it, mark it, train it, torture it, force it to carry our tasks, to perform ceremonies, to emit signs."[23] *Discipline and Punish* is Foucault's attempt to write a history of this political investment of the body. Despite the image of a body that is tortured and forced to carry out tasks, the novelty of Foucault's argument is that the political investment of the body, at least in the modern era, does not entail the sort of overt violence that we might associate, for instance, with state power.

When Foucault says that "power relations have an immediate hold upon" the body, he has in mind something quite other than a hold rooted in "instruments of violence or ideology." It may well be that a state turns its people into "subjects" through physical violence and ideological programming. Foucault notes, however, that "subjection"

> can also be direct, physical, pitting force against force, bearing on material elements, and yet without involving violence; it may be calculated, organized, technically thought out; it may be subtle, make use neither of weapons nor of terror and yet remain a physical order. That is to say there may be a "knowledge" of the body that is not exactly the science of its functioning, and a mastery of its forces that is more than the ability to conquer them: this knowledge and this mastery constitute what might be called the political technology of the body. . . . [I]t cannot be localized in a particular type of institution or state apparatus. . . . [I]n its mechanisms and in its effects, it is situated at a quite different level. What the apparatuses and the institutions operate is, in a sense, a micro-physics of power, whose field of validity is situated . . . between these great functionings and the bodies themselves in their materiality and their forces.[24]

This microphysical power operates according to what Foucault calls a *dispositif*.[25] The term appears in the above passage and is translated as "apparatus," although here it has not yet acquired the specific meaning it will have in Foucault's next work. Nonetheless, this is perhaps the best place to introduce the notion of the *dispositif*, since we can use Foucault's later definition of the term to make sense of his discussion of the microphysics of power as we encounter it in *Discipline and Punish.*

Foucault defines the notion of the *dispositif* most clearly in an interview from 1977:

> What I am trying to pick out with this term is . . . a thoroughly heterogeneous ensemble consisting of discourses, institutions, architectural forms, regulatory decisions, laws, administrative procedures, scientific statements, philosophical, moral and philanthropic propositions—in short, the said as much as the unsaid. Such are the elements of the apparatus. The apparatus itself is the system of relations that can be established between these elements . . . [W]hat I am trying to identify in this apparatus is precisely the nature of the connection that can exist between these heterogeneous elements.[26]

The notion of an apparatus, then, is Foucault's attempt to specify the relationship between discursive and nondiscursive practices. Thus he can say that "the apparatus in its general form is both discursive and non-discursive."[27]

Foucault's notion of the apparatus qualifies his earlier emphasis upon discursive practices and extends his analysis of the material reality of discourse by allowing him to begin an analysis of both the discursive and nondiscursive elements of power in its microphysical guise.[28] Power in this guise cannot be located in "a particular type of institution," nor can it be equated with the power of discourse itself—and yet it operates via both discourse and nondiscursive social structures.[29]

If all this seems murky, it is simply because Foucault is attempting to craft a vocabulary that will allow him to articulate the mechanisms of a kind of power that is, finally, invisible. To render the invisible visible in language is always a murky business, as we will see in the next chapter when we turn to the language of power in the New Testament; nonetheless, both Foucault and the authors of the New Testament suggest that to speak not simply of power but of power in its invisibility is also crucial business. Foucault calls this kind of power "disciplinary" or "pastoral" and offers a metaphorical depiction of its heterogeneous relations by invoking the image of the "Panopticon." The term refers to a particular architectural design first conceived by Jeremy Bentham and described in some detail by Foucault as follows:

> We know the principle on which it was based: at the periphery, an annular building; at the centre, a tower; this tower is pierced with wide windows that open on to the inner side of the ring; the peripheric building is divided into cells, each of which extends the whole width of the building; they have two windows, one on the inside, corresponding to the windows on the tower; the other, on the outside, allows the light to cross the cell from one end to the other. All that is needed, then, is to place a supervisor in a central tower and to shut up in each cell a madman, a patient, a condemned man, a worker or a school boy. By the effect of backlighting, one can observe from the tower, standing out precisely against the light, the small captive shadows in the cells of the periphery. . . . Each individual, in his place, is securely confined to a cell from which he is seen from the front by the supervisor; but the side-walls prevent him from coming into contact with his companions. . . . If the inmates are convicts, there is no danger of a plot, an attempt at collective escape . . . ; if they are patients, there is no danger of contagion; if they are madmen there is no risk of their committing violence upon one another; if they are school children, there is no copying, no noise, no chatter, no waste of time; if they are workers, there are no disorders, no theft, no coalitions, none of those distractions that slow down the rate of work, make it less perfect or cause accidents.[30]

Foucault goes on to say that "the major effect of the Panopticon [is] to induce in the inmate a state of conscious and permanent visibility that assures the automatic functioning of power."[31] To guarantee this effect, Bentham recommended the windows in the central tower be covered with blinds. The inmates would then not know if the tower was occupied and in time would internalize the surveillance of the tower, becoming their own guards.

Even though Bentham's design was in fact realized in a variety of buildings, some of which are still in operation as prisons, Foucault says that we must not understand the Panopticon in simply architectural terms but as "the diagram of a mechanism of power reduced to its ideal form."[32] It is, in other words, a diagram of the nondiscursive mechanisms of disciplinary power, a fact that will perhaps be more apparent if we relate the Panopticon back to Foucault's earlier account of the pure Gaze become pure Language.

When Foucault says that the Panopticon is the diagram of a mechanism of power, he has in effect returned to the myth of the pure Gaze. Now, however, it is not the myth of a Gaze become Language, of a Gaze that functions through discourse, but of a Gaze that functions in the nondiscursive field of institutions that work according to the mechanisms of the Panopticon. In his earlier works, Foucault argued that the discursive practices of the classical age silenced the mad, related the truth of disease to the depth of the body, and reduced language to its representative function. In *Discipline and Punish,* Foucault argues that the classical age also "discovered the body as an object and target of power. It is easy enough to find signs of the attention then paid to the body—the body that is manipulated, shaped, trained, which obeys, responds, becomes skillful and increases its forces."[33] More specifically, the classical age saw the birth of a

> technico-political register, which was constituted by a whole set of regulations and by empirical and calculated methods relating to the army, the school, and the hospital, for controlling or correcting the operations of the body. . . . The human body was entering a machinery of power that explores it, breaks it down and rearranges it. A "political anatomy", which was also a "mechanics of power," was being born; it defined how one may have a hold over others' bodies, not only so that they may do what one wishes, but so that they may operate as one wishes, with the techniques, the speed and the efficiency that one determines. Thus discipline produces subjected and practiced bodies, "docile" bodies. Discipline increases the forces of the body (in economic terms of utility) and diminishes these same forces (in political terms of obedience).[34]

By focusing his attention upon the army, the school, the hospital, and, most of all, the prison—and the way these institutions organized space and time as a means of training and disciplining individuals—Foucault begins to analyze "the effective formation of discourse"—in other words, the nondiscursive practices where discourse meets the body, finds its material reality, and becomes effective. This analysis is the work of genealogy, and it functions on a quite different plane than Foucault's earlier archaeological analysis of the discursive practices that created the human sciences. Foucault's overall argument about classical confinement, however, remains the same and is now simply nuanced by including in the argument an analysis of nondiscursive practices:

> The carceral texture of society assures both the real capture of the body and its perpetual observation; it is, by its very nature, the apparatus of punishment that conforms most completely to the new economy of power and the instrument for the formation of knowledge that this very economy needs. Its panoptic functioning enables it to play this double role. By virtue of its methods of fixing, dividing, recording, it has been one of the simplest, crudest, also the most concrete, but perhaps most indispensable conditions for the development of this immense activity of examination that has objectified human behaviour. . . . I am not saying that the human sciences emerged from the prison. But, if they have been able to be formed and to produce so many profound changes in the episteme, it is because they have been conveyed by a specific and new modality of power: a certain policy of the body, a certain way of rendering the group of men docile and useful.[35]

If today we find ourselves trapped in the order of the same, if we find that we have a penchant for excluding the other, for annihilating the wolf, the bear, the rain forest, for building bigger hospitals and more prisons, for averting our gaze from the homeless and voicing concerns about the gays on the streets and in the schools, then we can rest assured, says Foucault, that this is not only because we are obeying the anonymous rules of discourse but also because we live in "the carceral city" amidst "a modest, suspicious power, which functions as a calculated, but permanent economy."[36] At "the centre of this city, and as if to hold it in place, there is, not the centre of power, not a network of forces, but a multiple network of diverse elements—walls, space, institution, rules, discourse."[37] And centered within this "centre," says Foucault, is the prison—that place where walls, space, discourse, and the like meet to discipline the body in the most obvious way. The prison, however,

> is not alone, but linked to a whole series of "carceral" mechanisms which seem distinct enough—since they are intended to alleviate pain, to cure, to comfort—but which all tend, like the prison, to exercise a power of normalization. . . . [U]ltimately what presides over all these mechanisms is not the unitary functioning of an apparatus or an institution, but the necessity of combat and the rules of strategy. . . . In this central and centralized humanity, the effect and instrument of complex power relations, bodies and forces subjected by multiple mechanisms of "incarceration" . . . we must hear the distant roar of battle.[38]

It's hard to know what to make of Foucault's recourse to the dramatic language of battle and combat, and he himself later questions the use of terms like these to characterize the contested terrain of power.[39] In any case, this language seems to serve a double purpose. Certainly the idea that "the necessity of combat" presides over the disciplinary mechanisms of the carceral city drives home the point that at least since the classical age, and perhaps since Plato, there has been afoot in the world a determined and aggressive Apollinian effort to confine, exclude, and annihilate the other. And it may be that when Foucault speaks of the distant roar of battle, he means only to accentuate the point that this war against the other is underway. On the other hand, battles generally have two sides. Perhaps, then, Foucault's words about combat and battle are a call to arms. Consider these words from the first chapter of the text:

> Power is not exercised simply as an obligation or a prohibition on those who "do not have it"; it invests them, is transmitted by them and through them; it exerts pressure upon them, just as they themselves, in their struggle against it, resist the grip it has on them. This means that these relations go right down into the depths of society, that they are not localized in the relations between the state and its citizens or on the frontier between classes and that they do not merely reproduce, at the level of individuals, bodies, gestures and behaviour, the general form of the law or government. . . . The *overthrow* of these "micro-powers" does not, then, obey the law of all or nothing; it is not acquired once and for all by a new control of the apparatuses nor by a new functioning or a destruction of the institutions.[40]

When at the end of the text, Foucault perks our ears to the distant roar of battle, certainly he wants us to notice not only that an attack against the other is underway but also that the attack has met formidable resistance. Contrary to what some of Foucault's critics say, *Discipline and Punish* is not a dark and pessimistic description of our certain and inevitable confinement within the carceral city. Rather, it is a redescription of power that enables us to imagine resistance where previously none was imaginable. In fact, in this text Foucault begins to offer the details of a politics that he had been gesturing toward ever since the end of *Madness and Civilization.* For Foucault's redescription of power enables us to imagine what it might mean to say that the artist and the poet, and all those who have sought to dodge the incarcerating powers of the will to truth, must "serve as the signs of our daily work"—the "real work" of political resistance. In order to continue to describe the character of Foucault's politics, let me say a few more words about his redescription of power.

The Soul Is the Prison of the Body

At the core of Foucault's account of power are the related claims that we should no longer conceive of power as something that has a center and that "we must cease once and for all to describe the effects of power in negative terms: it 'excludes,' it 'represses,' it 'censors,' it 'abstracts,' it 'masks,' it 'conceals.'"[41] Instead we must imagine that power is positive and productive: "power produces; it produces reality; it produces domains of objects and rituals of truth. The individual and the knowledge that may be gained of him belong to this production."[42] The notion that power is productive and that, in particular, it produces the individual, is a crucial aspect of his redescription of power, and it needs elaboration—a task that requires we move beyond *Discipline and Punish* and into numerous interviews, lectures, and his next major work: Volume 1 of *The History of Sexuality.*[43]

In *The History of Sexuality,* Foucault spends more time than he did in *Discipline and Punish* discussing the assumptions that guide his analysis of power. "We shall try to rid ourselves," he says, "of a juridical and negative representation of power, and cease to conceive of it in terms of law, prohibition, liberty and sovereignty."[44] To conceive of power in terms other than these is in effect to conceive of "power without a king," without, that is, the notion that power resides at the center of things: "Power's condition of possibility . . . must not be sought in the primary existence of a central point, in a unique source of sovereignty from which secondary and descendant forms would emanate."[45] Rather, Foucault argues that we must think of power as

> the moving substrate of force relations which, by virtue of their inequality, constantly engender states of power, but the latter are always local and unstable. The omnipresence of power: not because it has the privilege of consolidating everything under its invincible unity, but because it is produced from one moment to the next, at every point, or rather, in every relation from one point to another. Power is everywhere; not because it embraces everything, but because it comes from everywhere.[46]

Power, then, is not centralized but dispersed; it is exercised not from the palace or the capitol, the White House or the Kremlin, but "from innumerable points, in the interplay of non-egalitarian and mobile relations."[47] Hence Foucault can say that "in thinking of power, I am thinking of its capillary existence, the point where power reaches into the very grain of individuals, touches their bodies and inserts itself into their actions and attitudes, their discourses, their learning processes and everyday lives . . . a synaptic regime of power, a regime of its exercise from *within* the social body, rather than from *above* it."[48]

To say that power is insidious and everywhere is not to say that it is anarchic. For "there is no power that is exercised without a series of aims and objectives."[49] Nonetheless, once we separate power from the sovereignty of the center, we cannot imagine that it rests in individual subjects nor even in institutions; therefore, "let us not look for the headquarters that presides over its rationality."[50] Instead, let us "be concerned with power at its extremities, in its ultimate destinations, with those points where it becomes capillary, that is in its more regional and local forms and institutions."[51]

To conceive of power without a headquarters and in its capillary existence is, of course, to return to the Panopticon. If the Panopticon, with its central tower and its isolated cells on the periphery, seems in fact to contradict the image of a decentralized power, then we need to recall the genius of Bentham's design: The inmates could not see into the tower; and the tower, therefore, did not, in principle, need to be occupied because in time the inmates would internalize the surveillance that the tower represented. Hence, the eventual evacuation of the tower provides us with a perfect image of power in a capillary form that is now dispersed and "everywhere," as the power that once sat in the tower comes to be the disciplined "soul" of each inmate. The Panopticon, then, is not only the perfect metaphorical depiction of power decentralized but also of the link between this dispersion of power and its productive character.

According to Foucault, what power produces, as it courses through institutions and apparatuses such as those of the army, the school, the hospital, and the prison, is a disciplined interiority that we might identify with the "soul." The soul, at least in its modern guise, is the product of power, which is not

> to say that the soul is an illusion. . . . On the contrary, it exists, it has reality, it is produced permanently around, on, within, the body by the functioning of a power that is exercised on those punished—and, in a more general way, on those one supervises, trains and corrects, over madmen, children at home and at school, the colonized, over those who are stuck at a machine and supervised for the rest of their lives. This is the historical reality of this soul, which, unlike the soul represented by Christian theology, is not born in sin and subject to punishment, but is rather born out of methods of punishment, supervision, and constraint.[52]

Foucault goes on to speak of the implications of the notion that individuals are, from the bottom up, the products of power and not pre-given natural entities that find themselves oppressed by power, from the top down.

We are oppressed, says Foucault, not by the heavy hand of the state pressing upon us from without (or at least not simply by this) but by a more subtle power that works in us from within. Foucault makes this point, memorably, in the following way:

> The man described for us, whom we are invited to free, is already in himself the effect of a subjection more profound than himself. A "soul" inhabits him and brings him to existence, which is itself a factor in the mastery that power exercises over the body. The soul is the effect and instrument of a political anatomy; the soul is the prison of the body.[53]

The notion that the soul is the prison of the body—that power does not simply capture us from without but also from within—has implications for how we think about resistance—as does the companion notion that power has no center. And it seems at this point that Foucault has delivered us into something of a fix. Perhaps his critics are right about the dark and pessimistic character of his narrative about power. For if power is as pervasive and insidious as he says it is, if it no longer has a headquarters that we can overthrow, if, as he puts it in an interview, it's "a machine in which everyone is caught . . . [but] that no one owns,"[54] then what possible hope do we have of resistance and escape? The rest of this chapter will occupy itself with the attempt to answer that question.

Below the Thresholds of Visibility

Foucault's short answer to the question of resistance is simply this: "Where there is power, there is resistance."[55] But what does this mean? To understand this statement we have to realize first that as Foucault conceives of it, power is not a substance: "it is not something that is acquired, seized, or shared, something that one holds on to or allows to slip away."[56] Power is a "relation," a "process," and not a thing; or rather, it is "a multiplicity of relations." It exists only when a second (or third or fourth) term is present: Where there is power, there is resistance. In fact, the existence of power "depends on the multiplicity of points of resistance: these play the role of adversary, target, support, or handle in power relations. These points of resistance are present everywhere in the power network. Hence there is no single locus of great Refusal, no soul of revolt, source of all rebellion, or pure law of the revolutionary. Instead there is a plurality of resistances, each of them a special case."[57]

This plurality of resistances, says Foucault, "by definition . . . can only exist in the strategic field of power relations,"[58] since a relational definition of power excludes the possibility that one could ever be "outside" power: Power has no "exterior."

When Foucault says that the man we are invited to free is already the effect of a subjection more profound than himself, he calls attention to the productive and capillary character of disciplinary power and to the fact that "there are no spaces of primal liberty between the meshes of its network."[59] This is not to say, however, that we are "doomed to perpetual defeat."[60] Rather, there is "always something in the social body, in classes, groups and individuals themselves which in some sense escapes relations of power, something which is by no means a more or less docile or reactive primal matter, but rather a centrifugal movement, an inverse energy, a discharge."[61]

In a curious way, if Foucault is right about the character of power, then the possibility of resistance is even greater than it was when our only hope was to unseat the king. Indeed, Foucault argues that far from precluding the possibility of resistance, his analytics of power leads to the conclusion that resistances "are all the more real and effective because they are formed right at the point where relations of power are exercised; resistance to power does not have to come from elsewhere to be real, nor is it inexorably frustrated through being the compatriot of power. It exists all the more by being in the same place as power; hence like power, resistance is multiple and can be integrated in global strategies."[62]

The last point is particularly important and deserves comment. For even though Foucault moves away from the idea that power has a center and that, therefore, resistance resides in a single locus of great Refusal or the pure all-or-nothing law of the revolutionary, Foucault does not mean to reduce either power or resistance to their capillary dispersion. Both power and resistance are capable of appropriating a multiplicity of capillary forces and building with this raw material a "global" network. Indeed, the State itself is an example of just such a phenomenon:

> The State can only operate on the basis of other, already existing power relations: The State is superstructural in relation to a whole series of power networks. . . . True, these networks stand in a conditioning-conditioned relationship to a kind of "meta-power" which is structured essentially round a certain number of great prohibition functions; but this meta-power with its prohibitions can only take hold and secure its footing where it is rooted in a whole series of multiple and indefinite power relations that supply the necessary basis for the great negative forms of power.[63]

Hence it is wrong to say that power has no center whatsoever. Insofar as the State appropriates successfully certain power relations in their capillary form—like those linked to the family, for instance—it can gather them into something like a center. But note that this centering of power is inherently unstable because it depends upon the ceaseless, strategic appropriation of power in its capillary form. The fact that resistance, like power, occurs both at a capillary level and at the level of global strategies, makes resistance more complex but also more potent than when it functioned according to the law of all or nothing. Foucault puts it this way:

> I would say that the State consists in the codification of a whole number of power relations which render its functioning possible, and that Revolution is a different type of codification of the same relations. This implies that there are many different kinds of revolution, roughly speaking as many kinds as there are possible subversive recodifications of power relations, and further that one can perfectly well conceive of revolutions which leave essentially untouched the power relations which form the basis for the functioning of the State.[64]

This image of proliferating revolutions indicates that far from dooming us to defeat, Foucault's account of power opens up countless new possibilities for resistance. But if this is true, then what are we to make of Foucault's use of the Panopticon as a metaphor for the mechanics of power? Indeed, as a way of summarizing Foucault's account of resistance so far, let's return to Bentham's Panopticon and the way it seems to preclude, as an image of power, the sort of resistance that we have just seen Foucault describe.

In a comment that sets up a question to Foucault during an interview, Michelle Perrot, speaking of people like Bentham who had hoped the Panopticon would revolutionize society, states the matter with precision:

> These thinkers generally misunderstood the difficulty they would have in making their system take effect. They didn't realize that there would always be ways of slipping through their net. In the domain of prisons, the convicts weren't passive beings. It's Bentham who gives us to suppose that they were. The discourse of the penitentiary unfolds as though there were no people confronting it, nothing except a *tabula rosa* of subjects to be reformed and returned to the circuit of production. In reality it had to work with a material—the prisoners—which put up formidable resistance.[65]

Foucault responds by agreeing that Bentham underestimated "the effective resistance of people."[66] We can say, then, that although the Panopticon serves fairly well as a metaphor for disciplinary power, it serves not at all as an image of how, as a centrifugal force "inside" power, resistance is always real.[67] In order to capture resistance metaphorically, then, let us leave behind the Panopticon and enlist instead the image of New York City, as Michel de Certeau describes it in the course of his own analysis of power and resistance:

> To be lifted to the summit of the World Trade Center is to be lifted out of the city's grasp. . . . It transforms the bewitching world by which one was "possessed" into a text that lies before one's eyes. It allows one to read it, to be a solar Eye, looking down like a god. . . . The 1370 foot high tower that serves as a prow for Manhattan continues to construct the fiction that creates readers, makes the complexity of the city readable, and immobilizes its opaque mobility in a transparent text. . . .
>
> The ordinary practitioners of the city live "down below," below the thresholds at which visibility begins. They walk—an elementary form of this experience of the city; they are walkers . . . whose bodies follow the thicks and thins of an urban "text" they write without being able to read it. These practitioners make use of spaces that cannot be seen . . . [that] elude legibility. . . .
>
> Escaping the imaginary totalizations produced by the eye, the everyday has a certain strangeness that does not surface, or whose surface is only its upper limit, outlining itself against the visible. . . . A *migrational*, or metaphorical, city thus slips into the clear text of the planned and readable city.[68]

In spite of the density of his prose, de Certeau provides us, I think, with an image that captures what the image of the Panopticon cannot. Like the guard in the tower of the Panopticon, the voyeur at the top of the World Trade Center has an uninhibited view of "the dark space where the crowds move back and forth" below. From this perspective, the city becomes a transparent, eminently readable text. This uninhibited view, however, is an optical artifact, for what it takes to be the clear text of the planned and readable city is in fact a much more complicated text that escapes the notice of this totalizing eye. Below the thresholds of visibility is an entirely different text, written by the ordinary practitioners of city life, who in the course of the opaque mobility of their daily life craft "unrecognized poems." In these poems and in this text, as they slip in between the lines and below the surface of the clear text, rest innumerable paths of escape from the imaginary totalization of the all-powerful eye.

By locating for us, even if only metaphorically, those practices that reside below the threshold of visibility, de Certeau alerts us to what Foucault calls the "underside" of power.[69] Of course the challenge now is to display those practices not metaphorically but concretely. A concrete display of such practices may help us understand how Foucault can say in the face of his detractors that "all of [his] investigations rest on a postulate of absolute optimism."[70]

One of the difficulties of offering a concrete display of Foucault's understanding of resistance is that, despite his optimism, he rarely gives us examples of concrete practices in his texts. His analyses of discourse and power are loaded with examples, but when it comes to resistance he rarely offers specifics. Indeed, Foucault never tired of reminding us that he had little interest in telling us what to do. Nonetheless, he was quite clear that his reticence in this regard was itself a "political choice"[71] and was in no way related to a belief that there was "nothing to be done." "On the contrary," he said, "there are a thousand things to do, to invent, to forge, on the part of those who, recognizing the relations of power in which they're implicated, have decided to resist or escape them."[72] Even if Foucault was not inclined to give us concrete examples, we can at least find in his texts the outline of what such resistance and escape might look like, and we can then provide examples of our own. Not surprisingly, Foucault's outline of resistance is fixed along the double axis of discourse and the body and can be divided therefore, at least for the sake of analysis, into its discursive and nondiscursive (bodily "committed") aspects.

Discursive Resistance, Heterotopia, and Subjugated Knowledges

In *The History of Sexuality*, Foucault, in effect revising the analysis of *Madness and Civilization*, has this to say about the role of discourse in resistance:

> We must make allowance for the complex and unstable process whereby discourse can be both an instrument and an effect of power, but also a hindrance, stumbling block, a point of resistance and a starting point for an opposing strategy. Discourse transmits and produces power; it reenforces it, but also undermines and exposes it, renders it fragile and makes it possible to thwart it. . . . There is not, on the one side, a discourse of power, and opposite it, another discourse that runs counter to it. Discourses are tactical elements or blocks operating in the field of force relations.[73]

These comments begin to shed light on Foucault's claims in *Madness and Civilization* that even as the mad were confined and silenced, they preserved in the fortresses of confinement a silent memory of protest that became eventually embodied in the works of mad artists, beginning most notably with the works of the Marquis de Sade, who stands for Foucault as the ultimate witness to the relationship between the practice of confinement and the birth of resistance:

> And it is no accident that sadism, as an individual phenomenon bearing the name of man, was born of confinement and, within confinement, that Sade's entire *oeuvre* is dominated by the images of the Fortress, the Cell, the Cellar, the Convent, the inaccessible Island which thus form, as it were, the natural habitat of unreason. It is no accident, either, that all the fantastic literature of madness and horror, which is contemporary with Sade's *oeuvre,* takes place, preferentially, in the strongholds of confinement.[74]

Even as discourse was used to silence and confine the mad, Sade stands as proof that there emerged a discourse that was a hindrance, a stumbling block, a point of resistance. Hence as Foucault puts it in *The Order of Things,* "Sade's works play the role of a silent murmur in our culture."[75] These works take the "violence of the name" that characterized the classical capturing of things and utter it, at last, "for its own sake." Oddly enough, this utterance shatters the presumptions that words can be reduced to their representative function, and it does so by manifesting "language in its brute being." What Sade represents according to Foucault is "the sovereignty of the mad heart that has attained, in its solitude, the limits of the world that wounds it." The fact that in Sade's works these limits are embodied in stories of "insane murders" and "unreasonable passions" simply brings the world to the doorstep of its own mad violence. In our own time and in a different medium, Oliver Stone's film *Natural Born Killers* attempts to do the same thing when it juxtaposes images of America's penchant for sex and violence with those of Hitler and Stalin.

Although it may be unclear exactly how Sade's works (or Stone's film) function as resistance, Foucault's analysis of discourse and power in *The History of Sexuality* brings us closer, nonetheless, to an understanding of the power of literature and art to contest the order of things.[76] For once we see that the world of discourse is not, as Foucault portrayed it in *Mad-*

ness and Civilization, divided against itself but is instead a single network of multiple discursive elements, then we can begin to imagine how a few words uttered in one place might alter the configuration of an entire discourse. The possibilities of resistance carried in the silent murmur of Sade's works will perhaps come into a better view if we consider briefly what Foucault has to say not about discourse but about space. For precisely because Sade's works came into being in the space of the prison and are therefore the voice of confinement, they are suggestive not only of the powers of resistance embodied in words but of the way certain words are rooted in a particular space.

Of course, the notion that space might have something to do with resistance comes as no surprise, given that in *Discipline and Punish* Foucault shows in some detail how the mechanisms of power depend upon a particular arrangement of space. The Panopticon, after all, works because of the way it arranges space. If power and resistance accompany one another at every point, then we have to assume that space, as well as discourse, is always contested ground. And indeed, de Certeau's image of the spaces in the city that "cannot be seen," that evade the panoptic gaze, is suggestive of just this fact. Foucault's way of calling our attention to the importance of these "other spaces," of spaces that contest the mechanisms of power, is to invoke the notion of a "heterotopia."

We live, he notes, in a time when space has been largely formalized, homogenized, and desanctified.[77] We live in the age of McDonald's, Burger King, and interstate highways. There remains, however, in some spaces, "the hidden presence of the sacred"—in the spaces, for instance, of the house, the bedroom, the beach.[78] More significantly, some spaces are not only "sacred" but "have the curious property of being in relation with all other sites, but in such a way as to suspect, neutralize, or invert the set of relations that they happen to designate, mirror, or reflect."[79] Foucault calls these spaces "heterotopias," by which he means to designate "something like counter-sites, a kind of effectively enacted utopia in which the real sites, all the other real sites that can be found within the culture, are simultaneously represented, contested, and inverted."[80]

Although we are not accustomed to thinking of prisons as "sacred" spaces and although this is not the place to argue the point, it is fruitful nonetheless to think of the prison as a heterotopia that represents our cultural arrangements, even as it simultaneously inverts and contests them. To think of the space of confinement as a heterotopia is fruitful because it helps to explain Foucault's notion that the voice of unreason was passed down through the centuries. If there is a link between the mad of an earlier time and Sade, and between Sade and Artaud and Nietzsche, it is not simply because words were passed along but because these words, as they contested confinement, had a place, a countersite, from which to launch their protest. Paradoxically, perhaps, the very spaces that were constructed to silence or normalize the other (the spaces, for instance, of prisons and asylums) became countersites that functioned to preserve the insurrection of a "silent memory," or better, "the insurrection of subjugated knowledges."[81] This latter notion brings us to another component in Foucault's outline of resistance.

Because of its multiple character, discourse is not once and for all subservient to power, but in the space of a countersite can become a counter-discourse that undermines, exposes, and contests power. To bring into play the idea of subjugated knowledges is to develop these thoughts with a bit more precision. For Foucault argues that "it is through the re-emergence of these low-ranking knowledges, the unqualified, even directly disqualified knowledges (such as that of the psychiatric patient, of the ill person . . . of the delinquent, etc.), and which would involve what I would call a popular knowledge . . . a particular, local, regional knowledge . . . that criticism performs its work."[82]

For Foucault, power and knowledge are linked in a crucial way; they are "articulated" upon one another.[83] To say, as Foucault does, that power is productive is to say, in part, that it produces "effective instruments for the formation and accumulation of knowledge—methods of observation, techniques of registration, procedures for investigation and research, apparatuses of control. All this means that power, when it is exercised through these subtle mechanisms, cannot but evolve, organise and put into circulation a knowledge, or rather apparatuses of knowledge."[84] The notion of subjugated knowledges helps refine Foucault's account of resistance because it allows us to see that words alone do not contest power, nor even words rooted in the space of a countersite, but rather words gathered into a what we might call a counterknowledge—words that compose what Foucault calls in another place a "popular memory."[85] Indeed, at stake in the struggles for discourse and for space are not just words or a place to stand but memory. As Foucault puts it, "There's a real fight going on . . . [o]ver what we can roughly describe as popular memory. . . . [M]emory is actually a very important factor in struggle. . . . [I]f one controls people's memory, one controls their dynamism. And one also controls their experience, their knowledge of previous struggles."[86]

If we use this notion of popular memory to gather the various aspects of resistance as Foucault describes it, then we can say that resistance is a discursive phenomenon, embodied in a local knowledge, launched from a countersite, and dependent upon the popular memory, the popular history, of a subordinate group. Although for Foucault the works of Sade are suggestive of resistance in this form, perhaps more obvious examples would be the church, particularly as it survived in the Soviet Union and Eastern Europe during decades of communist oppression, or on a different note, farmers in rural America, as they resist the functionalist reduction of industrial agriculture. Discourse is a single network of multiple discursive elements; within this network certain elements come together to form the site, say, of the State. Other elements gather on countersites such as the factory or the church, and a struggle is underway: The weapons are words and the stakes are knowledge and memory.

This summary of Foucault's account of discursive resistance should give us some idea about how the poet, for instance, contributes to resistance. But still something is missing—and that is a precise account of the relationship between discourse and the body, between the discursive and the nondiscursive. For Foucault, resistance, like power, does not function at the discursive level alone but is also inherently physical. Hence the genealogical analysis of power and resistance, as a supplement to the discursive analysis of archaeology, must "show how deployments of power are directly connected to the body."[87] Indeed, the task of genealogy is to write "a 'history of bodies' and the manner in which what is most material and most vital about them has been invested."[88]

Physically Committed Resistance

As we have seen already, to say that bodies are invested is to say that power is productive.

> But once power produces this effect [of investment], there inevitably emerge the responding claims and affirmations, those of one's own body against power, of health against the economic system, of pleasure against the moral norms of sexuality, marriage, decency. Suddenly, what had made power strong becomes used to attack it. Power, after investing itself in the body, finds itself exposed to a counter-attack in that same body.[89]

In other words, resistance, like power, is in part microphysical, or perhaps minutely physical, which is to say that the counterattack of "one's own body" may have more to do with the "soul" than the body or may involve seemingly insignificant acts, such as the subtle breach of a norm or a slowed pace on the assembly line. To recall de Certeau, the counterattacks of the body may occur below the threshold of visibility. Often, however, bodily resistance also involves a more obvious "physical commitment." The "essence of being radical," remarks Foucault, "is physical; the essence of being radical is the radicalness of [bodily] existence itself."[90] We can find examples of how Foucault envisions this radical physical commitment in anecdotes from his own life.

Consider, for instance, his comments about teaching in Tunisia in the late 1960s. Here Foucault is speaking of the Marxist students whom the police had attacked on the campus where he taught:

> During those upheavals I was profoundly struck and amazed by those young men and women who exposed themselves to serious risks for the simple fact of having written or distributed a leaflet, or for having incited others to go on strike. Such actions were enough to place at risk one's life, one's freedom, and one's body. And this made a very strong impression on me: for me it was a true political experience. . . . For those young people, Marxism did not represent merely a way of analyzing reality: it was a kind of moral force, an existential act that left one stupefied. . . . [W]hat on earth is it that can set off in an individual the desire, the capacity, and the possibility of an absolute sacrifice without our being able to recognize or suspect the slightest ambition or desire for power or profit? This is what I saw in Tunisia. The necessity for a struggle was clearly evident on account of the intolerable nature of certain conditions produced by capitalism, colonialism, and neo-colonialism. In a struggle of this kind, the question of direct, existential, physical commitment was implied immediately.[91]

Years later, Foucault witnessed with continued fascination this same physical commitment when he went to Iran during the revolution against the Shah and saw the "people take to the streets, in their hundreds of thousands, in their millions, and face the machine-guns bare-chested."[92] In another interview, speaking of the Soviet Gulag, Foucault again addresses the physical character of resistance:

> We must open our eyes . . . to what enables people there, on the spot, to resist the Gulag, what makes it intolerable for them, and what can give the people of the anti-Gulag the courage to stand up and die in order to be able to utter a word or a poem. . . . What is it that sustains them, what gives them their energy, what is the force at work in their resistance, what makes them stand and fight? . . . The leverage against the Gulag is not in our heads, but in their bodies, their energy, what they say, think and do.[93]

What enables people to stand up and die in order to utter a word or a poem? In this question and in the analyses of power and resistance that accompany it, Foucault has come close to defining the character of the politics that his work has gestured toward from the beginning.

At the end of *Madness and Civilization,* Foucault arraigned the world before mad works of art and declared a triumph for madness in the face of reason's military camp. The image was moving and was itself a call to arms, but the task was daunting: a few works of art against the world. Then in *The Order of Things,* Foucault both reissued the battle cry and clarified the task by speaking more specifically both about the power embodied in words and about literature and the poet as the inheritors of the struggle. But the possibility of effective resistance remained almost unimaginable, for it was still the poets against the world. In *The Archaeology of Knowledge,* Foucault tilted the odds slightly with both his analysis of the way words work and his argument for the existence of a counter-history that at least made the politics of the poet imaginable—but only imaginable, since concretely the poets didn't stand much of a chance. But then, beginning in "The Order of Discourse" and continuing through *The History of Sexuality,* everything changed, and in two ways. First, Foucault got physical, as it were, and turned his attention to the material reality of discourse. By the time he is done with this new analysis, the poets, now bare-handed, have taken to the field. Second, Foucault erased the image that had been so daunting: the image of the margins against the center, of the poets against the world, the revolutionaries against the State—the image of reason's vast and impregnable military encampment, dug in and secured against all possible attack. When the poets take to the field, they find no such camp but instead skirmish troops; and in a guerrilla war they imagine they might just have a chance.

By redescribing power as dispersed and relational and by linking the discursive power of poems to the physical commitment of bodies, Foucault makes the possibilities of resistance concrete. And even if Revolution is no longer thinkable, countless revolutions are. And perhaps it is here, with the image of the now physically committed, bare-handed poet fresh in mind, that I should stop to note what should already be noticeable: Foucault's redescription of power and resistance is also a redescription of politics—a redescription that Foucault continues to nuance in his last two major works: *The Use of Pleasure* and *The Care of the Self.*

A Technology of the Self

Foucault says in an interview that modern politics "has been dominated by the question of revolution" and that if "politics has existed since the nineteenth century, it's because there was revolution."[94] Foucault goes on to say that to the extent revolution is no longer thinkable—or in any case no longer "desirable"—then "we are perhaps living at the end of politics," and we find ourselves faced with the task of inventing "a substitute for it."[95] We should, I think, understand Foucault's analysis of power and resistance as precisely the invention of a new politics. By the mid-1970s, however, after the back-to-back publication of *Discipline and Punish* and the first volume of *The History of Sexuality,* as well as a plethora of interviews and lectures that centered upon discussions of power, the invention was not complete. Something was still missing, something that had to do with the whole notion of a body imprisoned by a soul, of a subject that had been produced as an effect of power. For, to echo Foucault's question about those who resist the Gulag, what enables subjects that are the products of power to stand up and resist their producer, whence the counterattack, the centrifugal force of the body against power? Where, in other words, does resistance come from in a world where power is everywhere and one can never get "outside" it? If something exists below the threshold of visibility and escapes the panoptic gaze and the disciplinary procedures, then what is it, and how does it operate? In the eight years that passed between the publication of the first volume of *The History of Sexuality* and its companion volumes—*The Use of Pleasure* and *The Care of the Self,* both published just before his death in 1984—it seems that just these questions must have been weighing on Foucault's mind. For in these works Foucault provides the final missing link in his analysis of power and resistance.[96]

In the first volume of *The History of Sexuality,* Foucault had rejected "the repressive hypothesis" and had argued that power is productive. In the confines of that particular study, this meant that he could no longer assume sexuality, with its desires, drives, and pleasures, was a constant human characteristic, which was then repressed in various ways at various times. Rather, sexuality—our relation to ourselves as sexual beings, as bodies full of desire—is the effect of both discursive and nondiscursive procedures of power. Speaking more broadly, the rejection of the repressive hypothesis entailed dismissing the idea that beneath the heavy hand of power is "a docile or reactive primal matter" that keeps open here and there "spaces of a primal liberty between the meshes of [power's] network."[97] Foucault's new model of power rests on the idea that subjects are not composed of a primal, natural substance, which then inevitably seems to find itself imprisoned by power. Rather, subjects are through and through, and from the bottom up, the effects of power.

But if there is no space of primal liberty, if there is no primal matter seeking release from imprisonment, then what can all this talk of resistance possibly mean? In a world that exists as the product of the totalizing network of power, who or what resists? Is it enough to say simply that resistance is always possible because it arises hand in hand with power as its relational counterpart? The trajectory of Foucault's final works seems to indicate that he decided he had not in fact yet said enough about the complexities of power and resistance. Something was still missing—something Foucault had already gestured toward when he made the double claim that power is productive and that there exists no docile, primal matter upon which power works.

If subjects are not, at bottom, composed of a docile, primal matter but are instead and in a sense always already underway as the products of a complex relation between power and resistance, then the implication seems to be that subjects are *active* in ways that Foucault had previously underestimated. From *Madness and Civilization* through the first volume of *The History of Sexuality,* Foucault's tendency had been to emphasize the passive nature of both subjects and objects by analyzing the complex systems of domination in which both discursive and nondiscursive practices mold the world. Hence, Foucault could say in "The Order of Discourse," for instance, that discourse is "a violence we do to things, or in any case a practice that we impose upon them."[98] In the early 1980s, Foucault began to suggest that this way of putting the matter is problematic and that in his earlier works perhaps he had "insisted too much on the technology of domination and power."[99]

In a lecture he gave at Dartmouth in 1982, Foucault offers the following account of this shift in his thought:

> Let me introduce a kind of autocritique. It seems according to some suggestions by Habermas, that one can distinguish three major types of techniques in human societies: . . . there are techniques of production, techniques of signification, and techniques of domination. . . . [S]ince my project was concerned with the knowledge of the subject, I thought that the techniques of domination were the most important, without any exclusion of the rest. But, analyzing the experience of sexuality, I became more aware that there is in all societies . . . another type of techniques: techniques which permit the individual to effect, by their own means, a certain number of operations on their own bodies, on their own souls, on their own thoughts, on their own conduct, and this in a manner so as to transform themselves, modify themselves, and to attain a certain state of perfection, of happiness, of purity, of supernatural power, and so on. Let's call this kind of techniques a technique or technology of the self.[100]

Foucault goes on to say that "if one wants to analyze the genealogy of the subject in Western civilization, he has to take into account not only techniques of domination but also techniques of the self. Let's say: he has to take into account the interaction between those two types of techniques."[101] Why? Because only in this way, Foucault suggests, will we arrive at a more expansive understanding of the way subjects have been produced historically. To consider only the techniques of domination, only the notion of a soul imprisoned by a body, is simply too limited a view of how selves come to be. As Foucault puts it in the Dartmouth lectures:

> Power consists in complex relations: these relations involve a set of rational techniques, and the efficiency of those techniques is due to a subtle integration of coercion-technologies and self-technologies. I think we have to get rid of the more or less Freudian schema . . . the schema of the interiorization of the law by the self. . . . [T]hings are more complicated than that.[102]

Things are more complicated because it's far too simple to say that the prisoners simply interiorize the discipline that emanates from the tower. Certainly the prisoners also "effect, by their own means, a certain number of operations on their own bodies, on their own souls, on their own thoughts, on their own conduct." To imagine it otherwise is to imagine that the prisoners are simply docile, reactive subjects, a possibility that Foucault's previous analysis of power has already rejected. But if the prisoners are not a sort of primal matter worked over by the techniques of domination, then what or who are they?

In his last works, Foucault concludes, in effect, that by focusing upon the techniques of domination, he had precluded an analysis of all those activities that lie below the threshold of visibility, he had limited himself unnecessarily to a narrow slice of the historical imprint upon the body. Foucault suggests as much when he offers the following commentary on the change of course that occurred after the first volume of *The History of Sexuality:*

> Let's say very briefly that through studying madness and psychiatry, crime and punishment, I have tried to show how we have indirectly constituted ourselves through the exclusion of some others: criminals, mad people, and so on. And now my present work deals with the question: How did we directly constitute our identity through some ethical techniques of the self which developed through antiquity down to now?[103]

As this comment indicates, Foucault's move from an analysis of the techniques of domination and the "indirect" production of the self to an analysis of those techniques that constitute the self directly is a move into the field of ethics, insofar as ethics is "understood as an elaboration of a form of relation to the self that enables an individual to fashion himself into a subject of ethical conduct."[104]

An Aesthetics of Existence

In the second and third volumes of *The History of Sexuality,* Foucault, really for the first time, leaves behind the classical period that had been the focus of all his previous books and turns his attention to antiquity. What Foucault found particularly fascinating in his study of the ancient Greeks and Romans was "a kind of ethics which was an aesthetics of existence."[105] The phenomena Foucault attempts to capture with the notion of an aesthetics of existence "are those intentional and voluntary actions by which men not only set themselves rules of conduct, but also seek to transform themselves, to change themselves in their singular being, and to make their life into an *oeuvre* that carries certain aesthetic values and meets certain stylistic criteria."[106] Intrigued by what he calls at one point the possibility of an "ethopoetics," Foucault, in his last works, began to align himself with "a history of 'ethics'," declaring in a late interview that what interested him was "much more morals than politics or, in any case, politics as an ethics."[107] It is in this conjunction of aesthetics, ethics, and politics that we begin to see yet more clearly an outline of Foucault's tragic politics—a politics that is evident in this comment from an interview in 1983:

> I think that ethics is a practice; ethos is a manner of being. Let's take an example that touches us all, that of Poland. If we raise the question of Poland in strictly political terms, it's clear that we quickly reach the point of saying that there's nothing we can do. We can't dispatch a team of paratroopers, and we can't send armored cars to liberate Warsaw. I think that, politically, we have to recognize this, but I think we also agree that, for ethical reasons, we have to raise the problem of Poland in the form of a nonacceptance of what is happening there, and the nonacceptance of the passivity of our own governments. I think this attitude is an ethical one, but it is also political; it does not consist in saying merely, "I protest," but in making of that attitude a political phenomenon that is as substantial as possible, and one which those who govern, here or there, will sooner or later be obliged to take into account.[108]

Foucault's nonacceptance of what was happening in Poland in the early 1980s took a variety of forms and included a trip to Poland.[109] But perhaps a biographical anecdote that reveals more clearly the character of Foucault's tragic politics involves a trip he took not to Poland but to Spain in the fall of 1975. In September of that year the Franco regime had declared its intention to execute ten militants by garroting them. Spurred on by other French intellectuals, Foucault drafted a statement of protest against the impending executions. After numerous other French intellectuals and artists signed the statement of protest, Foucault decided the statement should be turned into a leaflet and that it should then be delivered in person at a press conference in Madrid. On September 22, 1975, Foucault and six other prominent French personas flew to Madrid and, in the bar of a hotel there, read in French a statement that called for justice and a fair trial for the condemned and that ended with the following words: "We have come to Madrid to bear this message. Matters are so serious that we had to. . . . Our physical presence in Madrid must add to the seriousness of our demands, must demonstrate the indignation that moves us and has made us, and many others, demonstrate our solidarity with those whose lives are threatened."[110]

Before they could read the Spanish translation of their statement to the press, plainclothes policemen arrived and interrupted the press conference. When Foucault asked if they were under arrest, the police responded simply that everyone was to remain seated. The police then asked Foucault for the copies of the leaflet that remained in his possession. When Foucault refused to turn them over, the police pressed the issue. One of Foucault's compatriots, Claude Mauriac, later described Foucault's resistance: "pale, tense, trembling, ready to leap, to spring, to go on the attack, the most useless, the most dangerous, and the finest attack, and all the more admirable in his refusal, his aggressiveness, and his bravery because one felt (one knew) that for him it was both a physical reaction and a moral principle: the bodily impossibility of being subjected to the contact of a police officer and taking an order from him."[111] After Mauriac intervened, Foucault finally handed over the leaflets, and a few hours later the contingent of French intellectuals and artists were taken to the airport and expelled from Spain. Five days later, five of the Spanish militants were executed.

Although the story of Foucault's protest against the Franco regime is consistent with the kind of political activity in which he engaged from the early 1970s until his death in 1984, I do not mean to make too much of this anecdote. But if we combine this story with Foucault's comments about ethics, politics, and the question of Poland, and if we alter each scene just slightly, then we should experience something like a shock of recognition. For consider what happens if we both substitute Sarajevo for Poland and imagine that the text of the statement in Madrid was a poem—or better, a play.

Clearly, "in strictly political terms . . . there's nothing we can do" for Sarajevo, just as there was nothing we could do for Poland. And yet, "for ethical reasons," we have to do something, we have to express our "nonacceptance of what is happening there," and we have to turn this nonacceptance into "a political phenomenon that is as substantial as possible." And so what might we do in order "to raise the question of Sarajevo"? Well, we might, as Foucault did in the case of Poland, accompany a shipment of medical supplies to Sarajevo; or we might, particularly if "we" are prominent intellectuals, fly to Sarajevo and hold a press conference; or we might, and this seems to be the best option in the circumstances, stage a performance of *Waiting for Godot*.[112]

I said in the first chapter that one of my tasks was to explain the profoundly practical and political character of Sontag's staging of a play in Sarajevo. We are now in a position to see the political character of Sontag's act and, at the same time, to summarize Foucault's tragic politics.

Returning to the Theater in Sarajevo

Consider first that Sontag's staging of *Godot* involved immense physical commitment. Remember that some of the actors and actresses walked a four-hour round-trip to make it to the theater, that they were all undernourished, that they dropped to the stage for rest at every opportunity, and that both they and the audience had to risk sniper fire and mortar attacks in order to make the performance possible. Consider also that Sontag's staging of *Godot* displays an aspect of Foucault's politics that I have yet to mention: It is an inherently collective enterprise. In spite of Foucault's stress in his early works upon the transgressive power of the work of individual artists and, in his final works, upon the self as a work of art, Foucault is quite clear that even if resistance begins at the level of individuals it must become collective. As he said it in an interview when discussing the Iranian revolution, "To confront so fearsome an armed power, one mustn't feel alone";[113] or again, from a different interview and more tellingly, "It is necessary to clear the way for a transformation, a metamorphosis which isn't simply individual but which has a character accessible to others: that is, this experience must be linkable, to a certain extent, to a collective practice."[114] Sontag's staging of *Godot* is a wonderful example of a collective practice that depended upon the physical commitment and the physical sacrifice of bodies gathered together. Theater, however, involves more than bodies on stage and in the seats; it requires a text.

Some of the bodies must speak, and others must listen—and coursing between and through all these bodies, drawing them together, are words. These words are themselves bound to other words, and these words to other bodies—and so the dim-lit theater stands as an intersection in a complex network of words and bodies. This particular intersection is an interesting place because the words have been chosen carefully. They are not the words of a children's rhyme nor those of a railroad timetable. Rather they are the poetic words of a playwright that were crafted in the wake of a world war and the systematic annihilation of millions of human beings by other human beings. Not surprisingly, then, they are words that project both those who speak them and those who hear them toward an uncertain future. They are words that, forty years later and in the middle of another war and another genocide, call attention both to themselves and to the hungry and tired bodies that have gathered around them. In their own particular material reality these words call attention to these bodies and the way they now live at the mercy of a different set of words and a different set of bodies.

The intersection of the dim-lit theater is interesting, as well, because just as these are no ordinary words, so too they are not ordinary bodies. In the case of the actors and actresses they are bodies that have dedicated themselves to art; they are bodies that both on and off the stage forever seek to perfect their ability to express themselves. And in Sarajevo at least, we can imagine that things are not much different with the spectators. Have not they, too, dedicated their bodies to art, at least in the broad sense of what Foucault calls an aesthetics of existence? Why else would they risk the walk and the long wait gathered together in an enclosed and vulnerable space? As Sontag notes, "In Sarajevo, as anywhere else, there are more than a few people who feel strengthened and consoled by having their sense of reality affirmed and transformed by art."[115] And how is it that art affirms and transfigures our sense of reality? It does so precisely insofar as we do not remain passive in relation to it but rather engage it and take it up into our lives. In Sarajevo there are no spectators. There are only those people who, on and off the stage, seek "to effect, by their own means, a certain number of operations on their own bodies, on their own souls, on their own thoughts, on their own conduct, and this in a manner so as to transform themselves, modify themselves, and to attain a certain state of perfection, of happiness, of purity, of supernatural power."[116] Notice how Foucault's words resonate in a new way once we set them down in Sarajevo.

Indeed, not just these words but the whole of Foucault's tragic politics, as we have seen it develop from *Madness and Civilization* to the last works, gains a new clarity on the stage in Sarajevo. Think for a moment more about the way Sontag's staging of *Godot* gathers together the disparate elements of Foucault's politics. We have first a work of art as it arraigns the world and asks for the justification of genocide—the ultimate exclusion of the other. Then there is the use of discourse as "a point of resistance," and linked to this discursive resistance, we see displayed the physical commitment that such protest requires; and we see, too, that this is a collective enterprise, that we cannot arraign the world alone but must come together—from miles away and at the risk of sniper fire, if need be—in order to resist power. And note, all of this occurs in the heterotopic space of the theater, a countersite that becomes the native home of resistance and that keeps open the space of popular memory. This memory in turn bears within it a host of subjugated knowledges—the sort of memory and the kind of knowledge, for instance, that allows a culture to survive even the greatest of persecutions, the sort of memory and the kind of knowledge, for instance, kept alive in song and dance and poetry and story and that has allowed many of the so-called primal cultures of the world to survive in the face of genocide.

And note, as well, that the staging of *Godot* rests upon the unspoken assumption that power functions in the interstices of a complex network of relations and is, at every point, accompanied by resistance. Standing behind this unspoken assumption about the operation of power is the unspoken hope that because chance is the god of history and because nothing in history follows the simple logic of cause and effect, on any given day even the smallest acts might bring the wall crumbling down. Hence, although staging *Godot* in Sarajevo may be like fiddling while Rome burns, it is nonetheless an eminently *practical* thing to do. And even if the wall does not come crashing down and even if the war goes on and on, these acts themselves embody a transformation of power that renders lives dignified, even if the world around them is not. The world, and not the wall, may come crumbling down, having failed to justify itself as an aesthetic phenomenon; nonetheless, the lives of the individuals in the theater attained an aesthetic justification that the world itself did not.

There remains, of course, a decisive objection both to Foucault's politics as I have portrayed it and to my interpretation of Sontag's staging of

Godot. One can certainly argue, and some of Foucault's critics have done so, that such acts are a "refusal of politics," that they represent "a self-imposed exclusion from the political," and are "condemned to marginality."[117] After all, if Rome burns and if the world itself becomes rubble at our feet, then how can we possibly say, as Foucault does, that such acts are "all the more . . . effective because they are formed right at the point where relations of power are exercised"?[118]

The simple answer to this objection comes as the reply that to found a politics upon a counterhistory is also to redefine the meaning of effectiveness. Once history is loosed from the necessity of an unfolding, then anything is possible. However, the odds are still skewed; to invoke the words of Adorno, they remain the odds of an overwhelming number killed and a minimal number rescued. Both because we face these odds and because success and effectiveness, like everything else, are finally aesthetic determinations, politics is tragic. A politics of resistance as Foucault describes it is not a politics of effectiveness or reform nor exactly a politics of revolution; it is rather what Stanley Hauerwas has called in another context "the art of dying." [119] To recall *Young Men and Fire*, such a politics not only doesn't teach us how to get out of the way, it demands that we stand, physically committed, in front of the machine guns and the tanks. And such a politics makes sense only against the background of a metaphysics of tragedy. Only in this context can we begin to answer the question of what enables people to stand up and die in order to utter a word or a poem.

Indeed, because Foucault's politics is founded not upon the answer to this question but the posing of it, we arrive at metaphysics. For in the end, we cannot speak of this enabling power, of this centrifugal force that makes resistance possible; we can only analyze its effects and stand in awe of its existence. Of course with this comment I have arrived at the same place I stood at the end of my account of Nietzsche: Just when we most want a few more words, one more missing link, that will bring Foucault's politics into a final focus, we have only a question—a question that Foucault refused to answer, even if all of his works gather around it. Like Nietzsche, all Foucault can do in the end is point to the possibilities of life as art—and as we saw at the end of Chapter Four, life is rarely more beautiful than when it turns to face death as it races up the hill. Or as Foucault once put it:

> All the forms of freedom, acquired or claimed, doubtless find in revolt a last point on which to anchor themselves. . . . If there are societies which hold firm and live, that is to say, if there are powers that are not "absolutely absolute," it is due to the fact that behind all the submissions and coercions, and beyond the menace, the violence, the persuasion, there is the possibility of the moment when life will no longer barter itself, when the powers can no longer do anything, and when, before the gallows and the machine guns, men revolt.[120]

So it is that politics becomes tragic, which is to say that it becomes an art of dying.[121] In one last attempt to make Foucault's tragic politics compelling, let's turn once again to a work of literature: Ian MacMillan's novel *Orbit of Darkness*.[122]

A Politics of Dying

MacMillan's book is in fact not exactly a novel, for the weight of most of its pages is composed of fourteen short stories, whose only relationship with one another comes from a certain chronological and geographical order. The stories all take place on the eastern front during World War II. The first story occurs in western Poland in 1939, and the last in Berlin in 1945. Slightly past the midpoint of the book, we find ourselves somewhere "southeast of Moscow," during the winter of 1943. MacMillan's book, then, follows the ebb and flow of Germany's push to and retreat from the east.

The book contains one additional thing, however, that makes it more than a loosely bound collection of short stories. The fourteen stories are framed by and gathered around a further story about a priest in Auschwitz who volunteers to die in the place of another man.[123] Set in Auschwitz from July 30 to August 15, 1941, and delivered in installments, this story binds the disparate stories of *Orbit of Darkness* into a single narrative. *Orbit of Darkness* both opens and closes in Auschwitz, and in between each of the fourteen stories the reader is returned there, as MacMillan unfolds the story of these seventeen days in Auschwitz bit by bit, two or three pages at a time. At the end of Chapter Eight, I will recount the story of the priest in Auschwitz. Here I want to turn to two of the other stories.

The first story is that of a young artist living in Crakow in April of 1940, after the Nazis had begun to occupy the city but before the creation of the ghetto. Early in the story we learn that the artist had been an apprentice to a master, whom the Nazis had executed. The artist then sets out to avenge his master's death with art:

> My first work was on the smooth, stucco wall of a building not far from the studio, where I drew a Nazi soldier in his clean black uniform . . . sleeping in a bed with his arm around a huge, bloated rat, and above them hovered an angel, in this case the Master in a pose of foreshortened crucifixion. . . . The Nazi's sleep appears troubled; the figure above them dominates the world of his sleep. My intent . . . was to suggest that the murder of the Master was an act no Nazi would ever escape, unless he managed to avoid sleep. (50)

In the weeks after the master's death, the artist draws several such pictures, each time withdrawing a short distance to watch the Nazis' reaction when they discover his work. At first, the Nazis simply painted over the drawing; then they beat anyone caught looking at the artist's work. In response to the third drawing, the Nazis were more severe: After destroying the drawing itself, they hung a man and a woman, chosen at random from the streets of Crakow, in front of the space where the drawing had been. Horrified, the artist locks himself in his studio and stops drawing. A few pages later, however, as the story ends, we find the artist preparing to draw once again. In telling this story, MacMillan makes no overt comments about the artist's decision to begin drawing again, but the narrative does offer clues to his motive.

Early in the story, the artist reports that the master had taught him "to be emotionless where the world's daily business was concerned. Death has no meaning and life has no meaning. Only our art has meaning, and our identities are fashioned by that, bringing meaning to everything else" (52). Following this logic, we can suppose that the artist first draws his murals, which always include the figure of his master in the form of an angel, in order to lend meaning to his master's death.

However, when the third drawing serves not to avenge death but to cause it and so breaks all the boundaries the master had placed between art and the world, the artist ceases to draw. Having been led astray by his master's teaching, the artist had misunderstood the power of his art. The master was certainly right to say that art produces meaning; but he was wrong to suggest that the power of art to produce meaning exists at a remove from the daily business of the world. The man and woman hang as proof that the power of art is in fact caught up in the world's daily business. What the artist learns from these deaths is that far from requiring an emotional remove, art involves a physical commitment to the world's business—a commitment that may well involve not only one's own death but the death of others. When, in the closing pages of the story, the artist begins to draw again, it seems he does so because he has arrived at a new understanding of the relationship between art and the meaning of both life and death. The final clue to the artist's motivations for beginning to draw again lies in something that happens one day to a little girl in Crakow.

In the story, the artist was not alone in his artistic forays in the streets of Crakow. Someone else was wandering the streets trying to establish meaning amidst so much meaninglessness. This person did not draw caricatures of the Nazis on the side of buildings but sounded Crakow's noontime trumpet call, which in more ancient times had been the city's warning cry, its call to arms. In the days when he was sneaking through the streets, planning his next drawing, the artist would hear this call often, and he began to feel a certain affinity with the trumpeter, although he wondered why the call never came on the hour, as it was supposed to. One day, after he had ceased to draw, the artist asked an old man about this oddity of the mistimed trumpet call. The old man, offended by the question, suggested that the artist had missed the point, a point the artist himself finally understands a few days later, when the SS catch the trumpeter.

The trumpeter was a young girl of fourteen. They hung her with her trumpet around her neck and then abused her adolescent body as she died. It is in the wake of this incident that the artist begins to draw again and arrives, it seems, at an understanding of the link between art and the meaning of both life and death. It is not simply, as the master thought, that "identities are fashioned" by art in its remove and that through art both life and death become meaningful. Rather, life and death are meaningful to the extent that they fashion themselves as art—to the extent that, like art, they embody a physical commitment to the aesthetic character of existence. Let me explain.

MacMillan tells us that when the old man listened to the trumpet call, he did so "as if it were great music, Mozart or Chopin" (61). Her music was not, of course, like that of either Mozart or Chopin, but it shared with them that same insistence on beauty, an insistence all the more remarkable given that it is an insistence that requires a radical physical commitment in the face of Nazi power. When the artist returns to drawing, he embodies this same insistence and hopes the old man will admire his cartoons as if they, too, are both great art and a call to arms, a moment of meaning in an otherwise meaningless world. But the artist returns to drawing not only to give life meaning but death as well. In his new drawings the little trumpeter hovers with the master above the Nazis and the rats.

Of course the artist still has to face the fact that people will die because of his work. But he seems willing to risk the possibility that when people are hung in front of his drawings, life, death, and art—in a conjunction unimaginable to the master—will find meaning otherwise unavailable on the streets of Crakow in April of 1940. To paraphrase the words of a character from another of MacMillan's stories: In the face of radical evil, work to keep the living alive, and when that fails make death meaningful. To work to keep the living alive and to render death meaningful is the "real work" of a tragic politics governed by an art of dying. And it is fundamentally aesthetic work—as is evident in another of MacMillan's stories, that of a young girl marching amidst hundreds of others, naked, through a nameless meadow in the Polish countryside, listening to rifle fire ahead:

> Rachel Steiner felt the grass wet with evaporating dew under her feet. . . . She reached up ahead of her and touched her mother's shoulder. She recoiled so quickly that Rachel gasped. Her mother's eyes were so flat and glazed that she seemed not to recognize her daughter. . . . Off to her left were little red-orange flowers in one field. Poppies, for baker's seed. She remembered watching the women in the village sifting the tiny seed in screen boxes.

> Someone brushed up against her, and she pulled her arms closer around herself. It was a boy about her age. . . . Maybe he was younger than she was. His eyes had a wild, searching look in them.
>
> She had never made love. She would die without having done it. . . . The sense of resignation deepened, until she felt she could laugh. "Would you touch me," she whispered. The boy wasn't listening.
>
> Ahead she saw the woman with [a] baby walk forward in short, jerky steps. Through the brush she saw movement and heard the baby scream. Then the rifles fired, and she saw the mother's hair snap into a fan above her head as she fell forward.
>
> She placed her hand on the boy's bony shoulder, but he didn't respond. . . . She saw a flock of birds pass in the distance and that made her heart slam in her chest with such force that her vision dimmed and brightened with each beat. She realized that her mother was in the hole.
>
> Ahead the man in the ill-fitting boots said, "You, turn around!" Then the rifles. . . . There was no one in front of her. . . . She felt light, as if she had no substance. . . . Urine so hot that it felt almost scalding ran down the inside of her legs. Then the warm stock of a rifle gently urged her to the edge of the crevice. She approached it. Down three meters was the strange, pale tangle of bodies, twisted and intertwined, some still moving. "You, hold the braid away!"
>
> She reached behind her, hearing the clicking sounds of the rifles, and pulled the black braid across her eyes and smelled the scented soap she had used to wash her hair in the morning. (94–98)

Wet grass, fields of red-orange poppies, a longing to touch and be touched—to make love, a flock of birds passing in the distance, the smell of soap: Everywhere she turns Rachel seems to find a beauty so incredible that it makes her heart slam in her chest. And all this on her way to a pit of death and in contrast to a mother so filled with fear she cannot even see her daughter a few feet away—and to a boy so frightened he cannot speak nor respond to her touch.

This composure in the face of death, with its emphasis upon the unstoppable beauty of things, is the final display of a politics of dying, a politics rooted in what I called at the end of Chapter Four "an aesthetics of dignity." This composure in the face of death is also not unlike, as I imagine it, the sort of composure that Jesus displayed on the way to the cross. Certainly the cross is about a politics of dying. However, as we will see in the next chapter, it is a politics rooted not in a metaphysics of tragedy but in the theology of apocalypse. Before leaving tragedy behind, however, and as a way to prepare the ground for my discussion of apocalypse, let me attempt to say something about the difference between the tragic politics I have outlined in the course of the last two chapters and the apocalyptic politics that will be the focus of Chapters Seven and Eight.

A Difficult Hope and the Politics of Lamentation

The difference between tragedy and apocalypse is finally a difference between two kinds of hope. No doubt, Foucault's politics is not particularly hopeful. Hence the comment from one of Foucault's more sympathetic critics, Romand Coles, that Foucault's perception of the world gives

> rise to a skepticism that leads one to shy away from attempts to construct plausible alternatives. . . . That Foucault's rhetoric and ontology largely discourage the attempt to formulate alternatives is extremely significant. . . . Foucault himself calls us to create our existences as works of art, but the world he describes at the ontological level harbors little space for the inspiration of possibility which would help sustain this ethos—an ethos that requires an enormous degree of fortitude.[124]

"The inspiration of possibility" is, of course, simply another name for hope. According to Coles, the problem with Foucault's politics in the end is that it allows too little space for hope. In the course of the last two chapters I have attempted to argue that in fact this is not the case. My attempt to link Foucault's historiography to his politics was precisely an attempt to establish the fact that Foucault's politics makes sense in part because it does rest upon hope, the hope that Chance is the god of history and that, therefore, the inspiration of possibility necessary for resistance and revolt is ever present. As Foucault says, "It is always necessary to watch out for something, a little beneath history, that breaks with it, that agitates it. . . . While revolts take place in history, they also escape it in a certain manner."[125] For Foucault, this mysterious "something" beneath history that, in a certain sense, escapes it is the source of all hope, which is why it seems wrong to say that Foucault ever really leaves behind the metaphysical character of his early works.

Of course, the hope in question is no ordinary hope, and it is certainly not apocalyptic hope; it is rather what Wendell Berry calls "difficult hope." A brief look at the essay in which Berry coins this phrase will serve to make the point. Berry's essay focuses upon the following poem by Hayden Carruth titled "On Being Asked to Write a Poem Against the War in Vietnam."

> *Well I have and in fact*
> *more than one and I'll*
> *tell you this too*
>
> *I wrote one against*
> *Algeria that nightmare*
> *and another against*

Korea and another
against the one
I was in

and I don't remember
how many against
the three

when I was a boy
Abyssinia Spain and
Harlan County

and not one
breath was restored
to one

shattered throat
mans womans or childs
not one not

one
but death went on and on
never looking aside

except now and then like a child
with a furtive half-smile
to make sure I was noticing.[126]

This poem, says Berry, presents us with a problem: "Why do something that you suspect, with reason, will do no good?"[127] It seems at first the poem answers this question by saying that there is no reason to take on such futile tasks—and yet Carruth has, after all, written another poem about war. This fact causes Berry to remark that "the distinguishing characteristic of despair is absolute silence. There is a world of difference between the person who, believing that there is no use, says so to himself or to no one, and the person who says it aloud to someone else. A person who marks his trail into despair remembers hope—and thus has hope, even if only a little."[128] Hayden Carruth is a person who marks his trail into despair. Having said this, however, we have still not solved the problem of this poem. Berry puts it this way: "Why has this poet expended so much skill and care to tell us there is no use in doing what he has already done a number of times and is now, in fact, doing again? 'Is this a trick?' one is tempted to ask, for it is impossible not to see that the poet, in the act of refusing to write a poem against the war, has written one."[129]

After some musing, Berry concludes that what we recognize as the "problem" of this poem is in fact, more generally, the problem of political protest and that the poem, therefore, is "an unusually complex protest poem." It is unusually complex because "it complicates our understanding of what political protest is and means":[130]

> Much protest is naive; it expects quick, visible improvements and despairs and gives up when such improvement does not come. Protesters who hold out longer have perhaps understood that success is not the proper goal. If protest depended on success, there would be little protest of any durability or significance. History simply affords too little evidence that anyone's individual protest is of any use. Protest that endures, I think, is moved by a hope far more modest than that of public success: namely, the hope of preserving qualities in one's own heart and spirit that would be destroyed by acquiescence.
>
> A protest poem, then, had better confront not only the impossibility of restoring what has already been destroyed, but also the likelihood that it will be unable to prevent further destruction. This is simply one of the practicalities of political dissent and protest. And Mr. Carruth's poem takes up this practicality and makes music of it. He makes a protest poem that understands carefully the enforced, the inescapable, modesty of protest poems. And so his poem becomes necessarily more than a protest poem: it is also a lamentation for the dead who could not be saved, and for the poet who could not save them.[131]

The idea of a protest that is also and at the same time a lamentation for the dead is the perfect depiction of a tragic politics. And as Berry notes, since it marks its trail into despair, such a politics is not in fact without hope, but what hope there is remains both modest and difficult. It is modest because it has no illusions of success, or rather it understands that the real battle is not about success. Rather, "what we need to worry about is the possibility that we will be reduced, in the face of the enormities of our time, to silence or to mere protest. Mr. Carruth's protest poem is a poem against reduction. On its face, it protests—yet again—the reduction of the world, but its source is a profound instinct of resistance against the reduction of the poet and the man who is the poet."[132]

The real work of a tragic politics, of an aesthetics of existence, has its home in this profound instinct of resistance against reduction. Berry notes that this "poem preserves the poet's wholeness of heart in the face of despair."[133] A modest hope is one that expects no more than this preservation of heart.

Obviously, such a hope is not only modest but difficult. For as Coles reminds us, it requires an enormous degree of fortitude—a fortitude in the face of death, as it goes on and on, never looking to the side, except now and then like a child with a furtive half-smile to make sure we are watching.

Foucault's politics of tragedy is not a politics founded upon skepticism, as Coles and others have suggested, but one founded upon the difficult hope that chance is the god of history, that at some point life will no longer barter itself, and that humans will find the fortitude they need to stand up and die in order to utter a word or a poem. And here Camus, in his imaginary "Letters to a German Friend," is particularly instructive:

> Hundreds of thousands of men assassinated at dawn, the terrible walls of prisons, the soil of Europe reeking with millions of corpses of its sons—it took all that to pay for the acquisition of two or three slight distinctions which may have no other value than to help some among us to die more nobly. Yes, that is heart-breaking. But we have to prove that we do not deserve so much injustice.[134]

Two or three slight distinctions, distinctions that prove "there are things you cannot choke in blood" and that perhaps allow us only to die more nobly, such is the stuff of tragedy and of the difficult hope of a tragic politics. All of Foucault's works gather round these two or three slight distinctions. Distinctions that define what Foucault, in a short essay on the Iranian Revolution and its aftermath, called the "enigma of revolt":

> There was a striking discovery for the person who searched in Iran not for the profound reasons behind the movement but for the manner in which it was being lived, and who tried to comprehend what went on in the minds of the men and women who were risking their lives. Their hunger, their humiliations, their hatred of the regime and their will to overthrow it were registered on the borders of heaven and earth in a history which was dreamt of as being as much religious as political. . . . The famous demonstrations, which played such an important role, could genuinely respond to the menace of the army (to the point of paralyzing it), and proceed with the rhythm of religious ceremony and, finally, return to a timeless mode of performance where power is always cursed. It was in this striking superimposition that there appeared at the height of the twentieth century a movement so strong that it could overthrow a regime which seemed to be among the best armed in the world. It did this while staying so close to those old dreams which the West had known at another time, when it wanted to inscribe the figures of spirituality on the earth of politics.[135]

The enigma of revolt Foucault describes here with such passion and eloquence is, more generally, the enigma of a tragic politics—a politics of lamentation and dying that requires physically committed actions in the face of domination, even though such actions hold out no promise of "success." The politics of tragedy as we have found it in Foucault's works resides precisely on the border of heaven and earth. With that image in mind, let me turn now to the work of the next two chapters, where I will consider from another angle this same border and a similar politics by exploring the old dream of another time that sought, and seeks, to inscribe the figures of spirituality on the earth of politics.

7

Worthy Are the Slaughtered: Toward a Metaphysics of Apocalypse and an Apocalyptic Politics

The last three chapters have been an attempt to trace the path that leads from nihilism to tragedy. The sign that marked this path carried the name of Dionysus; and Nietzsche's metaphysics of tragedy took us some distance along the way. What Nietzsche began, Foucault finished, as he led us from a metaphysics to a politics of tragedy. As it turned out, the contours of this path from nihilism to tragedy were quite different from those on the confused map of John Milbank.

Recall that for Milbank no path, properly speaking, leads from nihilism to tragedy. Rather, on his map we find either the dead end of nihilism or the path that bears the name not of Dionysus but of the Crucified. For Milbank, nihilism is synonymous with a coding of the world that privileges the necessity of violence, a coding "whose practical expression must be fascism."[1] The nihilist code leads to fascism because it assumes that reason is always a ruse of power, that power is everywhere, and that the history of human society is thus reducible to a history of "universal military manoeuvres,"[2] as one cultural formation arbitrarily replaces another. According to Milbank, such are the conclusions of the absolute historicism that governs philosophical works such as those of Foucault. As a reading of history, these conclusions are benign, just a particular way of telling the story. However, as the governing assumptions of a politics, these conclusions lead to fascism because they cannot help but become the "joyful" and "celebratory" affirmation of power and violence.

At the end of Chapter Three, I offered a critique of Milbank's reading of the so-called nihilists by offering a brief account of Milbank's misreading of Gilles Deleuze. The last three chapters should make it clear that Milbank also misreads both Nietzsche and Foucault. Note, however, that this misreading of the so-called nihilists does not mean that Milbank is wrong about nihilism. In fact, as I suggested in Chapter Two, his account of the ontological ground of nihilism is quite helpful. Milbank's mistake lies not in his description of nihilism but in his categorization of certain philosophers as nihilists. Nietzsche and Foucault are not nihilists; rather, their works point beyond nihilism to a metaphysics of tragedy that achieves a practical expression not in a politics of terror but in the tragic politics of the poet. The poet, far from celebrating power in its most "naked" form, stands against power and violence with a physical commitment that may well lead to Dionysian martyrdom. When Milbank characterizes both Nietzsche and Foucault as nihilists and accuses them of fascism, he misses just this tragic character of their thought.[3]

Foucault's archaeological and genealogical diagnosis of our present is not a nihilistic promotion of dissonance. What may look like nihilism is simply the tragic affirmation of difference. "This affirmation is tragic," in the words of Gilles Deleuze, "because it affirms chance and the necessity of chance."[4] Foucault introduces chance into history not because he wants to make general claims about power and the arbitrary displacement of one cultural formation with another; rather, he wants to establish the fact that history is radically contingent and that we cannot, therefore, narrate it as the unfolding of necessity. On the basis of this fact, Foucault then hopes to make possible a counterhistory, a popular memory, that will enable people to resist the very powers Milbank has identified as the enemy.

In the wake of the foregoing account of Nietzsche and Foucault, I can now say that the "undecidability" that haunts Milbank's narrative resides not between nihilist dissonance and Christian risks of harmony but between the tragic affirmation of chance and the apocalyptic affirmation that what looks like chance is in fact the work of God. In other words, tragedy and apocalypse stand together as alternatives to nihilism. With an account of tragedy now at our backs, it is time to turn to apocalypse, which is to turn from Nietzsche to the New Testament, on one hand, and from Foucault to John Howard Yoder, on the other—as the metaphysics and politics of apocalypse replaces the metaphysics and politics of tragedy. Let me begin by saying a few words about my use of the term "apocalypse."

Toward an Apocalyptic Style

In Chapter Three, I called attention to the apocalyptic character of Milbank's narrative by pointing out his assertion that Christian counterhistory emerges from a logic that "involves the claim that the interruption of history by Christ and his bride, the Church, is the most fundamental of events."[5] This interruption of history is the most fundamental of events because it supplies us with a code that allows us to narrate the whole of history. As Milbank puts it, "all history before Christ can be narrated as anticipating his story, and all history since as situated within it."[6] Milbank offered an example of how this code functions by borrowing from Augustine's account of the stories of Cain and Abel and Romulus and Remus. The inhabitants of the earthly city, all of whom are descendants of Cain, interpret the events of the world according to a code of ceaseless and violent successions of power. Those who reside in the city of God, on the other hand, use as a code for the meaning of events the memory of Abel. As Milbank puts it, "the 'city of God on pilgrimage through this world' founds itself not in a succession of power, but upon the memory of the murdered brother."[7]

To say that Jesus' interruption of history is the most fundamental of events and that it supplies us with a code that allows us to discern the meaning of history is to say, in effect, that Jesus is the ultimate victim (who yet is not victimized)—and that in his life, death, and resurrection we find disclosed what it means for God to be involved in history. To say all of this is to say that the character of history is apocalyptic.

That "apocalypse" points to God's involvement in the events of history is apparent already in the term itself. The term comes from the Greek *apokalypsis*, which means simply "to reveal," "to disclose," or "to unveil."[8] To say that history is apocalyptic is to say both that its meaning depends upon certain disclosures of divinity and that the definitive such disclosure occurred at the cross. To speak of history as apocalyptic is also to say more than this, however, because the cross itself finds meaning only in the context of the apocalyptic character of certain strands of ancient Jewish thought.

As Richard Horsley says, apocalypticism "was the distinctive cultural form taken by imagination in late second Temple Jewish society. In that context apocalyptic traditions and literature carried crucial liberative functions of the imagination." Horsley goes on to note that this imagination was informed by

> the memory of God's promises of blessings to the people, particularly, the great divine acts of deliverance from foreign bondage and domestic exploitation and of their earlier independence in their own land. . . . [I]f life had not always been lived in subjection, then it need not remain in subjection for ever. Thus the apocalyptic imagination had a creative envisioning function. . . . Seemingly illusory fantasies of "new heavens and a new earth" in fact expressed the knowledge that life could again be human, that God, who willed human values such as justice and freedom from oppression, was still ultimately in control of history and faithful to the historic promises.[9]

In the Old Testament, we encounter this apocalyptic imagination most readily in the Book of Daniel; it is also present in numerous extrabiblical works.[10] But the Book of Revelation perhaps best expresses the character of this imagination (albeit now in Christian form) when John of Patmos recounts his vision of God's judgment of Rome:

> Then one of the seven angels who had seven bowls came and said to me, "Come, I will show you the judgment of the great whore who is seated on many waters, with whom the kings of the earth have committed fornication, and with the wine of whose fornication the inhabitants of earth have become drunk." So he carried me away in the spirit into a wilderness, and I saw a woman clothed in purple and scarlet, and adorned with gold and jewels and pearls. And I saw that the woman was drunk with the blood of the saints and the blood of the witnesses to Jesus. . . .
>
> Then I heard another voice from heaven saying the kings of the earth, who committed fornication and lived in luxury with her, will weep and wail over her when they see the smoke of her burning. And the merchants of the earth weep and mourn for her, since no one buys their cargo anymore.
>
> *Alas, alas, the great city,*
> *clothed in fine linen,*
> *in purple and scarlet,*
> *adorned with gold,*
> *with jewels, and with pearls!*
> *For in one hour all this wealth has been laid waste.*
> *Rejoice over her, O heaven,*
> *you saints and apostles and*
> *prophets! For God has given judgment for*
> *you against her.*
> *With such violence Babylon the*
> *great city*
> *will be thrown down,*
> *and will be found no more.*
> *In her was found the blood*
> *of the saints,*
> *and of all who have been*
> *slaughtered on earth.* (Revelation 17:1–18:24)[11]

Rejoice! The great whore, drunk with the blood of the saints, of all who have been slaughtered on earth, will be thrown down and burned. For God has given judgment against her. Such is John's apocalyptic proclamation that God is still in control of history. But is this proclamation anything more than the figment of an imagination so wild that it has ceased to address the realities of either history or politics? That is how Paul Hanson, for instance, understands such proclamations.

Hanson makes a distinction between the apocalyptic eschatology of books like Revelation and prophetic eschatology, which involves "the prophetic announcement to the nation of the divine plans for Israel and the world, which the prophet has witnessed unfolding in the divine council and which he translated into terms of plain history, real politics, and human instrumentality."[12] An apocalyptic eschatology, on the other hand, focuses upon "the disclosure (usually esoteric in nature) to the elect of the cosmic vision of Yahweh's sovereignty—especially as it relates to his acting to deliver his faithful—which disclosure the visionaries have largely ceased to translate into terms of plain history, real politics, and human instrumentality."[13]

As Hanson portrays the matter, when I use the term "apocalypse" to speak of the realities of both history and politics, I misuse it, since the flights of the apocalyptic imagination into fantastic metaphors signal a departure from "plain history" and "real politics." However, as several scholars have argued in recent years, the distinction between apocalyptic and prophetic eschatology is no less problematic than the popular notion that apocalypse simply designates the catastrophe at the end of time.[14] John Howard Yoder raises the issue in particularly memorable terms:

> When read carefully, none of the biblical apocalypses, from Ezekiel through Daniel to Mark 13 and John of Patmos, is about either pie in the sky or the Russians in Mesopotamia. They are about how the crucified Jesus is a more adequate key to understanding what God is about in the real world of empires and armies and markets than is the ruler in Rome, with all his supporting military, commercial, and sacerdotal networks.[15]

Despite appearances, the Book of Revelation is about real, plain history; or more accurately, it is about God's involvement in history.[16] As Yoder puts it, "The question laid before John by his vision of the scroll sealed with the seven seals is precisely the question of the meaning of history."[17] If we miss this fact and get lost in the fantastic images of the text, it is simply because we fail to acknowledge that according to the apocalyptic mind there is no such thing as "plain history"; for the meaning of history does not announce itself from the surface of events but lies in God's action "within" events. Yoder puts it this way:

> The substantial assumption that moves the seer is that God is an actor. *How* God acts can be expressed only in metaphors which our mechanically formed vision can only consider fantastic or poetic. Nonetheless, the addressees of "revelation" are expected or commanded to behave differently, *within* the system of the real world, because of that information which has been "disclosed" to them about God as a purposeful actor.[18]

The metaphorical character of the Book of Revelation, then, does not remove us from history; nor does it "assume that time will end tomorrow."[19] Rather, it draws our attention to the way God acts in history and "reveals why it is meaningful that history should go on at all."[20]

When I invoke the term "apocalypse" to characterize both a way of reading history and a politics, I may well be ignoring worthwhile aspects of distinctions between prophetic and apocalyptic eschatology, and I may express little interest in the tumultuous character of the final days. In these ways I may be employing the term "loosely." However, if there is a looseness in my employment of the term it stems from the fact that what I want to portray are not the subtleties of either the biblical term or the biblical text but rather what Yoder refers to as "an apocalyptic style" or "vision" that is rooted not only in the oddity of apocalyptic literature like the Book of Revelation but also in the oddity of the entire biblical text.[21] "It is," says Yoder, "not merely apocalyptic that is odd; it is the Bible whose world is strange."[22] An apocalyptic style is a way of acknowledging the strangeness of this biblical world and, by extension, the world generally. When I speak of an apocalyptic historiography and an apocalyptic politics, I have in mind a particular style, a particular way of life, that, much like Foucault's aesthetics of existence, founds itself not upon the identity of the same but upon the otherness of a world that never ceases to be strange. In this world, history continues not because of what kings and presidents might do but because ravens keep alive a prophet starving in the desert (1 Kings 17) and because even as kings and presidents count their people and take their polls and plan the future, the word of God comes into the wilderness (Luke 3).[23]

What the authors of both Kings and Luke knew is that ravens and peasants have more to do with the movement of history than all the best laid plans of kings. To adopt an apocalyptic style is to follow the biblical lead and turn our attention away from the power of kings and toward the power of ravens and peasant prophets in the wilderness. If this shift of vision sounds vaguely familiar, it should, for it is not unlike the shift that we have seen already in Foucault's archaeological and genealogical analyses. Let me begin, then, to say more about apocalypse by comparing Yoder's apocalyptic vision with Foucault's tragic one.

Politics as the Art of the Impossible

Perhaps the first indication that Foucault and Yoder share a vision or a style, if not exactly a method or a politics, comes in Yoder's insistence that an apocalyptic style will "free us to live without the myth of a complete systemic causal overview of how all that we do will work out for the best, because we see things whole and intervene 'responsibly'. The axiom of systemic causal perspicuity is part of the legacy of the enlightenment in its most sanguine phases."[24] Like Foucault, Yoder argues that we need to resist this legacy, for precisely in its "sanguineness" it has proved to be a legacy of violence driven by an overly confident sense of the direction history needs to take.[25] The apocalyptic style, says Yoder, "does us the service of ignoring and thereby striking down our confidence in system-immanent causal explanations for the past, and, even more, in system-immanent causal descriptions of how the future is sure to unfold from the choice we are just now making."[26] In other words, the apocalyptic style is something of an exercise in skepticism, as it seeks to destroy our confidence in traditional historical narratives.[27]

The undermining of our confidence in system-immanent causal explanations is, however, no easy task. For as Yoder notes,

> we take for granted a deterministic, even mechanistic vision of human affairs. From the micro level where DNA analysis explains more and more of who we are, to the macro level where statistics on resource depletion and global warming describe changes which no one can control, we assume our universe to be a massive causal nexus with no loopholes.
>
> In the middle range between the molecules and the greenhouse effect, we do still speak meaningfully of human agency, but the psychological and social sciences which deal with those activities are no less deterministic. That is what they mean by being called sciences. They make no room for "freedom" or for "God."[28]

Like Foucault, Yoder commits himself to an exercise in skepticism toward traditional history in order to discover the "loopholes" in the "massive causal nexus" and thereby free us from the illusion of historical necessity. Unlike Foucault, who locates these loopholes by introducing chance into the production of events, Yoder allows for our freedom and resistance by introducing God into history—or more accurately, by encouraging us to discern God's presence amidst events. Note, however, that introducing God into the production of events serves a purpose not unlike the introduction of chance, for God is full of surprises.[29] In his essay "Ethics and Eschatology" Yoder offers an anecdote that illustrates nicely the understanding of history's contingency that both he and Foucault share:

> I was one of a tableful of faculty colleagues privileged to host at Notre Dame, early in 1989, the first sociologist from the Soviet Union to visit our university. We plied him with questions about whether *perestroika* was going to work. He answered that it was not within his competence to say, since the sociologist is a scientist, and scientists deal with what can be generalized and replicated. Michael Gorbachev not only cannot be replicated; he cannot be explained. In terms of social science, he could not have happened. Politics is the art of the possible; history on the other hand is the realm of the unique, sometimes the impossible.[30]

Both Yoder's apocalyptic historiography and Foucault's archaeological/genealogical method assume that history is the realm of the unique and the impossible. Foucault calls this impossibility "chance"; Yoder calls it "God." Of course, to suggest this similarity between Foucault and Yoder is not to conflate their understandings of history. The difference between "chance" and "God" is significant, since to say "God," for Yoder at least, is to invoke the life, death, and resurrection of Jesus. Hence, as we will see in the next chapter, Yoder founds his account of a counterhistory upon a particularity missing in Foucault.[31] Still, for both Foucault and Yoder, this assumption of the irruption of an impossible event into the series of events makes a politics of resistance thinkable—a politics that we now need to call, taking our cue from Yoder, the art of the impossible.

Yoder says of the relationship between an apocalyptic reading of history and an impossible politics that "what the apocalyptic perspective enables the believing community to do is to 'deconstruct' the self-evident picture of how things are which those in power use to explain that they cannot but stay that way."[32] A "community playing the victim role within a society," Yoder continues, "needs first of all to know not what they would do differently if they were rulers, nor how to seize power, but that the present power constellation which oppresses them is not the last word."[33] Like Foucault, Yoder understands that politics as the art of the impossible requires the construction of a counterhistory that deconstructs the "self-evident picture of how things are." And like Foucault, Yoder links the demands of producing a counterhistory to the necessity of rethinking power, as will be apparent if we consider first Yoder's analysis of the link between history and politics and then the metaphysical background of this link, as we find it portrayed in the New Testament.

From the Politics of Effectiveness to the Politics of the Cross

Yoder notes that as moderns "we are obsessed with the meaning and direction of history."[34] And this obsession, he says, is linked inextricably to the way we think about politics, or our "social ethical concern":

> Social ethical concern is moved by a deep desire to make things move in the right direction. Whether a given action is right or not seems to be inseparable from the question of what effects it will cause. Thus part if not all of social concern has to do with looking for the right "handle" by which one can "get a hold on" the course of history and move it in the right direction.[35]

According to Yoder, the exact character of this handle varies widely, but still, "whichever the favored handle may be, the structure of this approach is logically the same. One seeks to lift up one focal point in the midst of the course of human relations, one thread of meaning and causality . . . [one] thread within history that is thought to be the most powerful."[36] Having selected a handle on history, one then attempts to move history in the right direction. And all such attempts, Yoder notes, are then subject to the tribunal of effectiveness, for in this approach effectiveness "is itself a moral yardstick"[37]: Did we, or did we not, fulfill our obligation to move history in the right direction?

Yoder raises several questions about the "strategic calculus" that links the handle on history to effectiveness. But most importantly, he asks the following: "Is there not in Christ's teaching on meekness, or in the attitude of Jesus toward power and servanthood, a . . . question being raised about whether it is our business at all to guide our action by the course we wish history to take?"[38] This question reminds us that, for all their similarities, Yoder's apocalyptic perspective is yet radically different from Foucault's tragic one, since both Yoder's counterhistory and his counterpolitics are rooted in the particularity of Jesus. From Yoder's apocalyptic perspective, the problem with the link between traditional historical narratives and the politics of effectiveness is not simply, as Foucault demonstrates, its violent and exclusionary character but also its departure from God's disclosure of *his* politics in the life, death, and resurrection of Jesus. Yoder argues that the politics of God is particularly apparent both in the story of Jesus' temptations at the beginning of his career and on the night of his arrest in the garden of Gethsemane.

The three temptations Jesus experiences in the wilderness just after his baptism and just before the beginning of his public ministry are all of a piece: He is tempted, as the words of the second temptation state clearly, with "all the kingdoms of the world" (Luke 4:5), which is to say with the opportunity to govern the whole of history.[39] Yoder's succinct formulation of the first temptation, the turning of stones into bread, conveys the same point: "Feed the crowds and you shall be king."[40]

The idea that the temptations involved the offer both of kingship and its accompanying power finds support in the rest of the narrative. Consider, for instance, the feeding of the five thousand as it is reported in both Luke 9 and John 6. Luke tells us first that Jesus and the disciples had withdrawn to the town of Bethsaida to escape the crowds. The crowds, however, discovered Jesus' whereabouts and "went after him." Jesus then proceeded to teach them about the Kingdom of God; and in the late afternoon, when the crowds were hungry, Jesus multiplied the five loaves and the two fish, producing enough food for five thousand people. John then tells us that after all the people "were satisfied" and the disciples had gathered the leftovers, the people "began to say, 'This is indeed the prophet who is to come into the world.' When Jesus realized that they were about to come and take him by force to make him king, he withdrew again to the mountain by himself" (John 6:11–15). Here we see clearly the link between the power of kingship and the ability to feed the people. In Luke, we see just as clearly that this is the kind of power Jesus rejects.

Following the miracle of the loaves, Luke moves us straight into Peter's confession of Jesus as the Messiah, as indeed, the king come, like David, to lead the people to victory and freedom. Jesus' response to Peter's confession, which serves also as his response to the crowd's desire to make him king, is to instruct the disciples about the cross, saying, "If anyone wants to become my followers, let them deny themselves and take up their cross daily and follow me. For those who want to save their life will lose it, and those who lose their life for my sake will save it. What does it profit them if they gain the whole world, but lose or forfeit themselves" (Luke 9:23–25).

In the story of the loaves and in Jesus' response to Peter's confession we see something that we did not see in the earlier story of the temptations, which is that Jesus' refusal of the kind of kingly power that Satan offered him was not a refusal of power itself, nor of kingship; it was, rather, an attempt to redefine power. This is again evident in Luke's account, where, after the instructions about the cross, Luke records the transfiguration and then almost without delay reports that Jesus, after this meeting with Elijah and Moses on the mountaintop, set his face toward Jerusalem. After the feeding of the five thousand, when the crowds clamored for him to be king, and after Peter's confession of Jesus as the Messiah, Jesus did not, as he was sometimes prone to do, withdraw from the crowds into the wilderness but instead set out upon a journey into the center of both Roman and Jewish power.[41]

Taken as a response to both the crowd's desires and Peter's confession, the journey to Jerusalem is not a refusal of kingship but an indication of the form this kingship will take. As Yoder puts it, we see what Jesus "proposes is not withdrawal into the desert or into mysticism; it is a renewed messianic claim, a mountaintop consultation with Moses and Elijah, and a march to Jerusalem. The cross is beginning to loom not as a ritually prescribed instrument of propitiation but as the political alternative to both insurrection and quietism."[42]

The cross is a political alternative to quietism because, as the disciples will discover soon enough, it is the result of a direct confrontation with the Powers. The cross is a political alternative to insurrection because it stands at the end of a path of resistance that refused violence. This refusal, present by implication in the temptations and throughout Jesus' ministry, becomes explicit on the eve of Passover, when, as he is arrested in the garden of Gethsemane, Jesus chastises one of his followers for drawing his sword and resorting to violence: "Put your sword back into its place; for all who take the sword will perish by the sword. Do you think that I cannot appeal to my Father, and he will at once send me more than twelve legions of angels?" (Matthew 26:52–53). Yoder offers the following commentary upon this scene:

> I have little qualification for what it would have looked like for twelve legions of angels—a Roman legion is said to have been 6,000 soldiers—to come into that garden. But what I can imagine is not very much to the point. Matthew's report is clear, and Matthew *could* imagine that this final encounter with Judas and the Jewish and perhaps Roman police would have been just the point at which God would unleash the apocalyptic holy war, where the miraculous power of the angelic hosts, Jesus' disciples as shock troops, and the crowds in Jerusalem with their long-brewing resentment would rise up in one mighty surge of sacred violence and would finally drive the heathen from the land.[43]

From beginning to end, then, Jesus rejects the temptation to grab hold of a handle on history and to move events in "the right direction." He refuses that kind of power and that kind of kingship that finds its support in violence; and he opts instead to resist just this kind of power by going to the cross. As Yoder says, for Jesus "the cross and the crown are alternatives."[44] As a political proposition what this means is that resistance against violence cannot itself be violent, and perhaps more importantly, that the politics of the impossible cannot be a politics of effectiveness.[45] For according to standard accounts of politics, the cross was, as the disciples on the road to Emmaus believed, absolutely ineffective: "Our hope had been that he would be the one to set Israel free," but now he has been crucified and is dead (Luke 24:21).

Yoder's reading of the Gospel narratives leads him to the conclusion that standard accounts of the relationship between history and politics stand in question not simply because with their simple logic of cause and effect they are inadequate to the task of explanation but also because, for Christians at least, it is not in fact "our business at all to guide our action by the course we wish history to take."[46] Rather Christians should seek to follow obediently Jesus' preference for the cross over the crown. To set the cross as an alternative to the crown is to suggest that "the cross and not the sword, suffering and not brute power, determines the meaning of history":[47]

> What Jesus renounced was . . . the untrammeled sovereign exercise of power in the affairs of that humanity amid which he came to dwell. His emptying of himself, his accepting the form of servanthood and obedience unto death, is precisely his renunciation of lordship, his apparent abandonment of any obligation to be effective in making history move down the right track. . . . Jesus was so faithful to the enemy-love of God that it cost him all effectiveness; he gave up every handle on history.[48]

An apocalyptic style that imagines politics to be the art of the impossible is rooted both in an *unwillingness* to grab hold of a handle on history and a *willingness* to accept the costs of this decision. Note, however, that the abandonment of effectiveness is not a recipe for despair, since to forgo all handles on history is not to abandon history to meaninglessness, but is rather to imagine that history works according to a different logic. As Yoder says, the "relationship between the obedience of God's people and the triumph of God's cause is not a relationship of cause and effect but one of cross and resurrection."[49] Hence the basis of a Christian politics "is one in which the calculating link between our obedience and ultimate efficacy has been broken, since the triumph of God comes through resurrection and not through effective sovereignty or assured survival."[50] Because this politics rests not upon calculation but upon obedience, "the cross is not a recipe for resurrection," and "suffering is not a tool to make people come around."[51] Rather, the cross is but the definitive expression of "the kind of faithfulness that is willing to accept evident defeat rather than complicity with evil [and therefore] is, by virtue of its conformity with what happens to God when he works among us, aligned with the ultimate triumph of the Lamb."[52]

The Metaphysics of Apocalypse

The language of "ultimate triumph" calls our attention to the fact that both Yoder's historiography and his politics rest upon metaphysical assumptions. As Yoder says, "'cross and resurrection' designates not only a few days' events in first century Jerusalem but also the shape of the cosmos":[53]

> The point apocalyptic makes is not only that people who wear crowns and who claim to foster justice by the sword are not as strong as they think—true as that is. . . . It is that people who bear crosses are working with the grain of the universe. One does not come to that belief by reducing social processes to mechanical and statistical models, nor by winning some of one's battles for the control of one's own corner of the fallen world. One comes to it by sharing the life of those who sing about the Resurrection of the slain Lamb.[54]

Here Yoder gestures toward what we might call a metaphysics of apocalypse—the kind of metaphysics displayed graphically in The Apocalypse itself, as John of Patmos recounts his vision:

> Then I saw in the right hand of the one seated on the throne a scroll written on the inside, and sealed on the back with seven seals; and I saw a mighty angel proclaiming with a loud voice, "Who is worthy to open the scroll and break its seals?" And no one in heaven or on earth or under the earth was able to open the scroll. . . . And I began to weep bitterly. . . . Then I looked, and I heard the voice of many angels . . . singing with full voice,
>
> *"Worthy is the lamb that was*
> *slaughtered*
> *to receive power and wealth and*
> *wisdom and might*
> *and honor and glory and*
> *blessing!"*

> . . . [Then] I saw under the alter the souls of those who had been slaughtered for the word of God and for the testimony they had given; they cried out with a loud voice, "Sovereign Lord, holy and true, how long will it be before you judge and avenge our blood on the inhabitants of the earth?" (Revelation 5:1–6:10)

When Yoder says that "people who bear crosses are working with the grain of the universe," he makes the same point that Augustine makes when he says that the city of God is founded upon the blood of Abel. And both Yoder and Augustine make the apocalyptic point that the testimony of the slaughtered makes history meaningful because the one worthy to open the scroll was himself slaughtered.

Yoder notes that when John of Patmos weeps, he weeps because if the scroll remains sealed, then history—and with it, suffering—remains meaningless.[55] But John does not weep for long because one worthy steps forward, and the angels sing "a new song": "You are worthy to take the scroll, and to open its seals, for you were slaughtered" (Revelation 5:9). Worthy is the Lamb; worthy are the slaughtered; such is the grain of the universe; so it is that the metaphysics of apocalypse reconfigures both history and politics. And note that this reconfiguration bears a resemblance to the change in scenery that we encountered in the work of Foucault.

Just as Foucault's archaeological historiography displaces the sovereign subject from the center of history and prepares the way for the subsequent genealogical account of power and politics, so too does Yoder's apocalyptic displacement of the crown with the cross lead to the notion that we are mistaken to imagine either that power operates from the center or that resistance involves frontal assaults upon power's citadel.[56] Hence Yoder argues that we must "dismantle the notion . . . that the Caesar is the privileged mover of history,"[57] which is also to say the center around which power gathers. Foucault calls this traditional model of power the sovereign or juridical model; Yoder aligns this understanding of power with the term "imperial." In any case, both Foucault and Yoder agree that to dismantle this model of power is to see new possibilities for resistance. In Yoder's words:

> If Caesar is not the only mover of history, we shall place more hope in non-imperial strategies and tactics: voluntary associations, churches, militant non-co-operation, and the models of community maintenance which have kept Jews and Baptists and authentic Orthodox believers in the Soviet Union morally more powerful than the party, or which have enabled Christian communities in China to outlive Mao and the Red Guards, and the blacks in South Africa to survive under the Boers.[58]

What Yoder refers to here as "non-imperial strategies and tactics" is the kind of resistance Foucault says always exists as the "underside" of power and that Yoder himself equates with the realities of "seeing things from below."[59] By calling our attention to the fact that power does not belong exclusively, or even primarily, to Caesar, Yoder, like Foucault, wants to convince us that resistance need not be equated with Revolution, insofar as Revolution involves an attack upon what Foucault calls the "State apparatus." This is not to say, as Foucault puts it, "that the State apparatus is unimportant."[60] What it is to say, again in Foucault's words, is "that power isn't localised in the State apparatus and that nothing in society will be changed if the mechanisms of power that function outside, below and alongside the State apparatuses, on a much more minute and everyday level, are not also changed."[61] Yoder's way of making the same point is to say that it "is not false when people who call themselves 'realists,' from Machiavelli to Klausewitz to Reinhold Niebuhr, tell us that power comes from the barrel of a gun. That is one kind of power; but the alternative is not weakness but other kinds of power."[62] Both to delineate how Yoder envisions these "other kinds of power" and to deepen my account of the metaphysics of apocalypse, I need to consider the language of power as we find it in the New Testament.

The Powers

Walter Wink, who perhaps has explored New Testament understandings of power more thoroughly than anyone else, says of the language of power in the New Testament that it "is imprecise, liquid, and unsystematic."[63] The imprecision of the language is due in part to the sheer number of terms that designate power and its relations, terms that often come in pairs and are interchangeable, since they all designate something that can be called simply "the Powers." We hear of "kings and those in authority," "angels and principalities," "principalities and powers," "power and name."[64] Not only are these pairings interchangeable, they are frequently grouped together in series, for instance in Ephesians 1:21, where we encounter rule, authority, power, dominion, and name; or Ephesians 6:12, where we hear of principalities, powers, world rulers, and spirits of wickedness.[65] When we confront power in the New Testament, it is, says Wink, "as if power were so diffuse and impalpable a phenomenon that words must be heaped up in clusters in order to catch a sense of its complexity."[66]

A good place to begin analyzing the complexity of power as it exists in the New Testament is Colossians 1:16: "for in him all things in heaven and on earth were created, things visible and invisible, whether thrones or dominions or rulers or powers—all things were created through him and for him." Here we learn two basic facts about the Powers: (1) God created them (indeed, as Paul suggests in Romans 8:38–39, the Powers are "creatures"), and (2) they are both visible and invisible, earthly and heavenly, material and spiritual.[67] Let me take the former point first.

To understand that God created the Powers is to remember that even though the New Testament usually casts them as the enemy, it nonetheless remains the case that they are God's creatures and, like all creatures, are simply fallen and rebellious. In fact, as Wink suggests, the temptations that Jesus experienced in the wilderness were real just to the extent the Powers were fallen, for it is the Powers in this condition that Satan offered him. Yoder notes that because we, like Jesus, always meet the Powers in their fallen and rebellious state, it is particularly important to begin thinking about them

> with the reminder that they were part of the good creation of God. Society and history, even nature, would be impossible without regularity, system, order—and God has provided for this need. The universe is not sustained arbitrarily, immediately, and erratically by an unbroken succession of new divine interventions. It was made in an ordered form and "it was good." The creative power worked in a mediated form, by means of the Powers that regularized all visible reality.[68]

Or as Wink puts it, the Powers "are still, despite themselves, inseparably bonded to the principle of rationality and cohesiveness in the universe. . . . Like a cancer dependent on the host organism for its very destructive energies, evil remains inescapably parasitic upon the whole."[69]

Of course, as the image of cancer is meant to convey, the whole, although at bottom God's creation, is not unchanged by the parasitic character of the Powers, since, as Yoder reminds us, the Powers are

> no longer active only as mediators of the saving creative purpose of God. . . . These powers have rebelled and are fallen. They did not accept the modesty that would have permitted them to remain conformed to the creative purpose, but rather they claimed for themselves an absolute value. They thereby enslaved humanity and our history. . . . They do not enable humanity to live a genuinely free, loving life. They have absolutized themselves and they demand from the individual and society an unconditional loyalty. They harm and enslave us. *We cannot live with them.* Looking at the human situation from within, it is not possible to conceive how, once unconditionally subjected to the Powers, humankind can ever again become free.
>
> We are lost in the world, in its structures, and in the current of its development.[70]

In a striking way, this account of the Powers bears a resemblance to Foucault's account of the Panopticon. And yet, like Foucault, Yoder does not think this account precludes resistance; it does, however, suggest that our resistance cannot take the form of an all-out rejection of, or assault upon, the Powers because in their ordering function the Powers remain a part of God's created order. We may be lost in the structures of the world and enslaved on all sides by the reach of the tyrannical order, but still, says Yoder, "it is in this world that we have been preserved, that we have been able to be who we are and thereby to await the redeeming work of God. Our lostness and our survival are inseparable, both dependent upon the Powers."[71]

The notion that the Powers are at once our masters and our means of survival and that resistance cannot, therefore, take the form of an all-out rejection of the Powers is not unlike Foucault's notion that power is everywhere, and yet where there is power there is also resistance. If this relationship between Foucault and Yoder remains less than apparent, it is because at this point we still have an inadequate understanding of the Powers as we find them portrayed in the New Testament, an understanding that will arrive if we turn now to the second lesson of Colossians 1:16: Not only are the Powers God's good, if fallen, creation, they are also both visible and invisible, of earth and of heaven.

The Power of the Air

Wink says that in their visibility the Powers can "be understood as institutions, social systems, and political structures."[72] However, such institutions and structures cannot be taken as the sole residence of the Powers, for if we limit our analysis of power to its visible manifestations, we will find that we always arrive at a "remainder" that will "not reduce to physical structures—something invisible, immaterial, spiritual, and very, very real."[73] In the New Testament this invisible remainder carries a variety of names, for instance: Satan, demons, angels, gods, elements, and perhaps most notably, *exousia*, which is sometimes translated simply as "power" and often refers to those invisible manifestations of power that Foucault deemed "microphysical."[74]

Wink notes that of the 102 uses of *exousiai* in the New Testament, 85 percent refer not to spiritual beings "but ideological justifications, political or religious legitimations, and delegated permissions":[75]

> It is a modern bias to single out just the supernatural Powers as if they alone were of significance. For the ancients, heaven and earth were a seamless robe, a single interacting and continuous reality. To read the literature on the subject, one would never have suspected that the spiritual Powers comprised only 15 percent of the uses of the term. *We* are fascinated with the supernatural forces the ancients described; *they* seem to have taken them for granted and to have been much more preoccupied with that more amorphous, intangible, indefinable something that makes it possible for a king to command subjects to voluntary death in war or for a priest to utter words that send a king to his knees.[76]

In the New Testament, then, the idea that power is in some way spiritual or heavenly does not usually refer to spirits, per se, but to what the author of Ephesians identifies as "the power of the air" (Ephesians 2:2), a term that specifies, in the words of Wink,

> the world-atmosphere . . . the invisible dominion or realm created by the sum total of choices for evil. It is . . . the invisible but palpable environment of opinions, beliefs, propaganda, convictions, prejudices, hatreds, racial and class biases, taboos, and loyalties that condition our perception of the world long before we reach the age of choice, often before we reach the age of speech. It "kills" us [according to Ephesians] precisely because we "breathe" it in before we even realize it is noxious. Like fish in water, we are not even aware that it exists, much less that it determines the way we think, speak, and act.[77]

The phrase "power of the air" summarizes nicely the New Testament understanding of power as an "indefinable something," an understanding accompanied by the insight that power acquires a hold on the way we think, speak, and act just to the extent it is amorphous and intangible. Indeed, the New Testament understands that it is in its amorphous character that power confronts us as such a formidable opponent. Wink's analysis of power in the New Testament is helpful because when he speaks, with an imprecision that matches that of the New Testament, of an invisible, intangible, spiritual power that nonetheless "determines the way we think, speak, and act," that "conditions our perceptions of the world . . . before we reach the age of speech," that becomes "the normative definition of our possibilities," that operates "from concealment, compelling, controlling, and constraining behavior," and that, despite its invisibility, takes effect only in the "concretion" of "material or tangible manifestations of power," Wink aligns the New Testament with Foucault's analytics of power.[78]

Recall, for instance, Foucault's notion of the *dispositif*—that "thoroughly heterogeneous ensemble consisting of discourses, institutions, architectural forms, regulating decisions, laws, administrative measures, scientific statements," and so on.[79] There is a remarkable similarity between Foucault's account of power and the principalities and powers of the New Testament. And where Foucault and the New Testament meet, both step into the glow of a new light that is itself the product of their convergence. In order to speak of this convergence in some detail, we need to move from the conception of power to the conception of resistance, as we find it in the New Testament. This move requires a return to Yoder's peculiar idea that because the Powers are God's good creatures, we cannot seek to destroy them—and yet because they are fallen and rebellious, we must seek to resist them. What might it mean to say that the Powers are at once our masters and, if not exactly the means, at least the location of our resistance? Or, as Yoder phrases the question, "If our lostness consists in our subjection to the rebellious powers of a fallen world, what then is the meaning of the work of Christ?"[80]

The Concreteness of the Cross, the Church, and the War in Heaven

Yoder has to phrase the question this way because it seems at first glance that the work of Jesus simply confirms our subjection to the Powers. After all, Jesus sought neither to escape them nor to resist them but allowed them to exercise power over him in the most fundamental way when he went willingly to his death. If anything, the cross seems to confirm that our lives, determined as they are by the structures of a fallen world, are irretrievably lost. In fact, however, Jesus' voluntary subjection to the Powers stands as an example of a brilliant strategy for resistance, given the fact that because of their necessary role in the order of creation, the Powers cannot be either evaded or destroyed. Yoder puts it this way:

> Subordination to these Powers is what makes us human, for if they did not exist there would be no history nor society nor humanity. If then God is going to save his creatures *in their humanity*, the Powers cannot simply be destroyed or set aside or ignored. Their sovereignty must be broken. That is what Jesus did, concretely and historically, by living a genuinely free and human existence. This life brought him, as any genuinely human existence will bring anyone, to the cross.[81]

Thus it is that the author of Colossians can declare that in Jesus and through the cross, God "disarmed the principalities and powers and made a public example of them, triumphing over them in him [or 'it']" (Colossians 2:15).[82] The image is that of a victory parade like those the Romans sometimes staged after a major success in war. And as Wink notes, "the most exciting part of the parade was dragging the defeated enemy through the streets and exposing them to public ridicule."[83] To say God triumphed over the principalities and powers is to say that he paraded them before the world as captives in their defeat; it is also to say that he defeated them precisely by thus exposing them. Indeed, the Greek term *apekdysamenos*, translated above as "disarmed," conveys the sense of "stripping off," or "undressing": The image is that of armor coming off.[84] The overarching message of Colossians 2:15, then, is that God defeated the Powers by "exposing" them. "Exposure" is the theme that runs throughout the entire verse; and the punch line is that Jesus exposed the Powers at the cross. Wink offers us the following image:

> If God is viewed as the *imperator mundi* who has bestowed on Christ this the highest of honors (for the triumph was considered the greatest distinction

Rome could confer) and Christ is conceived of as the *triumphator,* then the cross may be pictured as being carried before the entire procession as the trophy of victory, the paradoxical spoils of war by which the Powers were themselves despoiled. Hence the ambiguous *en auto,* which refers apparently simultaneously to Christ as the victor and the cross as the means to victory.[85]

Colossians 2:15 suggests that to force the Powers into a public display of their violent truth, as Jesus did at the cross, is already to have disarmed them. Despite appearances the cross is already victory (although the decisiveness of this victory is apparent only with the discovery of the empty tomb on the third day). Yoder puts it this way:

The Powers have been defeated not by some cosmic hocus-pocus but by the concreteness of the cross; the impact of the cross upon them is not the working of magical words nor the fulfillment of a legal contract calling for the shedding of innocent blood, but the sovereign presence, within the structures of creaturely orderliness, of Jesus the kingly claimant and of the church who herself is a structure and a power in society. Thus the historicity of Jesus retains, in the working of the church as it encounters the other power and value structures of its history, the same kind of relevance that the man Jesus had for those whom he served until they killed him.[86]

The meaning of the work of Christ in a fallen world, where we find ourselves lost amidst the structures of rebellious Powers, is to be found in this link between the "concreteness of the cross" and the church "who herself is a structure and a power within society." To explain the exact nature of this link between Jesus on the cross and the church in society requires that we leave behind for now the drama of the cross and return to what Yoder calls the nonimperial strategies and tactics that characterize Christian resistance, a topic that takes us once again to Ephesians.

Yoder implies that the image of the triumph of the cross in Colossians 2 is related in an important way to the murky notion found in Ephesians 3:10 "that through the church the manifold wisdom of God might now be made known to the principalities and powers in the heavenly places."[87] With this reference to "heavenly places" we find ourselves moving from the overt display of power and resistance embodied in the cross back to what Wink calls their "mythic dimension."[88] If we find ourselves moving back to this mythic dimension of power and resistance it is because, as the author of Ephesians reminds us, "we are not contending against flesh and blood, but against the principalities, against the powers, against the world rulers of this present darkness, against the spiritual hosts of wickedness in heavenly places" (Ephesians 6:12). Because the Powers are more extensive than their manifestation in "flesh and blood," because they reside not only in institutions and social structures but also in "heavenly places," resistance, too, must take on a spiritual character as the church confronts the Powers where they are, in fact, the most formidable.

But how is the church to confront the Powers in heavenly places? What does it mean to say, with Wink, that the church "must develop a fine-tuned sensitivity to what the ancients called 'the war in heaven'" or with the author of Ephesians that Christians must take up "the sword of the spirit" (Ephesians 6:17)? How, exactly, is the church, as herself a structure and power within society, to resist the Powers?

Put simply, and in a way that sounds something like Foucault, the church resists the Powers by making manifest the "sovereign presence" of Jesus in a concrete rearrangement of the social order, which serves simultaneously as a recodification of power relations in their intangibility. As Wink says, "there can be no spirit of Christ apart from its concretions in the world."[89] To take up the sword of the spirit, then, or to join the war in heaven, is not to imagine that resistance is, in Yoder's phrase, a "cosmic hocus-pocus"; it is simply to say that resistance, like power, always functions simultaneously at two levels. To paraphrase Wink, spiritual realities do not have an existence independent of their material counterparts, and it is for just this reason that rearrangements of the physical order serve also as recodifications of the spiritual relations of power. If this seems a somewhat murky thought, recall Foucault's account of the microphysics of power and of the link, for instance, between the physical arrangement of space and the insidious and invisible operation of disciplinary power.

The implication of the New Testament view of power and resistance is that subtle rearrangements of the social order are themselves already instances of resistance. What this means is that the church, simply by being the church—by being an alternative society in the midst of an existing social order—is in its very existence a point of resistance because of the way in which it recodifies power relations. The idea that this recodification of power relations is both possible and represents a moment of resistance rests upon the assumption that the Powers, even in their rebellion, remain God's creatures. Indeed, the New Testament understanding of the link between power and resistance recasts this link as we found it in Foucault. I can now say that the reason resistance always accompanies power and has at least the hope of success is that the Powers, even in rebellion, remain God's creatures. Hence, when Ephesians says that the church will make known God's manifold wisdom to the principalities and powers, we encounter the suggestion that the task of the church is to call the Powers "back to their origins."[90] The church can do this best by establishing itself as an alternative social order that better represents those origins, that better aligns itself with the grain of the universe. Indeed, only in this way can the church address the powers, since "the church has no hope of success in a frontal encounter."[91] As Hendrikus Berkhof argues:

> The very existence of the church . . . is itself a proclamation, a sign, a token to the Powers that their unbroken dominion has come to an end. . . . [T]he very presence of the church in a world ruled by the Powers is a superlatively positive and aggressive fact. . . . All resistance and every attack against the gods of this age will be unfruitful, unless the church herself is resistance and attack, unless she demonstrates in her life and fellowship how men can live freed from the Powers.[92]

Of course, to say with Yoder and Berkhof that the church resists the powers simply by being the church because it accomplishes a recodification of intangible power relations remains an extremely abstract answer to the question concerning the character of Christian resistance. To make this answer more concrete, we need to convert the mythic, metaphysical character of power and resistance, as we have found them in the New Testament so far, into more concrete terms. We need, in other words, to follow the metaphysics of apocalypse the final distance on its way to becoming a politics; to do this is to take up the work of the next chapter and turn to the apocalyptic politics of Jesus and the church.

8

Revolutionary Subordination: The Apocalyptic Politics of Jesus and the Church

The task of this chapter is to display the apocalyptic alternative to the tragic politics outlined in Chapter Six. The definitive display of an apocalyptic politics is to be found in the life and death of Jesus. An account of the life and death of Jesus, however, is not a sufficient display of an apocalyptic politics. Left to themselves, the events of Jesus' life and death lead, at best, to the story of a tragedy—and not to the story of the church. And yet to speak of an apocalyptic politics is, as Ephesians suggests, to tell the story of how the *church* resists the Powers in heavenly places. What's at stake, then, is an account not only of Jesus' life and death but also of the relationship between the Jesus who lived and died in first-century Palestine and the Jesus who lives on in the life of the church, as the church continues to resist the Powers. To speak of this relationship in general terms is, of course, to speak of the resurrection; to speak specifically of the political character of this relationship, however, is to speak of what John Howard Yoder calls "revolutionary subordination," a concept he distills from a reading of certain New Testament epistles.

My display of an apocalyptic politics, then, will involve a twofold inquiry both into the life and death of Jesus and into the life of the early church. In order to prepare for this inquiry, let me say a few words about the status of the claims I will make in this chapter by taking a brief detour into recent debates concerning the quest for the historical Jesus. Upon the terrain of these debates, I should be able to display clearly the assumptions that are part and parcel of my account of Jesus and the early church—assumptions that all come to rest in one way or another in a particular understanding of history.

The Messianic Pattern of New Testament Narrative

Since the first third of the nineteenth century, scholars have engaged in a quest for the historical Jesus. By standard accounts, this quest has three parts: It begins with the publication of David Friedrich Strauss's *Das Leben Jesu* in the 1830s and culminates with the numerous Jesus studies published in the last decade or so; at midpoint, and even now still binding one end of the quest to the other, stands Albert Schweitzer's *In Quest of the Historical Jesus,* published in 1906.[1] In spite of the numerous works and the divergent portraits of Jesus that have emerged from this quest, one assumption seems to hold throughout. In the words of Luke Timothy Johnson,

> From start to finish of the various quests for the historical Jesus, the four canonical Gospels have been regarded primarily as a problem to be overcome: they are written from the perspective of resurrection faith, and they offer divergent testimony. . . . The first quest began by eliminating anything that smacked of the "miraculous," then chose the Synoptics as more reliable than John, then sorted through the Synoptics in search of the earliest and presumably least-corrupted version. The latest quest dismantles the narrative structure of the Gospels, putting all the separate pieces of tradition in a pile with all the similar pieces from the extracanonical gospels, then testing according to "criteria of historicity" for the pieces that go back to Jesus. The premise for the last search as for the first is: the only way to find "the real Jesus" is to bypass the Jesus found in the canonical Gospels.[2]

In other words, whatever "facts" the quest for the historical Jesus has yielded have been acquired at the expense of narrative structure. But as Johnson argues, if "meaning derives above all from narrative, and if we remove the meaning of Jesus' ministry given it by the Gospels, we are left simply with a pile of pieces . . . discrete items—things 'Jesus said and did.'"[3] Because these now "free-floating" pieces "cannot by themselves form a new pattern," they must, if they are to amount to anything like a portrait of the historical Jesus, be placed within a new narrative structure.[4] But once the "narrative control" of the Gospels has been set aside, on what basis does one decide how the narrative should go?

Johnson offers a good example of the problem. Suppose that on the basis of various criteria for deciding the authenticity of what goes back to Jesus and what does not, we conclude, as most scholars indeed have, that he really did create a scene in the temple. Johnson argues that "we are not thereby allowed, without the synoptic framework, to place that event at the end of his ministry. Perhaps, as in John, it happened at the start of his public ministry. Still less can we legitimately deduce that this incident was the precipitant for Jesus' arrest, trial, and execution."[5] In the absence of the Gospel narratives, we can, of course, draw conclusions about the causal relationship between various pieces in the pile of "facts" about Jesus. And we can draw these conclusions upon the basis of a variety of evidence. But what we cannot do is claim that history itself determines the causal relationship between various pieces in the pile, as if history exists outside of narrative.

What these comments indicate is that the goal of recovering the Jesus of history is unattainable. Attempts to reach this goal can, at best, simply produce a pile of pieces that must then be recast into a narrative about Jesus. Although scholarly efforts may have rendered the pieces in the pile historically probable, the same probability does not carry over into the narrative itself. When scholars claim that it does, they have fallen victim to what Johnson calls "creeping certitude,"[6] as they move without warrant from a few isolated "facts" to a grand narrative that claims to be "an accurate but impartial account of the historical Jesus."[7] Johnson notes that the creeping certitude that leads to claims like this arises "from the need to find patterns of meaning."[8] Such patterns are the product of narrative; and what this suggests is that the quest for the historical Jesus has always been more than a quest for the facts; it has in fact been a quest for a story. As Johnson says, the "meaning of Jesus is given, not by any of the single pieces, or their historical probability, or the quantitative balance among them, but by the structuring of the narrative as such. The meaning is given by the story."[9]

But if the facts have no meaning without the story and the structure of the story does not rest in the facts, then the opposition between the historically unreliable Gospels and the historically accurate portrait of Jesus produced by academics is false. The opposition is not between the biased, fact-obscuring narratives produced by the early church and the impartial, factual account of events produced by scholars. What's at stake, rather, is the meaning of events as those events are embodied in competing narratives; it's not fact versus fiction but story versus story, pattern versus pattern. To see that the dispute lies here is to have a renewed appreciation for the Gospels, for as narratives that structure the events of Jesus' life and death into a meaningful pattern, they are remarkable.[10]

The story of the Gospels, perhaps displayed most clearly in the Gospel of Mark, is the story of a Messiah who suffers for others and calls everyone else to do the same. Johnson puts it this way:

> The four canonical Gospels are remarkably consistent on one essential aspect of the identity and mission of Jesus. Their fundamental focus is not on Jesus' wondrous deeds nor on his wise words. Their shared focus is on the *character* of his life and death. They all reveal the same *pattern* of radical obedience to God and selfless love toward other people. All four Gospels also agree that discipleship is to follow the same *messianic pattern*.[11]

My goal in this chapter is neither to recover the historical Jesus nor to recapture the history of the early church. I seek rather to display the messianic pattern of the New Testament in order to outline the character of a Christian politics. In the end, I will rest my case not on the historical Jesus but upon an imaginative reconstruction of a first-century Jew from the village of Nazareth in lower Galilee. This reconstruction is "historical" insofar as I assume that Jesus is not a fictional character in the way that Dorothy is, for instance, in *The Wizard of Oz.* I assume, as the creed asserts, that Jesus "was crucified under Pontius Pilate, suffered, died, and was buried." Indeed, as you will see, with the help of various studies of the historical Jesus, I assume even more than that. Unlike most of the studies I will draw upon, however, I do not assume that the life and death of Jesus are reducible to a handful of assertions about the historical probability of certain events. As Johnson argues, such a reduction leads us not to the "real Jesus" but to a pile of pieces. The pieces, of course, are important, and for that reason scholarly quests for the historical Jesus are not without merit. But without a narrative to bind them together, the pieces are meaningless.

What follows, then, is not an unbiased, impartial, historical reconstruction of events in the first century. Rather it is an imaginative attempt to display the messianic pattern of the New Testament that draws upon some of the fruits of recent scholarship but at the same time refuses to separate the discrete "facts" of Jesus' existence from the meaningful arrangement they receive in the New Testament.

The Tactical Calculus of Jesus' Provocative Acts

To speak of Jesus' life and death is to speak of what Walter Wink calls Jesus' "provocative acts." Before considering these acts in some detail, let me say something about the character of these acts by taking a detour into the work both Michel de Certeau and James Scott have done on political resistance.[12]

With the help of de Certeau, we can gather all of Jesus' acts under the single heading of "tactics." De Certeau distinguishes a tactic from a "strategy." He defines a strategy or a "strategic model" of "force relations" in a way akin to Foucault's account of the sovereign-juridical model of power. Hence, de Certeau says that "a strategy assumes a place that can be circumscribed as *proper* (*propre*) and thus serve as the basis for generating relations with an exterior distinct from it."[13] In other words, a strategic model is based upon "the calculus of force-relationships which becomes possible when a subject of will and power (a proprietor, an enterprise, a city, a scientific institution) can be isolated from an 'environment.'"[14] A recent event in the city of Missoula, Montana, where I teach, is a perfect example of a strategy as de Certeau conceives of it.

In the past few decades the city of Missoula has grown rapidly and the city limits have, accordingly, expanded, as what were once rural areas become suburbs and those suburbs are then annexed and become an official part of the city. According to Montana state law, annexation can occur in one of two ways: Either the people in a neighborhood can vote to become part of the city, or in those cases where the city already surrounds the neighborhood, the city can forcibly annex it. Recently, the city of Missoula, having failed to convince enough people in a neighborhood to vote for annexation, went ahead and annexed the neighborhood anyway, using the provision in the law that allowed them to do so. The calculus involved in this decision to forcibly annex an entire neighborhood is what de Certeau would call "strategic," since it involves the relations between an identifiable place—a city—and an exterior distinct from it—the peripheral neighborhood.

A "tactic," on the other hand, involves "a calculus which cannot count on a 'proper' (a spatial or institutional localization), nor thus on a border distinguishing the other as a visible totality."[15] A tactic

> has at its disposal no base where it can capitalize on its advantages, prepare its expansions, and secure independence with respect to circumstances. The "proper" is a victory of space over time. On the contrary, because it does not have a place, a tactic depends on time—it is always on the watch for opportunities that must be seized "on the wing." Whatever it wins, it does not keep. It must constantly manipulate events in order to turn them into "opportunities." The weak must continually turn to their own ends forces alien to them.[16]

A tactic, then, is "a way of using imposed systems":[17]

> Innumerable ways of playing and foiling the other's game, that is, the space instituted by others, characterize the subtle, stubborn, resistant activity of groups which, since they lack their own space, have to get along in a network of already established forces and representations. People have to make do with what they have. In these combatants' stratagems, there is a certain art of placing one's blows, a pleasure in getting around the rules of a constraining space. We see the tactical and joyful dexterity of the mastery of a technique.[18]

De Certeau goes on to say that "here," in the realm of tactics, "order is tricked by an art."[19] This art is the art of conforming to an order as a means of evading it, of escaping an order "without leaving it"; it is the art of what we will see Yoder call "revolutionary subordination"; and it is an art that Jesus perfected. He was, as we will see, a tactical master.

Although all of Jesus' provocative acts involved a tactical calculus, they were not all alike; and by enlisting the suggestive work of James Scott, we can make distinctions about the various forms of tactical resistance that Jesus employed in his struggle with the Powers.

Infrapolitics and the Hidden Transcript

In words that are reminiscent of Yoder's attempt in *The Politics of Jesus* to establish the political character of Jesus' life and death, Scott makes the following general comment about his own work:

> Until quite recently, much of the active political life of subordinate groups has been ignored because it takes place at a level we rarely recognize as political. To emphasize the enormity of what has been, by and large, disregarded, I want to distinguish between the open, declared forms of resistance, which attract most attention, and the disguised, low-profile, undeclared resistance that constitutes the domain of infrapolitics. . . . So long as we confine our conception of *the political* to activity that is openly declared we are driven to conclude that subordinate groups essentially lack a political life or that what political life they do have is restricted to those exceptional moments of popular explosion. To do so is to miss the immense political terrain that lies between quiescence and revolt.[20]

The immense terrain between quiescence and revolt is the terrain of what Scott calls infrapolitics, which involves "a fundamentally different logic of political action."[21] In an attempt to delineate the logic of infrapolitics, Scott makes a distinction between the "public transcript" and the "hidden transcript." The public transcript is

> the *self*-portrait of dominant elites as they would have themselves seen. Given the usual power of dominant elites to compel performances from others, the discourse of the public transcript is a decidedly lop-sided discussion. While it is unlikely to be merely a skein of lies and misrepresentations, it is, on the other hand, a highly partisan and partial narrative. It is designed to be impressive, to affirm and naturalize the power of dominant elites, and to conceal or euphemize the dirty linen of their rule.[22]

According to Scott, the problem with most discussions of power is that they limit themselves to the public transcript, but the "public transcript, where it is not positively misleading, is unlikely to tell the whole story about power relations. . . . At the very least an assessment of power relations read directly off the public transcript between the powerful and the weak may portray a deference and consent that are possibly only a tactic."[23] In other words, both to recall de Certeau and anticipate Yoder, if we read only the public transcript, we will see only the conformity of certain subjects to the dominating structures of a certain order. What we will not see is the way in which conformity and subordination might themselves be an art that has tricked this order.

To take a skeptical view of the public transcript and turn our attention to the hidden transcript is, says Scott, to discover

> the key roles played by disguise and surveillance in power relations. Subordinates offer a performance of deference and consent while attempting to discern, to read, the real intentions and mood of the potentially threatening powerholder. . . . The power figure, in turn, produces a performance of mastery and command while attempting to peer behind the mask of subordinates to read their real intentions. The dialectic of disguise and surveillance that pervades relations between the weak and the strong will help us, I think, to understand the cultural patterns of domination and subordination.[24]

As we will see, this dialectic also will help us understand Jesus, as does Scott's argument that the distinction between the public and hidden transcript allows us to distinguish four kinds of resistance, or what he calls "four varieties of political discourse among subordinate groups."[25]

One variety of resistance takes place wholly within public discourse, resistance that involves, for instance, mainstream political activities such as lobbying Congress in order to convince them that the lack of civil rights legislation goes against the grain of everything America, in its own self-made image, stands for. At the opposite pole stands the resistance "where subordinates may gather outside the intimidating gaze of power" and express their anger, plan their revenge, and so on.[26] This resistance takes place wholly offstage and, to anticipate the coming discussion, is equivalent to those private meetings Jesus had with the disciples. Although these two varieties of political discourse—the wholly public and the wholly private—are important to the overall character of resistance, neither of them embodies what is most interesting about the art of tricking the Powers. In between simply public and simply private resistance, lies a third kind of political discourse, "a politics of disguise and anonymity that takes place in public view but is designed to have a double meaning or to shield the identity of the actors."[27]

According to Scott, it "is one of the ironies of power relations that the performance required of subordinates can become, in the hands of subordinates, a nearly solid wall making the autonomous life of the powerless opaque to the elites."[28] Indeed, it is the "willful use of submissiveness" that produces "a thick and resilient hidden transcript," that is, a "discourse that takes place 'offstage,' beyond direct observations by powerholders," and not just discourse but "a whole range of practices."[29] The political strength of both this willful submissiveness and the attending transcript, however, rests not behind the opaque wall but in those places where subordinate groups breach the wall and go public. Most of the time, "going public" is a subtle matter, as subordinate groups "insinuate their resistance, in disguised forms, into the public transcript."[30] This politics of disguise characterizes what Scott calls "everyday forms of resistance" and involves "a partly sanitized, ambiguous, and coded version of the hidden transcript."[31] If we imagine the hidden transcript as the private, offstage meetings between Jesus and his followers, then we can imagine that both Jesus' public ministry and the mission of the twelve (or seventy) is the ambiguous, coded expression of this transcript. As we will see, the parables, in particular, serve as the best example of this disguised voicing of the hidden transcript.

Sometimes the hidden transcript goes public in another, less ambiguous way. This brings us to both the fourth type of political discourse and the place where politics is "the most explosive," as the opaque wall between elites and subordinates, between the public and the private transcripts, is not only breached but "ruptured."[32] This variety of political discourse involves a "declared refusal to comply" with an order and requires a "public declaration of the hidden transcript."[33] Whereas the more subtle and ambiguous voicing of the hidden transcript often takes the form of "willing submissiveness" or, as Yoder calls it, "revolutionary subordination," this voicing of the hidden transcript is, Scott says, insubordination:

> [The] term *insubordination* is quite appropriate here because any particular refusal to comply is not merely a tiny breach of a symbolic wall; it necessarily calls into question all the other acts that this form of subordination entails. . . . A single act of successful public insubordination . . . pierces the smooth surface of apparent consent, which is itself a visible reminder of underlying power relations. Because acts of symbolic defiance have such ominous consequences for power relations, the Romans, as Veyne reminds us, dealt more harshly with *indocilité* than with mere infractions of the law.[34]

Hence when early Christians refused to pay allegiance to the Roman emperor and instead prayed for him, they were engaging in just this sort of "symbolic defiance." Rome's response to such acts, which was often to throw Christians to the dogs or the lions, is itself a comment upon the power of such defiance. Scott notes one of the reasons that acts of symbolic defiance are so powerful:

> A direct, blatant insult delivered before an audience is, in effect, a dare. If it is not beaten back, it will fundamentally alter those relations. Even if it is beaten back . . . something irrevocable has occurred. It is now public knowledge that the relations of subordination, however immovable in practice, are not entirely legitimate. In a curious way something that everyone knows at some level has only a shadowy existence until that moment when it steps boldly onto the stage.[35]

The prayers of the Christian martyr not *to* the emperor but *for* him were, in effect, "a symbolic declaration of war," a declaration Rome met with immediate and decisive action, in spite of the seemingly innocuous character of prayer. Although such an act in the face of Roman might seems insignificant, it in fact signals "a public breaking of the ritual of subordination. So long as the elite treat such assaults on their dignity as tantamount to open rebellion, symbolic defiance and rebellion do amount to the same thing."[36]

Such symbolic challenges to the order of the public transcript are not, however, always taken as acts of insubordination. Hence Scott notes that "when it suits them, the dominant elite may ignore a symbolic challenge. . . . By the same token, the dominant may also choose to construe an ambiguous act as a direct symbolic challenge in order to make a public example of someone."[37] Because of the varying responses to symbolic defiance, it is, like the more ambiguous forays of the hidden transcript into the domain of public discourse, usually the result of a political calculation. In other words, both the more subtle practices of every day forms of resistance and more obvious acts of symbolic defiance function according to what de Certeau calls a tactical calculus. Or as Scott puts it, "material and symbolic resistance are part of the same set of mutually sustaining practices. . . . The logic of symbolic defiance is strikingly similar to the logic of everyday forms of resistance."[38] Both kinds of resistance are public manifestations of the hidden transcript and are part of a tactical calculus designed to subvert "the self-portrait of the dominant elites."

Scott says that "most of the political life of subordinate groups is to be found neither in overt collective defiance of powerholders nor in complete hegemonic compliance, but in the vast territory between these two polar opposites."[39] We know now that two distinct but related types of political resistance reside in this vast territory: the everyday practices of resistance that insinuate a disguised hidden transcript into public discourse, and the more rare and more explosive instances when the hidden transcript "storms the stage" in an act of symbolic defiance.[40]

After summarizing de Certeau's account of tactics, I declared that Jesus was a tactical master. Scott's notion of the hidden transcript allows us to see the exact nature of this mastery. For we can say now that the politics of Jesus rested upon the tactical deployment of both everyday forms of resistance and acts of symbolic defiance. With this general characterization in mind, let's turn to the specific character of Jesus' provocative acts, beginning with his acts of everyday resistance, which we can divide roughly into the categories of teaching, exorcisms, healings, and table fellowship.

Parables as Tactics of Resistance

Even though the hidden transcript is not limited to speech acts, we can perhaps recognize it most clearly in speech, and so the parables are a good place to begin looking for the hidden transcript in the Gospels.[41] Both de Certeau and Scott note that stories play a significant role in resistance. Scott offers the example of the Brer Rabbit stories told by slaves in the American South, which "at one level are nothing but innocent stories about animals" but at another level are a "coded version of the hidden transcript" and accomplish something altogether different.[42]

Jesus' parables, like the Brer Rabbit stories, can be taken at one level as nothing more than innocent, if somewhat confusing, stories about the sowing of seeds, yeast in bread, birds in the field, fish in the sea, and about the amazing qualities of mustard seeds. But what else might these stories accomplish? In what way might they be a subtle, intentionally ambiguous voicing of the hidden transcript? To answer this question, let me consider three parables as we find them recounted back-to-back in Mark's Gospel: the parable of the sower, the parable of the seed growing secretly, and the parable of the mustard seed. Taken together these parables display "a partly sanitized, ambiguous, coded version" of a hidden transcript, a transcript we encounter initially in the parable of the sower:

> A sower went out to sow. And as he sowed, some seed fell on the path, and the birds came and ate it up. Other seed fell on rocky ground, where it did not have much soil, and it sprang up quickly since it had no depth of soil. And when the sun rose it was scorched; and since it had no root, it withered away. Other seed fell among the thorns, and the thorns grew up and choked it, and it yielded no grain. Other seed fell into good soil and brought forth grain, growing up and increasing and yielding thirty and sixty and a hundred-fold. (Mark 4:3–8)

To recognize this parable as a voicing of the hidden transcript we need to imagine how it might have sounded in rural Galilee in the first century. To imagine this is, in part, to recognize in the closing words of the parable what Ched Meyers calls an "agrarian eschatology"[43]—an apt description, I think, of the "code" this parable (and others) puts into play. Borrowing words from Fernando Belo, Meyers notes that "in a social formation in which agriculture is the dominant production, blessing takes the form, first of all, of abundant fruits and the satiety these bring."[44] The closing words of the parable of the sower promise just such a blessing. A blessing that stands in stark contrast both to all the wasted seed mentioned in the parable and to the economic realities of first-century Palestine, where grain seed was equivalent to "cash" and where "wealthy landlords always extracted enough of the harvest to ensure that the farmer remained indentured to the land, strangling any prospects . . . of economic security."[45] "Against this background," notes Meyers, "the promise of an astounding harvest (to the sower, not the landowner) is poignant indeed"—and not only poignant but "subversive" because such a promise

> symbolically represents a dramatic shattering of the vassal relationship between peasant and landlord. With such surplus the farmer could not only eat and pay his rent, tithes, and debts, but indeed even purchase the land, and

> thus end his servitude forever. "The kingdom is like *this*," says Jesus: it envisions the abolition of the oppressive relationships of production that determined the horizons of the Palestinian farmer's social world. Such images strongly suggest that Mark is articulating an ideology of the land, and the revolutionary hopes of those who work it.[46]

As numerous scholars have argued in recent years, first-century Palestine was a place of social and economic unrest, as it moved into its second century of Roman rule and became bound more tightly to the economy of empire. Ben Witherington summarizes the cumulative economic effects of Roman rule when he notes that "the gradual integration into the wider Mediterranean economy . . . entailed a widening gap between rich and poor, a situation that was exacerbated by other factors, including famine, population growth (without comparable growth in arable land), and small farmers' loss of land to the wealthy who held it as collateral against loans."[47] In the context of these economic realities, it's not hard to imagine that parables about abundant harvests might have instilled in the inhabitants of rural Galilee the hope of better times. And the next two parables in Mark's sequence help us imagine that this hope might have been revolutionary. Consider the parable of the seed growing secretly:

> The kingdom of God is as if someone would scatter seed on the ground, and would sleep and rise night and day, and the seed would sprout and grow, he does not know how. The earth produces of itself, first the stalk, then the head, then the full grain in the head. But when the grain is ripe, at once he goes in with his sickle, because the harvest has come (Mark 4:26–29).

Here we encounter again a parable that ends with the promise of harvest and that thus aligns itself with the hope an agrarian eschatology. But we encounter something else, as well—namely, an indication that this hope is indeed revolutionary and subversive. The closing words of the parable call us back to these words from the prophet Joel:

> Put in the sickle, for the harvest is ripe. Go in, tread, for the wine press is full. The vats overflow, for their wickedness is great. Multitudes, multitudes, in the valley of decision! For the day of the Lord is near in the valley of decision. The sun and moon are darkened, and the stars withdraw their shining. (Joel 3:13–15)[48]

With the explicit reference to sickle and harvest, the parable of the seed growing secretly links itself implicitly to this text from Joel and thus, as Meyers notes, "invokes the prophetic-apocalyptic-holy war tradition":[49] "the day of Lord is near," the day when "the Lord roars from Zion" and when "Egypt shall become a desolation and Edom a desolate wilderness, because of the violence done to the people of Judah" (Joel 3:16; 3:19). The parable of the sower promises a harvest so abundant that those who work the fields might step from beneath the oppressive hand of those who own them. The parable of the seed growing secretly extends this good news and promises that at harvest time those responsible for the oppression, those who have done violence to the people, will hear the roar of the Lord.

On their face, neither of these parables about seeds and harvests is inspiring, let alone revolutionary and subversive. And yet encoded in these parables is the twofold promise both that those who have suffered violence and lived lives of desolation will soon suffer no more, and that those who perpetrated the violence will themselves be made desolate. This promise contained in the agrarian code of the first two parables in Mark's series reaches something of a crescendo in the parable of the mustard seed:

> With what can we compare the kingdom of God, or what parable will we use for it? It is like a mustard seed, which, when sown upon the ground, is the smallest of all the seeds on earth; yet when it is sown it grows up and becomes the greatest of all shrubs, and puts forth large branches, so that the birds of the air can make nests in its shade. (Mark 4:30–32)

In this case the words lurking within the words of the parable itself are those not of Joel but of Ezekiel:

> Thus says the Lord God: I myself will take a sprig from the lofty top of the cedar; . . . On the mountain height of Israel I will plant it, in order that it may produce boughs and bear fruit, and become a noble cedar. . . . In the shade of its branches will nest winged creatures of every kind. All the trees of the field shall know that I am the Lord. I bring low the high tree, I make high the low tree. (Ezekiel 17:22–24)[50]

To make high the low tree is to turn the sprig of Israel into a mighty cedar or, in Jesus' altered imagery, to turn the tiniest of seeds into the greatest of shrubs. Like the seed that fell into good soil and grew up and increased, the mustard seed "grows up and becomes the greatest"—"*of all shrubs*." It is odd that even as the parable reminds us of Ezekiel's image of the cedar it substitutes a shrub for a tree. Even "the greatest of all shrubs" is, as John Dominic Crossan notes, "hardly competition for the Lebanese cedar."[51]

Why, then, does Jesus tap the symbolic power of Ezekiel's allegory and then alter the symbol? Crossan suggests, in the company of Brandon Scott, that the altered imagery leads us away from "the whole apocalyptic tradition."[52] This suggestion comes as no surprise, given that Crossan is one of several scholars who have in recent years attempted to overturn the post-Schweitzer conclusion that Jesus' ministry, like that of John the Baptist, was founded upon an apocalyptic eschatology.[53] It seems more likely, however, that the substitution of the mustard plant for the cedar moves us even more deeply in the direction of an apocalyptic eschatology.

Note first that to "make high the low tree" is also to "bring low the high tree," and then consider this "tree" as we encounter it later in Ezekiel, as God instructs Ezekiel what to say to Egypt about its demise:

> Whom are you like in your greatness? Consider Assyria, a cedar of Lebanon. . . . The waters nourished it, the deep made it grow tall, making its rivers flow around the place it was planted, sending forth its streams to all the trees of the field. . . . All the birds of the air made their nests in its boughs, under its branches all the animals of the field gave birth to their young; and in its shade all great nations lived. (Ezekiel 31:2–6)

In this passage we see clearly that the image of the tree is, as Meyers calls it, "a two-edged sword."[54] On one edge we find the low tree made high—an image of Israel as the nation of nations; on the other edge, we find the high tree made low, for Israel's rise is also the fall of its enemies. By substituting the image of the mustard plant for that of the cedar, Jesus does not depart from these apocalyptic pronouncements. Rather, he sharpens both edges of the sword, since the contrast now is not between one tree (Israel) and another (Egypt or Assyria) but between the tiniest of seeds-become-a-shrub and the great tree that is now Rome. Just as the mustard seed replaces the cedar sprig, Rome replaces Egypt and Assyria as the target of an apocalyptic pronouncement. The parable of the mustard seed leads us to the image of Israel living in the shade of Rome, "one small client state being fed by the streams of Caesar."[55] And then the parable, like Ezekiel, leads us on to the image of Rome made desolate:

> I have cast it out. On the mountains and in the valleys its branches have fallen, and its boughs lie broken in all the water courses of the land; and all the peoples of the earth went away from its shade and left it. On its fallen trunk settle all the birds of the air. (Ezekiel 31:11–13)

By using the contrast between mustard and the great tree of empire, the parable of the mustard seed offers a decisive summary of the agrarian eschatology that characterizes both the parable of the sower and the parable of the seed growing secretly. The summary is decisive not only because it paints the promise of Israel's success against the background of Rome's demise but also because it symbolizes this success with what is, after all, a weed.

Drawing upon the first-century botany of Pliny the Elder, who describes the weed-like properties of mustard ("when it has once been sown it is scarcely possible to get the place free of it"), Crossan offers the following summary of the parable of the mustard seed: "The point . . . is not just that the mustard plant starts as a proverbially small seed and grows into a shrub of three, four, or even more feet in height. It is that it tends to take over where it is not wanted, that it tends to get out of control. . . . And that, said Jesus, was what the kingdom was like. Like a pungent shrub with dangerous take-over properties."[56] When combined with the agrarian eschatology that unfolds across all three of these parables in Mark, this image of the kingdom as a noxious weed offers us a final glimpse of the revolutionary and subversive hope encoded in the parables.[57]

One might reply to this account of these parables that it assumes too much. Can we really assume that a first-century audience would have recognized either the reference to Joel or the even more nuanced and complicated reference to Ezekiel and then combined these allusions with their knowledge of mustard to arrive at the understanding of these parables I have suggested here? It is tempting to concede the point and to answer that surely such a reading is a bit extravagant. And yet to concede the point would be to miss the importance of Scott's analysis of the role the hidden transcript plays in peasant resistance. It may appear I have gone beyond what one might infer legitimately from the parables, but if the parables are part of the hidden transcript of the landless poor of first-century Galilee, then the fact so much is *hidden* in them should not be surprising—indeed, it should even seem likely.

If we imagine that the hidden transcript of the Galilean peasantry in the first century would have involved endless offstage discussions about the injustices of tenant farming, as well as behind-the-back criticism of landlords and their wealth, and if we imagine that such talk was accompanied by the secretive pilfering of the crops and inaccurate reports of the yield, then what we see in parables like those about the sower, the secret seed, and the mustard plant is the coded surfacing of this transcript as it is voiced in public.[58] We should imagine, then, that from the perspective of the Galilean peasantry these parables are nothing less than a subtle call to arms, since hidden within them is the news that harvest time is coming, that the day of the Lord is near, that the high tree will be brought low—that, like a noxious weed, the kingdom of God has taken root in the fields of the dominant elite. To borrow words from John Meier, we should see the parables as "word events" charged with the power of the kingdom they talk about.[59]

I have begun not only with the parables but with *these* parables because they provide a clear display of what Scott has in mind when he speaks of the subtle surfacing of the hidden transcript as a politics of disguise and anonymity.[60] These parables are, therefore, the most obvious way to bring Scott's analysis of resistance to bear upon the actions of Jesus. Certainly it is plausible to see in these parables Jesus taking the hidden transcript of the Galilean peasantry public. As Ben Witherington notes, given the economic realities of rural life in Galilee, "parables about unlucky tenant farmers, day laborers in vineyards, absentee landlords, unscrupulous middlemen and the like would hardly have sounded like pious platitudes. They would have rung true to the realities of life, a social commentary on how the coming Dominion of God could ultimately change the situation."[61]

What is perhaps not yet clear is how the veiled stories of God's revolutionary defeat of the powerful amount to anything *political*. As Scott says, "A skeptic might very well accept much of the argument thus far and yet minimize its significance for political life. Isn't much of what is called the hidden transcript, even when it is insinuated into the public transcript, a matter of hollow posing that is rarely acted out in earnest?"[62] What, after all, can a few clever parables really amount to? Let me join Scott in saying that such a skeptical view of this politics of disguise

> embodies a fundamental idealist fallacy. . . . [I]t is impossible to separate veiled symbolic resistance to the ideas of domination from the practical struggle to thwart or mitigate exploitation. Resistance, like domination, fights a war on two fronts. The hidden transcript is not just behind-the-scenes griping and grumbling; it is enacted in a host of down-to-earth, low-profile stratagems designed to minimize appropriation. In the case of slaves, for example, these stratagems have typically included theft, pilfering, feigned ignorance, shirking of careless labor, footdragging, secret trade and production for sale, sabotage of crops, livestock, and machinery, arson, flight, and so on. In the case of peasants, poaching, squatting, illegal gleaning, delivery of inferior rents in kind, clearing clandestine fields, and defaults in feudal dues have been common stratagems.[63]

We have to imagine, then, that Jesus' parables, as a verbal expression of the hidden transcript, expressed not simply the hopes and feelings of a subordinate people but also affirmed the concrete, material resistance that was already underway on a daily basis in lower Galilee. It is, in part, when the parables are connected to this material resistance that they gain their political character.[64]

Itinerancy and the Articulation of a Poetic Geography

We can account further for the political character of the parables if we recall that Jesus' preaching was itinerant, that he did not settle down in a particular village, that he was, in the words of Gerd Theissen, a "wandering radical."[65] On this note both Scott and de Certeau help us see the political character of Jesus' public but coded expression of the hidden transcript.

According to Scott,

> the effective social reach of the hidden transcript under normal circumstances might not extend much beyond, say, one plantation, one hamlet of untouchables, the neighborhood pub, or perhaps merely the family. It is only when this hidden transcript is openly declared that subordinates can fully recognize the

> full extent to which their claims, their dreams, their anger is shared by other subordinates with whom they have not been in direct touch.[66]

Scott's analysis here allows us to imagine that Jesus' parables gathered together and united previously disparate groups of disgruntled peasants and social outcasts. This gathering power of the parables is particularly evident when we consider that by taking his message from village to village and house to house, Jesus was in effect linking together previously unrelated subordinate groups and thereby constructing a more extensive and more "resilient" hidden transcript.

Remember that, as de Certeau portrays it, tactical resistance does not have a proper place but rather functions within the space of a social order that is the work of the strategic calculus of those in power. Tactical resistance operates without any strategic base and is, therefore, inherently mobile. Pairing Foucault's terms with de Certeau's insights, we can say that this mobility comes in two forms: the "discursive" mobility of the story and the "nondiscursive" mobility of walking.

The world is full of places storied by what de Certeau calls "local authorities"—legends, tales, family histories, what we might call the local "color" that brings alive the otherwise gray places we pass as we rush by on the interstate. Part of the strategy of the Powers, however, is to homogenize space by homogenizing the stories we tell. Think, for instance, of the homogenized accounts of American history taught in grade schools across the country and of the way such accounts contribute to the almost total illiteracy of these children when it comes to the local stories that once colored places all across America. According to de Certeau, it "is a symptomatic tendency of functionalist totalitarianism (including the programming of its games and celebrations) that it seeks precisely to eliminate these local authorities, because they compromise the univocity of the system."[67] Hence American children can, perhaps, speak of the significance of the Fourth of July and, maybe, of President's Day. But by and large, they will know nothing of the history of their own town, let alone the legends concerning, for instance, the creatures and the gods of the surrounding forests and mountains.[68] The more our stories are homogenized, the more our memory is programmed, the more our mind is evacuated, and the more we come to live in the uncluttered clean space of the Panopticon.

De Certeau notes, however, that we do not ever really live in the homogenized space of the Powers because the "surface of this order is everywhere punched and torn by ellipses, drifts, and leaks of meaning: it is a sieve-order."[69] These ellipses, drifts, and leaks are in part the work of the stories of those local authorities that persist. Despite the leveling effect of functionalist totalitarianism, "there is no place," says de Certeau, "that is not haunted by many different spirits hidden there in silence, spirits one can 'invoke' or not. Haunted places are the only ones people can live in—and this inverts the schema of the Panopticon."[70]

When Jesus took his parables and proclamations on the road, he was, to borrow an image from de Certeau, "articulating a second, poetic geography on top of the geography of the literal, forbidden or permitted meaning"[71] that had been constructed in Palestine by centuries of first Greek and then Roman rule. He was in effect invoking the spirits that haunted lower Galilee and creating an alternative storied space in which people might live a life of resistance. As de Certeau says, it is in their capacity "to store up rich silences and . . . to create cellars and garrets everywhere, that local legends . . . permit exits, ways of going out and coming back in, and thus habitable spaces."[72] With his appropriation of the "local legends" that color his parables and his proclamations, we can imagine that Jesus sought to resist the homogenizing tendencies of the Roman Empire by resorting to the mobility inherent in stories. Note, however, that Jesus fostered anti-empire mobility in another way, as well: He both practiced and encouraged itinerancy.

De Certeau calls our attention to the importance of itinerancy by noting that "walking about and travelling substitute for exits, for going away and coming back, which were formerly made available by a body of legends. . . . Travel (like walking) is a substitute for the legends that used to open up space to something different."[73] As a "walking exile," Jesus not only gathered Israel's oppressed into a common cause by voicing their hidden transcript but also sought in both his parables and his itinerancy to invent haunted places where this newly gathered people might resist the homogenizing orders of Roman power. Scott's account of the hidden transcript and de Certeau's account of this twofold tactical mobility, taken together, serve to alert us to the political character of the parables. The politics of Jesus, however, is not limited to parables; it is embodied as well in exorcisms, healings, and table fellowship.

Of Demons and Lepers

The extent to which the politics of Jesus subverted the Powers, and Roman power in particular, is perhaps best evident, outside the parables, in the exorcisms, whereby Jesus "cast out" demons in the same way that Yahweh "cast out" Assyria and Egypt (Ezekiel 31).[74] Indeed numerous scholars have noted the connection between demon possession and the oppression characteristic of imperial or colonial rule.[75] Crossan states this connection succinctly when he says that "colonial exploitation is incarnated as demonic possession."[76] In the Gospels, the most glaring example of this relationship between possession and imperialism is the story of the Garasene demoniac, which begins when Jesus meets "a man with an unclean spirit" at the edge of the Sea of Galilee:

> For he had often been bound with fetters and chains, but the chains he wrenched apart, and the fetters he broke in pieces; and no one had the strength to subdue him. Night and day among the tombs and on the mountains he was always crying out, and bruising himself with stones. And when he saw Jesus from afar, he ran and worshiped him; and crying out with a loud voice he said, "What have you to do with me, Jesus, Son of the Most High God? I adjure you by God, do not torment me." For he had said to him, "Come out of the man, you unclean spirit!" And Jesus asked him, "What is your name?" He replied, "My name is Legion; for we are many." And he begged him eagerly not to send them out of the country. Now a great herd of swine was feeding there on the hillside; and they begged him, "Send us to the swine, let us enter them." So he gave them leave. And the unclean spirits came out, and entered the swine; and the herd, numbering about two thousand, rushed down the steep bank into the sea, and were drowned in the sea. (Mark 5:6–13)

This story is full of subtle clues that point to the tension between the imperial powers of Rome and the oppressed inhabitants of Palestine, hence the reference to "Legion" (a term for a division of Roman soldiers) that enters swine (one of the most unclean of all the animals) and then drowns in the sea (a scene that recalls Israel's triumphant escape from Egypt).[77] As Meyers says, the "conclusion is irresistible that we are here encountering imagery meant to call to mind the Roman military occupation of Palestine."[78] And if that is true, then the conclusion that Jesus' exorcism of the Garasene demoniac is politically subversive is equally irresistible. Of course it may be the case that Jesus never performed this particular exorcism.[79] But even if the story of the Garasene demoniac is "fiction," it is a fiction that demonstrates clearly that the early Christian community understood the political character of those exorcisms that Jesus did perform.

Like the parables, the exorcisms recorded in the Gospels convey the promise of a kingdom that frees people from the Powers. The Gospel accounts of Jesus' miraculous healings convey the same promise; but the images of weeds, abundant harvests, and of demons cast into the sea are now replaced with images of broken people made whole. Hence Matthew can summarize Jesus' ministry by noting that "Jesus went about all the cities and villages . . . proclaiming the good news of the kingdom, and curing every disease and every sickness" (Matthew 9:35); or again, now quoting Isaiah, "He took our infirmities and bore our diseases" (Matthew 8:17). Both Matthew and Luke report that when John sent his disciples to inquire of Jesus if he is "the one to come, or are we to wait for another? Jesus answered them, 'Go and tell John what you hear and see: the blind receive their sight, the lame walk, the lepers are cleansed, the deaf hear, the dead are raised, and the poor have good news brought to them'" (Matthew 11:3–5; Luke 7:20–22).

To appreciate the revolutionary and subversive character of such healings is to move beyond the impasse of debates about their status as miracles and to consider them instead in the context of the inherently political character of the human body.[80] Foucault, of course, alerted us to the relationship between politics and the body, but in the present instance it is the work of Mary Douglas that proves particularly instructive. Douglas argues that "the symbolism of the body, which gets its power from social life, governs the fundamental attitudes to spirit and matter"; "the body," she continues, "is a symbolic medium which is used to express particular patterns of social relations."[81] Indeed, according to Douglas, we should be "prepared to see in the body a symbol of society, and to see the powers and dangers credited to social structure reproduced in small on the human body."[82]

For both society and the body, the powers and dangers in question are most evident at the margins. "All margins," as Douglas says, "are dangerous. If they are pulled this way or that the shape of fundamental experience is altered."[83] Often a danger at the margins of society finds symbolic expression at the margins of the body itself:

> We should expect the orifices of the body to symbolise its especially vulnerable points. Matter issuing from them is marginal stuff of the most obvious kind. Spittle, blood, milk, urine, faeces or tears by simply issuing forth have traversed the boundary of the body. . . . The mistake is to treat bodily margins in isolation for all other margins. . . . To understand bodily pollution we should try to argue back from the known dangers of society to the known selection of bodily themes and try to recognize what appositeness is there. . . . [For instance] when rituals express anxiety about the body's orifices the sociological counterpart of this anxiety is a care to protect the political and cultural unity of a minority group. The Israelites were always in their history a hard-pressed minority. In their beliefs all the bodily issues were polluting, blood, pus, excreta, semen, etc. The threatened boundaries of their body politic would be well mirrored in their care for the integrity, unity and purity of the physical body.[84]

Douglas's recourse to the Israelites allows me to bring this discussion of the relationship between society and the symbolic powers of the body to bear upon Jesus' healings. Take, for instance, the healing of the leper as we find it reported in Mark:

> A leper came to him begging him, and kneeling he said to him, "If you choose, you can make me clean." Moved with pity, Jesus stretched out his hand and touched him, and said to him, "I do choose. Be made clean!" Immediately the leprosy left him, and he was made clean. (Mark 1:40)

From the perspective of a first-century Jew, who would have relied on detailed instructions like those found in Leviticus in order to negotiate the complex dangers of bodily boundaries, leprosy, as Crossan notes, presented an especially troubling problem:

> The standard bodily orifices can be clearly delineated and their incomings and outgoings categorized as clean or unclean. And that establishes, as it was meant to do, an intense concentration on social boundary. When, however, would-be orifices start to appear where no orifices are meant to be, then, unable to tell orifice from surface, or with all boundaries rendered porous, the entire system breaks down.[85]

Leprosy is a sign that the boundaries that guarantee the distinctive existence of Jews as a holy people set apart have been mysteriously breached.[86] The exclusion of the leper, and of all others who in a similar way indicate that the boundaries of the community are in danger, is then an attempt to restore these boundaries and preserve the social structure.

We are now in a position to understand the significance of Jesus' healing of the leper. When, in the midst of the dynamics of this particular understanding of the relationship between a leprous body and the social body, Jesus reaches out and *touches* a leper and declares him clean he has, in Crossan's words, "acted as an alternative boundary keeper in a way subversive to the established procedures of his society."[87] Jesus subverted the social order that had declared such people outcasts. Jesus thus made possible a new community that refused to be founded upon the exclusion of the other. Jesus' touch of the leper was a small, seemingly insignificant act of immense political importance, directed this time not at the order of Roman power but at the Powers of his own native social order.

The Weapon of Table Fellowship

In his healings and exorcisms, as well as in his parables, we see the nature of Jesus' provocative acts and the form of his politics. However, my account of Jesus' material, everyday resistance would be incomplete without a discussion of table fellowship, for it is here that we see most clearly the character of Jesus' everyday resistance. Indeed, the coded teachings of the parables and the bodily interventions of the healings and exorcisms converge in Jesus' table fellowship. As Marcus Borg notes:

> In his behavior, teaching and pictorial representations of the destiny of the people of God, Jesus accepted the central role assigned by his contemporaries to table fellowship. . . . Jesus did not simply accept the role of table fellowship, but used it as a weapon. From the fact that his teaching shows an awareness of the centrality of the meal, it is clear that his action was deliberately provocative . . . an "acted parable," a symbolic act, chosen as terrain on which to do battle.[88]

Given the presence of rituals that surround food in our own lives, we should not be surprised that Jesus would choose the table as a place to do battle. After all, just a few decades ago blacks in the South frequently made the same choice. Food, and this was particularly true in the ancient world, is freighted with meaning; and in the life of first-century Palestine it embodied the same social hierarchies and social boundaries that we have encountered already in leprosy. In Jesus' day, more so than in ours, food was a "boundary keeper." And just as Jesus usurped the right to define boundaries and subverted the "established procedures" when he touched the leper, so too did he subvert the procedures and breach the boundaries when, as we hear numerous times in the Gospels, he ate with "tax collectors and sinners" (Mark 2:15; Matthew 11:19; Luke 15:12, 19:7). For to speak of tax collectors and sinners is to designate all those people who posed either external or internal threats to Israel's bounded identity, from the gentiles, who probably lurk behind the reference to tax collectors, to the social outcasts, such as prostitutes, within Israel itself.[89]

The Gospels make it clear that Jesus' eating habits attracted both attention and bad press, which we perhaps see most clearly in the charge that he was "a glutton and a drunkard" (Matthew 11:19). This particular choice of words to characterize Jesus' practice of table fellowship will gain something of the weight it would have carried in Jesus' day if we look at one of Jesus' parables about table fellowship: the parable of the wedding banquet or the great feast, recorded somewhat differently in both Matthew and Luke, as well as in the Gospel of Thomas.[90]

Conflating the three versions, I can outline the parable as follows: Someone decides to have a great feast. When the food is ready, the host sends the servants to summon the guests, but all the invited guests offer excuses and do not come. So the host sends the servants into the streets, instructing them to "bring back whomever you find to have dinner" (as Thomas has it) or to "bring in the poor, the cripple, the blind, and the lame," (as it reads in Luke). Crossan offers the following commentary:

> The host replaces the absent guests with anyone off the streets. But if one actually brought in *anyone off the street,* one could, in such a situation, have classes, sexes, and ranks all mixed up together. . . . What Jesus' parable advocates, therefore, is an open commensality, an eating together without using the table as a miniature map of society's vertical discriminations and lateral separations. The social challenge of such equal or egalitarian commensality is the parable's most fundamental danger and most radical threat. It is only a story, of course, but it is one that focuses its egalitarian challenge on society's miniature mirror, the table, as the place where bodies meet to eat. Since, moreover, Jesus lived out his own parable, the almost predictable counteraccusation to such open commensality would be immediate: Jesus is a glutton, a drunkard, and a friend of tax collectors and sinners. He makes, in other words, no appropriate distinctions and discriminations.[91]

Both in his actual table fellowship and in many of his parables, Jesus enacted "a festive celebration of the return of the outcasts," to borrow an apt description from Borg.[92] All clues seem to indicate that the kingdom of God is precisely this ongoing festive celebration—not only of the return of the outcasts but also of the healing of the lepers and of the casting off of colonial chains and of the casting out of demons; in short, the kingdom of God is the ongoing festive celebration of the subtle, everyday victory of the peasants over the lords, the weak over the strong. From the parable of the mustard seed to the parable of the feast, from the cleansing of lepers and the exorcism of demons to the sharing of the table with outcasts, Jesus, the wandering radical, was engaged in a campaign of everyday tactical resistance, insinuating the hidden transcript into public discourse and "continually pressing against the limit of what [was] permitted on stage, much as a body of water might press against a dam."[93] This image is Scott's, and he notes that the pressure behind the dam "varies with the degree of shared anger and indignation experienced by subordinates"; but in any case, behind "the pressure is the desire to give unbridled expression to the sentiments voiced in the hidden transcript directly to the dominant."[94]

If we compare Jesus' everyday actions in Galilee to the constant pressure of water against a dam, then we can imagine that his decision to go to Jerusalem marked the moment when the pressure of the hidden transcript had increased to the point of an imminent rupture, and the tactics of everyday resistance thus gave way to those of symbolic defiance.[95] In order to understand the significance of Jesus' acts of symbolic defiance, as well as the response of the Powers to these acts, let's begin at the beginning and consider his baptism in the wilderness by John in the Jordan.

Jesus in Jerusalem: Symbolic Acts of Defiance

Just as the parables were more than innocent stories and the touching of the leper was not simply a magic trick, "the wilderness," as Crossan reminds us, "was not just sand and the Jordan was not just water."[96] The wilderness, of course, was Israel's home for the forty years during which they made their way from Egypt to the Promised Land. It was in this wilderness, and near this river, that Moses gave his great speech about both Israel's past and its future; and it was in this wilderness, just east of the Jordan, that Moses' successor, Joshua, prepared the people for the conquest of the Land. In other words, it was from out of this wilderness and across this river that Israel first entered the Land, in a triumphal procession that, as the waters of the Jordan parted, rivaled the Exodus event itself (Joshua 3). If we keep Israel's history in mind, then John's practice of baptizing people in the Jordan takes on a quite particular significance.

As Crossan puts it, "John did not . . . *baptize* in the Jordan; he baptized in the *Jordan*. . . . When people came to him, he kept sending them back *from* the wilderness, *through* the Jordan, *into* the Promised Land, there to await the imminent coming of the redeeming and avenging God."[97] John's baptisms, then, were symbolically charged events. Now recall what Scott says of such challenges to the public transcript: "the dominant may elect to ignore a symbolic challenge, pretend they did not hear it or see it . . . [or they] may also choose to construe an ambiguous act as a direct symbolic challenge in order to make a public example of someone." Shortly after John baptized Jesus in the Jordan, he met his death at the hands of Herod Antipas. The Gospels suggest that his death was the result of his criticism of Herod's marriage (Mark 6:17ff and parallels); however, it seems more likely that Herod chose to construe John's ambiguous acts at the Jordan as a direct symbolic challenge, a challenge he met with execution. Certainly this is how Josephus reports it:

> Herod, who feared lest the great influence John had over the people might put it into his power and inclination to raise a rebellion (for they seemed ready to do anything he should advise), thought it best, by putting him to death, to prevent any mischief he might cause. . . . Accordingly he was sent a prisoner, out of Herod's suspicious temper, to Macherus . . . and was there put to death.[98]

Consider, too, Josephus' account of the following event:

> Now it came to pass, while Fadus was procurator of Judea, that a certain magician, whose name was Theudas, persuaded a great part of the people to take their effects with them, and follow him to the river Jordan; for he told them he was a prophet, and that he would, by his own command, divide the river, and afford them an easy passage over it; and many were deluded by his words. However, Fadus did not permit them to make any advantage of his wild attempt, but sent a troop of horsemen out against them; who, falling upon them unexpectedly, slew many of them and took many of them alive. They also took Theudas alive, and cut off his head, and carried it to Jerusalem.[99]

Fadus was the procurator of Judea from 44–46 C.E., and so here we see, perhaps fifteen years after the execution of John the Baptist, both another symbolic challenge to the Powers involving the Jordan River and another execution. It is in the light cast by the response of the Powers to the symbolic acts of John and Theudas that we need to examine Jesus' own "symbolic declaration of war" in the face of these same Powers. Let's look first at his entrance into Jerusalem.

The Gospels report that Jesus came into Jerusalem riding on a donkey, a scene that recalls an oracle from Zechariah 9:9:

> *Shout aloud, O daughter*
> *Jerusalem!*
> *Lo, your king comes to you;*

triumphant and victorious is he,
humble and riding on a donkey.

Now surely it is possible, as some critics suggest, that the story of Jesus on the donkey has no basis in fact but was simply the product of the evangelists as they sought, retroactively, to make sense of Jesus.[100] However, it seems just as likely, and certainly consistent with Jesus' *modus operandi,* that Jesus tapped the symbolic charge of this scene from Zechariah in the same way John and Theudas tapped the symbolic charge of the Jordan River. What we have in Jesus' triumphant and yet humble entrance into Jerusalem is a tactically calculated symbolic challenge to the Powers. Look Jerusalem! Look Rome! Here comes the true king of Israel, the one who heals the sick, casts out demons, eats with the outcasts, the one who, triumphant and victorious, subverts orders and breaches boundaries.

As the Gospels tell it, Jesus followed this symbolic challenge with another:

> Then Jesus entered the temple and drove out all who were selling and buying in the temple, and he overturned the tables of the money changers and the seats of those who sold doves. (Matthew 21:12)

Because of the evangelists' own tendency to interpret this act as "the cleansing of the temple," we often miss the more aggressive nature of this symbolic challenge to the Powers. The overturning of the tables is a symbolic destruction of the temple and not simply a housecleaning.[101] Considered against the background of Israel's history, to symbolically destroy the temple is to level a challenge at the heart of power, insofar as the temple was, from Solomon to Jesus, both the practical and symbolic center of Israel's life.[102]

Given the fate of John and Theudas, we can hardly be surprised that seven days after he came to town on a donkey, and six days after he overturned the tables in the temple, Jesus found himself hanging from a cross.[103] Both the Jewish aristocracy and Rome had accepted his symbolic challenges and met his now blatant rupture of the public transcript with the force of death. To describe what happens next, let me amend Scott's account of the significance of such symbolic defiance.

Scott notes that a "small act of symbolic defiance, seemingly trivial but giving evidence of an enlarged public space, [often] touches off a flurry of bold assertions and claims."[104] The power of such an act, he notes, "is likely to come from the fact that it condenses some of the most deeply felt sentiments of the hidden transcript."[105] In other words, the power of acts of symbolic defiance, like Jesus' attack on the temple, is rooted in an offstage social "reservoir" of indignation.[106] The relationship between symbolic challenges and this offstage reservoir of sentiment helps explain, as Scott sees it, "the rapidity with which an apparently deferential, quiescent, and loyal subordinate group is catapulted into mass defiance" by small symbolic actions.[107] As Scott puts it:

> When the first declaration of the hidden transcript succeeds, its mobilizing capacity as a symbolic act is potentially awesome. At the level of tactics and strategy, it is a powerful straw in the wind. It portends a possible turning of the tables. . . . At the level of political beliefs, anger, and dreams it is a social explosion. That first declaration speaks for countless others, it shouts what has historically had to be whispered, controlled, choked back, stifled, and suppressed. If the results seem like moments of madness, if the politics they engender is tumultuous, frenetic, delirious, and occasionally violent, that is perhaps because the powerless are so rarely on the public stage and have so much to say and do when they finally arrive.[108]

Such is the case when symbolic challenges succeed. But what if they don't? According to Scott, if

> the first act of defiance meets with a decisive defeat it is unlikely to be emulated by others. The courage of those who fail, however, is likely to be noted, admired, and even mythologized in the stories of bravery, social banditry, and noble sacrifice. They become themselves part of the hidden transcript.[109]

No doubt, those who followed Jesus at first understood the cross as a decisive defeat, hence the reports that all the disciples fled, and Luke's account of the forlorn disciples on the road to Emmaus. And no doubt, too, Jesus' courage was "noted, admired, and even mythologized"—hence the Gospels, which we should now see are themselves but the hidden transcript of the next generation. And yet we have to amend Scott's account because, in an interesting twist, the Gospels do not proclaim that Jesus' public declaration of the hidden transcript was a failure and that his death on the cross was a "noble sacrifice"—something to be admired but not emulated. On the contrary, the Gospels suggest that Jesus' declaration of the hidden transcript was a success and that his death on the cross was a decisive victory. And they then do the unlikely thing and call upon those who would follow Jesus to emulate just *this* success and *this* victory, a thought that brings us back to the subject of the last chapter, that is, to the church and its methods of resistance.

In the last chapter, I offered an account of the Powers as we find them in the New Testament. This account led to two conclusions: First, because the Powers are God's creation, they cannot be destroyed; and second, because of their insidious invisibility, they cannot be resisted with a frontal assault. These conclusions led, in turn, to the conclusion that the church is "herself resistance and attack" insofar as the church is the "sovereign presence" of Jesus within the structures of society. The definitive example of Jesus' sovereign presence is the cross: his willing subjection to the Powers, even unto death.

Recall, however, that the church is called not simply to the cross but also to the much more mysterious task of making known God's wisdom to the Powers. Long before the church contends with the Powers at the cross, it must contend with them in "heavenly places." Thus at the end of the last chapter, we arrived at the rather abstract notion that the church, simply by being the church, reconfigures the social order and therefore recodifies power relations in their invisibility. The work of this chapter so far has been an attempt to make this notion more concrete.

Using both the theoretical work of de Certeau and Scott (both of whom are extending the work of Foucault) and specific examples of the provocative acts that comprised Jesus' ministry, I have offered a concrete display of the kinds of resistance the church is called to imitate. There remains one task still unfulfilled. For although I have now placed the cross in the context of a wide field of tactical resistance, I have yet to translate Jesus' resistance into the everyday life of the church. To undertake this final task is to return to Yoder and take up his notion of "revolutionary subordination."

Revolutionary Subordination

The place to begin a discussion of Christian resistance is the declaration in Romans 13: "Let everyone be subject to the Roman authorities" (13:1)—or again, from Ephesians,

> Be subject to one another out of reverence for Christ. Wives be subject to your husbands as you are to the Lord. . . . Husbands, love your wives, just as Christ loved the church and gave himself up for her. . . . Slaves, obey your earthly masters with fear and trembling, in singleness of heart, as you obey Christ. . . . Render service with enthusiasm. . . . And, masters, do the same to them. Stop threatening them, for you know that both of you have the same Master in heaven. (Ephesians 5:21–6:9)[110]

No doubt, such instructions may seem an odd place to begin thinking about the form of resistance the church should embody, since such words were once used to sanction slavery and continue to sanction both Christian participation in state violence and the subjugation of women. How else can we possibly understand both Paul's command to be subject to that state and the instructions in Ephesians that wives should be subject to their husbands (5:22)? Yoder argues that in fact there is another way to understand the call for subjection, an understanding that is both more true to the character of the early Christian communities as they attempted to embody the example of Jesus and more fruitful for understanding the character of Christian resistance.

As a first step of reinterpreting these passages, Yoder notes that the Greek term *hypotassesthai* "is not best rendered by *subjection,* which carries a connotation of being thrown down and run over, nor by *submission,* with its connotation of passivity."[111] Yoder argues that a better translation of the Greek is in fact *subordination*: "Sub*ord*ination means the acceptance of an *order,* as it exists, but with the new meaning given to it by the fact that one's acceptance of it is willing and meaningfully motivated."[112] When the epistles call upon the early Christians to be subordinate both to the state and to one another, they call them to the voluntary acceptance of an existing order. If we imagine that this call is synonymous with the justification of Christian participation in war, for instance, or the sanction of slavery and the domination of women, then, says Yoder, we have missed not only the "revolutionary innovation" of New Testament instructions about subordination but also the meaning of the cross.[113] Or rather, we have missed the fact that the New Testament understanding of the cross is itself revolutionary—a revolution we owe largely to Paul. Wayne Meeks puts it this way:

> Paul's most profound bequest to subsequent Christian discourse was his transformation of the reported crucifixion and resurrection of Jesus Christ into a multipurpose metaphor with vast generative and transformative power. . . . In that gospel story Paul sees revolutionary import for the relationships of power that control human transactions. . . . If God's power is manifested in the weakness of the cross and God's wisdom in the foolish claim that the crucified was the Messiah, then it is no longer obvious that the high-born, wealthy, well-educated, rhetorically sophisticated should always have their way, while those who are socially "nothing," those who are "weak"—the women, the slaves, the poor, the uneducated—are simply to obey.[114]

Standard accounts of Paul often praise him for his progressive teaching that in Christ there is "no longer Jew or Greek, slave or free, male and female" (Galatians 3:28) and then chastise him (or the authors of other epistles) for subverting this insight by reinstating the structures of domination with the command to be subordinate.[115] Yoder argues, however, that in fact the call to subordination does not subvert these insights but instead, following the logic of the cross, affirms the status of the early church as a radically reordered society.

Dale Martin not only lends support to Yoder's argument but helps us see the apocalyptic character of this new order:

> As is well known, making a crucified criminal the honored, central figure of devotion ran completely counter to common assumptions. It therefore pro-

> vides Paul with an appropriate jumping off place for introducing a system of values that he will oppose to that of the dominant culture. . . . This is where we see the importance of apocalyptic for Paul's argument. In order to oppose the dominant ideology, with its value system and its way of attributing status, Paul must advance an alternative system. He finds one, to some extent, ready to hand in the dualism of Jewish apocalypticism, which had for centuries countered the imperialistic ideologies of Greece and Rome with a narrative that depicted an alternative, hidden, and vastly more powerful empire: the kingdom of God. . . . The image that Paul adds to this traditional apocalyptic portrait is that of the crucified Christ as the central icon of the Gospel. . . . Without apocalypticism and his interpretation of the cross in apocalyptic terms, Paul would have had no alternative to oppose to the overpowering ideology of the Greco-Roman ruling class. But with it, Paul can propose the existence of a world that is more real than the one the Corinthians see around them.[116]

Martin has in mind here not the household codes of Ephesians and Colossians but the rhetoric of 1 Corinthians. Nonetheless, what Martin says of Paul applies, I think, to the household codes. And indeed, it is important to see that Paul's alternative to Greco-Roman society rests not simply on the apocalyptic discourse that early Christians borrowed from their Jewish heritage but upon an application of this discourse to the crucifixion. The call to subordination is the logical unfolding of this apocalyptic interpretation of the cross. And note, although this "logic" subverts the socioeconomic hierarchies of the Greco-Roman world, it does so in a most peculiar way. For it is not simply the case that the weak will now be strong and the strong weak, that the low tree will be made high and the high tree brought low. Rather, this apocalyptic reversal requires the willing subordination of the weak to the strong.[117]

Keeping in mind the instructions to both men and women, free and slave, to be subordinate to one another and to the state, it is worth recalling de Certeau's notion that tactical resistance, because it does not have a strategic space of its own, is an art of conforming to an order as a means of evading it. If we place the apocalyptic understanding of the cross in the context of what de Certeau and Scott teach us about tactical resistance, then we should be able to see the link between the "sovereign presence of Jesus within the structures of creaturely orderliness" and "the church who herself is a structure and a power within society." Let me expand upon this point by recalling what I said earlier about Jesus' exorcisms.

Subordinate groups, who find themselves captives of both superior power and a lack of alternatives, face a dilemma: Either they simply submit to exploitation and domination, or they hate the Powers that oppress them while at the same time imagining that if only they had enough power they could escape. Hence, even as they despise their oppressors, they admire their power. Should we be surprised that this combination of submission, hate, and admiration in the face of an overwhelmingly powerful oppressor sometimes leads to "possession," or in the language of our own time, to "mental illness," a term that no doubt falls short of the phenomenon in question?

Mark actually captures this phenomenon quite well when he says of the Garasene demoniac that "no one could bind him anymore, even with a chain; for he had often been bound with fetters and chains, but the chains he wrenched apart, and the fetters he broke in pieces. . . . Night and day among the tombs and on the mountains he was howling and bruising himself with stones." If you are in the cell of an oppressive social order, it seems you have two options: You can simply accept your chains as your lot, or you can wrench them apart and break them, only to find that the cell remains. You are indeed *possessed.*

According to Yoder, revolutionary subordination offers a way out of this dilemma. For it enables a person to overcome hate and resentment and to realize, as the man among the tombs demonstrates, that the wrenching apart of chains is not itself the path to freedom, since beyond the chains are simply the bars of a still oppressive social order. Perhaps this point will be more clear if I reverse it and say that demonic possession is what occurs when subordination fails to be revolutionary.

Let me punctuate Yoder's understanding of revolutionary subordination—and attempt to link it back to the discussion of the last chapter, with recourse to the following words from Wink:

> When the Roman archons (magistrates) ordered the early Christians to worship the imperial spirit or *genius,* they refused, kneeling instead and offering prayers on the emperor's behalf to God. This seemingly innocuous act was far more exasperating and revolutionary than outright rebellion would have been. Rebellion simply acknowledges the absoluteness and ultimacy of the emperor's powers and attempts to seize it. Prayer denies that ultimacy altogether by acknowledging a higher power. Rebellion would have focused solely on the physical institution and its current incumbents and attempted to displace them by an act of superior force. But prayer challenged the very spirituality of the empire itself and called the empire's "angel," as it were, before the judgment seat of God.
>
> Such sedition could not go unpunished. With rebels the solution was simple. No one challenged the state's right to execute rebels. . . . *But what happens when a state executes those who are praying for it?* When Christians knelt in the Colosseum to pray as lions bore down on them, something sullied the audience's thirst for revenge. Even in death these Christians were not only challenging the ultimacy of the emperor and the "spirit" of empire but also demonstrating the emperor's powerlessness to impose his will even by death. The final sanction had been publicly robbed of its power. Even as the lions lapped the blood of the saints, Caesar was stripped of his arms and led captive in Christ's triumphal procession.[118]

In the wake both of this dramatic example of Christian martyrdom and a discussion of Yoder's concept of revolutionary subordination, we can now answer the question Yoder posed earlier: "If our lostness consists in our subjection to the rebellious powers of a fallen world, what then is the meaning of the work of Christ?" Christ's work means that resistance does not involve standing over and against the Powers but *with* them. As Yoder puts it, "We subject ourselves to government because it was in so doing that Jesus revealed and achieved God's victory."[119] And we subject ourselves to one another because "it is in every situation a free, extremely aggressive way of acting . . . founded in an ethical theme that runs clear through the New Testament, in the person and the way of the Lord, who is at the same time the norm and the realization of self-abasement."[120] The meaning of the work of Christ is that we are not in fact lost amidst the Powers if we transform our previously unconditional subjection into a subjection conditioned by our voluntary acceptance of their order. For once we replace domination with "willing servanthood," we have altered the configuration of power at the very point of its application. And we have in fact accomplished something more far-reaching than if we had stormed the palace or the Pentagon. For we have engaged the Powers where they are the most formidable.

When the martyr prays for the emperor in the Colosseum as the lions rush on, he or she, although physically committed, can accomplish nothing against power in its material guise: The emperor is not unseated; the Colosseum does not come crashing down; the lions don't drop dead; the spectators don't leap into the ring out of sympathy, save the prisoner, and launch a revolt against Rome. In the material world of things, nothing occurs that is not supposed to occur. And yet, at another level, in heavenly places, the spirit of an entire empire is called to account and meets a decisive challenge, one that in its material form was no more than the posture of a body and a few words of prayer: the sword of the spirit.

Of course, as Wink notes, the lesson here is not that our response to power should be simply to kneel and pray; "in most circumstances prayer is not enough, but in that situation it was the most radical response imaginable," since it met power where it is the most powerful: in its invisibility.[121] The institution of the Colosseum depended for its functioning upon the spectators who enjoyed witnessing the gore, just as Americans enjoy watching football. And their enjoyment depended, like that of the football fan, upon a proper performance by the "players." When the victim in the Colosseum met the lions with prayer, he or she had performed improperly and ruined the game, even though the game went on. The game depended upon a particular kind of death; and when the saint refused to die in the right way, the very logic of the Colosseum had been thrown into radical question. "What good," asks Wink, "is a sword made of words, in the face of such monolithic evil—unless evil is not merely so much a physical phenomenon as a spiritual construct, itself born of words, and capable of destruction by the Word of God?"[122]

With the martyr in the Colosseum we have returned to Foucault's physically committed poet—with the difference that the poem is now a prayer and death is faced not with the difficult hope of tragedy but with the Christian hope of apocalypse. To make one last attempt to display this apocalyptic hope and the politics it enables, I return to the text that occupied us at the end of Chapter Six: Ian MacMillan's *Orbit of Darkness.*

Resisting Auschwitz

At the end of Chapter Six, I offered a literary display of Foucault's tragic politics by turning to the stories MacMillan has crafted about the young artist in Crakow and the young girl in the Polish meadow. These stories, together with the story I had recounted in Chapter Four about the Mann Gulch fire, allowed me to speak of an "aesthetics of dignity" and a "politics of dying." To return now to MacMillan's text and to a story that offers a display of an apocalyptic politics is to speak again of the relationship between death and dignity, but this time we find ourselves neither in Crakow nor in a Polish meadow but in Auschwitz. Because to return to MacMillan's text is to arrive in Auschwitz, it is fitting, I think, to give the first word to Elie Wiesel:

> I was there. And I still do not understand. . . . I still do not understand why I did not throw myself on the Kapo who was beating my father before my very eyes. In Galicia, Jews dug their own graves and lined up, without any trace of panic, at the edge of the trench to await the machine-gun barrage. I do not understand their calm. And that woman, that mother, in the bunker somewhere in Poland, I do not understand her either; her companions smothered her child for fear its cries might betray their presence; that woman, that mother, having lived this scene of biblical intensity, did not go mad. I do not understand her: why, and by what right, and in the name of what, did she not go mad?
>
> I do not know why, but I forbid us to ask her the question. The world kept silent while the Jews were being massacred, while they were being reduced to the state of objects good for the fire; let the world at least have the decency to keep silent now as well. Its questions come a bit late; they should have been addressed to the executioner. Do they trouble us? Do they keep us from sleeping in peace? So much the better. We want to know, to understand, so we can turn the page: is that not true? So we can say to ourselves: the matter is closed and everything is back in order. Do not wait for the dead to come to our rescue. Their silence will survive them.[123]

As I approach the end of my reflections on nihilism, tragedy, and apocalypse and find that I have arrived in Auschwitz, I realize that I have been waiting for the dead to come to my rescue. I realize that I have been asking them questions. Like Norman Maclean, I want to know "what it was like on the way." Like Foucault, I want to know what gave them the courage "to stand up and die." I want to know these things because, like Vladimir and Estragon, I have a vague but persistent sense that if I can only wait to see what the dead have to say, then perhaps all will come clear. And yet all this waiting has led me to Auschwitz.

But perhaps this is as it should be. We can forget neither that Sontag staged *Godot* as a response to genocide nor that Beckett first put Vladimir and Estragon on the stage in the wake of the Holocaust. In a sense, Auschwitz has been a presence in this text from the beginning, and so perhaps it is fitting that we have now arrived there. And yet does not Auschwitz threaten to destroy everything that I have attempted to accomplish: *not* tragedy, *not* apocalypse, only *meaninglessness.* To invoke again the words of Elie Wiesel:

> In truth, Auschwitz signifies not only the failure of two thousand years of Christian civilization, but also the defeat of the intellect that wants to find a Meaning—with a capital M—in history. What Auschwitz embodied has none. The executioner killed for nothing, the victim died for nothing. No God ordered the one to prepare the stake, nor the other to mount it. During the Middle Ages, the Jews, when they chose death, were convinced that by their sacrifice they were glorifying and sanctifying God's name. At Auschwitz the sacrifices were without point, without faith, without divine inspiration. If the suffering of one human being has any meaning, that of six million has none. Numbers have their importance; they prove, according to Piotr Rawicz, that God has gone mad.[124]

Perhaps I should end my reflections here. Perhaps I should stop waiting for the dead to come to my rescue, particularly these dead, these six million Jewish dead who died because of Christian failure. Perhaps I should not attempt what has been forbidden. Perhaps I should have the decency to keep silent. And yet I want desperately to tell one more story, the story of the suffering of one human being.

MacMillan's central story begins on the parade grounds in Auschwitz in 1941, on a hot summer afternoon in late July, during a roll call.[125] The prisoners have been gathered so that the deputy commandant can select ten men to die as recompense for the escape of one of their fellow prisoners. The ten men are to be led away to a cell to starve to death. As the tenth man chosen begins to protest, another man, a Catholic priest, steps out of line and requests to speak to the deputy commandant. MacMillan does not record the conversation, but the reaction of the commandant signals that the priest had said something extraordinary. In fact he had: He had volunteered to die in the place of the other man. Recovering from his shock, the commandant agrees. It was a decision he would come to regret.

Once in the starvation cell, the priest and the nine other men begin to sing and pray, and the sounds of their songs emanate through part of the camp. Some prisoners sneak to the windows of the cell to listen to these amazing sounds. One of the guards, Vierck is his name, begins to grow weary and edgy; the singing and praying are so incessant that it seems the building itself is starting to murmur.

Meanwhile, word spreads among the prisoners. Soon they are telling one another stories about other unusual things the priest had done: He had often given his rations to others; and some had seen him remain composed even when receiving a severe and nearly death-causing beating.

Six days go by and the priest and most of the others are still alive, though some have died. The other prisoners in camp continue to talk about the priest. Some of the guards, the more superstitious, when they have to remove one of the ten who has died, approach the cell in fear. Witness this scene:

> One guard dragged a corpse by one arm. The other guard stopped and yelled, "Look at the floor, not at us!" The Father looked down, then up again. Oh . . . the eyes seared their flesh. "Down, I said, don't look at us!" Then they left. . . . [Prisoner] 10,151 stared at the priest, whispering: They are afraid of you. . . . 10,151 laughs at the simplicity of it—the priest overcame their excess of power with an excess of selfless love, and now it is as if they are gathered over a table staring at this formula written on a piece of paper. They whisper, question each other. The formula is too elemental to contradict. One of them, Fritsch it would be, walks to the window, thinking. Then he says, "Put that paper away—let me think." (103–104)

Two days later, the eighth day after the selection, a guard named Guerber, having found recently that the priest is the same age as he, begins to wonder about the priest's motivation for volunteering:

> What after all would possess a man to go to the extremes he did? . . . Clearly the act had no other motivation than a spiritual one. . . . [And yet] clearly his doing it in the manner he did was in a way a revolutionary act, because of the way he called attention to himself. . . . And now Guerber, used to casually watching men shot or beaten to death, has found himself worrying about the priest, as if he were keeping a secret vigil on someone ill, holding a secret space in his mind that cultivated expectations of recovery. (127–129)

On the ninth day, talk among the prisoners escalates: "I saw him at the selection," Grudzinski says. "When he requested the switch, Fritsch backed up . . . Fritsch looked like"—he pauses—"I don't know . . . you should have seen Fritsch's face . . . Fritsch lost his composure. Do you know what that means?" (152).

On the tenth day, the guard Vierck, now convinced that the walls really are singing, requests a transfer, and we see exactly what Fritsch's loss of composure meant, as the commandant denies the request:

> "No. I will not have soldiers of the Reich turning into whining babies over something as foolish as this. You stay at your post. You will leave him to starve as ordered. . . . A priest . . . and look what he has done to you." Then he understands why this has become a problem in the first place. "He's made self-sacrifice a virtue, and by doing that he's fogging our certainty, don't you see? He's using himself as an example to make men out of vermin. Don't you see it in the prisoners' eyes? . . . Now they all walk around acting as if there's some sort of virtue in martyrdom, and all because of this one little man." (172–173)

At this point in the story, we have already seen both Vierck and Guerber exhibit this fogged certainty on the part of the SS. On day thirteen, MacMillan returns us to the barracks and records the following conversation between prisoners Szweda and Kalucki, after Szweda complains first that Kalucki is wasting his food by sharing it with a sick prisoner, and then that Kalucki is only doing this because that deranged mystic of a priest says he should. Kalucki responds:

> "Yes, my deranged mystic speaks to me in the night, and I know that it is probably my imagination. He might already be dead. So when I drag another slippery corpse toward the oven, or when I wake up in the morning and find another of us dead and half eaten by rats, I do what my deranged mystic tells me to do—pray over the dead and work to keep the living alive. There is no other choice."
>
> "A pretty sentiment," Szweda says. . . . "But when it comes to saving myself in the dark, I couldn't care who or what it costs. It takes a sense of self-preservation to keep from becoming smoke."
>
> "No," Kalucki says. "That deranged mystic offered himself to save another and in so doing made it possible for us to save ourselves. The move was calculated and brilliant. Because of it we are no longer the same and the Germans are no longer the same." (237–238)

And indeed they were not. On day fourteen, the guard Vierck committed suicide by throwing himself on the electric fence. The suicide presented the commandant with something of a public-relations problem. The loss of composure was now more evident than ever. Hence the commandant gave the following orders: "I want you to inform the German Kapos that anyone mentioning the priest's name shall be beaten to death. . . . In addition, I want them to watch for people helping each other or for people giving food away. . . . When these acts are observed both parties shall be beaten to death" (261).

MacMillan then describes the commandant's thoughts:

> He is furious that the little weakling Vierck would allow himself to be affected this way. Underneath the fury, he is bothered by something else: the priest had compromised the stability of a good system. . . . [H]e understands the worst of it now—what the priest has done is a profound secret that is hidden only because it is so obvious, and it is Nehring's job to see that the secret is kept. (262)

On the fifteenth day, they finally kill the priest with a shot of carbolic acid, and the commandant remarks to Guerber that at least now it is over:

> Guerber nods, and then thinks, no, it is not over. He knew the previous night when he saw the look on Nehring's face—it was a combination of anger, shock, disbelief. The whole thing went too far.
>
> And now, as Guerber walks back toward the penal block entrance, he is aware that his feet do not feel right on the ground under him, that just a little way beyond the limits of his understanding there is something obviously wrong. (280)

MacMillan's book ends on the following day, when Guerber stops a Kapo from beating a young boy and finds himself unusually aware of "the heavy smoke coming from the crematorium chimney."

Perhaps the best way to begin to comment on MacMillan's story is to recall the way I had to amend Scott in order to account for the "success" of Jesus' attacks on the public transcript. By Scott's account, Jesus' voicing of the hidden transcript was a decisive failure, since Jesus was executed. By Scott's logic, Jesus' provocative acts would have been admired, and even mythologized, but not emulated, since they led to death and defeat. For all his insights into the mechanisms of power and resistance, Scott reveals at this point that he has retained at least a vestige of standard accounts of politics. For he fails to arrive at either the tragic or apocalyptic insight that death is not equivalent with defeat.

What both Wink's account of martyrs in the Colosseum and, even more, MacMillan's account of the priest in Auschwitz display is that there are times when success requires death because there are times when death itself becomes the last bit of contested terrain. Hence, in the end, apocalyptic politics is, like its tragic counterpart, a politics of dying.

Think for a moment about the priest in Auschwitz. What does one do to resist Auschwitz, given that it was nothing more than a factory designed to produce corpses. The answer, as the SS realized too late, is simple. Volunteer to die. Willingly submit yourself to the system. Subvert the very logic of the camp. Fog the certainty of the Powers—trick them, as it were.

Of course, as was true with Jesus, the trick involves more than voluntary death, as the prisoners understood after the priest was led away to the starvation cell. Hence they began to recall the other, more subtle things the priest had done long before he stepped out of line and asked to die. For instance, he had remained mysteriously composed when beaten; he had prayed and sang; and most importantly, he had shared his food. These seem like such small things. And they are. But in Auschwitz they were revolutionary; and as always, the proof is the reaction of the Powers: "watch for people helping each other or for people giving food away. . . . When these acts are observed, both parties shall be beaten to death." Like Jesus, the priest went to Galilee before he went to Jerusalem. And as we see clearly in the commandant's orders, success in Galilee leads inevitably to Jerusalem and the cross. Of course, the cross is the ultimate trick. For it is at the cross that the Powers lose the one thing left to them—the power to kill in such a way that death is robbed of its meaning.

Immeasurable Victory

The prospect that the politics of resistance is, in the end, reduced to the art of meaningful death assaults all our modern political sensibilities. A fact that became fully apparent to me a few years ago when I used MacMillan's book in an introductory theology course and discovered that most of the students were simply repulsed by MacMillan's subtle suggestion, in story after story, that in the end all is reduced to the possibility of making death meaningful. The students were not able to articulate their objections to *Orbit of Darkness* until, by chance, *Schindler's List* arrived in local theaters. They all flocked to see it and then returned to inform me that if I wanted to teach them about the Holocaust, I should have assigned *Schindler's List* instead of MacMillan's text. When I asked them why, they replied that it was simply a much better story. I came to find that what they meant by "better" was that it was a story of success rather than defeat.

In defense of *Orbit of Darkness,* I tried to convince my students that the power of MacMillan's narrative rests precisely in the juxtaposition of the horrors of radical evil and the mystical power of meaningful deaths, the latter most clearly depicted in the story of the priest but also in the stories about the artist in Crakow and the young girl in the Polish meadow, which I recounted in Chapter Six. Many of my students were not persuaded and tried to convince me that *Schindler's List* is simply a better story about both good and evil—better, finally, because it is more hopeful. I thought for some time about what my students were seeing in *Schindler's List* and concluded that they were seeing what they—indeed, what *we*—have been trained to see. And what *do* we see in *Schindler's List*? In *Schindler's List* we see the horror, certainly, but in the movie at least, not too much of it, and then we see in the end what we have been looking for all along: a happy ending, some good news, a final settling of the plot that does not leave our heart in our throat or our stomach on edge.

In the end we see Schindler (a man portrayed as daringly confident throughout the film) collapse and cry because he realizes he could have saved more. And then we see those he did save gather around him and embrace him and convince him that he did all he could. After Schindler drives away, we see a lone Russian soldier on horseback liberate the camp. And when the prisoners tell him they need food, he points to the horizon and says, "Isn't there a town over there?" And so Schindler's Jews begin to spread out of the camp and fan out across a meadow and march toward the town; and then the film, which has been black-and-white almost from the beginning, returns to color, and the people we see, locked arm and arm and marching toward us with a happy-sounding Jewish song playing in the background, are the real Schindler Jews and their descendants. Finally, we watch as those whom Schindler saved march by his tomb in Israel. And as we watch, subtitles give us the math of it all: 6,000 descendants of Schindler Jews; only 4,000 Jews living in Poland today; more than 6,000,000 Jews perished—an overwhelming number killed, a minimal number rescued. But the delivery of the numbers in this order—in combination with the music, the return to color, and the march of the survivors—places an emphasis upon the saved.

To craft this ending, Spielberg had to depart significantly from Thomas Keneally's book. The moment Spielberg has Schindler collapse in tears, he departs from the book; and in making this departure he, in the closing minutes of the movie, fails miserably, a failure that Keneally himself identifies for us in the opening pages of his text.[126]

In the prologue to *Schindler's List,* Keneally says of his book that it "is the story of the pragmatic triumph of good over evil, a triumph in eminently measurable, statistical, unsubtle terms" (14). But the challenge to the novelist (and I assume to the filmmaker) is, he says, to tell such a story without wandering into sentimentalism. To tell the good news without sap is a difficult thing. Keneally puts it this way:

> When you work from the other end of the beast—when you chronicle the predictable and measurable success evil generally achieves—it is easy to be wise, wry, piercing, to avoid bathos. It is easy to show the inevitability by which evil acquires all of what you could call the *real estate* of the story, even though good might finish up with a few imponderables like dignity and self-knowledge. . . . But it is a risky enterprise to have to write of virtue. (14)

In spite of the difficulty, Keneally clearly succeeds in avoiding bathos, but Spielberg does not. Spielberg wandered into bathos. Had he stuck to the book in the end, he could have avoided this story-destroying sentimentalism.

In the movie, a few hours before the end of the war, Schindler gives a speech to the camp—guards as well as prisoners. Keneally mentions that two people present, perhaps sensing the history of it all, took down the speech in dictation, so we have a good idea of what Schindler said—and he did not say what Spielberg has him say.

In the film, Schindler praises the prisoners for their fortitude and tells the SS to go home in peace—and as men, rather than slaughter the prisoners and go home as murderers. When the SS leave, Schindler asks the prisoners to observe three minutes of silence in honor of the dead.

In the book—and according to Keneally, in fact—Schindler's speech praised both the prisoners *and* the SS for their fortitude, as if they had all been captive there; and he then asked the *prisoners* not to take justice into their own hands. He asked them to let the SS go in peace; he told them not to plunder the nearby town. And when he was done, he asked them all, SS included, to honor the dead in silence. The SS, no less than the prisoners, complied with his command.

After Oskar left the camp and the lone Russian soldier had liberated the prisoners, they did not simply march, en masse, out of the camp. Most of them stayed there for days, not knowing where to go or what to do. In this time of uncertainty, they hung one of the German guards from the rafters; retreating tanks from a German Panzer division lobbed two shells into the middle of the camp, wounding a few of the prisoners; and a contingent of SS officers in retreat drove up to the camp and pleaded for gasoline, which the prisoners, now armed, finally gave generously. When the prisoners did go to town, they did so with guns, and when one baker insisted he had no bread, they threatened to kill him unless he told the truth and gave them food. Then, upon witnessing the fear in the eyes of the baker's family and realizing that the whole scene looked too much like the SS in Crakow's ghetto, the man with the gun was crushed by shame, as many of the prisoners had been when the German Kapo was hung in the camp a few days earlier.

Of course by crafting his own ending, Spielberg was able to avoid the continued fear and uncertainty and horror that persisted after the war was over and that, if we have the eyes and the stomachs for it, persists in our time. Spielberg's ending leaves us feeling uplifted, even while we try to envision six million deaths, an impossible image, but one obscured in any case by the faces of the survivors. For those who have seen the movie, I ask you to imagine how different it would have been if Spielberg had ended the film with images of the SS, heads bowed in tribute to the dead, with images of bursting tank shells and prisoners giving gasoline to desperate SS officers, even while they hang a Kapo from the rafters. And then imagine that all these scenes are cast against the background not of the few who survived but of the millions who did not, as well as against the background of the million or more now dead in Bosnia and Rwanda.[127]

For my students, *Schindler's List* is a story, as Keneally himself intended it to be, about the eminently measurable, statistical, unsubtle victory of good over evil, whereas *Orbit of Darkness* leaves them with those imponderables like meaningful death, those two or three slight distinctions that Camus speaks of. My students don't want to hear of meaningful death; they don't want to hear, from Hegel, of the truth that Spirit finds in utter dismemberment; they don't want to hear about dignity; and they certainly don't want to be left amidst the corpses in Auschwitz or Bosnia. To put it in theological terms, they don't, finally, want to hear about the cross. They want simply to bask in the glory of the resurrection. They want results. They want to see the dead raised. They want heroes who get up and walk away in the end. *Orbit of Darkness* simply does not give them that kind of story.

Orbit of Darkness does, in its final major story, take us to the end of the war and to liberation, but the final pages of the book return us to Auschwitz in 1941. The priest is dead; and although the Germans and the prisoners will never be the same, Auschwitz will last for almost four more years, and a million people, mostly Jews, will die inside its wire. There is a profound difference, then, between *Orbit of Darkness* and Keneally's *Schindler's List* and an insurmountable difference between MacMillan's book and Spielberg's film. Good's victory, no less than evil's onslaught, cannot be measured in statistics. Any such measurement, unless of course it waxes sentimental, will always weigh in evil's favor: an overwhelming number killed and a minimal number rescued. Indeed, it is a difficult thing to write of virtue.

What my students liked about *Schindler's List* is that it allowed them to measure success. They liked this because, like all of us, they have been trained to think in terms of a politics of effectiveness—in terms of measurable, statistical, and visible victories. MacMillan's stories, and particularly the story of the priest, ask us to think differently both about success and politics. The story of the priest invites us to imagine that victory is in fact immeasurable, nonstatistical, and ever so subtle. This invitation is announced most clearly on day thirteen of the priest's ordeal, as MacMillan describes the priest's thoughts about what it's like to die of starvation in Auschwitz:

> *Behold, O Lord, this dreaming skeleton in its feast of the spirit.* He lines his eye along the foreshortened view of the ghost of his body, dry and hard like cooling lard, and thinks: pray for those who torture us, pray tenfold for the masters of this empire. It is as if the hard floor and wall of the cell have softened to accommodate the angularity of his emaciated body. He feels a throbbing numbness, one of few sensations left to a moribund body that is the sleeve of a mind which has doggedly held its hands cupped under the water of peace. . . .
>
> It comes again: the pain begins in the solar plexus and radiates outward in a slow burst, searing his organs in the path of its expanding sphere. At first

> there was sweat, but no more. The pores of the skin open and seem to groan, one by one, until all of his skin prickles in a long shudder of desire. Most of earth is covered with water, O Lord, behold thy obedient, empty shell. Come and see. They are all here in this one cell: conquest, starvation, pestilence, death. Come and see then inside this concrete box. (218)

"We are afflicted," proclaims Paul, "in every way, but we are not crushed; perplexed, but not driven to despair; persecuted, but not forsaken; struck down, but not destroyed; always carrying in the body the death of Jesus, so that the life of Jesus may also be made visible in our bodies" (2 Corinthians 4:8–10). "Suddenly," says Foucault, "what had made power strong becomes used to attack it. Power, after investing itself in the body, finds itself exposed to a counter-attack in that same body":

> The sergeant is drawn from the row, but just as he is about to be pushed toward the small group of doomed men, another man, only four paces from Szweda, emerges from the row. The move is so out of place that the guards' rifles and machine pistols snap up. Speaking German, the man says, "I request permission to speak to the deputy commandant."
>
> Szweda smirks—it is that little priest, the one the more devout prisoners are always talking about, because he holds services and sometimes gives away his rations. . . . Now the priest moves toward Fritsch, followed by a guard who is ready to shoot. Fritsch is annoyed at the interruption. The priest now faces him and begins to speak, gesturing once behind him at the sergeant. Then Fritsch steps back, momentarily both suspicious and surprised. The expression is so uncharacteristic that Szweda wonders what the priest could have said that would crack the exterior of superiority and absolute power. Why isn't the man shot?
>
> "You are insane," Szweda hears Fritsch say. The priest stares back without flinching. Fritsch then says something else, still with that peculiarly disarmed expression. Then he kicks the sergeant and snaps, "Back to ranks, you!"
>
> The priest turns and stares across the faces of the men and seems for a moment to catch Szweda with his eyes—his face is absolutely composed, as if he is standing in a crowded train station thinking of something harmless but mentally perplexing. His eyes move across the men with a steady, contemplative stare. Then he turns to join the group of men selected for execution. (4–5)

Epilogue: Returning to Sarajevo

Toward the end of the first chapter, I left Vladimir and Estragon on the stage in Sarajevo, awaiting a decision on the character of the universe. When we last see Vladimir and Estragon in Beckett's play they are contemplating suicide, hoping that tomorrow they can remember to bring some rope. Most immediately, they are contemplating suicide because Godot has once again failed to arrive. Haunting their musings about remembering rope, however, seems to be something less immediate and more frightening, and that is the conclusion that Pozzo was right when he declared in his anguish that "one day he went dumb, one day I went blind, one day we'll go deaf, one day we were born, one day we will die, the same day, the same second. . . . They give birth astride a grave, the light gleams an instant, then it's night once more." It is this specter of meaninglessness that brings Vladimir and Estragon to thoughts of suicide. Indeed, as Camus understood, in a meaningless world, the question of suicide remains the one truly philosophical question.

Of course another word for the specter of meaninglessness that delivers Vladimir and Estragon into thoughts of suicide is "nihilism." Whence nihilism, the uncanniest of guests?[1] That is the question that presses to the front of all questions once we witness the plight of Vladimir and Estragon. How did they arrive on this stage, in this fix, facing these problems? Before I could even begin to offer them a decision on the character of the universe, I had to confront nihilism. It turned out that there is general agreement that "nihilism" is a descriptive term for a world where value, meaning, and desirability have been radically repudiated. No agreement, however, was forthcoming about the origins of nihilism. Hence for Nietzsche it originates the moment humans step from the abyss; for Gillespie, it derives from nominalist conceptions of God in the fourteenth century; and for Milbank, nihilism begins with the rejection of Jesus as the Lord of history, a rejection that begins at the moment of Jesus' arrival on the stage of the world in the first century. To explain to

Vladimir and Estragon how they got to be where they are thus proved to be a difficult matter.

Nonetheless, my search for the origins of nihilism had unexpected consequences. For the existence of conflicting narratives about nihilism led to the conclusion that the descriptive character of the term is tied to prescriptive assumptions. Or to put it a bit differently, I discovered that to attempt to explain to Vladimir and Estragon how they arrived in this meaningless world is already to suggest that the world might not be meaningless. But if the world is not meaningless, then whence its meaning? If not nihilism, then what—given that any talk of meaning cannot escape the brute fact of the torment and suffering that Pozzo voices so powerfully?

The answer unfolded as a choice between tragedy and apocalypse, an answer rooted in Nietzsche's description of the contest between Dionysus and the Crucified. Nietzsche declared this contest to be one that would determine the meaning of suffering, since both Dionysus and the Crucified met their end at the hands of a murderous world. It is not a question, he said, "in regard to their martyrdom—it is a difference in the meaning of it." Contrary to Nietzsche's conclusions, however, I discovered, with the help of John Milbank, that this contest has yet to be decided and that any declarations about the character of the universe are far from simple. Thus Milbank sought to offer an apocalyptic account of the world, over and against nihilism. But in Milbank's narrative both apocalypse and nihilism finally faded into tragedy. All declarations about the meaning of suffering seem to exist, then, in a moment of inherent undecidability. Still, even given the tenuous nature of such declarations, any suggestion of the possibility that suffering might mean something is the beginning of an answer to the plight of Vladimir and Estragon: Martyrdom is *not* suicide.

By following the path Nietzsche places beneath the sign of Dionysus, I discovered that if suffering has meaning, it might be because the world is an aesthetic phenomenon and that we need not, therefore, find ourselves mumbling about remembering the rope. Instead, we might come to the conclusion that life, particularly when it comes up against the explosive forces of the universe, takes on the shape of art. To say that life takes on the shape of art, that suffering finds meaning in a world justified as an aesthetic phenomenon, is to say with Nietzsche that as human beings "we have our highest dignity in our significance as works of art." In his story about young men and fire, Norman Maclean offered us a picture of such dignity. Dignity, so defined, is, in Maclean's memorable words, "courage struggling for oxygen"; it is the "firm intention to continue doing forever and ever what we last hoped to do on earth"—an intention that may even involve stopping to take pictures of the forces of the universe as they sweep up the hillside to consume us.

This display of the world as art and of dignity as an aesthetic phenomenon—in short, this display of the tragic character of the universe—is compelling when the suffering in question is that of thirteen young men on a hillside in Montana. But one wonders about such metaphysical descriptions of the world when the suffering in question is not that of thirteen men who died in a fire but that of the millions of men, women, and children who died in the Holocaust. It is not an accident that after leaving behind Nietzsche's metaphysics of tragedy, I moved on to an account of the politics of tragedy to see if I could thicken this description of the world—to see if I could give it more purchase on events of more significance than the fire in Mann Gulch. And it is not an accident that the display of a tragic politics brought us not to a grassy hillside in Montana in 1949 but to the streets of Crakow in 1940 and to a nameless meadow in Poland in 1941.

In an extended discussion of the work of Michel Foucault, I discovered that a metaphysics of tragedy did hold out the possibility of becoming a politics. And I discovered that such a politics did seem to promise a new purchase on events—at least as long as we were willing to admit that in the face of "the enormities of our time," politics is defined as the art of dying. Politics is an art of dying because in our times—and perhaps in all times—protest can be, as Wendell Berry showed us, little more than "a lamentation for the dead . . . and for those who could not save them." But to say that politics is little more than lamentation is to understate the significance of tragic politics; it is to misrepresent the power of seemingly insignificant acts, such as Sontag's staging of *Godot*. Near the end of Chapter Six, I returned briefly to the stage in Sarajevo to make precisely this point. What I did not do there, however, that I must do now is offer Vladimir and Estragon one possible declaration about the character of the universe: It's a tragic place, but it's not meaningless, which is not to say that Godot will finally arrive. In fact, Godot will not arrive; so you can stop waiting. But you can also forget about the rope because even without Godot you can approach your suffering with dignity. All may not be well with the world, but the world is not lost, at least not as long as chance is the god of history.

Of course, Vladimir and Estragon may find no comfort in this declaration about tragedy. They may, like so many critics of Foucault, find it too dark a picture; they may find the hope here too difficult; they may find no inspiration of possibility. So it goes, but the offer is there in any case. And it is, of course, not the only offer. For if not tragedy, then apocalypse—or so the narrative went.

And what's the difference between tragedy and apocalypse? For Vladimir and Estragon the difference is that Godot will finally arrive. For Nietzsche, the difference lies between Dionysus and the Crucified. John Howard Yoder sums up this difference in a word: Jesus, the slain lamb, the one who took up the cross and not the crown. Of course what this means for Vladimir and Estragon is not only that Godot will arrive one day, perhaps one day soon, but that he has already come and that they can, therefore, wait with confidence and patience; it means that even in Sarajevo they can protest their suffering with dignity. Indeed, such dignified protest, as the priest showed us, is possible even in Auschwitz.

And so it is that Vladimir and Estragon have their answer, or rather, their answers. And perhaps both answers are right. Perhaps that's why we arrive at a moment of undecidability. Perhaps we should say to Vladimir and Estragon that their lives, like ours, are both tragic and apocalyptic. For maybe the lesson of Milbank's struggle with these issues is that even when our lives as a whole are cast within an apocalyptic frame, moments—even extended moments—in our lives may be tragic, since some of the paths we walk are simply paths of dissonance that have yet to be resolved back into harmony. Maybe. Perhaps. Nothing is certain.

Nothing is certain; and yet we must act. Hence it has been my work in these pages to map the terrain of that uncertainty, a vast terrain, to be sure, but one full of possibilities—possibilities that stand out in the glow of that new light that comes to be just at the point where Foucault and Jesus meet.[2] Surrounding this light, however, and sometimes engulfing it, is darkness. For Vladimir and Estragon live on in Beckett's play as if they had yet to hear of either tragedy or apocalypse. And the priest is one of the first and not one of the last of the million or more to die inside Auschwitz. And even as I write these words, almost three years after Sontag went to Sarajevo to stage *Godot,* and two years after I began these reflections, the suffering in Bosnia continues, even though recent months have brought a cease-fire and the lifting of the siege on Sarajevo. There is hope in this turn of events, no doubt. But even if this cessation of war continues, what of a city destroyed? What of a city, now in ruins, that was once, in the words of Dzevad Karahasan, "a metaphor for the world . . . the planet's little heart . . . a new Jerusalem."[3]

In his book on the siege of Sarajevo, Karahasan relates the reason that a Jewish friend of his had given for not moving to Jerusalem:

> For two thousand years now, on the eve of our greatest holiday, my ancestors have repeated this sentence: "Next year in Jerusalem." That sentence preserved them; that sentence is the vertical axis of their experience of the world and their place in it; that sentence is an unavoidable part of our identity. Spoken in the city of Jerusalem itself, it simply makes no sense. And it is stupid to renounce a two-thousand-year-long dream, to renounce one's own identity, for the sake of a certain number of buildings that make up the real city of Jerusalem.[4]

Karahasan reports that his friend's words caused him to reflect upon the plight of Sarajevo. He began to wonder, he says, if Sarajevo "had already moved toward the imaginary quarters where . . . Jerusalem [has] dwelled for two thousand years":

> With lowered eyelashes I saw Sarajevo, so much ruined and so much loved—loved as never before—rising up from the earth, taking off and flying away, somewhere beyond, where everything is gentle and tranquil. It flew toward the deepest recesses of reality, where it can be loved and dreamed about, and from where it can shine back upon us, rich with meaning, like a beckoning destination.[5]

Karahasan's words here lead us inexorably, it seems, to the end of John's vision in Revelation:

> Then I saw a new heaven and a new earth. . . . And I saw the holy city, the new Jerusalem. . . . And the city has no need of sun or moon to shine on it, for the glory of God is its light, and its lamp is the Lamb. The nations will walk by its light, and the kings of the earth will bring their glory into it. Its gates will never be shut by day—and there will be no night there. People will bring into it the glory and the honor of the nations. (Revelation 21:1–26)

In words that express the stark contrast between the open gates of this city and the city of Sarajevo—"semi-destroyed and surrounded by heavy artillery, so that not even a bird could enter"—Karahasan ends his book with a question that seems a fitting place for me to end as well: "Shall we . . . on the eve of every holiday, when the day that we wish to be beautiful is about to begin, repeat as a dream, as an oath, and as a prayer: 'Next year in Sarajevo'?"[6]

Notes

Preface

1. Obviously, this is a suggestive, and not exhaustive, list of the atrocities of the twentieth century.

2. Dzevad Karahasan, *Sarajevo, Exodus of a City,* trans. Slobodan Drakulic (New York: Kodansha International, 1994).

3. "Nihilism," as Nietzsche understands it, is a term that expresses the prospect that suffering might be meaningless. "Tragedy," for Nietzsche, bespeaks the possibility that suffering might be meaningful, if only we can affirm the untamed character of the forces that both create us and destroy us.

4. The reader will come to understand in due course what I mean by "apocalypse." Let me simply offer the reminder at this point that the term has more to do with the "revelation" or "unveiling" of God's intentions for the course of history than it does with the cataclysmic *end* of history.

5. Friedrich Nietzsche, "The Twilight of the Idols" in *The Portable Nietzsche,* ed. and trans. Walter Kaufmann (New York: Penguin Books, 1982), 483.

6. Michel Foucault, *The Order of Things: An Archaeology of the Human Sciences,* trans. unnamed (New York: Vintage Books, 1973), 298.

7. Michel Foucault, *Power/Knowledge: Selected Interviews and Other Writings, 1972–1977,* ed. Colin Gordon, trans. Colin Gordon, Leo Marshall, John Mepham, Kate Soper (New York: Pantheon Books, 1980), 136.

8. Michel Foucault, *Remarks on Marx: Conversations with Duccio Trombadori,* trans. R. James Goldstein and James Cascaito (New York: Semiotext(e), 1991), 27; see also, 42.

9. Ibid., 40.

10. Ibid., 36.

11. Ibid.

12. Ibid.

13. Michel Foucault, *The Birth of the Clinic: An Archaeology of Medical Perception,* trans. A. M. Sheridan Smith (New York: Vintage Books, 1975), xvi.

14. Foucault, *Power/Knowledge,* 53–54, and Michel Foucault, *Politics, Philosophy, Culture: Interviews and Other Writings, 1977–1984,* ed. Lawrence D. Kritzman, trans. Alan Sheridan and others (New York: Routledge, 1988), 326.

Chapter One

1. Sontag's account of her experience in Sarajevo appears in "Godot Comes to Sarajevo," *New York Review of Books,* October 21, 1993, 52–59.

2. Sontag uses Vladimir and Estragon in the plural because in her staging of the play, in order to allow more people to participate, she had several actors on stage in these roles at the same time.

3. Kant's essays on history, some of which are collected in *Kant's Political Writings,* ed. Hans Reiss, trans. H. B. Nisbet (Cambridge: Cambridge University Press, 1970) are fascinating. On the point in question, see "The Contest of the Faculties," 188.

4. Friedrich Nietzsche, *The Will to Power,* trans. Walter Kaufmann and R. J. Hollingdale, ed. Walter Kaufmann (New York: Random House, 1967; Vintage Books edition, 1968), 3.

5. Jan Kott, *The Eating of the Gods* (Evanston: Northwestern University Press, 1987), xviii.

6. See Theodor W. Adorno, *Negative Dialectics,* trans. E. B. Ashton (New York: Continuum Press, 1973), 364.

7. Alasdair MacIntyre, *After Virtue* (Notre Dame: University of Notre Dame, 1981, 1984). In an interview in *Cogito* (Summer 1991), 67–73, MacIntyre notes that he has been involved in a "single project" since 1977, when he was writing the final draft of *After Virtue*; the other works that are "central" to that project are *Whose Justice? Which Rationality?* (Notre Dame: University of Notre Dame, 1988) and *Three Rival Versions of Moral Enquiry: Encyclopaedia, Genealogy, and Tradition* (Notre Dame: University of Notre Dame, 1990). MacIntyre's overall narrative has not changed in the course of this project, although some of the details have. It would be interesting to explore the precise changes MacIntyre's thought has undergone from the first to the third of these works. I will, however, treat his narrative as a single narrative, noting changes from text to text only where not to do so would radically distort the narrative.

8. Any strong distinction between the account of the moral life as we find it in a text like the *Summa* and that embodied in the lives of real people in a community is in fact a false distinction, given that the *Summa* was itself written as a practical guide to the Christian life; see MacIntyre, *Three Rival Versions,* 129, 132–133. MacIntyre is not unaware of the kinds of assumptions he makes in placing so much weight upon a fall. In fact, he anticipates this objection to his narrative on page 11 of *After Virtue,* and the whole discussion of emotivism that follows in the next twenty pages is in effect a response to such criticism, insofar as such criticism, as MacIntyre sees it, amounts to the claim that we have been emotivists from the beginning—since, in other words, the sophists. He also makes helpful comments about what we might call his historical method in *Three Rival Versions,* 117, 150.

9. In *After Virtue,* MacIntyre speaks of the fall as an event that took place across three centuries, whereby the teleology crucial to both Aristotelian science and Aristotelian ethics was displaced and rejected by scientific revolution and theological reformation (see, for example, page 117). In *Three Rival Versions,* MacIntyre is much more specific about the moment of the fall and dates it from about 1277, when the bishop of Paris rejected 219 of Aquinas's theses (149–169). Of course within a few decades Pope John XXII canonized Aquinas, and then within four years of his death the Dominicans imposed his teaching on the order. Nonetheless, MacIntyre argues that the Middle Ages mostly misunderstood Aquinas, allowing, for instance, the fragmentation of his systematic enquiry. "What defeated

Aquinas," says MacIntyre, "was the power of the institutionalized curriculum" (151). If we merge MacIntyre's account of the fall in *After Virtue* with that of his account in *Three Rival Versions,* we arrive, it seems to me, at the radical argument that the closing decades of the thirteenth century were watershed years for the history of the world. In any event, the rejection of Aquinas—and hence of Aristotle—is *the* pivotal event in MacIntyre's narrative.

10. MacIntyre, *After Virtue,* 4–5.

11. Ibid., x.

12. Ibid., 263.

13. Ibid.

14. Ibid., 262–263.

15. MacIntyre, *Three Rival Versions,* 18.

16. Ibid., 19.

17. Ibid.

18. This analysis of liberalism, which I owe to John Milbank, *Theology and Social Theory: Beyond Secular Reason* (Cambridge: Basil Blackwell, 1990), 238, seems to me to contribute to an understanding of the various movements in the United States, such as the militia movement, that are rebelling at one and the same time against government bureaucracy and corporate America in the name of freedom. Aside from the advocacy of violence and their paranoia, these people seem to be fairly acute critics of liberalism as it has become embodied in our institutions. Ironically, however, integral to their critique is an invocation of the Founding Fathers in an attempt to prove that America has somehow left behind its principles. What they do not see is that what America has become is precisely the logical conclusion that follows from its principles.

19. MacIntyre, *Three Rival Versions,* 56.

20. Ibid.

21. For MacIntyre on Nietzsche, see *After Virtue,* 112–113; for the quotation from Nietzsche, see *The Will to Power,* 7.

22. Because I will offer my own reading of Nietzsche in a later chapter, I will let MacIntyre's reading of Nietzsche stand as is, although I do not think, finally, his account of Nietzsche is satisfactory.

23. For MacIntyre's discussion of these issues see *Whose Justice? Which Rationality?* 352–353.

24. MacIntyre, *After Virtue,* 111.

25. Ibid., 113.

26. To my knowledge, MacIntyre has not declared one way or another on pacifism. However, I assume that he is not a pacifist, for nothing in his work indicates that he might be—and much suggests that he is not.

27. MacIntyre, *Three Rival Versions,* 231–232.

28. Ibid., 234.

29. Ibid.

30. It may be too strong to say that MacIntyre celebrates such a world, but he certainly does think that given the choice between the facade of agreement and radical conflict, the latter is preferable—if for no other reason than that in the current climate of the university, where what amounts to a surreptitiously constrained agreement masquerades as an exercise in diversity, voices like those of

Aquinas are marginalized. See the closing paragraph of *Three Rival Versions* on pages 235–236 and also pages 171–172.

31. Ibid., 171.

32. For a more detailed account of the status of the mode of dialectical enquiry that MacIntyre makes central to the moral life and that we see here institutionalized in a forum for debate, see my "Flyfishing, Farming, and Grace: How to Survive in a Postnatural World Without Going Mad," *Soundings* 76 (Spring 1993):85–104. Some of these issues will also be taken up in the next chapter.

33. MacIntyre, *Three Rival Versions,* 234–235.

34. See, for example, Louis Ruprecht, Jr., *Tragic Posture and Tragic Vision: Against the Modern Failure of Nerve* (New York: Continuum, 1994), 20.

35. Alasdair MacIntyre, "*Kinesis* Interview with Professor Alasdair MacIntyre," interview by Thomas Pearson, in *Kinesis: Graduate Journal in Philosophy* 20, no. 3 (1994):34–47.

36. MacIntyre, *After Virtue,* 145.

37. Ibid., 262.

38. Samuel Beckett, *Waiting for Godot* (New York: Grove Press, 1954, 1982), 7.

39. Ibid., 57.

40. Ibid., 58.

41. Arthur Schopenhauer, *The World as Will and Representation,* trans. E.F.J. Payne (New York: Dover Publications, 1966), vol. 1, 322. I was alerted to this quotation from Schopenhauer by Bert States, *The Shape of Paradox: An Essay on Waiting for Godot* (Berkeley: University of California, 1978).

42. In the original version Beckett wrote that in the second act the tree should be covered with leaves, but he pared this down to just a few in later versions. The leaves suggest, it seems, a hint, but only a hint, of hope. And this hint is countered in the second act by the desperate turn in the fate of Pozzo and Lucky, making the play all the more ambiguous, as I note later. I should also point out that when Sontag staged the play in Sarajevo she performed only Act I. Her reasons for doing this had in part to do with time constraints; however, she also decided that it made sense in Sarajevo just then to do only the first act.

43. Nietzsche, *The Will to Power,* 542–543.

44. Ibid., 7.

45. Ibid., 14.

Chapter Two

1. Friedrich Nietzsche, *The Will to Power,* trans. Walter Kaufmann and R. J. Hollingdale, ed. Walter Kaufmann (New York: Vintage Books, 1968), § 7.

2. Friedrich Nietzsche, *On the Genealogy of Morals,* trans. Walter Kaufmann and R. J. Hollingdale, ed. Walter Kaufmann (New York: Vintage Books, 1989), Essay 3, § 24.

3. Michael Allen Gillespie, *Nihilism Before Nietzsche* (Chicago: University of Chicago, 1995), xii.

4. See for instance, Phillip R. Fandozzi, *Nihilism and Technology: A Heideggerian Investigation* (Washington, D.C.: University Press of America, 1982); Karen L. Carr, *The Banalization of Nihilism: Twentieth-Century Responses to Meaninglessness* (Albany: State University of New York, 1992); James C. Edwards, *The Authority of*

Language: Heidegger, Wittgenstein, and the Threat of Philosophical Nihilism (Tampa: University of South Florida Press, 1990); Gianni Vattimo, *The End of Modernity: Nihilism and Hermeneutics in Postmodern Culture,* trans. Jon R. Snyder (Baltimore: Johns Hopkins University Press, 1988); Nishitani Keiji, *The Self-Overcoming of Nihilism,* trans. Graham Parkes with Setsuko Ahiara (Albany: State University of New York, 1990); and Gillespie, *Nihilism Before Nietzsche.*

5. Nietzsche, *The Will to Power,* § 585 A. The fact that this note appears some two hundred pages after the rest of Nietzsche's explicit musing on nihilism is a good indication of the problematic organization of Nietzsche's notes; it also raises the question, much debated by Nietzsche scholars, about the status of these notes within Nietzsche's body of work.

6. Ibid., § 12.

7. Friedrich Nietzsche, *The Portable Nietzsche,* ed. and trans. Walter Kaufmann (New York: Penguin Books, 1982), 32–39.

8. Ibid., 32.

9. Ibid., 33.

10. Ibid.

11. Ibid., 34, 38.

12. Ibid., 34–35.

13. Nietzsche, *On the Genealogy of Morals,* Essay 3, § 28.

14. Ibid.

15. Nietzsche, *The Portable Nietzsche,* 31–35

16. Nietzsche, *The Will to Power,* § 1067.

17. Ibid., § 114.

18. Ibid., § 55.

19. Friedrich Nietzsche, *Beyond Good and Evil: Prelude to a Philosophy of the Future,* trans. Walter Kaufmann (New York: Vintage Books, 1989), § 257.

20. With this Nietzschean view in mind, it is worth noting that Elaine Pagels, from a completely different perspective, constructs a similar narrative about the origins of Jewish and Christian conceptions of evil in her book *The Origin of Satan* (New York: Random House, 1995).

21. Nietzsche, *Beyond Good and Evil,* § 265.

22. Nietzsche, *On the Genealogy of Morals,* Essay 1, § 11.

23. Nietzsche, *Beyond Good and Evil,* § 259.

24. Ibid.

25. Ibid.

26. Nietzsche, *On the Genealogy of Morals,* Essay 1, § 11.

27. Ibid.

28. Ibid., § 2.

29. For Nietzsche's synopsis of this, see "Twilight of the Idols," *The Portable Nietzsche,* 485. What follows is a partial summary of the section in "Twilight of the Idols" called "How the 'True World' Finally Became a Fable: The History of an Error," 485–486.

30. Nietzsche, *The Will to Power,* § 12.

31. Ibid.

32. Ibid.

33. Ibid.

34. Martin Heidegger, "The Word of Nietzsche: 'God Is Dead,'" in *The Question Concerning Technology and Other Essays,* trans. William Lovitt (New York: Harper and Row, 1977), 53–112. The quotation comes from page 61.

35. See Friedrich Nietzsche, *The Gay Science,* trans. Walter Kaufmann (New York: Vintage Books, 1974), § 343.

36. Heidegger, "The Word of Nietzsche," 60, 64, 61.

37. Nietzsche, *The Gay Science,* § 125.

38. Nietzsche, *The Will to Power,* §1.

39. Ibid., § 3.

40. Ibid., § 23.

41. Ibid., § 28.

42. Heidegger, "The Word of Nietzsche," 64, 69.

43. On this note see Nietzsche, *The Will to Power,* § 12, § 30, § 32, § 55; *On the Genealogy of Morals,* Essay 1, § 12, Essay 2, § 24.

44. Nietzsche, *The Will to Power,* § 13.

45. Ibid.

46. Ibid., § 112.

47. Ibid., § 1041.

48. Ibid., § 26. Sometimes Nietzsche does not speak of new goals but rather of affirming the process, sheer becoming, after having removed the idea of a goal. See *The Will to Power,* § 55.

49. John Milbank, *Theology and Social Theory: Beyond Secular Reason* (Cambridge, Mass.: Basil Blackwell, 1990). All references to this text will occur parenthetically in the body of my text, unless otherwise noted.

50. I would like to remind the reader that at this point I am simply offering an exposition of Milbank's position. Later, I will have occasion to challenge his reading of the so-called nihilists, who do not, it seems to me, reduce the world to warfare.

51. The references to Jacques Derrida come from his essay on the work of Emmanuel Levinas, "Violence and Metaphysics," in *Writing and Difference,* trans. Alan Bass (Chicago: University of Chicago, 1978).

52. Ibid., 117, 147–148.

53. Ibid., 117.

54. Ibid., 133. Derrida's qualification here should not be missed, for the placing of violence within the very possibility of discourse itself obviously demands that we rethink what we mean by the term "violence." As we will see, Derrida here wants to speak of what he calls a transcendental or preethical violence (an ontological violence), which then becomes the basis for thinking about what we might mean, in the context of ethics, about both violence and nonviolence: "For this transcendental origin, as the irreducible violence of the relation to the other, is at the same time nonviolence, since it opens the relation to the other" (128–129). These are complex issues, and I do not intend to work them out here. I did, however, want to call the reader's attention to these matters, since questions about violence and nonviolence lurk throughout this book. In any event, one needs to understand that however these issues are decided, the core of Milbank's case lies in his insistence that such issues are determined at the ontological level, and only later as matters of ethics. On this point, he and Derrida agree.

55. Ibid., 129.

56. Ibid., 128.
57. Ibid., 125.
58. Ibid., 147.
59. Ibid.
60. Ibid., 129.
61. Ibid., 130.
62. Heidegger, "The Word of Nietzsche," 62–63. For Nietzsche's similarities to Heidegger with regard to the relationship between nihilism and the technological modern world see Nietzsche, *The Will to Power,* § 12, § 32–34.
63. Heidegger, "The Word of Nietzsche," 70.
64. Nietzsche, *The Will to Power,* § 715.
65. Heidegger, "The Word of Nietzsche," 73.
66. Ibid., 80–81.
67. Ibid., 83–84.
68. Martin Heidegger, "The Question Concerning Technology," in *The Question Concerning Technology and Other Essays*, 3–35.
69. Ibid., 14–15.
70. Ibid., 16–17.
71. Heidegger, "The Word of Nietzsche," 95.
72. Ibid., 96–97.
73. Ibid., 100.
74. Ibid., 102–104.
75. Ibid., 109.
76. As we will see later in this chapter, it seems to me that Nietzsche agrees with Milbank and Heidegger on this note.
77. Gillespie, *Nihilism Before Nietzsche,* xii.
78. Ibid., 255–256.
79. Ibid., 24.
80. Ibid., 28, 33, 62.
81. Quoted in Gillespie, *Nihilism Before Nietzsche,* 66.
82. Ibid., 64–65.
83. Ibid., xx.
84. Ibid., 173.
85. Ibid., xxiii.
86. Ibid.
87. Ibid., 171.
88. Ibid., 143, 160.

Chapter Three

1. John Milbank, *Theology and Social Theory: Beyond Secular Reason* (Cambridge, Mass.: Basil Blackwell, 1990), 282. All references to this text will occur parenthetically in the body of my text and in the notes, unless otherwise noted.
2. I should note that my account of Milbank is limited almost entirely to his first book. He has since published numerous essays and two other books. I note this because I do not want to be accused of the offense that so many people have made, for instance, with regard to MacIntyre. Many commentators on MacIntyre

speak as if MacIntyre never wrote another word after *After Virtue.* My concern in this chapter is not to offer a definitive exposition of the whole of Milbank's corpus nor to reduce Milbank to this one book. Rather, I have intentionally limited myself to this particular work by Milbank because his narrative in *Theology and Social Theory* helps to advance my own.

Indeed, it may help if I alert the reader to the fact that my exposition of Milbank's narrative in *Theology and Social Theory* is a foundational part of my own narrative; hence in spite of the difficulty that parts of this chapter may present to the reader, I encourage her to press ahead. In the end, if not in the beginning, the purpose of this journey through *Theology and Social Theory* should become clear. I have labored for clarity in my account of Milbank, but the fact is that even a distilled Milbank makes for difficult, but I think rewarding, reading.

3. The full title of Augustine's major work is *Concerning the City of God Against the Pagans.* And note not only that one of Nietzsche's last works is called *Der Antichrist* but also that *The Genealogy of Morals,* in which Nietzsche develops much of his case against Christianity, is subtitled "A Polemic," or an "attack." Clearly the attack is launched against Christianity.

4. To say that all events are in some way a manifestation of the work of God is not to say that God is the cause of all events. Hence it would be wrong to conclude that God caused either the Holocaust or the Allied attempts to defeat Germany and Japan with massive bombing campaigns that were responsible for thousands upon thousands of civilian deaths. As we will see when I turn to Yoder, however, although God is not the source of this violence, to think apocalyptically is to be willing to face the challenge of discerning the ways in which he nonetheless remains "involved" in events like the Holocaust.

5. Saint Augustine, *City of God,* trans. Henry Bettenson (New York: Penguin Books, 1972), XV, 5.

6. Milbank refers to his own work as a "postmodern critical Augustinianism" in "A Short *Summa* in Forty-Two Responses to Unasked Questions," *Modern Theology* 7 (April 1991):225–237.

7. Saint Augustine, *City of God,* XV, 5.

8. Ibid., IV, 16.

9. Ibid.

10. Ibid., XV, 1, 5.

11. Ibid., III, 13.

12. It is worth noting that the reported last words of Romulus were as follows: "Go and tell the Romans that it is the gods' will that my city of Rome should be the capital of the world. Let them exercise their military skill and let them know—and let them tell their descendants—that no mortal power can resist the Romans." I quote this part of the myth from *Classical Mythology,* 5th ed., Mark P. O. Morford and Robert J. Lenardon, editors (White Plains, N.Y.: Longman Publishers, 1995), 550.

13. Actually Milbank says this not of his entire project but of his eleventh chapter. Nonetheless, I think the comment applies to his work as a whole.

14. MacIntyre does of course think of himself as an "Augustinian Christian" in *Whose Justice? Which Rationality?* (Notre Dame: University of Notre Dame, 1988), 10. And perhaps we should now call him not simply Augustinian but also, or perhaps more so, a Thomist. MacIntyre's theological commitments and their role in his work

deserve attention that I cannot give here. For a display of those commitments, see *Three Rival Versions of Moral Enquiry: Encyclopaedia, Genealogy, and Tradition* (Notre Dame: University of Notre Dame, 1990), 26, 101, 146, 200, where MacIntyre exposes his theological commitments and their relationship to tradition. Although these commitments are still less than clear in *Three Rival Versions,* they are exposed in a way that they were not in his earlier works. It is also worth noting this exchange from an interview MacIntyre had with the journal *Kinesis* (Alasdair MacIntyre, "*Kinesis* Interview with Professor Alasdair MacIntyre," interview by Thomas Pearson, in *Kinesis: Graduate Journal in Philosophy* 20, no. 3 [1994]: 34–47):

> ***Kinesis:*** So how would you depict your religious faith?
> ***MacIntyre:*** I am Roman Catholic. Period.
> ***Kinesis:*** In a traditional and orthodox sense?
> ***MacIntyre:*** There is no other sense. I believe what I am taught to believe by God, through the Church. And, when God speaks, there is nothing to do but obey or disobey. I don't know in what other way one could be a Roman Catholic. If Roman Catholicism is a theory of mine, or of some group of people, about how the world might be construed, then it's not a particularly interesting philosophy.

Nonetheless, at the level of his intellectual enterprise, MacIntyre falls theologically short, according to Milbank, who also notes that philosophy generally is "subsumed," "finished and surpassed" by theological speculation: See Milbank, *Theology and Social Theory,* 430.

15. On page 78 of *Whose Justice? Which Rationality?* MacIntyre says, "To engage in intellectual enquiry is then not simply to advance theses and to give one's rational allegiance to those theses which so far withstand refutation; it is to understand the movement from thesis to thesis as a movement toward a kind of *logos* which will disclose how things are, not relative to some point of view, but as such." When paired with the words on page 363 ("The concept of truth, however, is timeless") MacIntyre's epistemology appears to be an almost untempered realism. In fact, his realism is complex: see in particular *Whose Justice? Which Rationality?* pages 349–403, where he argues in some detail for what he calls on page 357 "a developing complex conception of truth." See also my article, "Flyfishing, Farming, and Grace: How to Survive in a Postnatural World Without Going Mad," *Soundings* 76 (Spring 1993):85–104, for an account of MacIntyre's understanding of truth.

16. Milbank puts it nicely when he says that MacIntyre's historicism (embodied in his stress on narrative) is in conflict with, and submissive to, his realism (embodied in his commitment to dialectics); see Milbank, *Theology and Social Theory,* 339, 345.

When Milbank wrote his book, MacIntyre had not yet published *Three Rival Versions of Enquiry,* and it is interesting to note that in that work he has moved closer to Milbank's notion that it is not "possible to defend the notion of 'traditioned reason' in general, outside my attachment to a tradition which grounds this idea in the belief in the historical guidance of the Holy Spirit" (328). See in particular page 92, where MacIntyre says, speaking of Augustine but also, I think, of himself: "So in the Augustinian scheme when I first believe in order that I may go on to understand, I do not evaluate evidence, but put my trust in certain persons authorized to represent the apostolic testimony." See, too, MacIntyre's *First Principles, Final Ends, and Contemporary Philosophical Issues* (Milwaukee: Marquette University Press, 1990), 35–36, where he says, "It cannot be a matter of dialectic and nothing more, since the strongest conclusions of dialectic remain a matter of belief, not of knowledge." I am not at all sure that MacIntyre would disagree with Milbank's qualification about tradition, although the fact remains that MacIntyre's work remains "philosophical" in a way that Milbank's is not.

17. Milbank devotes an entire chapter to this claim about science: "Science, Power, Reality," 259–276. For an even better account of science as narrative see the introduction to Donna Haraway's book, *Primate Visions* (New York: Routledge, 1989), 1–15. See also John Dupré, *The Disorder of Things: Metaphysical Foundations of the Disunity of Science* (Cambridge: Harvard University Press, 1993; paperback, 1995).

18. Milbank, *Three Rival Versions*, 144.

19. For Deleuze on this notion see Gilles Deleuze, *Difference and Repetition*, trans. Paul Patton (New York: Columbia University Press, 1994), 59; and Gilles Deleuze, *Logic of Sense*, trans. Mark Lester with Charles Stivale, ed. Constantin V. Boundas (New York: Columbia University Press, 1990), 262.

20. Deleuze, *Logic of Sense*, 132.

21. Gilles Deleuze and Felix Guattari, *A Thousand Plateaus*, trans. Brian Massumi (Minneapolis: University of Minnesota Press, 1987), 84. The notions of "indirect discourse" and "incorporeal transformations" are crucial for Deleuze, and both are adopted by Milbank. Milbank explains indirect discourse well when he says on page 234: "All personal relations embody an 'indirect' moment in so far as they are mediated by language, which is the *residium* of previous social encounters." Or as Deleuze puts it more radically: "My direct discourse is still the free indirect discourse running through me, coming from other worlds or other planets." It is this indirect discourse, coming from elsewhere, that makes our conversations possible and lends to them the nuances of meaning that are absent from the words per se. Thus V. N. Vološinov, from whom Deleuze borrows (not without alteration) the notion of indirect discourse, says in *Marxism and the Philosophy of Language*, trans. Ladislav Matejka and I. R. Titunik (Cambridge: Harvard University Press, 1986), 128–129: "The direct utterance, 'Well done! What an achievement!' cannot be registered in indirect discourse as, 'He said that well done and what an achievement.' Rather, we expect: . . . 'He said, delightedly, that had been done well and was a real achievement.'" Direct discourse is full of "ellipses" and "omissions" of vital "orders" which are yet present indirectly as "implicit presuppositions" within each word. Hence Deleuze speaks of an "order-word" within every word, an indirect discourse pulsing through direct discourse.

"Order-words" designate this "instantaneous relation between statements and the incorporeal transformations" they express. For instance, to borrow examples from Deleuze, when the judge states a guilty verdict, she transforms the body of a free man into the body of an imprisoned one (complete with all the subtle and horrific implications of such a transformation), and yet all of this with the utterance of a single word—incorporeally. Or when the priest turns the body of the bread and the wine into the spiritual body and blood of Christ, which is no less real for being spiritual, he does not produce a chemistry set but says of the bread and wine what Jesus did: "Take, eat, this is my body. Drink it, all of you. For this is my blood." This sort of incorporeal transformation, which in speech-act theory is called a "performative," will be crucial to Milbank later when he needs to give an account of a nonviolent punishment, that is, a punishment erased as such by the retrospective consent of the punished.

22. Deleuze, *Logic of Sense*, 257–258.

23. Ibid., 261, 262.

24. The following discussion should make clear what Milbank means by "idealism"; however, what he means by "linguistic" is less obvious and really has to do with aspects of the philosophy of language that I have chosen to leave to the side. Suffice it to say that Milbank is indebted to the work of Hamann and Herder in the eighteenth century and "the post-Renaissance discovery that language creates rather than reflects meaning" (150):

"Their argument is that because we only think in language, and only grasp the world through language, it is impossible even to disentangle the knowledge we have of ourselves from the knowledge we have of the world (or 'nature'), or vice versa . . . It follows that access to this 'truth' of both humanity and nature can only be an aesthetic one: as all knowledge occurs through the expression of reality in signs, it is never possible to 'compare' the sign with the reality, and the fundamental function of language cannot be referential. Unless, in consequence, we 'trust' our creative expressions not as arbitrary, but rather as fulfilling a goal which is not our own, there can be no truth of any sort. The aesthetic decision for a particular linguistic content . . . is to be taken as also the instance of the manifestation of truth. One can properly speak here of a kind of 'aesthetic necessity'" (149).

25. Immanuel Kant, *Critique of Judgment*, trans. Werner S. Pluhar (Indianapolis: Hackett Publishing, 1987), Paragraph 49, 181–188. All the quotations from Kant in the next few paragraphs are from this section.

26. For Milbank's comment on Kant in this regard, see page 149.

27. Of course the language of presentation is deceiving, for as both Kant and Milbank acknowledge, these ideas are, finally, ineffable and yet necessarily mediated by language. To say it again, "narratives only identify God because they simultaneously invent the unpresentable 'idea' of God." The idea of God is unpresentable because only thus can we hold that "'God' is both imaginatively projected by us and known, though with a negative reserve which allows that our initiative, precisely *as* an initiative, is a response, and a radical dependency" (426).

28. Milbank does not say that textuality is the condition of all creation but only of culture. But given his understanding of culture as participation in creation, and given also the implications of his view that the world happens to us as narrative, "and not primarily the cultural world which humans make" (359)—this seems a fair assumption.

29. For more on this notion of formal structure (and its relation to indirect discourse) see page 234. Also I should note that one might put it the other way and say that it is the invitation of narrative and the resistance of ideas, depending on where in the sequence you were, since this is a never-ending and cyclical process.

30. Milbank says of nihilist philosophy that it works with a univocal code that produces an "absolute indifference to each particular difference." As we will see when we discuss Deleuze again later, this is simply a misunderstanding on Milbank's part.

31. Quotations from Milbank in this, as well as the next three paragraphs, come from pages 303–306.

32. A central aspect of Milbank's postmodernism involves an elaborate argument about the need, on the one hand, to jettison any allegiance to the traditional metaphysical notions of subject, substance, essence, presence, and the priority of idea over copy, while on the other hand to keep the equally traditional notions of transcendence, participation, analogy, hierarchy, and teleology. We can, says Milbank, accept the postmodern critique of notions like substance and essence without at the same time assuming that this critique necessarily leads to the rejection of notions of transcendence and teleology: See 295–296.

33. In Milbank's more difficult idiom, we can say that there is a tension between the "paradigmatic setting" of narrative portrayed as ideal and the "syntagmatic development" of narrative in different historical moments. A narrative "is always already internally torn between 'staying in the place' of its assumed frame of reference, or breaking out of this frame to project a new one through the temporal course of events. . . . [Thus] the paradigmatic is sketched in vaguely, and gets constantly revised in response to the syntagmatic unfolding" (386). This play between the paradigmatic and the syntagmatic, between "already realized" ideals and the syntactical ordering of historically embodied narratives is the non-identical repetition posited by Milbank's linguistic idealism and metanarrative realism.

34. This is the title of chapter nine, page 109.

35. In *Three Rival Versions*, page 215, MacIntyre says that it is not yet due time to declare Thomism the victor. Nonetheless, he indicates in a variety of places that as someone who attests to the truth of Thomism, he has to expect the incommensurable alternative account of things offered by the likes of Nietzsche and Foucault will founder on incoherence and end in failure. See, for instance, pages 55, 125, and 215. See also MacIntyre, *First Principles, Final Ends*, 22, 50–51, 65–67. MacIntyre's critique of Nietzsche and Foucault is complex, but in a nut shell it revolves around problems of the self, such that Nietzsche and Foucault cannot offer coherent arguments for their view of things because, finally, they cannot offer a coherent account of the self that makes those arguments; see *Three Rival Versions*, 32–57, 196–215.

36. On page 260 Milbank characterizes an ontology of difference as inseparable from narratives of power. However, on page 430, he characterizes his own ontology as an ontology of difference that does not rest on narratives of power. My account of the relationship between Milbank's ontology and the challenge of thinking difference emerges from this seeming contradiction in Milbank's text. The contradiction occurs in part because Milbank does not think that, properly speaking, nihilist ontology is ontology at all. See also pages 212, 219.

37. God's speech from the whirlwind in Job raises interesting questions about the proliferation of difference. On one hand, it is not unlike the creation we find in Genesis 1 and 2, only recounted with a poetic vengeance. On the other hand, God speaks here of himself as providing prey to lions and ravens, which makes us wonder about the peaceful coexistence that is our image of paradise, where both humans and animals ate only the green plants.

38. To speak this way is really to miscount, for the calling of Israel is surely the second time God speaks, and the sending of his son is then the third time.

39. Milbank's account of the Trinity is expressed, in addition to page 387, on pages 309, 385, 424, and 426.

40. From Fredrick Bauerschmidt, "The Wounds of Christ," *Journal of Literature and Theology* 5 (March 1991):87. My use of the language of "wound" throughout this chapter I owe to Bauerschmidt's insightful and eloquent essay, although Milbank does, as already noted, refer to the wound of history. I also owe the language "crucified logos" to Bauerschmidt. As Bauerschmidt puts it: "Because it is the body of the crucified Logos, we carry in our body corporate both the wound of violence and the wound of love." Bauerschmidt also says: "It is my contention that without the death on the Cross of the Logos, one cannot distinguish the wound of love from the wound of violence." After the crucifixion, Christians learn to speak in a "wounded language" with "wounded words," words that, by reflecting upon their own woundedness, name precisely but never escape the violence of a fallen world.

41. Ibid.

42. Milbank also misreads Foucault, but since I devote two chapters to Foucault later, I will hold to the side for now where Milbank goes wrong in this regard.

43. Gilles Deleuze, *Spinoza: Practical Philosophy*, trans. Robert Hurley (San Francisco: City Lights Books, 1988), 126.

44. Deleuze and Guattari, *A Thousand Plateaus*, 220.

45. Ibid., 230, 506. I should note that Deleuze, too, is aware of the "uselessness of violence"; see page 403.

46. Elsewhere, Milbank says—in a moment that contradicts his view that Christian theology is "unique" and so "can position itself as a gaze at once above, but also alongside, (with or against) other, inherited human gazes" (248)—both that "theology is just another socio-historical gaze, just another perspective, alongside other gazes" (247) and that nihilism and Christianity are two different "gazes" on the world, two mythical conjectures, and "as to what we should conjecture, nothing helps us decide" (306). Of course in other places in the text Milbank does suggest that something helps us decide: hence the notions of a persuasion intrinsic to the Christian logos, of an aesthetic necessity, and of an analogical ordering of the world.

47. In rare moments, Milbank does not speak with such confidence of the possibilities of rearrangement; see, for instance, pages 341–342, 413.

48. The tragic character of Milbank's theology is apparent not only, as I argue here, in *Theology and Social Theory* but also in his essay "'Between Purgation and Illumination': A Critique of the Theology of Right," in *Christ, Ethics, and Tragedy: Essays in Honour of Donald MacKinnon*, ed. Kenneth Surin (Cambridge: Cambridge University Press, 1989), 161–196; see especially pages 190–192, where Milbank, drawing on the work of Donald MacKinnon and addressing the Christian pacifism of Stanley Hauerwas, speaks of "a tragic refusal of the pacifist position." This essay also appears, in revised form, as "A Critique of the Theology of Right," in John Milbank, *The Word Made Strange: Theology, Language, Culture* (Cambridge, Mass.: Blackwell Publishers, 1997), 7–35.

49. Milbank understands the lines between Church and world, Church and State, to be hazy, or one might even say that Milbank would prefer a world in which the line between Church and State were blurred. See, in particular, page 408.

50. The notion that punishment can be redeemed by retrospective consent is rooted in Milbank's understanding of the way in which the world is endlessly

arranged and rearranged by the "incorporeal transformations" I discussed earlier in the chapter.

51. It is an important point, I think, to say with Milbank that the difference between coercion in the service of a disciplinary action within the church and the more obvious violence of state power is a matter of degree and does not therefore amount to a qualitative distinction.

52. These words were written before the end of the war.

53. Thucydides, *The History of the Peloponnesian War,* Book V, § 105; I have taken the quotation from Thucydides, *On Justice, Power, and Human Nature: Selections from "The History of the Peloponnesian War,"* trans. Paul Woodruff (Indianapolis and Cambridge: Hackett Publishing, 1993), 106.

54. Of course, it is only a matter of emphasis, since, as the creed makes plain, to recount the whole story is to include the incarnation, the crucifixion, and the resurrection. As we will see when we get to Yoder, to think apocalyptically requires a move from the crucifixion to the resurrection—for without the resurrection, we would be left at best with a tragedy. In any event, as a needed corrective to Milbank's narrative, I have chosen for now to move from the incarnation to the crucifixion. Walter Kasper in *Jesus the Christ,* trans. V. Green (New York: Paulist Press, 1976) has a helpful way of putting it, when he suggests that properly speaking the crucifixion and the resurrection are components of, or together make up, the Incarnation, which then serves, as Milbank wants it to, as the lens through which all history is viewed. As Kasper puts it: "Where the Cross and the Resurrection become the midpoint, that also means however an adjustment of a one-sided Christology oriented to the Incarnation" (37). It is precisely this kind of adjustment that I am attempting to make to Milbank's at times one-sided Christology.

55. Bauerschmidt, "The Wounds of Christ," 99, n. 1.

56. Ibid., 83.

57. Ibid.

58. Here, and in the first sentence of this paragraph, I am borrowing words and images, if not concepts and arguments, from Jacques Derrida, "Violence and Metaphysics," in *Writing and Difference,* trans. Alan Bass (Chicago: University of Chicago, 1978).

Chapter Four

1. Friedrich Nietzsche, *The Birth of Tragedy,* trans. Walter Kaufmann (New York: Vintage Books, 1967).

2. Ibid., 52. Nietzsche, of course, is not alone in this move toward aesthetics. He was preceded most immediately by Schopenhauer and before that by the early German Romantics, who themselves owed much to Kant's account of aesthetics in *The Critique of Judgment.* Indeed, one could tell a long and interesting story about the rise of aesthetics in eighteenth- and nineteenth-century thought, particularly in Germany, a rise that seems to have occurred along with the corresponding fall of God. For at least the sketch of such a story see Charles Taylor's *Hegel* (Cambridge: Cambridge University Press, 1975), 3–50, and also his *Sources of the Self* (Cambridge: Harvard University Press, 1989), particularly, 368–493. Michael Allen Gillespie's *Nihilism Before Nietzsche* (Chicago: University of Chicago, 1995) is also suggestive here.

3. Nietzsche, *The Birth of Tragedy,* 143.
4. Ibid., 141.
5. Ibid.
6. John Milbank, *Theology and Social Theory: Beyond Secular Reason* (Cambridge, Mass.: Basil Blackwell, 1990), 428.
7. Ibid., 428, 429.
8. From the transcript of a speech Marsalis gave to the National Press Club on November 21, 1995.
9. Nietzsche, *The Birth of Tragedy,* 143.
10. Ibid., 33.
11. Ibid., 38.
12. Friedrich Nietzsche, *The Portable Nietzsche,* ed. and trans. Walter Kaufmann (New York: Penguin Books, 1982), 33–34.
13. Nietzsche, *The Birth of Tragedy,* 42–43.
14. This occurs in Book VII, line 54ff. I quote here the Rieu translation, as it is recorded in Walter Kaufmann's *Tragedy and Philosophy* (Princeton: Princeton University Press, 1992), 145.
15. Ibid.
16. Nietzsche, *The Birth of Tragedy,* 43–44.
17. Ibid., 45.
18. Ibid., 46.
19. Ibid.
20. Ibid., 46–47.
21. Ibid., 49–50, 55.
22. Ibid., 108.
23. See Aristotle, *Poetics,* 1449a, 11. I have quoted from the translation of R. Kassel in *The Complete Works of Aristotle,* ed. Jonathan Barnes (Princeton: Princeton University Press, 1984).
24. Nietzsche, *The Birth of Tragedy,* 56.
25. Ibid., 61.
26. Ibid., 59.
27. Ibid., 60.
28. Ibid., 65.
29. I will refer to the translation by William Arrowsmith collected in *The Complete Greek Tragedies: Euripides V* (Chicago: University of Chicago, 1968). All references will offer the line numbers parenthetically in the body of my text.
30. Jan Kott, "The Eating of the Gods, or *The Bacchae,*" in *The Eating of the Gods* (Evanston: Northwestern University Press, 1987), 188.
31. I should note that the question of Nietzsche's accuracy with regard to ancient Greek views of Dionysus transcend my present concerns. It is perhaps worth noting, however, a word of caution from the French classicist, Jean-Pierre Vernant: "The *Bacchae* has been, and still is, read in the light of a particular idea that we ourselves have of Dionysism. And that idea—whatever it is that we call Dionysism—is not a piece of factual evidence: It is a product of the history of religions produced, from Nietzsche onward, in our modern age. It was, to be sure, on the basis of the documentary evidence that the historians of Greek religion constructed this category (of Dionysism), but they did so using conceptual tools and

a framework of reference whose bases, inspiration, and implications were affected at least as much by their own religious system and spiritual horizon as by those of the Greeks of the classical period." From Jean-Pierre Vernant, "The Masked Dionysus of Euripides' *Bacchae,*" in Jean-Pierre Vernant and Pierre Vidal-Naquet, *Myth and Tragedy in Ancient Greece* (New York: Zone Books, 1990), 383. For more detail about the issues Vernant mentions, see Albert Henrichs, "Loss of Self, Suffering, Violence: The Modern View of Dionysus from Nietzsche to Girard," in *Harvard Studies in Classical Philology* 88 (1984):205–240.

32. Kott, "The Eating of the Gods," 187–230.
33. Ibid., 190.
34. Ibid., 195.
35. Ibid., 194.
36. Ibid., 196–197.
37. Ibid., 200–201.
38. Ibid., 202–203.
39. Ibid., 207, 219.
40. Ibid., 222.
41. Ibid., 221–222.
42. Ibid., 226.
43. Ibid., 226–227.
44. Ibid., 227.
45. Ibid., 227–228.
46. Nietzsche, *The Birth of Tragedy*, 37.
47. Ibid.
48. Kott, "The Eating of the Gods," 229.
49. Vernant, "The Masked Dionysus," 381–412.
50. Ibid., 401–402.
51. Ibid., 402.
52. Ibid.
53. Ibid., 394, 390.
54. To avoid confusion, note that this apocalyptic vision is not the same as the apocalyptic vision that I will develop as an alternative to tragedy later in the book.
55. Perhaps this is the place to pause and note that my reading of Nietzsche, although true to the Nietzsche of *The Birth of Tragedy,* runs against the grain both of what Nietzsche himself said later of his work and what some scholars say. Hence in the "Attempt at Self-Criticism" that Nietzsche places at the beginning of *The Birth of Tragedy* in 1886, he denounces the notion of metaphysical comfort that is central to that work, saying, "No! You ought to learn the art of *this-worldly* comfort first" (26). Some commentators—Gilles Deleuze, for instance, in *Nietzsche and Philosophy,* trans. Hugh Tomlinson (New York: Columbia University Press, 1983)—argue that Nietzsche's work stands against all metaphysics and is not finally metaphysical itself. Although I am persuaded in general terms by such arguments, I do not find it particularly fruitful for my purposes to ignore either the unarguably metaphysical nature of *The Birth of Tragedy* or the metaphysical tendencies that persist even in Nietzsche's later works.

On this note, let me say one more thing. Even more conservative commentators on Nietzsche, such as Walter Kaufmann and Michael Gillespie, make a strong distinction between the Dionysus of Nietzsche's early work and Dionysus as we meet him at the end of *The Will to Power.* Hence Gillespie says in *Nihilism Before Nietzsche* (Chicago: University of Chicago, 1995) that the later "Dionysus differs from Nietzsche's early Dionysus, who offered a kind of metaphysical solace and forgetfulness in the face of suffering and death. The later Dionysus offers not solace but the vitality of life itself that transcends the death of all individuals, that reproduces individuality in the face of death and the dissolution of individuality" (223). And Walter Kaufmann, in *Nietzsche: Philosopher, Psychologist, Antichrist* (Princeton: Princeton University Press, 1974), says, "It has been overlooked that the Dionysus whom Nietzsche celebrated as his own god in his later writings is no longer the deity of formless frenzy whom we meet in Nietzsche's first book. Only the name remains" (129).

Although I have no interest in denying that Nietzsche's conceptions changed in the course of his life, I do think that the distinction between an early and a late Dionysus is unduly emphasized—after all, Nietzsche himself as late as 1886 still considered *The Birth of Tragedy* to be a book that answered the question "What is Dionysian?" I also think that this distinction precludes one from recognizing that in *The Birth of Tragedy* Nietzsche is already laying the groundwork for a tragic politics.

What all of this means is that as I read Nietzsche, everything he writes after *The Birth of Tragedy* is simply a commentary on that work, since it contains already at least sketches of everything from the will to power to the eternal recurrence to the notion of slave morality. Although the argument necessary to support this contention does not belong in the current work, I at least wanted to call the reader's attention to what from certain perspectives is an idiosyncratic reading of Nietzsche—a reading, however, that will enable us to understand the tragic politics that Nietzsche envisioned and that Foucault embodied.

56. Vernant, "The Masked Dionysus," 404.

57. Ibid., 406.

58. Nietzsche, *The Birth of Tragedy,* 104.

59. Ibid., 67.

60. Ibid., 60.

61. Ibid., 104.

62. Ibid., 104–105.

63. Friedrich Nietzsche, "What I Owe to the Ancients," § 5 in *Twilight of the Idols/The Anti-Christ,* trans. R. J. Hollingdale (New York: Penguin Books, 1990).

64. My account of Schopenhauer relies heavily on Gillespie's account in *Nihilism Before Nietzsche.*

65. Nietzsche, *The Birth of Tragedy,* 24. For an account of Nietzsche's dependence on Schopenhauer, see Gillespie's *Nihilism Before Nietzsche,* 181–202.

66. Gillespie, *Nihilism Before Nietzsche,* 187.

67. Arthur Schopenhauer, *The World as Will and Representation,* 2 vols., trans. E.F.J. Payne (New York: Dover Publications, 1966), vol. 1, 165.

68. Ibid., 146–147.

69. Gillespie, *Nihilism Before Nietzsche,* 189–190.

70. Ibid., 192.

71. Schopenhauer, *The World as Will and Representation,* vol. 2, 433–434.

72. Nietzsche, *The Birth of Tragedy,* 112.

73. For instance, by failing to take into account Nietzsche's tragic vision, Heidegger misses the fact that the will to power and the will to life are not, for Nietzsche, simply synonymous, and for this reason the will to power is not simply about preservation and enhancement but also about its own tragic self-overcoming, whereby life is lost. Hence Nietzsche says in *Thus Spoke Zarathustra,* trans. Walter Kaufmann (New York: Penguin Books, 1978): "There is much that life esteems more highly than life itself" (115). More on this follows.

74. Nietzsche, *Thus Spoke Zarathustra,* 114–115.

75. Vernant, "The Masked Dionysus," 411.

76. Nietzsche, *Portable Nietzsche,* 72.

77. Nietzsche, *The Birth of Tragedy,* 94.

78. Norman Maclean, *Young Men and Fire* (Chicago: University of Chicago, 1992). All page references to this text will occur parenthetically in the body of my text.

79. Each space between paragraphs indicates that I am skipping a portion of Maclean's text.

80. Nietzsche, *The Birth of Tragedy,* 59.

81. Ibid., 142.

82. Richard Manning, "The Failure of Literature," in *Northern Lights* 9 (Fall 1993):25–26.

83. Nietzsche, *The Birth of Tragedy,* 95–96.

84. Ibid., 97–98.

85. Note that this will prove true for Foucault as well. Hence both Nietzsche and Foucault can be disputed at the level of the "facts." Nietzsche, after all, was "wrong" about many of the things he said about tragedy. Nonetheless, his work on tragedy is, in my view, unsurpassed.

86. Kott, "The Eating of the Gods," x.

Chapter Five

1. Michael Allen Gillespie, *Nihilism Before Nietzsche* (Chicago: University of Chicago, 1995), 253–254.

2. Ibid., xxiii.

3. Ibid.

4. See, for instance, John Milbank, *Theology and Social Theory: Beyond Secular Reason* (Cambridge, Mass.: Basil Blackwell, 1990), 279, 315, 319.

5. Michael Walzer, "The Politics of Michel Foucault," in *Foucault: A Critical Reader,* ed. David Couzens Hoy (New York: Basil Blackwell, 1986), 61.

6. Ibid., 62.

7. Walzer's criticism of Foucault's unwillingness to make what amount to metaphysical declarations about the ways of the world is echoed, in various ways, by a number of Foucault's critics. See, for instance, Alasdair MacIntyre, *Three Rival Versions of Moral Enquiry: Encyclopaedia, Genealogy, and Tradition* (Notre Dame: University of Notre Dame, 1990), 32–57, 196–215; Charles Taylor, "Foucault on Freedom and Truth," in *Foucault: A Critical Reader,* 69–102; Jurgen Habermas, "Some Questions Concerning the Theory of Power: Foucault Again," in *The Philosophical Discourse on Modernity: Twelve Lectures,* trans. Frederick G. Lawrence (Cambridge: MIT Press, 1987), 266–293; and Nancy Frazier, "Foucault on Modern Power:

Empirical Insights and Normative Confusions," *Praxis International* 1.3 (1981): 272–287.

8. Walzer, "The Politics of Michel Foucault," 63.

9. "An Interview with Michel Foucault" by Charles Ruas published as the postscript to Michel Foucault, *Death and the Labyrinth: The World of Raymond Rousell,* trans. Charles Ruas (Berkeley: University of California Press, 1986), 174.

10. Ibid.

11. "The Minimalist Self," an interview published in Michel Foucault, *Politics, Philosophy, Culture: Interviews and Other Writings, 1977–1984,* ed. Lawrence D. Kritzman (New York and London: Routledge, 1988), 6–7.

12. Michel Foucault, *Remarks on Marx: Conversations with Duccio Trombadori,* trans. R. James Goldstein and James Cascaito (New York: Semiotext(e), 1991), 47–48.

13. Michel Foucault, *Foucault Live: Interviews, 1966–1984,* ed. Sylvère Lotringer, trans. John Johnston (New York: Semiotext(e), 1989), 149.

14. Charles Juliet, "Meeting Beckett," *TriQuarterly* 77 (Winter 1989–1990). I take this quotation from James Miller, *The Passion of Michel Foucault* (New York: Simon & Schuster, 1993), 65.

15. Juliet, "Meeting Beckett," 65.

16. See for instance his comments about the notion of the author in Michel Foucault, "What Is an Author?" in *Language, Counter-Memory, Practice: Selected Essays and Interviews by Michel Foucault,* trans. Donald F. Bouchard and Sherry Simon (Ithaca: Cornell University Press, 1977), 113–138; and in Michel Foucault, "The Order of Discourse," trans. Ian McLeod, in *Language and Politics,* ed. Michael Shapiro (New York: New York University Press, 1984), 116–117; see also Foucault's criticisms of the practice of commentary in *The Birth of the Clinic: An Archaeology of Medical Perception,* trans. A. M. Sheridan Smith (New York: Vintage Books, 1975), xvi–xvii, and in "The Order of Discourse," 114–117.

17. Gary Gutting, "Introduction to Michel Foucault: A User's Manual," in *The Cambridge Companion to Foucault* (Cambridge: Cambridge University Press, 1994), 1–27.

18. Ibid., 1–3.

19. Ibid., 5.

20. Foucault, *Politics, Philosophy, Culture,* 326.

21. See, for instance, Foucault, *Politics, Philosophy, Culture,* 250.

22. Friedrich Nietzsche, *The Birth of Tragedy,* trans. Walter Kaufmann (New York: Vintage Books, 1967), 46–47.

23. Michel Foucault, *Madness and Civilization: A History of Insanity in the Age of Reason,* trans. Richard Howard (New York: Vintage Books, 1973), ix.

24. Ibid., 15.

25. Ibid., 15–16.

26. Ibid., xii.

27. Ibid.

28. Ibid., 8.

29. Ibid., xi.

30. Ibid., 261–262.

31. Ibid., 32.

32. Ibid., 35.

33. Ibid., 6.
34. Ibid., 58.
35. Ibid., 64.
36. Ibid., x–xi.
37. Ibid.
38. Ibid., xii.
39. "The classical age" refers roughly to the period from the middle of the seventeenth century to the end of the eighteenth century and is a common designation in French scholarship.
40. Ibid., 109.
41. Ibid., 109–110.
42. Ibid., 110.
43. Ibid., 111.
44. Ibid., 110.
45. Ibid., 64.
46. Ibid., 110–111.
47. Ibid., 111.
48. Ibid., 110.
49. Michel Foucault, *Mental Illness and Psychology,* trans. Alan Sheridan (Berkeley: University of California Press, 1987), 69, 67.
50. Foucault, *Madness and Civilization,* 83.
51. I use the term "apocalyptic" here in its ordinary sense and not in the more specific sense that it will have later in my narrative.
52. Foucault, *Madness and Civilization,* 198.
53. Ibid., 225–226.
54. Ibid., 212.
55. Ibid., ix.
56. Ibid., 209.
57. Ibid., 281.
58. Ibid., 278.
59. Ibid., 285.
60. Ibid., 288.
61. Ibid., 107.
62. Ibid., 288.
63. Both John Rajchman, *Michel Foucault: The Freedom of Philosophy* (New York: Columbia University Press, 1985), and Gary Gutting, "Introduction to Michel Foucault: A User's Manual," which serves as the introduction to *The Cambridge Companion to Foucault,* have noted that Foucault's heroes change significantly as his work progresses: See Rajchman, *Michel Foucault,* 9–42 and Gutting, "Introduction to Michel Foucault: A User's Manual," 24. Obviously, when I say the mad represent all others for Foucault I am conflating all of his heroes from later works into one. Indeed, where Rajchman and Gutting emphasize the changes, I want to emphasize the continuity, as becomes apparent as I proceed.
64. Foucault, *Madness and Civilization,* 289.
65. Michel Foucault, *The Archaeology of Knowledge,* trans. A. M. Sheridan Smith (New York: Pantheon Books, 1972), 16. Translation altered slightly.
66. Foucault, *Foucault Live,* 149.

67. Ibid.

68. Gutting, "Introduction to Michel Foucault," 20–21.

69. Foucault, *Foucault Live,* 150.

70. Michel Foucault, *Discipline and Punish: The Birth of the Prison,* trans. Alan Sheridan (New York: Vintage Books, 1979), 31.

71. Foucault, *Madness and Civilization,* 25.

72. The curious nature of Foucault's histories and the question, for instance, of the way their "mythical" character seems to rest on the sacrifices of historical "accuracy" has been raised by numerous critics. See, for instance, Edward W. Said, "Michel Foucault, 1927–1984," *Raritan* 4, no. 2 (1984):1–11; Allan Megill, "The Reception of Foucault by Historians," *Journal of the History of Ideas* 48, no. 1 (1987):117–141; and J. G. Merquior, *Foucault* (Berkeley: University of California Press, 1985). My own view on this matter is that those who search Foucault's texts in an attempt to refute this or that "fact" have completely missed the spirit of his works. Foucault was certainly interested in historical truth, but the truth of his works does not lie in the details but rather in the experience the details make possible (see the Preface to this work). In other words, reading Foucault is akin to reading Scripture. One can bring one's modern concern for facts and literalness to his texts, discover disturbing discrepancies, and then dismiss his narratives as false. Or one can look for the truth of his narrative, taken as a whole. Obviously, I prefer to do the latter.

73. Michel Foucault, *The Order of Things: An Archaeology of the Human Sciences,* trans. unnamed (New York: Vintage Books, 1973), xxiv.

74. Foucault, *The Birth of the Clinic,* xiii–xiv.

75. Ibid., 115.

76. Ibid., 114.

77. Foucault uses these words to characterize madness in *Madness and Civilization,* 70.

78. Foucault, *The Order of Things,* 36–37.

79. Ibid., 59, 38.

80. Ibid., 56.

81. Ibid., 59, 40.

82. Ibid., 41.

83. Ibid., 40.

84. Ibid., 298.

85. Ibid., 79.

86. Ibid., 311.

87. Ibid., 117.

88. Ibid., 311, 117, 64.

89. Ibid., 239.

90. Ibid., 296.

91. Ibid., 296.

92. Ibid., 300.

93. Ibid.

94. Ibid., 383.

95. Ibid., 49.

96. Ibid., 49–50.

97. Ibid., 312.
98. Ibid., 313.
99. Ibid., 312.
100. Ibid., 316.
101. Ibid., 316, 315.
102. Ibid., 314.
103. The phrase "ultimately unworkable" comes from Hubert L. Dreyfus and Paul Rabinow, *Michel Foucault: Beyond Structuralism and Hermeneutics,* 2nd ed. (Chicago: University of Chicago Press, 1983), 30. Dreyfus and Rabinow offer a helpful exposition of Foucault's notion of the "analytic of finitude"; see pages 26–43. Romand Coles, *Self/Power/Other: Political Theory and Dialogical Ethics* (Ithaca and London: Cornell University Press, 1992), 67–75, also offers a good exposition of the simple and yet amazingly confusing point that Foucault tries to make with the notion of an analytic of finitude.
104. Foucault, *The Order of Things,* 314.
105. Ibid., 330.
106. Ibid., 370–371.
107. Ibid., 370.
108. Foucault, *The Archaeology of Knowledge,* 9.
109. Ibid., 10.
110. Ibid., 9.
111. Ibid., 12.
112. Ibid., 27.
113. Ibid., 117. According to Foucault, four kinds of rules determine enunciation, determine, that is, what can be said or stated at a certain time and location and within a certain "discursive formation": rules concerning "the formation of objects, the formation of subjective positions, the formation of concepts, and the formation of strategic choices" (*The Archaeology of Knowledge,* 116). A discursive formation is a group of statements that are linked together not by a common grammar or a common concern but by common objects, subjects, concepts, and theories, all of which are themselves determined by the rules of enunciation. In other words, to take just the first two rules of enunciation, statements within the discourse of medicine will be recognized as such—that is, will qualify as medical statements—insofar as they are enunciated from certain "subjective positions" (that of the doctor, for instance) and are directed toward certain recognizable objects (such as "heart disease" or "schizophrenia"). Statements, for Foucault, are not the same as sentences or propositions, although some sentences and propositions are statements. According to Foucault, one of the distinguishing characteristics of statements is that they are rare and unique (although they are inherently repeatable)—that they stand out from amongst all the things said. Another distinguishing characteristic is that if they stand out, it is because they are "effective," which is to say that, unlike most of the things said, they actually move the world.

These are difficult matters, and I can attempt here neither an exposition nor a critical analysis of Foucault's theory about statements, discursive formations, and the rest. Perhaps it would help to remember that *The Archaeology of Knowledge* is in part an account of the method that Foucault had already put to work in *Madness and Civilization, The Birth of the Clinic,* and *The Order of Things.* Hence the abstractions of *The Archaeology of Knowledge* gain clarity if we keep in mind that the analysis of enunciation and discursive practices and formations enables Foucault to offer an account of why, for instance, the notion of "mental illness" arises in our culture, or why modern medicine depends so thoroughly upon complete visibility for its *modus operandi*, or how the discourses of the human sciences have come to define us in the last two centuries.

In any case, what matters for my purposes is that we see the way archaeology, by freeing statements from their imprisonment in already existing and authoritative narratives of continuity, allows for the possibility of a counterhistory.

114. James Bernauer, *Michel Foucault's Force of Flight: Toward an Ethics for Thought* (London: Humanities Press International, 1992), 107.

115. Foucault, *The Archaeology of Knowledge*, 26–27.

116. Ibid., 28.

117. Ibid., 170.

118. Ibid., 29.

119. Thomas Flynn, "Foucault's Mapping of History," in *The Cambridge Companion to Foucault* (Cambridge: Cambridge University Press, 1994), 32.

120. Foucault, *The Archaeology of Knowledge*, 14.

121. Ibid., 208.

122. Ibid., 209.

123. Ibid., 209–210.

124. Michel Foucault, "The Order of Discourse," 109.

125. Gilles Deleuze, *Foucault*, trans. Sean Hand (Minneapolis: University of Minnesota Press, 1988), 9.

Chapter Six

1. Michel Foucault, *The Archaeology of Knowledge*, trans., A. M. Sheridan Smith (New York: Pantheon Books, 1972), 162, 164–165.

2. Foucault does address change explicitly in *The Archaeology of Knowledge*, 166–177, but not in the terms of the concern as I present it here.

3. Foucault, *The Archaeology of Knowledge*, 27.

4. Michel Foucault, *Discipline and Punish: The Birth of the Prison*, trans. Alan Sheridan (New York: Vintage Books, 1979).

5. Michel Foucault, "Nietzsche, Genealogy, History," in *Language, Counter-Memory, Practice: Selected Essays and Interviews by Michel Foucault*, trans. Donald F. Bouchard and Sherry Simon (Ithaca: Cornell University Press, 1977), 139–164.

6. Ibid., 114.

7. Ibid.

8. Ibid.

9. Ibid., 109.

10. Ibid., 125–126.

11. Ibid., 125.

12. Ibid., 109.

13. Ibid., 110.

14. Ibid., 128–129.

15. Foucault, "Nietzsche, Genealogy, History," 148.

16. Ibid., 154.

17. Michel Foucault, "The Order of Discourse," trans. Ian McLeod, in *Language and Politics,* ed. Michael Shapiro (New York: New York University Press, 1984), 129.

18. Foucault, "Nietzsche, Genealogy, History," 154–155.

19. Ibid., 155.

20. Ibid., 160.

21. Ibid., 148.

22. Foucault, *Discipline and Punish,* 25.

23. Ibid.

24. Ibid., 26.

25. For a discussion of the role of this concept in Foucault's work that exceeds the limited account that follows, see Gilles Deleuze, "What Is a *Dispositif*?" in *Michel Foucault: Philosopher,* trans. Timothy J. Armstrong (New York: Routledge, 1992), 159–168.

26. Michel Foucault, *Power/Knowledge: Selected Interviews and Other Writings, 1972–1977,* ed. Colin Gordon, trans. Colin Gordon, Leo Marshall, John Mepham, Kate Soper (New York: Pantheon Books, 1980), 194.

27. Ibid., 197.

28. Hence Foucault says of the *dispositif* that it "is a much more general case of the episteme," which together with the "archive" is the term he used in earlier works to refer to the domain of discursive practices. He can now say that "the episteme is a specifically discursive apparatus, whereas the apparatus in its general form is both discursive and non-discursive"; see Foucault, *Power/Knowledge,* 197.

29. Foucault says of the term "institution" that it "is generally applied to every kind of more-or-less constrained, learned behaviour. Everything which functions in a society as a system of constraint and which isn't an utterance, in short, all the field of the nondiscursive social, is an institution" (Foucault, *Power/Knowledge,* 197–198).

30. Foucault, *Discipline and Punish,* 200–201.

31. Ibid., 201.

32. Ibid., 205.

33. Ibid., 136.

34. Ibid., 136, 138.

35. Ibid., 304–305.

36. Ibid., 307, 170.

37. Ibid., 307.

38. Ibid., 308.

39. See, for instance, Foucault, *Power/Knowledge,* 164.

40. Foucault, *Discipline and Punish,* 27; my emphasis.

41. Ibid., 194.

42. Ibid.

43. Michel Foucault, *The History of Sexuality,* vol. 1, *An Introduction,* trans. Robert Hurley (New York: Vintage Books, 1990).

44. Ibid., 90.

45. Ibid., 91.

46. Ibid., 93.

47. Ibid., 94.

48. Foucault, *Power/Knowledge*, 39.
49. Foucault, *History of Sexuality*, vol. 1, 95.
50. Ibid., 95.
51. Foucault, *Power/Knowledge*, 96.
52. Ibid., 29.
53. Ibid., 30.
54. Ibid., 156.
55. Foucault, *History of Sexuality*, vol. 1, 95.
56. Ibid., 94.
57. Ibid., 95–96.
58. Ibid., 96.
59. Ibid., 142.
60. Ibid., 96.
61. Foucault, *Power/Knowledge*, 138.
62. Ibid., 142.
63. Ibid., 122.
64. Ibid., 122–123.
65. Ibid., 162.
66. Ibid.
67. Foucault himself was well aware of the limits of the image of the Panopticon, as well as the limits of the notion of disciplinary power, which he did not think in any way was the only kind of power. See Foucault, *Power/Knowledge*, 108, 146–148, 155; and Michel Foucault, "Politics and Ethics: An Interview," in *The Foucault Reader*, ed. Paul Rabinow, trans. Catherine Porter (New York: Pantheon Books, 1984), 380.
68. Michel de Certeau, *The Practice of Everyday Life*, trans. Steven Rendall (Berkeley: University of California Press, 1988), 92–93.
69. Foucault, *Power/Knowledge*, 138.
70. Michel Foucault, *Remarks on Marx: Conversations with Duccio Trombadori*, trans. R. James Goldstein and James Cascaito (New York: Semiotext(e), 1991), 174.
71. Ibid., 157.
72. Ibid., 174.
73. Foucault, *The History of Sexuality*, vol. 1, 101–102.
74. Michel Foucault, *Madness and Civilization: A History of Insanity in the Age of Reason*, trans. Richard Howard (New York: Vintage Books, 1973), 210.
75. Michel Foucault, *The Order of Things: An Archaeology of the Human Sciences*, trans. unnamed (New York: Vintage Books, 1973), 118. The rest of the short quotations in this paragraph come from this page and from page 119.
76. Indeed, my own sense is that Stone's film, which was certainly meant to be social critique, may well have simply appeared to most viewers as just another movie full of sex and violence.
77. Michel Foucault, "Of Other Spaces," trans. Jay Miskowiec, *Diacritics* 16 (Spring 1986):22–27.
78. Ibid., 23.
79. Ibid., 24.
80. Ibid.
81. Foucault, *Power/Knowledge*, 81.

82. Ibid., 81–82. The notion of subjugated knowledges refers not only to the disqualified knowledge of psychiatric patients, delinquents, and so on, but also "to the historical contents that have been buried and disguised. . . . Subjugated knowledges are thus those blocs of historical knowledge which were present but disguised within the body of functionalist and systematizing theory." Here we might envision, for instance, the knowledge of primal peoples who have been overrun by imperialism, or the knowledge of slaves in the American South, or the knowledge of women in various cultures around the world.

83. See Foucault, *Power/Knowledge*, 51–52.

84. Ibid., 102.

85. Michel Foucault, *Foucault Live: Interviews, 1966–1984*, ed. Sylvère Lotringer, trans. John Johnston (New York: Semiotext(e), 1989), 89–106.

86. Ibid., 91–92.

87. Foucault, *History of Sexuality*, vol. 1, 151.

88. Ibid., 152.

89. Foucault, *Power/Knowledge*, 56.

90. Foucault, *Foucault Live*, 191.

91. Foucault, *Remarks on Marx*, 134–137.

92. Michel Foucault, *Politics, Philosophy, Culture: Interviews and Other Writings, 1977–1984*, ed. Lawrence D. Kritzman (New York and London: Routledge, 1988), 217.

93. Foucault, *Power/Knowledge*, 136.

94. Foucault, *Foucault Live*, 151.

95. Ibid., 152.

96. Note that my use of Foucault's last two works does not require me to discuss the specifics of those works, although a more elaborate account of Foucault's politics than I can offer here might be aided by some of those specifics. *The Use of Pleasure* focuses upon the ancient Greek approaches to the self and tries to discern in particular how they thought about the self in conjunction with desire. *The Care of the Self*, volume three of *The History of Sexuality*, continues this exercise but moves forward from the Greeks to the Romans in the first two centuries, A.D.

97. Foucault, *Power/Knowledge*, 142.

98. Foucault, "The Order of Discourse," 127.

99. Michel Foucault, "Technologies of the Self," in *Technologies of the Self: A Seminar with Michel Foucault*, eds. Luther H. Martin, Huck Gutman, Patrick H. Hutton (Amherst: University of Massachusetts Press, 1988), 19.

100. Michel Foucault, "About the Beginning of the Hermeneutics of the Self: Two Lectures at Dartmouth," *Political Theory* 21 (May 1993):203.

101. Ibid.

102. Ibid., 204.

103. Michel Foucault, "The Political Technology of Individuals," in *Technologies of the Self: A Seminar with Michel Foucault*, eds. Luther H. Martin, Huck Gutman, Patrick H. Hutton (Amherst: University of Massachusetts Press, 1988), 146.

104. Michel Foucault, *The History of Sexuality*, vol. 2, *The Use of Pleasure*, trans. Robert Hurley (New York: Random House, Vintage Books edition, 1990), 251. Note that Foucault's recourse to the individual is not, as many of his critics have suggested, a lapse into some form of Enlightenment individualism—as should be

apparent when we remember that for Foucault the self is never a primal entity waiting to be freed but is always already, and to the core, a *relation.* As a relation the self is caught up in power and resistance and can perform maneuvers that change its status in the larger network of relations. The self has agency, then, but not an agency in any way connected to either a primal liberty or autonomy.

105. Michel Foucault, "On the Genealogy of Ethics: An Overview of Works in Progress," published as the Afterword in Hubert L. Dreyfus and Paul Rabinow, *Michel Foucault: Beyond Structuralism and Hermeneutics,* 2nd ed. (Chicago: University of Chicago Press, 1983), 231.

106. Foucault, *History of Sexuality,* vol. 2, 10–11.

107. See Foucault, *History of Sexuality,* vol. 2, 13, 251; and Foucault, "Politics and Ethics: An Interview," 375.

108. Foucault, "Politics and Ethics: An Interview," 377.

109. For an account of Foucault's trip to Poland, see Didier Eribon, *Michel Foucault,* trans. Betsy Wing (Cambridge: Harvard University Press, 1991), 300–305; and David Macey, *The Lives of Michel Foucault* (New York: Pantheon Books, 1993), 446–448.

110. Macey, *The Lives of Michel Foucault,* 344–346.

111. Eribon, *Michel Foucault,* 265.

112. It is worth noting that after the staging of *Godot* in the summer of 1993, Susan Sontag returned to Sarajevo repeatedly (nineteen times, I think, and usually on a cargo plane carrying medical supplies) and staged numerous other plays.

113. Foucault, *Politics, Philosophy, Culture,* 224.

114. Foucault, *Remarks on Marx,* 38–39.

115. Susan Sontag, "Godot Comes to Sarajevo," *New York Review of Books,* October 21, 1993, 52.

116. As the reader may have noticed already, whenever I quote a passage for the second time in a relatively short space, as I do here, I do not always note the reference—and in some cases, particularly where I have altered the passage slightly, I omit the quotation marks.

117. See Duccio Trombadori's introduction to his interviews with Foucault, *Remarks on Marx,* 22–23.

118. Foucault, *Power/Knowledge,* 142.

119. Stanley Hauerwas, *After Christendom? How the Church Is to Behave If Freedom, Justice, and a Christian Nation Are Bad Ideas* (Nashville: Abingdon Press, 1991), 43. See also Rowan Williams, "Politics and the Soul: A Reading of the *City of God,*" *Milltown Studies* 19, no. 20 (1987):55–72.

120. Michel Foucault, "Is It Useless to Revolt?" trans. James Bernauer, *Philosophy and Social Criticism* 8 (Spring 1981):1–9.

121. One could object that Foucault's politics seems to make sense only at the extremes, hence my recourse to dramatic examples. In Chapter Eight, however, I will confront just this problem when speaking of Christian resistance, and I will use the work of James Scott to address the ways in which such a Foucaultian politics in fact also works at the mundane levels of everyday life.

122. Ian MacMillan, *Orbit of Darkness* (San Diego: Harcourt Brace Jovanovich, 1991); I will note page references to this work parenthetically after each quotation. The following discussion of *Orbit of Darkness,* as well as the discussion of this

work in the final chapter, has been published in a different form as "Witnesses and Voyeurs: The Perils of Remembrance in *Orbit of Darkness* and *Schindler's List,*" *Soundings* 77 (Fall/Winter 1994):201–223.

123. This portion of MacMillan's book is based upon the story of a priest named Maxmillian Kolbe, who in fact did do something like this in Auschwitz and who has since been canonized as a saint by the Catholic Church.

124. Romand Coles, *Self/Power/Other: Political Theory and Dialogical Ethics* (Ithaca and London: Cornell University Press, 1992), 191, 190. This is perhaps the place to note that Rom Coles first introduced me to the work of Foucault by leading me through a close reading of *The Order of Things.* Although my reading of Foucault is quite different from his, Coles has, no doubt, influenced my reading of Foucault in ways I cannot even recognize.

125. Foucault, "Is It Useless to Revolt?" 9, 5.

126. Quoted in Wendell Berry, " A Poem of Difficult Hope," *What Are People For?* (San Francisco: North Point Press, 1990), 58–63.

127. Ibid., 59.

128. Ibid.

129. Ibid., 61.

130. Ibid.

131. Ibid., 62.

132. Ibid., 63.

133. Ibid.

134. Albert Camus, "Letters to a German Friend," *Resistance, Rebellion, and Death* (New York: Random House, Vintage Books, 1974), 31–32, 24.

135. Foucault, "Is It Useless to Revolt?" 6-7.

Chapter Seven

1. John Milbank, *Theology and Social Theory: Beyond Secular Reason* (Cambridge, Mass.: Basil Blackwell, 1990), 279.

2. Ibid., 282.

3. It is worth noting that both Foucault and Deleuze speak explicitly of their own work as an attempt to confront the reality of fascism. See, for instance, Foucault's preface to Gilles Deleuze's work (with Felix Guattari), *Anti-Oedipus,* trans. Robert Hurley, Mark Seem, Helen R. Lane (Minneapolis: University of Minnesota Press, 1983), xiii, where Foucault says that Deleuze's book is about the "art of living counter to all forms of fascism." See also Gilles Deleuze, with Felix Guattari, *A Thousand Plateaus,* trans. Brian Massumi (Minneapolis: University of Minnesota Press, 1987), 214–215, where Deleuze speaks in some detail about the difficulty of being "antifascist." See, as well, Michel Foucault, *Power/Knowledge: Selected Interviews and Other Writings, 1972–1977,* ed. Colin Gordon, trans. Colin Gordon, Leo Marshall, John Mepham, Kate Soper (New York: Pantheon Books, 1980), 139, where he says that the "non-analysis of fascism is one of the most important political facts of the past thirty years."

4. Gilles Deleuze, *Nietzsche and Philosophy,* trans. Hugh Tomlinson (New York: Columbia University Press, 1983), 36. Dorothea Olkowski, in her essay "Nietzsche's Dice Throw: Tragedy, Nihilism, and the Body Without Organs," in *Gilles Deleuze and*

the Theater of Philosophy, eds. Constantin V. Boundas and Dorothea Olkowski (New York: Routledge Press, 1994), 119–140, reminded me of this passage in Deleuze.

5. Milbank, *Theology and Social Theory,* 388.

6. Ibid., 383.

7. Ibid., 392.

8. For a brief account of the term, see Wilhelm Schneemelcher, ed., *New Testament Apocrypha,* vol. 2, rev. ed., trans. R. McL. Wilson (Louisville, Ky.: Westminster/John Knox, 1992), 544.

9. Richard Horsley, *Jesus and the Spiral of Violence: Popular Jewish Resistance in Roman Palestine* (Minneapolis: Fortress Press, 1993), 143–144.

10. Exactly which texts can and cannot be classified as apocalyptic is up for debate, as is the prior issue of the criteria that we might use to decide what counts as apocalyptic and what does not. For a good review of the evolution of twentieth-century scholarship on the subject, see Stephen Cook, *Prophecy and Apocalypticism: The Postexilic Social Setting* (Minneapolis: Fortress Press, 1995). Other Old Testament texts that express apocalyptic themes are Isaiah 24–27, Ezekiel 38–39, Joel 2, and the Book of Zechariah. Many of the extrabiblical apocalyptic texts have been gathered in James H. Charlesworth, ed., *The Old Testament Pseudepigrapha,* vol. 1 (New York: Doubleday, 1983), as well as in Schneemelcher, *New Testament Apocrypha,* vol. 2.

Stephen Cook's book is important because, based upon his reading of Ezekiel, Zechariah, and Joel, he challenges the widely held notion that the apocalyptic imagination is always the imagination of the disenfranchised, which, all debates to the side, is surely how I have cast things in my narrative.

11. The translation here is that of the NRSV, as will be the case with all biblical quotations, unless otherwise noted. Note that here I have condensed a much longer passage from Revelation, and without using the customary ellipses . . . since they were so numerous they proved too great a distraction.

12. See Paul Hanson, *The Dawn of Apocalyptic: The Historical and Sociological Roots of Jewish and Apocalyptic Eschatology,* rev. ed. (Philadelphia: Fortress Press, 1979), 11. Leslie Allen, in the article "Some Prophetic Antecedents of Apocalyptic Eschatology and Their Hermeneutical Value," *Ex Auditu* 6 (1990):15–25, initially drew my attention to these quotations from Hanson.

13. Hanson, *The Dawn of Apocalyptic,* 11.

14. See the entire issue of *Ex Auditu* 6 (1990), which is devoted to a discussion of prophetic and apocalyptic eschatology and is a useful guide through the literature on this subject.

15. John Howard Yoder, *The Politics of Jesus: Vicit Agnus Noster,* 2nd ed. (Grand Rapids, Mich.: Wm. B. Eerdmans, 1994), 246.

16. Of course, to speak of God's involvement in history is not quite right, since this kind of language assumes that history remains something apart from God, which He is then involved with. The whole point of an apocalyptic style is precisely an unwillingness to grant history a status apart from God: It is God's-story.

17. Yoder, *The Politics of Jesus,* 231–232.

18. Ibid., 245. Of course, it is not only God's actions that we can express only in metaphors; we can speak of action generally—indeed, we can speak of the world and our lives in it—only metaphorically.

19. Ibid., 105.

20. Ibid.

21. For Yoder's reference to an apocalyptic style/vision see "Ethics and Eschatology," *Ex Auditu* 6 (1990):125, 119. Michael C. Cartwright, in his essay "Radical Reform, Radical Catholicity: John Howard Yoder's Vision of the Faithful Church," first called my attention to this article by Yoder, as well as others that I will mention later. Cartwright's essay serves as the Introduction to John Howard Yoder, *The Royal Priesthood: Essays Ecclesiological and Ecumenical,* Michael C. Cartwright, ed. (Grand Rapids, Mich.: William B. Eerdmans, 1994).

For a biblically based display of an apocalyptic style as I describe it in this chapter, see Dale Aukerman, *Reckoning with Apocalypse: Terminal Politics and Christian Hope* (New York: Crossroads Press, 1993). For another account of apocalypse, as well as an overt display of how Aukerman has influenced my own thinking about apocalypse, see my essay "Divine Ecology and the Apocalypse: A Theological Description of Natural Disasters and the Environmental Crisis," *Theology Today,* forthcoming.

22. Yoder, "Ethics and Eschatology," 127.

23. I owe these biblical examples and the following point to James Sanders and his discussion of Luke in lectures he gave at Duke University in 1988.

24. John Howard Yoder, "Armaments and Eschatology," *Studies in Christian Ethics* 1/1 (Edinburgh: T. and T. Clark, 1988), 54.

25. Note Yoder's choice of words: The use of "sanguine" in this context draws our attention both to the optimism and the blood that are the legacy of the Enlightenment.

26. Yoder, "Ethics and Eschatology," 122.

27. See John Howard Yoder, *The Priestly Kingdom* (Notre Dame: University of Notre Dame Press, 1984), 3.

28. Yoder, "Ethics and Eschatology," 120.

29. On the subject of God's surprises, Wayne A. Meeks puts it well, I think, when he says the following: "One of the most remarkable things about the biblical story is that God, who is represented as being faithful to his covenant, is forever surprising and often dismaying his people. The quality of the story was wonderfully convenient to the first Christians, who were able thus to assert that the crucifixion and resurrection of God's Son, the Messiah, might be the greatest surprise of all, but not out of character. Naturally Christians then liked to presume that it was also the final surprise; henceforth God would act just as the Christian understanding of that revelatory event requires. But that presumption, in light of God's previous record, appears unwarranted" (Wayne A. Meeks, *The Origins of Christian Morality* [New Haven: Yale University Press, 1993], 218). Meeks may mean this to be more of an attack on Christian doctrine than I take it to be. But in any case, it is a good reminder that although always faithful, God remains unpredictable.

30. Yoder, "Ethics and Eschatology," 122.

31. Indeed, because such particularity is missing in Foucault I spent two chapters trying to construct the figure of the poet who, in the end, serves as the model for Foucault's politics, whereas to display Yoder's politics, I need only turn to Jesus.

32. Yoder, "Armaments and Eschatology," 53. Yoder credits Larry Rasmussen, "Bonhoeffer and the Public Vocation of an Eschatological Community," unpublished, presented to the Bonhoeffer section of the American Academy of Religion,

Atlanta, November 23, 1986, with the idea of borrowing the term "deconstruct" from the field of literary theory.

33. Ibid.

34. Yoder, *The Politics of Jesus*, 228.

35. Ibid.

36. Ibid., 229.

37. Ibid., 230.

38. Ibid.

39. Yoder applies this interpretation of the temptations to the third temptation—jumping from the temple—as well and asserts that we see here the temptation of revolutionary violence. I think matters here are more obscure, and I am not completely persuaded by Yoder's reading; nonetheless, his overall argument is still convincing and fits well, as we will see, with the tenor of the narrative as a whole. Note that when I number the temptations, I have followed Luke's order.

40. Yoder, *The Politics of Jesus*, 26.

41. Technically, the "center" of Roman power in Palestine was in Caesarea, where the prefect of Judea resided. Nonetheless, because of the presence of the temple there, Roman power was ever present in Jerusalem, particularly during the festival of Passover, which is when Jesus came to town.

42. Yoder, *The Politics of Jesus*, 36.

43. Ibid., 47.

44. Ibid., 35.

45. This is not to say that Christians are uninterested in results and that they do not seek "success"; it is to say, rather, that they refuse to make success a matter of calculation—and they refuse to allow seemingly negative results to deter them from holding the course. Yoder puts it this way: "The people who say 'You must simply be true to God' . . . and 'let the heavens fall' . . . [speak out] of a conviction about Providence, trusting that if the heavens fall God has another better set of better heavens ready, which is part of the process, so even that is not thumbing your nose at results"; from *Christian Attitudes Toward War, Peace, and Revolution* (436–437), quoted in Stanley Hauerwas, "A Pacifist Response to the Bishops," which serves as the epilogue to Paul Ramsey, *Speak Up for Just War and Pacifism* (University Park and London: Pennsylvania State University Press, 1988), 180.

46. Yoder, *The Politics of Jesus*, 230.

47. Ibid., 232.

48. Ibid., 235, 233.

49. Ibid., 232.

50. Ibid., 239.

51. Ibid., 238.

52. Ibid.

53. Ibid., 160.

54. Yoder, "Armaments and Eschatology," 58.

55. Yoder, *The Politics of Jesus*, 232.

56. One could object that comparing Foucault's account of modern power with an account of power rooted in ancient, largely feudal social systems is simply comparing apples and oranges. There are certainly times when it appears Foucault restricts his analysis of power to a small domain; and in fact *Discipline and*

Punish is founded upon the contrast between the feudal operation of power in the late Middle Ages and a distinctly modern form of power. Nonetheless, as we will see, I think exporting Foucault's analysis of power is quite fruitful. Foucault himself allowed that something like disciplinary power existed at least as early as the eleventh century; see Foucault, *Power/Knowledge*, 201, 207; and in the last volume of *The History of Sexuality*, he extended his analysis of power in this guise back to the Romans. Hence I see no reason to assume that Foucault's analysis has to remain bound to the particular domain in which it was born. What Foucault would object to, it seems to me, is any attempt to turn his analysis of power into a general and universal theory about power that would hold for all times and all circumstances. I am in no way involved in that sort of operation.

57. Yoder, "Armaments and Eschatology," 53, 55.

58. Ibid., 56.

59. Yoder, "Ethics and Eschatology," 124.

60. Foucault, *Power/Knowledge*, 60.

61. Ibid.

62. Yoder, "Ethics and Eschatology," 124.

63. Walter Wink, *Naming the Powers: The Language of Power in the New Testament* (Philadelphia: Fortress Press, 1984), 9. This is the first volume of Wink's three volume work on power and the New Testament. The other two volumes are *Unmasking the Powers: The Invisible Forces That Determine Human Existence* (Philadelphia: Fortress Press, 1986); and *Engaging the Powers: Discernment and Resistance in a World of Domination* (Philadelphia: Fortress Press, 1992). As will be apparent, my account of power in the New Testament relies heavily upon Wink's work.

64. See Wink, *Naming the Powers*, 7, for a more complete list and for references to chapter and verse.

65. Most New Testament scholars place Ephesians outside the authentic Pauline corpus; hence I sometimes refer simply to "the author of Ephesians." Later, I treat Colossians in the same way, for the same reason.

66. Wink, *Naming the Powers*, 8.

67. This distinction between the material and the spiritual reflects a distinctively modern dichotomy that was not in fact present in the ancient world. Nonetheless, since language of any sort falters here and since I think something can be gained in our times by thinking of a spiritual aspect of power and resistance, I will use this language occasionally. For a good account of how this dichotomy fails to capture Greco-Roman conceptions that serve as the background of New Testament understandings of the material and the spiritual, see Dale B. Martin, *The Corinthian Body* (New Haven and London: Yale University Press, 1995), especially 3–15.

68. Yoder, *The Politics of Jesus*, 141.

69. Wink, *Naming the Powers*, 64.

70. Yoder, *The Politics of Jesus*, 141–143.

71. Ibid., 143.

72. Wink, *Naming the Powers*, 5.

73. Ibid.

74. In *Unmasking the Powers*, Wink devotes all his efforts toward defining the spiritual powers that carry specific names like Satan, demons, etc.

75. Wink, *Naming the Powers*, 16.

76. Ibid.
77. Ibid., 84.
78. Most of the quotations are drawn from passages quoted previously. But see also Wink, *Naming the Powers*, 83, 146.
79. Foucault, *Power/Knowledge*, 194.
80. Yoder, *The Politics of Jesus*, 143.
81. Ibid., 144–145.
82. Wink notes that the Greek *en auto* can be translated here as either in "him" or in "it" (the cross) and, as we will see, really implies both; see Wink, *Naming the Powers*, 59.
83. Ibid., 57.
84. I owe this point to a comment Dale Martin made on an earlier draft of my manuscript.
85. Wink, *Naming the Powers*, 59.
86. Yoder, *The Politics of Jesus*, 158.
87. Here I am following the RSV.
88. Wink, *Naming the Powers*, 103.
89. Ibid., 138.
90. Ibid., 65.
91. Ibid., 94.
92. Hendrikus Berkhof, *Christ and the Powers* (Scottdale, Pa.: Herald Press, 1977), 41–42, quoted in Yoder, *The Politics of Jesus*, 147–148.

Chapter Eight

1. Albert Schweitzer, *In Quest of the Historical Jesus*, trans. W. Montgomery (New York: MacMillan, 1968). For both a brief account of the three quests and a critical and helpful overview of many of the most recent works, see Ben Witherington III, *The Jesus Quest: The Third Search for the Jew of Nazareth* (Downers Grove, Ill.: Intervarsity Press, 1995); see also Marcus Borg, *Jesus in Contemporary Scholarship* (Valley Forge, Pa.: Trinity Press International, 1994).
2. Luke Timothy Johnson, *The Real Jesus: The Misguided Quest for the Historical Jesus and the Truth of the Traditional Gospels* (San Francisco: HarperSanFrancisco, 1996), 143–144.
3. Ibid., 151, 124.
4. Ibid., 127, 131.
5. Ibid., 125.
6. Ibid., 131.
7. This is how John Dominic Crossan refers to his work, *Jesus: A Revolutionary Biography* (San Francisco: HarperSanFrancisco, 1994), xi.
8. Johnson, *The Real Jesus*, 131.
9. Ibid., 154.
10. Of course to shift the burden to the patterns of narrative and away from history may seem to beg all the important questions. I mean not to discredit the importance of history but rather to make the point that history does not exist outside narrative—and narrative, as Foucault teaches us, is inherently political—both in its initial production and later when narratives already produced are interpreted.

Both Ched Meyers, *Binding the Strong Man: A Political Reading of Mark's Story of Jesus* (Maryknoll, N.Y.: Orbis Books, 1988) and Gerd Theissen, *Sociology of Early Palestinian Christianity*, trans. John Bowden (Philadelphia: Fortress Press, 1978) provide helpful models here. Both Meyers and Theissen assume that the Gospel narratives tell us more about the social, political, and economic conditions at the time of their production (decades after Jesus) than they do about the historical Jesus. In Meyers's words, "the text is a production first of the 'historical reality' of *Mark's* time, and only very indirectly that of *Jesus'* time. But such is the nature of *all* our knowledge of the past." Nonetheless, Meyers assumes that "there is a reliable continuity between Mark, his sources, and Jesus"; hence "to 'read' Mark is to 'read' Jesus" (31). Theissen makes a similar point when he says that "we may leave open the question about whether the traditions about Jesus are true or false [on the assumption that] there is a correspondence between the social groups which handed down the tradition and the tradition itself. . . . [W]e should assume a continuity between Jesus and the Jesus movement and in so doing [open] up the possibility of transferring insights into the Jesus movement to Jesus himself" (3–4).

Of course when Meyers and Theissen say that there is both an insurmountable gap and yet also a reliable continuity between Jesus and the tradition about Jesus recorded in the Gospels, they are stating a methodological assumption—an assumption that can be, and has been, challenged, perhaps most vehemently by Burton Mack in both *A Myth of Innocence: Mark and Christian Origins* (Philadelphia: Fortress Press, 1988) and *The Lost Gospel: The Book of Q and Christian Origins* (San Francisco: HarperSanFrancisco, 1993). But to return to the point, Mack can challenge this assumption and offer an account of the disparity between the Gospels and Jesus only by first creating a pile of pieces (in this case, the pieces of "Q") and then plugging them into his own highly speculative narrative about Jesus and his original followers—a narrative that has a decidedly political (and, it seems, anti-Christian) agenda (see, for instance, page 10 of *The Lost Gospel*). Obviously, these are thorny debates, and I cannot hope to resolve them here; I do, however, want the reader to have some sense of where I stand amidst them.

11. Johnson, *The Real Jesus*, 157–158. Johnson notes that this pattern extends beyond the Gospels and into the epistles; he concludes, therefore, that we find "a deep consistency in the earliest Christian literature concerning the character of Jesus as Messiah" (165). And this consistency occurs despite literary independence in many cases—Paul, for instance, did not know the Gospels, and John did not know the Synoptics.

12. Both de Certeau and Scott owe a debt to Foucault, although both extend Foucault's insights to create works that are very much their own. Nonetheless, because of the kinship between their works and Foucault's, it is perhaps best to see my recourse to their work as an attempt to bring Foucault into conversation with the New Testament. What Scott, especially, allows me to do that Foucault does not is address the concrete particulars of resistance.

13. Michel de Certeau, *The Practice of Everyday Life*, trans. Steven Rendall (Berkeley: University of California Press, 1984), xix.

14. Ibid.

15. Ibid.

16. Ibid.

17. Ibid., 18.
18. Ibid., 26, 18.
19. Ibid., 26.
20. James C. Scott, *Domination and the Arts of Resistance: Hidden Transcripts* (New Haven: Yale University Press, 1990), 198–199. Although I don't refer to it here, Scott's earlier work, *Weapons of the Weak: Everyday Forms of Peasant Resistance* (New Haven: Yale University Press, 1985), upon which his later work draws, is also helpful in rethinking politics and resistance.
21. Scott, *Domination and the Arts of Resistance*, 199.
22. Ibid., 18.
23. Ibid., 2–3.
24. Ibid., 3–4.
25. Ibid., 18.
26. Ibid.
27. Ibid., 19.
28. Ibid., 132.
29. Ibid., 133, 132, 14.
30. Ibid., 136.
31. Ibid., 196, 19.
32. Ibid., 19.
33. Ibid., 203, 202.
34. Ibid., 205.
35. Ibid., 215–216.
36. Ibid., 196.
37. Ibid., 205.
38. Ibid., 184–196.
39. Ibid., 136.
40. Ibid., 16.
41. I do not mean to suggest that all of the parables fit this description; nonetheless, a significant number of them do and these parables are the most obvious place to locate the *voicing* of a hidden transcript in the Gospels. A more elaborate account of the transcript as *spoken*, however, would include a thoroughgoing analysis of Jesus' sayings that are not in the form of parables, or at least not fully so. John Meier has undertaken an analysis of these sayings that could, I think, be used to extend what I say here about the parables; see John P. Meier, *A Marginal Jew: Rethinking the Historical Jesus*, vol. 2, *Mentor, Message, and Miracles* (New York: Doubleday, 1994), 237–506. Gerd Theissen's imaginative rendering of Jesus and his times in *The Shadow of the Galilean: The Quest of the Historical Jesus in Narrative Form*, trans. John Bowden (Philadelphia: Fortress Press, 1987) is also helpful in thinking not only about the parables but the words and acts of Jesus generally, as a voicing of the hidden transcript, as is Ched Meyers, *Binding the Strong Man: A Political Reading of Mark's Story of Jesus* (Maryknoll, New York: Orbis Books, 1988).
42. Ibid., 19.
43. Meyers, *Binding the Strong Man*, 177.
44. Ibid. Here Meyers is relying on the work of Fernando Belo, *A Materialist Reading of the Gospel of Mark* (Maryknoll, N.Y.: Orbis Books, 1981), 124ff.
45. Meyers, *Binding the Strong Man*, 176.

46. Ibid. Note that Meyers refers to Mark here and not Jesus, for reasons I explained previously in note 10.

47. Witherington, *The Jesus Quest*, 27. Witherington here relies on the work of Sean Freyne, "The Geography, Politics, and Economics of Galilee," in *Studying the Historical Jesus: Evaluations of the State of Current Research*, eds. Bruce Chilton and Craig A. Evans (Leiden: Brill, 1994), 75–122. Numerous other works support this portrait of the economic realities of Galilee in the first century; see, for example, Richard A. Horsley, *Jesus and the Spiral of Violence: Popular Jewish Resistance in Roman Palestine* (Minneapolis: Fortress Press, 1993); and Gerd Theissen, *Sociology of Early Palestinian Christianity* (Philadelphia: Fortress Press, 1978). Scholars are not, of course, in complete agreement about the social, political, and economic realities of first-century Palestine. For a position somewhat at odds with the conclusions of these works, see E. P. Sanders, *The Historical Figure of Jesus* (New York: Penguin Press, 1993); Sanders does not think conditions were as dire as these scholars have made them out to be.

48. Note, I have converted the stanzas of the poetry as they occur in the text to prose.

49. Meyers, *Binding the Strong Man*, 179.

50. Once again, I have converted the poetic arrangement of the text to prose.

51. John Dominic Crossan, *The Historical Jesus: The Life of a Mediterranean Jewish Peasant* (New York: HarperSanFrancisco, 1991), 277. Note he is quoting himself from his earlier work on the parables, *In Parables: The Challenge of the Historical Jesus* (New York: Harper and Row, 1973), 48.

52. Ibid. For Scott on this point, see Bernard Brandon Scott, *Hear Then the Parable: A Commentary on the Parables of Jesus* (Minneapolis: Fortress Press, 1989), 386.

53. See, for example, Marcus Borg, *Jesus: A New Vision* (San Francisco: HarperSanFrancisco, 1987); and *Jesus in Contemporary Scholarship* (Valley Forge, Pa.: Trinity Press International, 1994); as well as Robert W. Funk, Roy W. Hoover, et al., *The Five Gospels: The Search for the Authentic Words of Jesus* (New York: Macmillan, 1993); and Burton Mack, *A Myth of Innocence* and *The Lost Gospel*.

54. Meyers, *Binding the Strong Man*, 180.

55. Ibid.

56. John Dominic Crossan, *Jesus: A Revolutionary Biography*, 65; *The Historical Jesus*, 278–279. The words from Pliny that I have inserted parenthetically I quote from Crossan, but they can be found in *Natural History* 19:170–171. Crossan is relying here on the work of Douglas Oakman, *Jesus and the Economic Questions of His Day* (Lewiston, N.Y.: Edwin Mellen Press, 1986). Oakman says of the parable, "It is hard to escape the conclusion that Jesus deliberately likens the rule of God to a weed" (127). Crossan says as well that the mustard plants attracted birds to the fields and so proved to be a double threat to the crops. I have omitted this portion of his claim, since I am not convinced that certain birds actually show such a preference for mustard.

57. Note, this combination is important because it links the hope to the possibility of God's action (the seed grows, but the sower "knows not how"), thereby overcoming the otherwise "unrealistic" character of the promises embedded in the parables. The shortcoming of Crossan's analysis is precisely that in his attempt to distance himself from an apocalyptic Jesus, he separates the good news of the parable from its divine referent.

58. Gerd Theissen's *The Shadow of the Galilean* is helpful here because in his imaginative reconstruction of first-century Palestine he records just this sort of conversation; he also displays well how the parables might have been linked to what Scott calls the hidden transcript.

I should also note here that it is crucial that we search for the connection between the discursive voicing of the hidden transcript as I have described it so far and nondiscursive, material resistance.

59. Meier, *The Marginal Jew,* vol. 2, 146; this is almost, but not quite, a direct quote from Meier, hence the lack of quotations marks.

60. One could easily extend this analysis both to other parables and, as I noted earlier, to other sayings in the Gospels that do not have the form of parables—sayings such as "the measure you give will be the measure you get, and still more will be given to you" (Mark 4:24) (see Meyers's analysis in *Binding the Strong Man,* 178–179) or The Lord's Prayer (see the discussion in Meier, *The Marginal Jew,* vol. 2, 290ff). The other parables that come to mind most immediately are those of the Wheat and the Weeds (Matt. 13:24–30)—see Crossan's *The Historical Jesus,* 279–280; the Vineyard (Matt. 21:33–41 and parallels); the Laborers in the Vineyard (Matt. 20:1–16); the Talents (Matt. 25:14–30 and parallels); and the Great Banquet (Matt. 22:1–14 and parallels).

61. Witherington, *The Jesus Quest,* 27.

62. Scott, *Domination and the Arts of Resistance,* 184.

63. Ibid., 187–188.

64. Again, much of the recent scholarship on the socioeconomic conditions of Galilee in the first century gives us good reason to imagine such material resistance, as do the works of Josephus—upon which much of the recent scholarship depends.

65. See Gerd Theissen, *Social Reality and the Early Christians: Theology, Ethics, and the World of the New Testament,* trans. Margaret Kohl (Minneapolis: Fortress Press, 1992), 33ff; and Theissen, *Sociology of Early Palestinian Christianity,* 8–16.

66. Scott, *Domination and the Arts of Resistance,* 223. In Scott's text the last sentence is italicized for stress. Note, when Scott speaks here of the public declaration of the hidden transcript, he is speaking specifically not of the ambiguous, disguised breaching of the public transcript but of the more aggressive rupture that results from an act of symbolic defiance. Nonetheless, these words apply more generally, I think, to *any* public expression of the hidden transcript.

67. De Certeau, *The Practice of Everyday Life,* 106.

68. Seen in this light, recent attempts to alter the curriculum in both universities and public schools appear to be an attempt to combat homogenization. Given the stake the Powers have in homogenized space, it is not surprising that debates about the curriculum have become so contentious. The recent interest in regionalism is also a sign of resistance to homogenization. In an odd co-opting of this interest, I have noticed that the local Burger King has decorated its walls with black-and-white photographs of the city from the nineteenth century, as if to disguise its truly homogenizing effect upon the life of local people.

69. De Certeau, *The Practice of Everyday Life,* 107.

70. Ibid., 108.

71. Ibid., 105.

72. Ibid., 106.

73. Ibid.

74. Meyers, *Binding the Strong Man,* 141ff, offers a convincing case for seeing the exorcisms as subversive of both Roman *and* Jewish power. In the name of simplicity, I will discuss only the Roman half of the subversion, saving my comments about Jesus' attack on Jewish power for my account of the aspects of Jesus' resistance that I discuss later.

75. Crossan, *The Historical Jesus,* 313–320, offers a summary of some of the sociological and anthropological studies; see also Meyers, *Binding the Strong Man,* 190ff; and Michael T. Taussig's *The Devil and Commodity Fetishism in South America* (Chapel Hill: University of North Carolina Press, 1980). For other works that speak on this topic with specific reference to the New Testament, see Gerd Theissen, *The Gospels in Context: Social and Political History in the Synoptic Tradition,* trans. Linda M. Maloney (Minneapolis: Fortress Press, 1991), 99–112; Sanders, *The Historical Figure of Jesus,* 138; Horsley, *Jesus and the Spiral of Violence,* 184–190; and Paul W. Hollenbach, "Jesus, Demoniacs, and Public Authorities: A Socio-Historical Study," *Journal of the American Academy of Religion* 49, no. 4:567–588. For a scathing critique of the latter article, see Meier, *The Marginal Jew,* vol. 2, 640, 677.

76. Crossan, *Jesus, A Revolutionary Biography,* 91.

77. Meyers expands upon this list of clues; see *Binding the Strong Man,* 190–192.

78. Ibid.

79. See Meier, *A Marginal Jew,* vol. 2, 650–653.

80. One can get a sense of these debates by reviewing Meier, *A Marginal Jew,* vol. 2, 509–970; Sanders, *The Historical Figure of Jesus,* 132–168; Crossan, *The Historical Jesus,* 303–353, and *Jesus: A Revolutionary Biography,* 75–101; and Meyers, *Binding the Strong Man,* 141–157. There are questions about whether Jesus was a magician and about whether all or some of the miracles recorded in the Gospels are historical. But whatever the outcome of these debates, all the scholars mentioned here seem to agree that Jesus was a healer, that these healings were often taken by his contemporaries to be miraculous, and that the understanding of miracles in the first century was different then the understanding that accompanies the modern mind.

81. Mary Douglas, *Natural Symbols: Explorations in Cosmology* (New York: Pantheon Books, 1970), xiii.

82. Mary Douglas, *Purity and Danger: An Analysis of Concepts of Pollution and Taboo* (London: Routledge and Kegan Paul, 1966), 116. For a good and thorough account of the relationship between the body and society in the ancient Greco-Roman world, see Dale B. Martin, *The Corinthian Body* (New Haven and London: Yale University Press, 1995).

83. Douglas, *Purity and Danger,* 122.

84. Ibid., 122–123, 125.

85. Crossan, *Jesus, A Revolutionary Biography,* 79.

86. Indeed, it is worth noting that Leviticus devotes more space to the dangers of "leprosy" than it does to any other bodily problem. And, as if to perfectly depict the relationship between the individual body and the social body, Leviticus speaks not only of people contracting the disease but of clothing and *houses,* as well (see Leviticus 13:47 and 14:34).

87. Crossan, *Jesus: A Revolutionary Biography,* 82.

88. Marcus Borg, *Conflict, Holiness, and Politics in the Teachings of Jesus* (Lewiston, N.Y.: Edwin Mellen Press, 1984), 82–83. If we could speak of anything even close to a scholarly consensus on the importance of any aspect of Jesus' ministry it would be with regard to the significance of Jesus' table fellowship, and this in spite of the fact that, as Meier notes, "the Gospel material that has a good claim to historicity is not plentiful" (Meier, *A Marginal Jew,* vol. 2, 1036, note 317). Nonetheless, as Meier also notes, sometimes scandalous table fellowship "is a widely accepted aspect of the historical Jesus, supported by critics as various as Joachim Jeremias (*New Testament Theology,* 115–116), Günther Bornkamm (*Jesus of Nazareth,* 80–81), Norman Perrin (*Rediscovering the Teaching Jesus,* 102–108), E. P. Sanders (*Jesus and Judaism,* 208–9, though more restrained on the issue than many others), and John Dominic Crossan (*The Historical Jesus,* 332–33, 341–44)." And we could add to this list not only Borg but also Horsley, *Jesus and the Spiral of Violence,* 178–180; Meyers, *Binding the Strong Man,* 157, 218, 443; and Witherington, *The Jesus Quest,* 67, 208.

89. There are debates about the exact identity of the tax collectors and sinners; for some of the possibilities see Borg, *Conflict, Holiness, and Politics,* 83–85; Sanders, *Jesus and Judaism,* 174ff, and *The Historical Figure of Jesus,* 227ff; Horsley, *Jesus and the Spiral of Violence,* 212ff; and Meier, *A Marginal Jew,* vol. 2, 149.

90. Matt. 22:1–13; Luke 14:15–24; Thomas 64.

91. Crossan, *Jesus: A Revolutionary Biography,* 68–69. Witherington suggests that Crossan goes too far when he argues that this parable is but a display of the radically egalitarian character of Jesus' ministry as whole. As Witherington sees it, Crossan has simply turned Jesus into a good American liberal who despises hierarchy in all its forms. While acknowledging the radical character of Jesus' table fellowship, Witherington argues that a more cautious view would lead to the conclusion that Jesus maintained an allegiance to certain hierarchies—the hierarchy between God and his creation, for instance—and between parents and their children; see Witherington, *The Jesus Quest,* 68ff.

92. Borg, *Conflict, Holiness, and Politics,* 91; Borg uses this phrase to summarize his compelling reading of the parable of the Prodigal Son.

93. Scott, *Domination and the Arts of Resistance,* 196.

94. Ibid.

95. This is not to say that Jesus' daily acts of resistance were not also symbolic; hence we saw Borg refer to Jesus' table fellowship as a symbolic act. But there is a difference in degree, if not in kind, between the acts of everyday resistance, which may well be symbolic, and more blatant acts of symbolic defiance. For a good account of the political character of symbolism generally, see Meyers, *Binding the Strong Man.*

96. Crossan, *Jesus: A Revolutionary Biography,* 43.

97. Ibid.

98. See Flavius Josephus, *The Antiquities of the Jews* in *The Works of Josephus: Complete and Unabridged,* trans. William Whiston (Peabody, Mass.: Hendrickson Publishers, 1987), 18.5.

99. Ibid., 20.5.

100. This is, for example, how Crossan (*Jesus: A Revolutionary Biography,* 129) understands it; on the other hand both Sanders, *The Historical Figure of Jesus,* 254,

and Borg, *Jesus: A New Vision,* 174, see it as a symbolic act performed by Jesus, as does Meier, at least provisionally, *A Marginal Jew,* vol. 2, 628.

101. As with the issue of table fellowship, this understanding of Jesus' action in the temple is supported by what seems to be a near consensus in recent scholarship. Borg, Crossan, Horsley, Meier, Sanders, and Theissen all support this view, as does Raymond Brown in *The Death of the Messiah,* 2 vols. (New York: Doubleday, 1994). This is not to say, of course, that these scholars agree with each other about the *meaning* of this symbolic act. Sanders, for instance, relates it to Jesus' apocalyptic eschatology, whereas Borg and Crossan do not.

102. See E. P. Sanders, *Jesus and Judaism,* 61–76. For an even more extensive account of the operation of the temple and why the idea that Jesus set out to cleanse it makes no sense, see Sanders's work *Judaism: Practice and Belief, 63 BCE–63CE* (Philadelphia: Trinity Press International, 1992), 45–170. Obviously, the temple was not the center of Israel's life during the Exile, and the Old Testament makes it clear that it was never the undisputed center of Israel's life. Nonetheless, the point stands that both its significance and Jesus' challenge to it should not be underestimated.

103. This chronology assumes that Jesus entered Jerusalem on Friday, the eighth of Nissan, overturned the tables on the next day (as in Mark), and was crucified the following Friday, the fifteenth of Nissan. For a discussion of this chronology, see Sanders, *The Historical Figure of Jesus,* 249ff.

104. Scott, *Domination and the Arts of Resistance,* 225.

105. Ibid., 226.

106. Ibid., 226–227.

107. Ibid., 224.

108. Ibid., 227.

109. Ibid.

110. This passage from Ephesians is an example of the so-called "household code" common in a general form in the Greco-Roman world and found also in Colossians (3:18–4:1) and 1 Peter (2:11–3:12). Both the exact role of this code in early Christian communities and the relationship between this Christian code and its secular counterparts is subject to debate. Yoder makes a strong distinction between this code and similar secular codes (John Howard Yoder, *The Politics of Jesus: Vicit Agnus Noster,* 2nd ed. [Grand Rapids, Mich.: Wm. B. Eerdmans, 1994], 162–187), arguing that both by addressing the person of lower status first and by directing the command also to the dominant member, the form of the code is a Christian innovation patterned after the cross. Elizabeth Schussler Fiorenza, *In Memory of Her: A Feminist Theological Reconstruction of Christian Origins,* 10th anniversary ed. (New York: Crossroad, 1994) argues that the code, which appears in its earliest Christian form in Colossians, is a patriarchal intrusion into the otherwise egalitarian early church; see, in particular, 251–284. Wayne Meeks, *The Origins of Christian Morality: The First Two Centuries* (New Haven and London: Yale University Press, 1993) seems to strike a middle position between Yoder and Fiorenza; see 78–79.

The works of both Gerd Theissen, *The Social Setting of Pauline Christianity,* ed. and trans. John H. Schutz (Philadelphia: Fortress Press, 1982) and *Sociology of Early Palestinian Christianity,* and Dale Martin, *Slavery as Salvation: The Metaphor of*

Slavery in Pauline Christianity (New Haven: Yale University Press, 1990) and *The Corinthian Body* (New Haven and London: Yale University Press, 1995) bear on this debate, particularly their different readings of Paul's Corinthian correspondence. For Theissen the household codes would fall within the purview of what he calls "love patriarchalism," a sure sign that the Greco-Roman world had co-opted the radical message of Jesus. But Martin argues that Theissen fails to appreciate the subtleties of Paul's rhetoric, whereby Paul "uses patriarchal rhetoric to make an anti-patriarchal point" (*Slavery as Salvation,* 142). In the end, I think Martin does a better job of sorting through the complexities here than any of the other scholars I have mentioned. Hence, Martin acknowledges that the revolutionary character of Paul's apocalyptic reading of the cross altered social relationships in the early church significantly; but Martin then demonstrates that Greco-Roman understandings of the body constrained Paul's theological innovations: "Paul's apocalyptic revolution is constrained by his physiology" (Martin, *The Corinthian Body,* 131).

111. Yoder, *The Politics of Jesus,* 172.

112. Ibid.

113. Ibid., 171.

114. Meeks, *The Origins of Christian Morality,* 196–197.

115. Fiorenza argues that Galatians 3:28 is an apt summary of the egalitarian character of both Jesus' message and the earliest Christian communities. She then traces the gradual erosion of this message through 1 Corinthians to Colossians, 1 Peter, and 1 Timothy ("Let a woman learn in silence with full submission. I permit no woman to teach or to have authority over a man," 2:11–12). Although in its general outline Fiorenza's narrative is persuasive, I again think Martin offers a better account of the complexities of early Christian understandings of social relations. Of course, I should confess that Fiorenza's conclusions allow no room for Yoder's understanding of revolutionary subordination (see pp. 8–9), whereas Martin lends some, though not total, support to Yoder. Obviously, Martin allows me to advance my own narrative in a way that neither Fiorenza nor Theissen would. On the other hand, even though I side with Yoder against Fiorenza in my understanding of the radical character of Jesus and the early church, I certainly acknowledge the importance of her demonstration that the early church was quickly co-opted by the Powers.

116. Martin, *The Corinthian Body,* 59–61.

117. I should stress that subordination is not equivalent to obedience: "The conscientious objector who refuses to do what government demands, but still remains under the sovereignty of that government and accepts the penalties which it imposes, or the Christian who refuses to worship the Caesar but still permits the Caesar to put him or her to death, is being subordinate even though not obeying" (Yoder, *The Politics of Jesus,* 209).

118. Walter Wink, *Naming the Powers: The Language of Power in the New Testament* (Philadelphia: Fortress Press, 1984), 110–111.

119. Ibid., 209.

120. These are the words of Johannes Hamel, from "Erwagungen zur urchristlichen Paraenese . . ." in *Christusbekenntnis im Atomzeitalter?* THEX, 70 (1959), 159–161, quoted in Yoder, *The Politics of Jesus,* 180.

121. Wink, *Naming the Powers*, 111.

122. Ibid.

123. Elie Wiesel, "A Plea for the Dead," in *Legends of Our Time* (New York: Schocken Books, 1982), 174–197. Peter Ochs not only brought this piece by Wiesel to my attention but also suggested that I use it here in order to acknowledge that, as he put it quite bluntly, "your Christian saint is standing on the blood of the Jewish people, and no where in your narrative do you acknowledge that fact." Indeed, I owe Peter a debt for alerting me to the conspicuous absence of the Jews in my narrative, in spite of the fact that I have chosen, here at the end, to display my Christian politics upon the terrain of a death camp designed to exterminate the Jews.

Peter's well-placed criticism led me not only to intrude upon my narrative, however briefly, with Wiesel's words about Auschwitz but also to wonder about a flaw that exists at the heart of my narrative. Certainly one of the reasons that I have excluded the Jews is that I have let Nietzsche's dualism become my own: Dionysus versus the Crucified. It is worth thinking about how this book would have been different had I not let Nietzsche's "either/or" determine the course of my narrative. Indeed, I wonder if a serious consideration of Jewish thought would not provide a third alternative to nihilism: neither tragedy nor apocalypse but . . . ?

124. Ibid.

125. The following story is drawn from Ian MacMillan, *Orbit of Darkness* (San Diego: Harcourt Brace Jovanovich, 1991); all references to this work occur parenthetically in the body of my text.

126. Thomas Keneally, *Schindler's List* (New York: Simon and Schuster, Touchstone edition, 1993). Page numbers of quotes are cited parenthetically.

127. Spielberg's failure to politicize—or at least universalize—his story is shocking, especially since he has, in interviews, made explicit connections between the Holocaust and Bosnia, for instance. As Jason Epstein asks in his critique of the film: "Will anyone be drawn by the film to see the connection between Nazi crimes and those in China and elsewhere and risk his factory and fortune as Schindler risked his?" See Jason Epstein, "A Dissent on *Schindler's List*," *New York Review of Books* 41, April 21, 1994.

Epilogue

1. This is how Nietzsche refers to it in *The Will to Power*, trans. Walter Kaufmann and R. J. Hollingdale, ed. Walter Kaufmann (New York: Random House, 1967; Vintage Books edition, 1968), § 1.

2. It is striking to me that no one else, or at least no one I have encountered, has sought to explore the constructive possibilities of this convergence between Foucault and the New Testament. Scholars from the world of theology and the New Testament have begun, in recent years, to engage Foucault's work, but usually it seems that they do so in one of two ways. Either they adopt his account of disciplinary power to further their own critical (in the more negative than positive sense) readings of Christian origins, or they use a critically altered Foucault as a launching pad for their own accounts of power. An example of the latter is Kyle A. Pasewark, *A Theology of Power: Being Beyond Domination* (Philadelphia: Fortress Press, 1993); two examples of the former are Elizabeth A. Castelli, *Imitating Paul: A*

Discourse on Power (Louisville, Ky.: Westminster/John Knox, 1991); and Stephen D. Moore, *Post-Structuralism and the New Testament: Derrida and Foucault at the Foot of the Cross* (Minneapolis: Fortress Press, 1994). Both of these works offer what I take to be accurate readings of Foucault on power, but they use his work in exactly the opposite way I have used it here. Hence, where I use Foucault to illuminate the character of resistance in the life and death of Jesus and in the early Christian communities, Castelli and Moore use Foucault to show what they take to be the negative effects of the discipline required for discipleship.

3. Dzevad Karahasan, *Sarajevo: Exodus of a City,* trans. Slobodan Darkulic (New York: Kodansha International, 1994), 3, 96, 5.

4. Ibid., 96.

5. Ibid., 96–97.

6. Ibid., 95, 97.

Index

Abyss, 29, 30, 43, 44
glancing into, 111, 117, 121, 125, 126, 129
nihilism and, 34, 36
noble/slave morality and, 31
pre-Homeric, 24–27, 32
suffering and, 28, 138
world-building force of, 122
Achilles, 33, 94
violence and, 25
virtue/honor and, 26
Acteon, 103, 104
Adler, Mortimer J.: *Encyclopedia* and, 8
Adorno, T. W., 4, 196
Aeschylus, 26, 104
Aesthetic, 64, 65, 89–93, 283(n24)
ethical and, 73
Aesthetic phenomenon, 90
world as, 96
After Virtue (MacIntyre), 13, 71
publication of, 4–6
Agave, 100, 102, 103, 105
Agrarian eschatology, 236, 237, 240
Aimlessness, 33, 114
Analogical code, 66–69, 79, 80
Andromache, 25
Antagonism, pagan code of, 55
Antigone (Sophocles), MacIntyre's treatment of, 13–15
Apekdysamenos, 222
Apocalypse, xiv, 19–21, 81, 85, 136, 254, 258, 269
Dionysian, 103–108, 109–110
history and, 207, 210, 217
hope of, 257
metaphysics of, 206, 216–218, 225
nihilism and, 130, 206
politics of, 83, 200, 206, 210, 217, 225, 257, 261
theology of, 200
tragedy and, 92, 201, 268
Apocalyptic eschatology, 83, 238
prophetic eschatology and, 208–209, 210
Apocalyptic style, 211
moving toward, 206–210
Apocalyptic thought, 84, 86
Apollinian impulse, 95, 99, 137
tragedy and, 111
Apollo
Dionysus and, 93, 94, 96–99, 137, 138, 147, 148
tragedy and, 96–99
world creation by, 93–94
Aquinas, Thomas, 4, 5, 8, 10, 12, 58, 71
rejection of, 9
Archaeology, as counterhistory, 160–163
Archaeology of Knowledge, The (Foucault), 133, 160–165, 167, 168, 170, 171, 187
Aristotle, 71, 275(n9)
dithyramb and, 97
rejection of, 9
tragedy and, 112–115
Art
death and, 197–198, 199
Dionysian impulse and, 149
madness and, 156, 187
meaning and, 198
origins of, 89–90
reality and, 194
reason and, 145, 146, 149

redemptive powers of, 114–115, 122
world as, 126–28, 269
Artaud, 146
madness and, 145, 169
Sade and, 184
Artistic impulse, 94, 127
Art of dying, 196, 269
tragic politics and, 199–200
"Attempt at Self-Criticism" (Nietzsche), 113
Augustine, 12
on Being, 69–70
on city of God, 217
coercion and, 82
on evil, 76
history and, 55, 58
Pagans and, 54
on Roman/Christian myth/ritual/history, 57
on Rome's foundation, 56
on violence, 70
Auschwitz, 19, 81, 135, 197, 265, 270
resisting, 257–262
revolutionary subordination at, 262

Bacchae, The (Euripides), 89, 99–106, 110, 115, 141
reading of, 106, 109
Sarajevo and, 108
Bad copies, 63
Baroque music, 91–92
dissonance in, 92
Bauerschmidt, Fredrick, 86
crucified logos and, 285(n40)
uncrucified logos and, 85
on wounds of violence/love, 76–77
Beckett, Samuel, xiv, xvi, 1, 134, 258, 270
Holocaust/World War II and, 19
impact of, 21
on tragicomedy, 18
Being, 69–70, 74, 75
as analogical, 66–67
univocity of, 66
will and, 48
Belo, Fernando: agrarian eschatology and, 236
Bentham, Jeremy
Panopticon and, 173, 174, 181
power and, 178
Berkhof, Hendrikus: on Powers, 224–225
Bernauer, James: on discursive practice, 161
Berry, Wendell, 201
despair and, 203
on protest, 203, 269
Birth of the Clinic, The (Foucault), 150, 151, 154
transitional quality of, 152
Birth of Tragedy, The (Nietzsche), 27, 89, 90, 93, 94, 110, 113, 115, 120, 137, 148
Madness and Civilization and, 147
Schopenhauer and, 115
Body
discourse and, 186
politics and, 245
society and, 245, 310(nn82, 86)
words and, 194
Book of Revelation, 273(n4)
apocalypse and, 208, 210
metaphorical character of, 209
real, plain history and, 209
vision from, 271
Borg, Marcus, 246, 248, 311(n95), 312(n101)

Cadmus, 99, 100, 102, 105
Cain and Abel story, 58, 69, 207, 217
violence and, 56, 57
Camus, Albert, 204, 265
on suicide, 267
Carceral city, 171–176
Care of the Self, The (Foucault), 188, 189, 298(n96)
Carruth, Hayden, 203
despair and, 202
poem by, 201–202
Catastrophe, tragedy and, 121–123, 125, 126
Chance, 201, 211
God and, 212
history and, 171, 204

Charity
flow of, 75, 79, 86
forgiveness and, 73–75, 85
sin and, 73, 74, 78
Chorus, 104
satyr and, 97–98
Christian difference, narration of, 72
Christianity
abyss and, 30
logic of, 42
morality and, 31
nihilism and, 28, 52, 53, 70, 71, 78, 87
peaceful code of, 55
self-understanding of, 53–54
suffering and, 29
Christology, 84–85, 286(n54)
City of God (Augustine), 55, 57, 58, 207, 280(n3)
Civility, 6, 15
Coercion, 82–83
church and, 286(n51)
Coles, Romand, 203, 300(n124)
on Foucault, 201
Confinement, 145, 153, 155, 156
critics of, 143
as heterotopia, 184
madness and, 142–143
resistance and, 164, 183
Conflict
assumption of, 60
history and, 57–58
violence and, 76
Conjugation, connection and, 79
Constrained disagreement, university of, 11
Continuity
narratives of, 164
tyranny of, 171
Counterhistory, 42, 55, 164, 188, 196, 206, 212, 213
archaeology as, 160–163
genealogy and, 170
resistance to, 163
Countermemory, building, 171
Countersites, 185, 186
Creon, 14, 15
Cross
apocalyptic interpretation of, 254
concreteness of, 222–225
crown and, 215
politics of, 212–216
Powers and, 252
resurrection and, 216
Crossan, John Dominic, 238, 243, 312(n101)
analysis by, 308(n57)
on John the Baptist, 248–249
on mustard seed parable, 239
on parables, 308(n56)
on social boundaries, 246, 247
on wilderness, 248
Cross of the Logos, 85, 285(n40)
Crucified
Dionysus and, 19, 20, 86, 106, 205, 268, 269
suffering and, 87
Crucifixion, 86, 286(n54)
meaning of, 76

Das Leben Jesu (Strauss), 228
Death
art and, 197–198, 199
dignity and, 257
meaningful, 262, 265
politics of, 197–200, 257, 261
See also Art of dying
De Certeau, Michel, 184, 186, 252
force relations and, 230, 231
on functionalist totalitarianism, 242–243
on itinerancy, 243
on poetic geography, 243
on power, 181, 182
public transcript and, 232
on resistance, 181, 230, 235, 254
on tactics, 231, 243
Defiance, Jesus and, 248–252
Deleuze, Gilles, 39, 62, 80, 205
on affirmation of difference, 206
Being and, 67
on lines of flight, 79
misreading of, 77–79
Plato and, 66

political philosophy and, 165
on simulacrum, 63
symphony and, 79
Demons, casting out, 243–246, 248, 255
Derrida, Jacques, 39, 54, 69
on discourse as war, 40, 41
on violence, 41, 42, 56, 278(n54)
Descartes, René: thought of, 49
Despair, 130, 202
paralysis of, 129
Dialectics, 11, 282(n16)
rhetoric and, 58–61
Difference, 156
aesthetic relation of, 91
affirmation of, 206
Christian, 72
created, 80
ontology of, 284(n36)
proliferation of, 73, 284(n37)
Dignity, aesthetics of, 131, 200, 257, 269
Dionysian apocalypse, 109–110
visions of, 103–108
Dionysian artist, 98
primal unity and, 97
Dionysian cult, 104, 108
Dionysian dithyramb, 110
music of, 97
Dionysian impulse, 99, 133, 137
art and, 98, 149
Dionysus, 87, 105, 116
Apollo and, 93, 94, 96–99, 137, 138, 147, 148
caging of, 149
Crucified and, 19, 20, 86, 106, 205, 268, 269
mysteries of, 100
Pentheus and, 100, 101, 102, 109, 141
polis and, 133
tragedy and, 89, 90, 91, 96–99, 103, 109, 205
world creation by, 93–94
Disciplinary power, 171–176, 297(n67)
Discipline and Punish (Foucault), 149, 150, 168, 170, 171, 172, 174, 176, 177, 184, 188
Discontinuity, 163
general theory of, 160
Discourse, 98, 174, 183–184
analysis of, 163
autonomy of, 167
body and, 186
changing, 164
infinite continuity of, 162
institutional/material conditions and, 167
internal/external, 168
material reality of, 170, 188
political, 233, 234
power and, 169, 185
resistance and, 195
rules of, 161
true/false, 169
war and, 40
Discursive practices, 164, 186, 242, 294(n113)
nondiscursive practices and, 168, 172, 173
Dispositif, 172, 221, 296(n28)
Dissonance, 206
harmony and, 93
nihilistic promotion of, 91, 92
See also Musical dissonance
Domination, techniques of, 190, 191
Dominium, 82
ecclesia and, 83
violence of, 84
Douglas, Mary: on body/society, 245
Duns Scotus, 66

Eating of the Gods, The (Kott), 103
Ecclesia, *dominium* and, 83
Effectiveness, 170
politics of, 212–216, 265
Eliade, Mircea, 103–104
Encyclopaedic enterprise, 6–7, 12
Encyclopedia Britannica
Ninth Edition of, 6–7, 12
Fifteenth Edition of, 7
Enlightenment
encyclopaedic enterprise of, 12
legacy of, 2–3, 5, 7
nihilism and, 8, 16
Enslaved sovereignty, 157–160

Epstein, Jason: on *Schindler's List*, 314(n123)
Eschatology
agrarian, 236, 237, 240
apocalyptic, 83, 208–209, 210, 238
prophetic and, 208–209, 210
Estragon, 16, 18, 19, 83, 136, 137, 165, 258, 268, 269, 270
Godot and, 17, 20, 21, 81, 84, 130–131
Sontag use of, 274(n2)
suffering and, 20
suicide and, 267
Eteocles, 13, 14
Ethics, 90, 191, 192
aesthetic and, 73
"Ethics and Eschatology" (Yoder), 211
Ethopoetics, 191
Ethos, 192, 201
Euripides, 89, 99–103, 108, 141
Evil, 31
origins of, 76
violence and, 79
Existence
aesthetics of, 137, 191–193, 194, 203, 210
terror/horror of, 94
Exorcisms, 246
political character of, 244
Exousia, 220
Experience-book, described, xvi-xviii
Expressible, visible and, 151
Ezekiel, 239

Fadus, 249
Fascism, 79
Fichte, Johann Gottlieb, 49, 51
nihilism and, 50
Fideism, 8
Finitude, 158, 294(n103)
Flynn, Thomas: on archaeology/counterhistory, 163
Force relations, strategic model of, 230
Forgiveness, charity and, 73–75, 85
Forms, philosophy of, 63
Foucault, Michel, 12, 39, 71, 128, 242, 252, 258, 269
aesthetics of existence and, 191, 194, 210
archaeological/genealogical method of, 211, 217
on archaeology, 162–163, 167, 168
chance and, 212
on confinement, 143
on counterhistory, 163
on criticism, 136–137
diffuse naturalism and, 147–148
on discourse, 161, 162, 168–169, 170, 173, 174, 175, 183
dispositif and, 172, 221, 296(n28)
on enslaved sovereigns, 157
on genealogy of subject, 190
Godot and, 134–137, 194, 195
on history, 159, 160–161, 293(n72), 305(n10)
on language, 152, 153–154
madman and, 156, 164
on madness, 139–144, 146, 154
nihilism and, xiv, 132, 133, 206
on nondiscursive practices, 175
on Panopticon, 173, 174
on poetry, 167
on Poland, 192, 193
on politics, 135, 150, 165, 201, 195–196, 245
on power, 172, 176–183, 185, 188, 189, 190, 191, 217, 220, 221, 224, 266
reading of, 129, 134, 136
on reason, 139, 141, 155, 156
on resistance, 179, 180, 181, 182, 185–189, 196, 217
Sade and, 183, 185
on subjection, 172
techniques of domination and, 191
thought of, xv, 134–135
tragedy and, 21, 141, 213, 257, 290(n85)
tragic politics and, 52, 103, 133, 149, 192–193, 195, 197, 203, 204, 210
on unreason, 142, 144, 155, 156
on visible/expressible, 151

on words/things, 153
on writing, 154, 171–172
Franco regime, nonacceptance of, 192–193
Franz Ferdinand, assassination of, xiii, 134
Functionalist totalitarianism, 242–243

Garasene demoniac, 244, 255
Gaze, 159, 175, 189
language and, 150–152, 154, 155, 160, 174
madness and, 151
myth of, 151
pure, 158, 160
Genealogy
counterhistory and, 170
task of, 171, 186
Genealogy of Morals, The (Nietzsche), 27, 39, 280(n3)
Genocide, 83, 194, 195, 258
Gillespie, Michael, 42, 115, 165, 267, 288(n55)
on Descartes, 49
on Dionysus, 107, 131–132
modern radicalism and, 52
on Nietzsche, 47, 48, 50, 51, 52, 131–132
on nihilism, 23, 50, 51, 52, 131–132
on politics, 133
on Schopenhauer/will, 114
tragedy and, 116
God
chance and, 212
history and, 207, 208, 209
Holocaust and, 280(n4)
Man and, 49
narrative and, 63
picture of, 64
Powers and, 218, 220, 221, 222–223, 251
power of, 29, 67–68
will of, 48
God incarnate, 64, 65, 86
God is dead, 35
Godot, 16, 17, 19, 267, 270
in Sarajevo, 20–21
waiting for, 84
Goethe, Johann Wolfgang von, 50
Gospels
extracanonical, 228
hidden transcript and, 251, 307(n41)
narrative control of, 228
Goya
madness/tragedy and, 145
unreason and, 146
Grief, wonder-altered, 121–123, 125
Gulag, xv, 135
resisting, 187, 188
Gutting, Gary, 292(n63)
on Foucault, 136, 148

Hanson, Paul: on apocalyptic/prophetic eschatology, 208–209
Harmony
dissonance and, 93
risk of, 80–84, 91
Hauerwas, Stanley, 285(n48)
on art of dying, 196
Healing, 244, 245, 246, 248
Hegel, G.W.F., xviii, 50, 55, 57, 84, 265
Heidegger, Martin, 23, 34, 39, 41, 48, 168
on Being, 69–70
on classical nihilism, 42–44
Dionysus and, 107
on God is dead, 35
on loss of values, 36
metaphysics and, 47
on nature/technology, 46
on Nietzsche, 44–47, 279(n76)
on nihilism, 38, 46–47, 51, 279(n62)
on technology, 45, 46, 279(n62)
tragedy and, 116, 290(n73)
true world and, 35
on violence, 70
Western thought and, 50
Hera, 103, 104
Herod Antipas, John the Baptist and, 249

Heterotopia, 182–186
Hidden transcript, 251, 307(n41), 309(nn58, 66)
  ambiguous voicing of, 234, 235
  disguised voicing of, 234
  infrapolitics and, 232–235
  parables and, 236, 240
  public discourse and, 235, 248
  public transcript and, 232–233, 241
  social reach of, 241–242
  as symbolic defiance, 235
  verbal expression of, 241
Historicism, absolute, 38–42, 53
Historiography, 160
  apocalyptic, 210, 211
  archaeological, 217
History
  apocalypse and, 207, 212
  Caesar and, 217
  chance and, 171, 204
  conflict and, 57–58
  effective, 170
  God and, 207, 208, 209
  homeland of, 157–160
  Jesus and, 214–215, 229
  meaning of, 215
  murdering, 160–161
  nihilism and, 43
  politics and, 209, 212, 215, 217
  violence and, 41, 42, 54
  writing of, 147–150, 159, 160, 171–172
History of Madness, The (Foucault), 148
History of Sexuality, The (Foucault), 134, 177, 182, 183, 188, 189, 191
Hitler, Adolf, xiii, 135, 183
  answering, 165
Hölderlin, madness/tragedy and, 144, 145
Holocaust, 258, 262, 269
  God and, 280(n4)
  symbolism of, 134
Homer, 14, 95, 138
  artistic impulse and, 94
  redemption by, 96
  on violence/suffering, 25
"Homer's Contest" (Nietzsche), 24, 28, 38, 94
  writing of, 27
Horrible, taming of, 110–112, 121
Horsley, Richard
  on apocalypticism, 207
  on imagination, 207
Household codes, 254, 312–313(n110)
Hypotassesthai, 253

Iliad, The (Homer), 25, 94, 96
Imagination, apocalyptic, 207–208
Imperium, 6, 13–15, 16
Incarnation, 65
  doctrine of, 63–64, 76
Incorporeal transformation, 76, 282–283(n21), 286(n50)
Infrapolitics, hidden transcript and, 232–235
In Quest of the Historical Jesus (Schweitzer), 228
Insubordination, 234, 235
Itinerancy, 241–243

Jacobi, Friedrich: on idealism, 49
Jean Paul: absolute autonomy and, 49–50
Jesus
  apocalyptic politics and, 227
  baptism of, 249
  entrance to Jerusalem by, 249–250
  healing by, 244, 245, 246
  hidden transcript and, 251
  historical, 228, 229–230
  history and, 214–215, 229
  parables of, 235–241, 242, 243, 248
  Powers and, 222, 223, 243, 252, 256
  provocative acts of, 230–234, 246, 247, 248–252, 261
  public transcript and, 261
  table fellowship and, 246, 247
Jews
  abyss and, 30
  morality and, 31
  nihilism and, 28
  suffering and, 29
John XXII, Aquinas and, 274(n9)

John of Patmos, on apocalypse, 208, 216–217
Johnson, Luke Timothy
on Gospels, 229
on historical Jesus, 228, 229, 230
John the Baptist, 238, 250
baptisms by, 248–249
death of, 249
symbolic challenge by, 249
Josephus, 249, 309(n64)
Joshua, 248

Kant, Immanuel, 7, 49
aesthetic idea and, 64, 65, 68, 286(n2)
animating principle and, 64
on finitude, 158
noumenal world of, 32
on religious differences/reason, 3
thing-in-itself and, 113
violence and, 60
Karahasan, Dzevad: on Sarajevo, xiii, 270, 271
Kaufmann, Walter, 94, 288(n55)
Keneally, Thomas, 263, 264
Kenesis, MacIntyre interview in, 281(n14)
Kott, Jan, 109
on *Bacchae,* 103, 104–105, 106, 107–108
on Chorus, 104
on Dionysus, 100, 104, 106–107, 133
quote of, 3–4
ritual and, 110
on tragedy, 128

Lamentation, politics of, 201–204
Language
analysis of, 161
art and, 152
confinement of, 152–154
demotion of, 154, 155
gaze and, 150–152, 154, 155, 160, 174
history of, 152, 157
moral, 5
myth of, 151
pure, 160
reason and, 152
rebirth of, 156
redemption and, 152–153
representative role of, 153–154
transparent, 154, 155–156
writing and, 154
Latent suggestions, 66, 68
Lear, King: as tragic figure/madman, 142
Left-Hegelianism, 51
Lepers
healing of, 248
Jesus and, 243–246
social boundaries and, 245–246
"Letters to a German Friend" (Camus), 204
Liberalism, 6, 7, 70
nihilism and, 52
violence and, 60
Linguistic idealism, 63–66, 284(n33)
Linguistic realism, 63
analogical code and, 66
Local community, new forms of, 15
Logos, 281(n15)
Christian, 58, 84, 85, 285(n46)
cross of the, 85, 285(n40)
Greek, 59, 60
incarnate, 77, 84–85
logos crucified and, 85
platonic, 60
uncrucified, 77, 85
Logos crucified, 75–77, 86, 285(n40)
logos and, 85
Lucky, 16, 17, 18, 276(n42)

MacIntyre, Alasdair
Antigone and, 13–15
on Aquinas, 9, 10–11, 274–275(n9)
Augustinian Christianity of, 280–281(n14), 281–282(n16)
dismantling of, 70–73
on *Encyclopedia Britannica,* 6, 7–8
on Enlightenment, 8
local communities and, 15
on modern radicalism, 5
on moral life, 11
narrative and, 58, 59, 61–62, 274(n7)
on new dark ages, 13
Nietzsche and, 8–11, 16, 71, 275(n22), 284(n35)

nihilism and, 71
philosophical realism of, 60
publication of, 4–6
on tradition, 10, 281(n14)
on university, 11, 12
on violence, 11, 60
Machiavelli, Niccolo: power and, 218
Maclean, Norman, 89, 258
consolation by, 123, 124
dignity and, 268
Mann Gulch fire and, 117–127
tragedy and, 119, 122, 123, 126
truth/art and, 127
MacMillan, Ian, xvi, 197, 198, 199, 257, 260
on Auschwitz, 258–259, 261, 265–266
on meaningful death, 262
Madman, poet and, 156, 163
Madness, 251
art and, 156, 187
in Classical Age, 140–143
confinement of, 142–143, 154
Dionysian, 141
gaze and, 151
history of, 150, 152, 157
Reason and, 138, 139–140, 141, 148
silencing, 144
tragedy and, 142, 145, 146
triumph of, 143, 146, 147
truth and, 142–143, 144
unreason and, 142, 143, 144, 147
Madness and Civilization (Foucault), 133, 137–140, 148, 150, 152, 155–156, 159, 160, 163
Birth of Tragedy and, 147
closing words of, 146, 147, 149
metaphysical gestures in, 147
Maenads, 99, 106
Maimonides, 5
Mann Gulch fire, 257, 269
story of, 117–122, 126–127
Manning, Richard: on Maclean/Mann Gulch fire, 122, 123, 128
Margins, danger at, 245
Marsalis, Wynton: on classical music/jazz, 92
Martin, Dale, 313(nn110, 115)
on Paul/apocalypse, 253–254
Marx, Karl, 52, 55, 57
Mauriac, Claude: on Foucault's resistance, 192–193
Meaning, 75–76, 258
repudiation of, 39
Meaninglessness, 24, 28, 32
escaping, 37
originary morality and, 33–34
radical morality and, 33–34
tragedy and, 20
values and, 36
Meeks, Wayne A., 302(n29)
on cross/revolutionary innovation, 253
Meier, John P., 307(n41)
on gospel/historicity, 311(n88)
on parables/word events, 240
Metanarrative realism, 60–63, 284(n33)
analogical code and, 66
Metanarratives, postmodern, 72
Metaphysical comfort, 97, 98, 115, 117, 147, 288(n55)
Metaphysics
necessity of, 147–150
as nihilism, 47
politics and, 131, 133, 148, 149
Meta-power, 180
Meyers, Ched, 239, 244, 306(n10)
agrarian eschatology and, 236
on prophetic-apocalyptic-holy war tradition, 237
Milbank, John, xviii, 23, 41, 48, 51, 69, 133, 165, 205, 270
on absolute historicism, 39
analogical code and, 66
on Augustine, 55, 56
Christianity and, 53, 55, 58, 81, 285(nn46, 48)
Christology of, 84–85
on coercion, 82–83
crucified logos and, 77
Dionysus and, 107
on evil, 76
on harmony, 80
on image of God, 86

on Jesus/history, 207
linguistic idealism of, 64, 65
on MacIntyre, 59, 60, 62, 70
meaning and, 75–76
musical dissonance and, 91, 92–93
narrative and, 58–61, 62–64, 68, 81, 82, 85, 87
Nietzsche and, 54, 72, 279(n76)
nihilism and, 39, 42, 47, 63, 54, 71, 77–79, 91, 130, 206
nonviolence and, 69
ontology of, 40, 73, 284(n36)
on philosophical realism, 60
postmodernism of, 55–58, 284(n32)
on punishment, 83
on socially aesthetic harmony, 81–82
theological project and, 52
tragedy and, 83, 116, 130
on unity, 91
on violence, 54, 79
Miller, James: on Foucault, xvi
Mobility, discursive/nondiscursive, 242
Modern radicalism, 5, 52
Modern subject, total history and, 161
Moral community, 15
Morality, 5, 7, 8
noble, 29, 30, 31
originary, 33–34
radical, 33–34
slave, 28–33
sustaining, 6
Moral life, university and, 11–13
Moses, 214, 248
Musical dissonance, 89–93
wonderful significance of, 91, 92–93
Mustard seed, parable of, 236, 238, 239, 240
Myth, 151
politics and, 150

Narrative, 61–62, 76, 81, 293(n72), 305(n10)
excess of ideas and, 68
God and, 63
ontology and, 72, 73
ordering of, 65, 68
world as, 64–66
Natural Born Killers, 183
Nature
demonization of, 123
technology and, 46
Nerval, madness/tragedy and, 144, 145
New Testament, 21
Christian politics and, 230
messianic pattern of, 228–230
power and, 173, 217, 218, 220, 221, 224, 251
on resistance, 224
revolutionary subordination and, 253, 256
Niebuhr, Reinhold: power and, 218
Nietzsche, Friedrich, xvi, xviii, 12, 19, 39, 146, 168
abyss and, 25, 27, 122
on Apollo, 93, 94
on art, 89–90, 127
on choral energy, 111
on Christianity, 53–54
Dionysus and, 89, 90–91, 97, 98, 99, 105, 106, 107, 109, 110, 131–132, 141, 147, 268
Enlightenment and, 8, 9
genealogy of, 39
horrible and, 111–112
on *Iliad,* 25
madness/tragedy and, 144, 145, 169
on meaning/value, 41–42, 44
on morality, 28, 29, 31
musical dissonance and, 92–93
nihilism and, xiv, 3, 16, 19–21, 23, 24, 27, 28, 32–38, 43, 44, 50–52, 94, 130, 206
on satyr, 97–98
Socratic insight and, 124–125
on suffering, 27, 86
on terror/horror of existence, 94
tragedy and, xiv, 21, 52, 102–103, 110, 112, 113, 116, 117, 119, 120–121, 127, 137–138, 144, 145, 169, 205, 269
tragic drama and, 98–99, 112–113

true world and, 27, 32, 34
Western thought and, 32–33, 50
on will to power, 30
"Nietzsche, Genealogy, History" (Foucault), 168, 171
Nihilism, xiv, 19–21, 98, 136, 257
abyss and, 34, 36
apocalypse and, 130, 206
Christianity and, 53, 70, 71, 78, 87, 91, 285(n46)
classical, 42–44
complete, 37
confronting, 38, 267
death of God and, 51
defining, 23, 51
development of, 3–4, 23, 27–29, 38, 48, 50, 268
Enlightenment and, 8, 16
ethical, 38–42, 53
final forms of, 35–38
incomplete, 36, 37, 45
as insurrection, 44–47
language of, 130
liberalism and, 52
before Nietzsche, 47–50
as normal condition, 51
originary, 31–32, 36
passive, 45
politics of description and, 50–52
radical, 28, 31–32, 34, 36
Russian, 51–52
self-understanding of, 23
tragedy and, 205, 206
as transitional stage, 19–20
violence and, 60, 75
Nihilism Before Nietzsche (Gillespie), 47–48
Noble morality, 29–32
defeat of, 31
Nondiscursive practices, 164, 170, 174, 242
analysis of, 175
discursive practices and, 168, 172, 173
material reality of, 168
Non-identical repetition, 66, 67, 68, 284(n33)
Nonviolence, 69, 278(n54)
logos and, 86
violence and, 85

Objective surface presence, 62, 63
Odyssey, The (Homer), 96
Oedipus, 13, 112
Omophagia, 103, 106
"On Being Asked to Write a Poem Against the War in Vietnam" (Carruth), 201–202
"On Self-Overcoming" (Nietzsche), 116
Ontology, 40, 74, 284(n36)
narrative and, 72, 73
Orbit of Darkness (MacMillan), 300(n122)
Auschwitz and, 197, 257
meaningful death and, 262, 265
"Order of Discourse, The" (Foucault), 134, 168–171, 188, 190
Order of Things, The (Foucault), 150–152, 156, 157, 159, 161, 162, 163, 169
Orpheus, 26, 28, 38
abyss and, 30
nihilism of, 32
Other, 73, 150, 156, 160
completely, 135

Panopticon, 171–176, 178, 182, 184, 242, 243
described, 173
power and, 181, 219
Parables, 246, 307(n41), 308(n56)
hidden transcript and, 236, 240, 309(n58)
political character of, 243
power of, 242
as tactics of resistance, 235–241
as word events, 240
Paul
apocalypse and, 254
progressive teaching of, 253–254
Pentheus, 104, 105, 110, 137
death of, 103

Dionysus and, 100, 101, 102, 108, 109, 141
Perrot, Michelle, 181
Perspectivism, 8, 12
relativism and, 9
truth and, 9
Phenomenology, 111, 134
Plain history, real politics and, 209
Plato, 12, 62–63, 168, 176
nihilism of, 32
violence and, 60
Platonism, 67
overturn of, 62, 63, 66
Pliny the Elder, 308(n56), 239
Poet
madman and, 156, 163
politics of, 188
Poetic geography, articulation of, 241–243
Poetics (Aristotle), 97
Poland, nonacceptance of events in, 192, 193
Polis, Dionysian subversion of, 108–110, 133
Politics
apocalyptic, 215
as art of impossible, 210–212
body and, 245
of cross, 212–216
of description, 50–52
of dying, 197–200, 269
of effectiveness, 212–216
as ethics, 191
history and, 209, 212, 215, 217
metaphysics and, 131, 133, 148, 149
myth and, 150
nihilism and, 52
redescription of, 188
refusal of, 196
spirituality and, 204
suffering and, 20
tragedy and, 133, 196
See also Infrapolitics; Tragic politics
Politics of Jesus, The (Yoder), 232
Polynices, 13, 14
Pontius Pilate, 230
Popular memory, notion of, 185–186
Positivism, 39, 158
Postmodernism, 54, 284(n32)
Power
analyzing, 186, 217
centering of, 180
discourse and, 169, 183, 185
dispersal of, 177–178, 188
knowledge and, 185
language of, 173, 217
microphysics of, 172
narratives of, 73, 284(n36)
productivity of, 177, 178, 186
redescription of, 176, 188, 214
resistance and, 179–181, 186–190, 217, 223, 224
spiritual, 220–221, 304(n67)
technology of, 190
transformation of, 195
underside of, 182
violence and, 172
Powers, 214, 233, 242, 254, 261
cross and, 252
God and, 218, 220, 221, 222–223, 251
Jesus and, 222, 223, 243, 256
Pantopticon and, 181, 219
resistance to, 220, 222, 224, 227, 231, 244, 246, 248, 249, 250, 256, 262
understanding of, 217–220
Pozzo, 16, 17, 18, 267, 268
Preservation-enhancement, 46
will to power and, 44
Primal unity, 97
Primordial law of things, 30
Princip, Gavrilo, xiii
Prophetic eschatology, apocalyptic eschatology and, 208–209, 210
Protest, 203
lyricism of, 144–147
Public transcript
challenges to, 249, 261
hidden transcript and, 232–233, 235, 241, 248
Punishment, 83
redeeming, 285–86(n50)

"Question Concerning Technology, The" (Heidegger), 45

Rawicz, Piotr, 258
Realism
  linguistic, 63, 66
  philosophical, 60
  metanarrative, 60–63, 66, 284(n33)
Real politics, plain history and, 209
Reason
  art and, 145, 146, 149
  dialectical, 10, 59–60
  history of, 150–151
  language and, 152
  Madness and, 138, 139–140, 141, 148
  Nietzschean critique of, 10
  silencing and, 150
  totalizing character of, 152
  tradition-constituted/tradition-constitutive, 59
  truth and, 9
  tyranny of, 145
  unreason and, 139, 140, 155, 156
  words and, 162
Redemption, language and, 152–153
Relativism, 8
  perspectivism and, 9
Resentiment, 51, 53
Resistance, 214, 233, 242, 252
  Christian, 253
  confinement and, 183
  discursive, 182–186, 195
  genealogical analysis of, 186
  parables and, 235–241
  physically committed, 186–188
  plurality of, 179
  politics of, 196
  power and, 179–180, 181, 186, 187, 188–190, 217, 220, 222, 223, 224
  redescription of, 188
  revolution and, 217
  tactical, 254
Revolutionary subordination, 227, 234, 252–257
Rhetoric, dialectics and, 58–61
Roman Empire, foundation of, 56–57
Romantics, nihilism and, 50
Romulus and Remus story, 55, 58, 69, 207, 280(n12)
  violence and, 56–57
Russian Revolution, nihilism and, 51–52

Sade, Marquis de, 183, 184
  madness/tragedy and, 145
  unreason and, 146
St. Benedict, 6
Same, 150, 156
Sarajevo
  destruction of, xiii
  dignity in, 270
  Godot in, 129, 130
  nonacceptance of events in, 193
  symbolism of, 134
  theaters in, 1
Satyrs, tragic chorus and, 97–98
Schindler, Oskar, 264
Schindler's List (Keneally), 265
  meaningful death and, 262
  prologue to, 263
Schindler's List (movie), 262
Scholastic theology, God of, 48–49
Schopenhauer, Arthur, 37, 50, 286(n2)
  on aimless world-will, 114
  on Kant, 114
  tragedy and, 18, 112–115
Schweitzer, Albert, 228
Scott, Brandon, 238
Scott, James, 252, 299(n121)
  on hidden transcript, 232, 233, 235, 240–243, 251
  on infrapolitics, 232
  on politics of disguise, 241
  on public transcript, 232, 233, 241, 261, 249
  on resistance, 230, 231, 233, 235, 250, 251, 254
Seed, parable of, 237, 238, 239
Self, 299(n104)
  technology of, 188–191
Self-understanding, Christian, 53–54
Semele, 99, 100, 103, 104
Ship of Fools, 138, 141

Simulacra, 62–63
Sin, charity and, 73, 74, 78
Slave morality, 28–32
  nihilism of, 33
Social ethical concern, 212
Social structure
  boundaries and, 246
  leprosy and, 245–246
  oppressive, 255
  subversion of, 246, 247
Society
  body and, 245, 310(nn82, 86)
  carceral texture of, 175
  margins of, 245
Socrates, 84, 124–125, 126
Sontag, Susan, xvi, 18
  on actors, 1–2
  criticism of, 2
  Godot and, xiv, 4, 15, 193–197, 258
  motivation for, 2
  in Sarajevo, 1, 2, 131, 134, 194, 270
Sophists, banishment of, 169
Sophocles, 14, 15
Soul, as prison of body, 176–179
Sower, parable of, 236, 238, 239
Spain, nonacceptance of events in, 192–193
Sparagmos, 103, 104, 105
Speculative theology, 68–69
Speech
  power of, 155
  violence and, 40
Spielberg, Steven, 265, 314(n123)
  Keneally and, 263
  Schindler's List and, 263, 264
Spiritual
  material and, 304(n67)
  politics and, 204
Stalin, Josef, xiii, 51, 132, 135, 183
  answering, 165
Stone, Oliver, 183, 297(n76)
Stout, Jeffrey: on MacIntyre, 12
Strauss, David Friedrich, 228
Subjection, 253
  violence and, 172
Subjugated knowledges, 182–186, 298(n82)
Subordination, 253, 254
Suffering, 29, 33, 96, 117, 217
  abyss and, 28, 138
  action and, 20
  Crucified and, 87
  meaning of, 26, 32, 86
  politics and, 20
  question of, 24–27, 31
  susceptibility to, 121
  tragic culture and, 116
  transfiguring, 94
Suicide, nihilism and, 267
Summa Theologica (Aquinas), 4, 5, 10, 59
  moral life and, 274(n8)
Superabundant life, 43, 44
Suprasensory world, 35, 36, 37
Symbolic defiance, 234, 235, 248, 250–251
Synoptics, 228
Systemic causal perspicuity, axiom of, 210, 211

Table fellowship
  parables about, 247–248
  weapon of, 246–248
Tactic, defining, 231
Technology
  nature and, 45, 46
  nihilism and, 279(n62)
Terror, 94, 113
  politics of, 133
Theissen, Gerd, 241, 306(n10), 313(n115)
  on household code, 313(n110)
Theology, xiv, xv, 4
Theology and Social Theory: Beyond Secular Reason (Milbank), 39, 84–85, 280(n2)
Thing-in-itself, 113, 114
Three Rival Versions of Moral Enquiry (MacIntyre), 6, 11
  quote from, 12–13
Thucydides, 107–108
Total history, 160
  modern subject and, 161

Tragedy, xiv, 18, 19–21, 102–103, 112–115, 127, 136, 258, 269
apocalypse and, 92, 201, 268
birth of, 96–99
catastrophe and, 121–123, 125, 126
in Classical Age, 140–142
hope of, 257
language of, 81, 83, 86, 130
madness and, 142, 145, 146
metaphysics of, 128, 130, 131–134, 148–149, 196, 200, 205, 206, 269
nihilism and, 205, 206
pity/terror and, 113
recovery of, 147
ritual and, 110
violence in, 82
way of the cosmos and, 110–111
Tragic culture
moving toward, 115–117
suffering and, 116
Tragic drama, 110–112
emergence of, 98–99
Tragic hero, 112, 141
Tragic insight, scientific insight and, 123–126
Tragic politics, 52, 103, 128, 131–134, 149, 191–192, 195–197, 203, 206, 269
apocalyptic alternative to, 227
art of dying and, 199–200
enigma of, 204
Tragic profundity, 82, 83
Trinity, Augustinian account of, 75
Truth
discourse and, 169
madness and, 144
reason and, 9
unreason and, 143
Twilight of the Idols (Nietzsche), 112

Unconstrained agreement, 11–12
Undecidability, moment of, 80–84
University, moral life and, 11–13
Univocal code, 66, 68, 283(n30)
Unreason
art and, 146
confinement of, 145
frenzied, 141
lyrics of, 144
madness and, 142, 143, 144
reason and, 139, 140, 155, 156
truth and, 143
voice of, 143, 145
Use of Pleasure, The (Foucault), 188, 189, 298(n96)

Value, 34
life and, 43–44
incomplete nihilism and, 37
loss of, 36, 37
meaninglessness and, 36
repudiation of, 36, 39
Van Gogh, Vincent, 146
Vernant, Jean-Pierre
Dionysus and, 108, 109–110, 287–288(n31)
metaphysics/politics and, 133
on mortal condition, 116
Violence, 11, 25–27, 30, 32, 47, 56, 58–60, 71, 81, 82, 132, 214
alien moment of, 77
conflict and, 41, 76
evil and, 79
guilt and, 70
history and, 41, 42, 54
logos and, 86
as misdirected desire, 70
nihilism and, 75
nonviolence and, 85
ontological, 38–42, 53, 72
as presence of being, 70
speech and, 40
state, 172, 252
subjection and, 172
Visibility, below thresholds of, 179–182
Visible, expressible and, 151
Vladimir, 16, 19, 83, 136, 137, 165, 258, 268, 269, 270
Godot and, 17, 20, 21, 81, 84, 130–131
Sontag use of, 274(n2)
suffering and, 20
suicide and, 267

Waiting for Godot (Beckett), 165
criticism of, 2
genocidal war and, 4
meaning of, 19
Sarajevo performance of, xiv, 1, 2, 4, 13, 15–19, 130, 131, 134, 193–197, 269, 270
success of, 18–19
tragedy/comedy of, 18
Walzer, Michael: on Foucault, 132, 133
Weaker souls, 29, 30
Wedding banquet, parable of, 247–248
Wiesel, Elie, 314(n123)
on Auschwitz, 257, 258
Wilderness, 248, 249
Will, Being and, 48
Will to power, 30
preservation-enhancement and, 44
Will to Power, The (Nietzsche), 23, 24, 27, 33
quote from, 19
Wink, Walter
on Colosseum/martyrs, 261
on *exousia,* 220
on Jesus' provocative acts, 230
on power, 217, 218, 221, 222–223, 224, 256–257
on revolutionary subordination, 255
Witherington, Ben
on Crossan, 311(n91)
on economic effects/Roman rule, 237
on parables, 240–241
Women, domination of, 252, 253
Words
bodies and, 194
progressive imprisonment of, 159
reason and, 162
things and, 153
wounded, 85, 285(n40)
World
as aesthetic phenomenon, 149
as it is, 27–28
as it ought to be, 32–35
as narrative, 64–66
as standing reserve, 45
true, 32, 34, 35, 36
as works of art, 90
World-building force, 122
Wounds of violence, wounds of love and, 76–77

Yoder, John Howard, xiv, xvi, 21, 206, 214, 269
on apocalypse, 209, 210, 211, 213
counterhistory and, 213
on cross, 215, 216
God and, 212
on history/politics, 212, 217
on Powers, 218, 221–222, 223, 225
public transcript and, 232
reading of, 129
on resistance, 217, 219
revolutionary subordination and, 227, 231, 255, 256
on subjection, 252–253
system-immanent causal explanations and, 211
on temptations, 213
Young Men and Fire (Maclean), 89, 117, 127, 196
remarkability of, 118

Zarathustra (Nietzsche), 7, 116
Zeus, 94, 99, 104